Creating Societies
Immigrant Lives in Canada

The birth of Canada as a society and a nation has often been told from the narrow perspective of the "founding nations." These versions have left little room for the everyday experiences of a wide variety of individual immigrants who have had to adjust old-world lifestyles to the promising but harsh and drastically different environments of the city's urban neighbourhoods or the farmland's lonely expanses.

Dirk Hoerder shows us that it is not shining railroad tracks or statesmen in Ottawa that make up the story of Canada but rather individual stories of life and labour – Caribbean women who care for children born in Canada, lonely prairie homesteaders, miners in Alberta and British Columbia, women labouring in factories, Chinese and Japanese immigrants carving out new lives in the face of hostility.

Hoerder examines these individual experiences in *Creating Societies*, the first systematic overview of the total Canadian immigrant experience. Using letters, travel accounts, diaries, memoirs, and reminiscences, he brings the immigrant's experiences to life. Their writings, often recorded for grandchildren, neighbours, and sometimes a larger public, show how immigrant lives were entwined with the emerging Canadian society.

Hoerder presents an important new picture of the emerging Canadian identity, dispelling the Canadian myth of a dichotomy between national unity and ethnic diversity and emphasizing the long-standing interaction between the members of different ethnic groups.

DIRK HOERDER teaches in the Department of History at the University of Bremen in Germany.

McGILL-QUEEN'S STUDIES IN ETHNIC HISTORY
DONALD HARMAN AKENSON, EDITOR

1 Irish Migrants in the Canadas
A New Approach
Bruce S. Elliott

2 Critical Years in Immigration
Canada and Australia Compared
Freda Hawkins
(Second edition, 1991)

3 Italians in Toronto
Development of a National Identity, 1875–1935
John E. Zucchi

4 Linguistics and Poetics of Latvian Folk Songs
Essays in Honour of the Sesquicentennial of the Birth of Kr. Barons
Vaira Vikis-Freibergs

5 Johan Schrøder's Travels in Canada, 1863
Orm Øverland

6 Class, Ethnicity, and Social Inequality
Christopher McAll

7 The Victorian Interpretation of Racial Conflict
The Maori, the British, and the New Zealand Wars
James Belich

8 White Canada Forever
Popular Attitudes and Public Policy towards Orientals in British Columbia
W. Peter Ward
(Second edition, 1990)

9 The People of Glengarry
Highlanders in Transition, 1745–1820
Marianne McLean

10 Vancouver's Chinatown
Racial Discourse in Canada, 1875–1980
Kay J. Anderson

11 Best Left as Indians
Native-White Relations in the Yukon Territory, 1840–1973
Ken Coates

12 Such Hardworking People
Italian Immigrants in Postwar Toronto
Franca Iacovetta

13 The Little Slaves of the Harp
Italian Child Street Musicians in Nineteenth-Century Paris, London, and New York
John E. Zucchi

14 The Light of Nature and the Law of God
Antislavery in Ontario, 1833–1877
Allen P. Stouffer

15 Drum Songs
Glimpses of Dene History
Kerry Abel

16 Louis Rosenberg
Canada's Jews
Edited by Morton Weinfeld

17 A New Lease on Life
Landlords, Tenants, and Immigrants in Ireland and Canada
Catherine Anne Wilson

18 In Search of Paradise
The Odyssey of an Italian Family
Susan Gabori

19 Ethnicity in the Mainstream
Three Studies of English Canadian Culture in Ontario
Pauline Greenhill

20 Patriots and Proletarians
The Politicization of Hungarian Immigrants in Canada, 1923–1939
Carmela Patrias

21 The Four Quarters of the Night
The Life-Journey of an Emigrant Sikh
Tara Singh Bains and Hugh Johnston

22 Resistance and Pluralism
A Cultural History of Guyana, 1838–1900
Brian L. Moore

23 Search Out the Land
The Jews and the Growth of Equality in British Colonial America, 1740–1867
Sheldon J. Godfrey and Judith C. Godfrey

24 The Development of Elites in Acadian New Brunswick, 1861–1881
Sheila M. Andrew

25 Journey to Vaja
Reconstructing the World of a Hungarian-Jewish Family
Elaine Kalman Naves

McGILL-QUEEN'S STUDIES IN ETHNIC HISTORY
SERIES TWO: JOHN ZUCCHI, EDITOR

Inside Ethnic Families
Three Generations of Portuguese-Canadians
Edite Noivo

A House of Words
Jewish Writing, Identity, and Memory
Norman Ravvin

Oatmeal and the Catechism
Scottish Gaelic Settlers in Quebec
Margaret Bennett

With Scarcely a Ripple
Anglo-Canadian Migration into the United States and Western Canada, 1880–1920
Randy William Widdis

Creating Societies

Immigrant Lives in Canada

DIRK HOERDER

McGill-Queen's University Press
Montreal & Kingston · London · Ithaca

ISBN 0-7735-1882-7

Legal deposit fourth quarter 1999
Bibliothèque nationale du Québec

Printed in Canada on acid-free paper

Canada

This book has been published with the help of a grant from the University of Bremen.

McGill-Queen's University Press acknowledges the financial support of the Government of Canada through the Book Publishing Industry Development Program (BPDIP) for its activities. We also acknowledge the support of the Canada Council for the Arts for our publishing program.

Canadian Cataloguing in Publication Data

Hoerder, Dirk
Creating societies: immigrant lives in Canada
(McGill-Queen's studies in ethnic history)
Includes bibliographical references and index.
ISBN 0-7735-1882-7
1. Immigrants–Canada–History. 2. Canada–History. I. Title. II. Series.

FC25.H63 2000 971 C99-901049-2
F1005.H63 2000

This book was typeset by Typo Litho Composition Inc. in 10/12 Sabon.

Contents

Preface ix
Introduction xi

PART ONE CONTEXTS 3

1 Settings 5
2 Sources 15
3 Transitions 27

PART TWO THE MARITIMES AND THE ST LAWRENCE VALLEY 37

4 Immigrants in a Settled Society: the Maritimes 39
5 French-Canadian Migrations 49
6 The Coming of the Irish 58

PART THREE URBAN LIFE, FARMING, AND LUMBERING IN CENTRAL CANADA 69

7 Immigrants in Montreal 71
8 Life on the Ontario Frontier 85
9 Northward-Bound to the Lumbering and Mining Frontier 96
10 The Labouring and Lower Middle Classes in Toronto 105

PART FOUR THE PRAIRIES: LABOURERS, SETTLERS, ENTREPRENEURS 119

11 Immigrant Crossroads at Winnipeg 121
12 The Opening of the West 137
13 Community-Building: Homesteading and Bloc Farming 151
14 Storekeepers and Small Entrepreneurs 176
15 Building and Imagining Western Society 190

PART FIVE THE ROCKIES AND THE PACIFIC COAST 205

16 Mining in the Rockies 207
17 East and West Do Meet 218

PART SIX DISCRIMINATION AND EXCLUSION, 1920S–1950S 237

18 From Dislocation to Politics of Protest 239
19 The Depression Thirties and Discriminatory Forties 259

PART SEVEN PERSPECTIVES: FROM MANY CULTURES TO MULTICULTURALISM 279

20 Years of Change and Redefinition 281
21 Multicultural Lives in Canada 295

Notes 309
Index 365
Index of Migrants 373

Preface

This study was initially conceptualized as a bottom-up test of the validity of the acculturation theory I had developed after years of research on immigration from all European cultures to North America and on internal migration in Europe.[1] The life-writings of the immigrants and their children did not contradict the theory but told a much more powerful story. The comprehensive views of their lives would have had to be compartmentalized into analytical categories, systematized into recurrent processes, and generalized beyond recognition of individuality.

I have chosen to immerse myself in the perspective of the people who committed their memories to writing, to follow a life-course approach.[2] The record of many lives permitted a composite view of societies in the process of being created. Separate from the immigrants' experiences, a layer of institutions existed where boundaries were drawn, where group coherence was used as a political resource, where calls for retention of culture of origin as understood by spokesmen and gatekeepers were voiced. For example, in Hamilton, Ontario, local newspapers of the early 1850s mentioned only about 6 percent of the inhabitants.[3] Above this arena of publicized discourse and structures was a British-cultured national polity and a distinct French-cultured regional polity. The immigrant life-writings hardly ever reflected the middle and top layers of society. Rather they expressed a slowly emerging attachment to the societies and society they helped to build.[4]

We look at immigrants' *views* of their lives, since even life-writings separate us from experienced lives, by narrator imposition, order imposition, and language imposition. I use the personal memory and collective patterns that emerge from it to illustrate aspects of the immigrant experience that scholarship in Canadian ethnic studies, in United States migration history, and in European research on acculturation has considered important. I revise scholars' findings when the life-writings suggest different approaches. I do not intend to create the "average" persons of sociological studies or a socio-politically correct schoolbook family. A social scientist could, of course, develop a group of statistically correct personages – for example, an immigrant working-class couple of medium age, with an average number of children as detailed by the census – and hand these data over to a literary writer who would then inflate them with feelings: fact-fiction, docu-drama, reportage. Immigrant self-writings portray a complex picture of a broad range of experiences. Some three hundred or more published accounts of first-generation immigrant men, women, and children who left accounts for the period from 1840s to the 1940s have been examined. Some one hundred from many cultural backgrounds and all colours of skin have found their place in this study. I have tried to remain true to individual experiences, and to respect the identities of the men, women, and children who grant us a glimpse of their life-worlds.

I am grateful to the authors of the many life-writings used in this book and to the researchers and publishers who made them available to the public. I interpret them in my own scholarly frame of reference and humanistic view of social relations. This means that I am highly critical of some actions, decisions, and constructions, and deeply sympathetic to others.

I am grateful to my students at York University in 1991–92, at the University of Toronto, in 1996–97, and my immigrant students at the University of Bremen, Germany, for sharing their ideas and experiences with me. Women's history and its offshot, gender history, opened vistas that in my student years in the 1960s were never as much as hinted at. A sabbatical from the University of Bremen provided time for research, and the Diefenbaker Fellowship of the Canada Council gave me the time to write this book. Deborah Allen helped as research assistant. Gabe and Kathy Scardellato provided opportunities to discuss ideas and a home in Toronto. Jean Burnet reviewed the manuscript with her scholarly and editorial experience. Two anonymous readers provided encouragement and comments. Diane Mew skilfully edited and pruned the manuscript and the bilingual and diligent typesetters from Typo Litho pointed out remaining errors. My colleagues and friends in interdisciplinary ethnic studies at York University, the University Toronto, the University of Calgary, the Multicultural History Society of Ontario, the life-course research unit of the University of Bremen, and at many other institutions provided opportunities for discussion and exchange of views. Colleagues from Memorial University, Newfoundland, via Saskatoon, to Simon Fraser, British Columbia, permitted me to present parts of my research in progress and gave feedback. I have learned much.

Introduction

The history of Canada has been viewed as nation-building by laying railway tracks, organized by great white men, or in economic terms as a country producing staples for world markets. But who laid the tracks, who grew the wheat, who clothed the great white men? Did not women and men, in addition to producing staples, raise new generations of Canadians? In the last decades, scholars have answered such questions by detailed studies of life in villages and urban neighbourhoods; they have examined ethnic groups and dominant structures, gender roles and life-cycles. Understanding Canadian society has advanced from abstractions to people.

Native-born and immigrant people alike had hopes for their future and perspectives on their everyday toil. They had to communicate across cultural and language barriers. They had to build homes and cities; they had to deal with local factory conditions or unseasonable frosts, with unstable wages and price fluctuations in world markets. They raised children in many-cultured communities and kept transnational family relationships intact. Some of these men and women felt their lives were worth recording. While the social sciences tell us what is specific to one family and what of general relevance, it is the specific life-world that counts for individual men and women and it receives meaning by being told in a particular way to others. From these local relations, productive and reproductive, regional societies were built, expanded, and joined into a Canadian whole.

Viewed through the life-writings of immigrants and internal migrants, Canadian societies were created by men, women, and children, who built isolated shacks, scattered like dots on a map. By hard work, shacks grew into towns, trading posts into cities, urban fringes into densely settled neighbourhoods. Small regions coalesced into larger social spaces. These, however, did not coincide with modern provinces; for example, the Irish social space extended from the Maritimes to southwestern Ontario, the Italian from Montreal along railway lines to the Crowsnest Pass, the "Galician" from working-class Toronto across the prairies and to the mines of the Rockies.

The dichotomy between an English and a French Canada, so present in political history and in 1990s politics, is not visible in these life-writings. French-speaking peoples were many: the Acadians, the St Lawrence valley French Canadians, the French Métis nucleus in the Red River Valley, the immigrants from Belgium, France, and French Switzerland. Internal migration and intermarriage contributed to heterogeneity, a shared Catholic faith to cooperation with culturally different people. The notion of the English, viewed as conquerors and nation-builders, was but a figure of speech, an image. Scots, Irish, English, Welsh, Cornish, spoke the same language, but in school the children had to learn to get along with those of other cultures. Since most English- and French-speakers were already well established, immigrants from other cultures had to learn French or English to find a job, or to be able to yell back at an abusive foreman, or to shop for food without being ridiculed.

The newcomers, too, came from heterogeneous societies. The so-called Galicians included Poles, Ukrainians, and Jews. They often spoke more than one language and formed mixed settlements on the prairies. The language of one particularly large group was often adopted by the others, or all changed to a pidgin English or to a French patois. Mennonites and Russian-Germans, the other two large groups in the West, were just as heterogeneous and traversed multiple trajectories to the new society and within it. At the turn of the century, racial stereotyping divided society. East and South European immigrants as well as Jews were non-white peoples, "dagoes," or "dark people." "Negroes" faced more discrimination than "dark" Europeans, and immigrants from Asia faced the worst segregation, being dismissed as "Chinamen" or "Orientals." Although these hierarchies of colour and power are reflected in the life-writings, cooperation and mutual support across ethnic boundaries and colour lines is even more evident.

The boundaries between ethnic identities remained fluid and permeable. A multilingual immigrant could decide which church to attend and where to look for a marriage partner. When some immigrants were labelled "enemy aliens" in wartime, they chose another ethnic identity or began to organize to counter the appellation and regain the power to define themselves. To come together as ethnic groups, women and men from vital regional cultures in the old worlds had to surmount differences. Thus the ethnic groups that seem to be so clearly delimited in modern Canadian history formed themselves within processes generic to Canadian society.

The process of settling in, whether in urban or rural environments, occurs on a local level by reliance on the labour power of a single person or a single family. Immigrant letters show that the broadening of the economic base precedes the extension of emotional ties. From among friends or relatives, those whose labour power is needed most are brought in first by prepaid tickets. Wage-earning bachelors usually bring over other single men to strengthen the pool of persons with earning capacity in those labour markets to which they have access. Women come in smaller numbers, usually to serve the men as boardinghouse keepers or cooks. Single self-supporting women in domestic service bring over other women, for whom they can find jobs in their line of work. On farms, or rather on land that is to become farms, men send for their wives or prospective wives because the social division of labour in agriculture makes the presence of both sexes imperative. Only when some kind of economic security has been established will children or, more rarely, elderly parents join the family, the group, the community. Parents structured local societies to permit their own survival and an improved future for their daughters and sons. In the process Canadian societies emerged.

The need for material survival suggests that after a temporary separation the family has no free time for an adjustment of personal relations, for reflection on new circumstances. Emotional relationships have to be resumed on the spot and function immediately. The entry into the new surroundings is not a conscious move into different societal institutions, into capitalist economic conditions, or into a polity of democratic character. It is rather a move into one particular segment of the labour market or one particular area with cheap tillable land. Migrants' experiences in global labour markets and on internationally accessible agricultural land suggest that men and women function in similar work environments even if the surrounding culture differs.

But changes are made necessary by exigencies of the new worlds. Settling in may demand an intense adaptation, including the shedding of many old-country habits. Among rural immigrants in urban environments, a loss of traditional customs was brought about by the need to earn a living in industry. Only after these enforced changes and the establishment of economic stability does self-directed acculturation occur.

Canadianization of the many-cultured, multi-ethnic newcomers occurs through cooperation or conflict with multiple-origin neighbours and conformity with structures and patterns established by earlier arrivals and dominant powers. The cultural practices that immigrants carry with them are adjusted through interaction with others. A society is an interactive whole rather than a multicultural mosaic. Within this interaction, culture is not only a lifestyle, it is also an organizing principle. In both functions, culture is adjusted to the goals that individuals, families, and groups intend to achieve. Some boundaries cannot be crossed easily. Irish and Poles were not admitted to English-Canadian country clubs, women could not go to street-corner pubs, Blacks and women could not enter the better-paying labour markets, and immigrants from Asia could not form social relationships in the communities that used them as labourers or laundrymen. The 1990s assumption of the divisiveness of ethnicity overlooks the cultural interaction of everyday lives as well as the segmentation dictated by established power hierarchies.

Present-day Canadian society emerged from many regional societies, created along the trails of settlement and urbanization and hammered out in conflict. Our narrative, starting in the mid-nineteenth century, will begin in the Maritimes, even though British Columbia had also just been placed on the map of Europeans. The chronological and the spatial will be connected with the cultural. Retrospectives will present the framework newcomers entered, and the alternatives that were available for constructing societies. The westward "trail of settlement" connected with chronological time does not imply a linear development of society, from family homestead to complex urban centre. Different stages of development were experienced alongside one another. When Halifax people lived in a developed urban society, Ontario settlers were clearing the bush. When Montreal, Toronto, and Vancouver had become vibrant urban centres, the Maritimes had begun to stagnate economically and a rudimentary pioneer society was emerging in the Peace River District. Changes specific to the 1920s, the Depression 1930s, and the Discriminatory 1940s will be reflected in a separate section. A concluding section will discuss the new immigration and new policies from the 1960s to the present.

Creating Societies

PART ONE

Contexts

CHAPTER ONE

Settings

By the 1850s, profound changes were affecting the Atlantic world. Peoples in Europe had unsuccessfully rebelled against their rulers in 1848 and 1849. Under the concept of Manifest Destiny expansionist groups in the United States had annexed part of Mexico and were negotiating for the Northwest, including the future British Columbia. From the core areas of the Russian Empire settlers moved into Siberia, and from Siberia trappers and fishermen came to the Pacific coast of North America. In this world of empires, the future Canada consisted but of an interconnected string of settlements ranging from the Maritimes via the St Lawrence valley to Georgian Bay. The Canadian Shield barred direct contact to the Red River Colony, and the prairies were only accessible via the United States. On Vancouver Island, reached by East India Company ships from Asia as early as 1788, the English came in contact with Spanish from Latin America and Russians from Siberia, and above all with the several Native cultures. Canada-to-be was part of worldwide trading patterns and migration systems, and inhabited by peoples of many ethnicities.

First Peoples

The First Peoples of North America had, by the eighteenth century, become part of a Europe-centred world. At first their integration was economic. The Inuvialuit of Labrador and Baffin Island joined in commercial whaling and walrus hunting until commercial slaughter deprived them of their subsistence base. Along the Atlantic coast, Native peoples had lost land to settlers. Inland fur-harvesting connected Amerindian peoples to European demand. The Hudson's Bay Company (HBC) and the North-West Company (NWC) extended their influence from James Bay via Norway House on Lake Winnipeg to Vancouver Island. Spanish horse imports changed the traditional Native buffalo-hunting culture, which collapsed with the destruction of the herds. Subsequent starvation paralleled that among the Inuvialuit. Only on the Pacific Coast did the Native Peoples continue their traditional lifestyles into the second half of the nineteenth century.

While trade provided the First Peoples with desired goods, the cultural imports of Europeans met with less acceptance. Missionaries met with disinterest and resistance, since conversion too often coincided with demonstrations of Christian power. On the political level, attempts by the Natives to forge alliances among themselves came to naught, notwithstanding temporary successes or long-term regional alliances such as that of the Six Nations. On the level of legal codification, the Amerindian "custom of the country" clashed with HBC regulations and British–North American laws such as the Canada Jurisdiction Act of 1803. With an increasing and second-generation immigrant population, Native peoples came to be viewed as children. In Europe, utopian thought responded to working-class dislocation and poverty resulting from industrialization by establishing rural colonies of the dispossessed classes of England and Scotland in North America. Similarly, dispossessed Native peoples were settled in or transported to model villages and left to subsist by European-type agriculture.

By the mid-nineteenth century, European fur-traders, HBC factors, and women of many Amerindian peoples across the continent had intermarried or cohabited, the men often adopting Native lifestyles. Such unions, based on genuine affection as much as on convenience and economic interest, were part of the development of a future Canadian culture. Two distinctive cultures emerged, the French-Métis *coureurs de bois* and the Scots "halfbreeds." Scottish traders, often from the Orkneys, and Cree Indians of the Hudson Bay and other northwestern communities formed a distinctive but scattered and impermanent culture. The Métis developed their culture along the fur routes of the Montreal-based NWC, in particular in the Red River valley and farther west. Their self-determination was crushed during what white people called the Riel rebellions of 1869–70 and 1885, but what in fact was military conquest and suppression of local autonomy.

Migration Systems

The economic linkages with Europe involved large regions and common trading patterns over much of the North American continent. Similarly, penetration eastward linked the Siberian fur trade to Moscow and, via Archangel, to the London Muscovy Company. Politically, the Russian Empire extended its reach to Alaska and to short-lived agricultural colonies in California. From the opening of the Siberian frontier in the mid-sixteenth century to the nineteenth century, a Russo-Siberian migration system developed. In a North Atlantic migration system migration patterns of settlers, indentured servants, and free labourers coalesced, with destinations ranging from the St Lawrence to the Caribbean and to South America. The two other intercontinental migration systems, the Afro-Atlantic slavery system and the Asian contract labour system, touched pre-Confederation Canada but lightly. Afro-Americans, free and unfree, reached Halifax or came with the United Empire Loyalists. The first British forts on the northwest coast were constructed by Chinese artisans crossing the Pacific under British captains in the 1780s. Two centuries later, in the 1980s, the Pacific migration system was to surpass the Atlantic one in importance.

While the mid-nineteenth-century culture of northern Canada and the prairies emerged out of the interaction of French, Scottish, and English newcomers with Huron, Cree, Ojibwa, Sioux, and Assiniboine peoples, that of the Pacific northwest arose from a different set of cultural influences. Newcomers from the Spanish and Russio-Siberian empires competed with HBC influences. Russian vessels carried Aleutian fishermen, British ships from East Asia brought Chinese craftsmen and labourers. All interacted with the Native peoples on the coast – the Nootka, Haida, Tlingit, and others. The second generation of fur-hunters was of mixed Russian-Aleutian parentage. The English remained sojourners, whereas many of the Chinese settled. By the late eighteenth-century, perhaps a hundred English-Chinese migrants lived on the Northwest Pacific coast, as well as Spanish-Chinese and Amerindian-Chinese.

Faced with these newcomers from many different cultures, the Native peoples had to adapt. An example of voluntary adaptation was the emergence of horse-based hunting cultures on the prairies or trading to obtain European goods. In the East, the formation of Indian confederacies to oppose French and English rule led to war between the Iroquois and Huron nations. The Native peoples, not resistant to European diseases, were devastated by infections. The survivors of once viable cultures had to retreat and merge with culturally different peoples. By the 1830s, few Amerindians survived in the Maritimes, and perhaps only twelve thousand in the two Canadas.

The Atlantic migration system had been contested ground between the European powers. Rivalry between Spain, France, and England in Europe extended to their colonies in North America. By the eighteenth century, the Dutch and Swedes had been eliminated; the Basques and Portuguese soon would be.[1] Competition was between Great Britain and France, both countries which included people of many cultures, languages, and dialects within their borders.

First-Coming Immigrants

The complex cultural mosaic on the North American continent before the arrival of Europeans, the input of many cultures in the first centuries of contact and migration, and the establishment of new mixed cultures has been simplified by reference to the two powers, France and England. Much of Canadian history has been constructed as hinging on this dualism: conflict and conquering, mercantile competition between English and French Montreal merchants or between Toronto and Montreal, two legal systems, two cultural solitudes. However, to lump together the immigrants as "the English" and "the French" is as wrong as lumping together all of the Native peoples as "the Indians" and all later immigrants as "the Others" or the Allophones.

French immigrants came from widely varying French regions; they settled in the Maritimes and the St Lawrence valley and developed the distinct Acadian and Quebec cultures. From Alsace-Lorraine, German-speaking families migrated into the settlements of French speakers. Under British rule, the Acadians were deported and dispersed in 1755, but many returned and today New Brunswick and Nova Scotia still combine French- and English-speaking cultures. The French of the St Lawrence valley, on the other hand, were granted a degree of autonomy. Compact bloc settlement, the hierarchical social structures of seigneurs and habitants, and the overpowering influence of the Catholic Church prevented social change. Quebec fur-traders, rebelling against the rigid social system and, encouraged by a freer lifestyle in the West, established the French presence in the Great Lakes and Red River regions. The remaining Quebec French, lacking new arrivals from France, became a tradition-centred group which, unlike the Anglo-Canadians, turned in on itself.

Migrants from Great Britain and Ireland also came from many cultures. The Welsh had been brought under English rule in 1536; with the union of 1707, England and Scotland became Great Britain; and the legislative union with Ireland in 1801 established the United Kingdom. Ulster Scots-Irish, urban Scots, Highlanders, and Orkneymen came. Their numbers and cohesion led to an early founding group myth. William J. Rattray's four-volume *The Scot in British North America* (1880–3) and Ralph Connor's Glengarry novels have recorded the contribution of the Scots: "The independent self-assertion, the sensitive pride, the delicate sense of honour, the indomitable perseverance, the unflinching courage and the rigid integrity of the Scot, are inherited possessions of which they may surely boast."[2] Irish immigrants, pushed out by internal colonialism of the English governing class, were culturally divided into Catholics and Protestants, Gaelic-Irish and Anglo-Irish.

English immigrants came from many districts and were joined by Cornish people and Channel Islanders. Since the Hanoverian dynasty had acceded to the British crown, their German-speaking subjects joined the migrations. But the majority of immigrants had come from the American colonies during their war of independence. The first arrivals were political refugees; the late Loyalists were motivated more by love of a land grant than the desire to live under British rule. The English-English, Loyalist- or American-English, and Scots-English; as well as the Loyalists of other ethno-cultural backgrounds, settled in clusters from the Maritimes to Ontario. Judging from the way the group has been discussed in Canadian historiography, it might be considered an ethno-political group by itself, multi-ethnic American in origin, politically conservative, and adept in inflating losses to negotiate compensation. Characterized by a sense of superiority, they set out to join British elites and to dominate institutional structures of the new society.

The concept of two founding peoples, one enclosed and one expansive, is not supported by the geography of settlement. Many English-speakers settled in Quebec, in the Gaspé, the Eastern Townships, and the Ottawa River valley. French-speakers moved into the Great Lakes area, into Ontario, and into the multicultural Red River valley, where they mixed with Indian peoples and lived alongside Lord Selkirk's colony of Scots, Norwegians, and Swiss. The deconstruction of the self-proclaimed homogeneity of the two founding peoples into their ethno-cultural components, and the analysis of mixed-settlement patterns in the Maritimes, and Lower, and Upper Canada is a prerequisite for understanding the subsequent contributions of immigrants of other cultural backgrounds, just as the exposure of the false stereotype of the typical "Indian" permits an assessment of the many-cultured input of the original peoples.

Immigrants who came without the backing of an imperial culture, though sometimes in the service of either the British or the French empires as mercenaries or settlers, included in particular German-speaking Swiss and inhabitants from Hesse, Brunswick, Hanover, and other German principalities. Some formed a compact group in Lunenburg, others intermarried with native-born French-speakers in Quebec. Polish, Italian, Dutch, and Jewish families came. Jews, excluded from settlement in New France after 1615, encountered no such discrimination after the British Conquest. Africans came under slavery, as bound servants, or as free sailors and craftsmen directly from Africa, from the Caribbean, or from the southern United States.

Internal migration brought other changes: Irish labourers moved into many communities; Irish settlers came into Ontario, and French Canadians worked in the lumber camps. Men and women of one ethnic culture were often divided by religion. Protestant Irish and Germans associating with co-religionists rather than with Catholic co-ethnics. Workers in the lumbering camps and in railway or canal construction banded together by class, as did the urban "lower sort," to oppose bosses and patricians of the same ethnicity but a different class. Gender cultures were as distant from each other within an ethnic group as one culture might be from another. In political discourse, however, ethnicity became the most important signifier.

Canadian-American Borderlands

By the mid-nineteenth century, Canada consisted of several distinct entities joined by a common allegiance to the British Empire – a reluctant one in the case of Quebec and the Native peoples. To form a united country, compromises were hammered out, bounties offered to provinces lagging behind. But regional peculiarities, multiple ethnicities, gender and class were supplemented by one more factor of diversity. The boundary with the United States had been established but was hardly controlled. Immigrants arriving in Halifax or Montreal used the provinces as a stopover, a *pays d'escale* (Ramirez), before moving to the United States. Others, intending to settle the prairies, arrived in American ports and moved by rail to St Paul. Ontarians intending to relocate westward did so via Detroit, Chicago, and St Paul. Before the 1870s, Winnipeg, the future distribution centre for settlers, was but a tiny community. Along the border a belt of mixed Canadian, American and immigrant settlements emerged, just as a Mexican and American belt exists along the southern United States border.

The most dramatic migration was that of French-Canadian families who began to move to the textile mills of New England in the 1840s. Both English- and French-Canadians settled in upstate New York, Ohio, and in Michigan. In Washington, Montana, and North Dakota, Canadians were among of the largest immigrant groups in 1900. Migrants going back and forth across the border, first-generation immigrants listed in statistics as Americans or Canadians, make any quantitative assessment of ethnicity impossible in the prairie borderlands. To make matters even more difficult, during the main period of arrival, Canadian immigration statistics counted newcomers only at the ocean ports and not along the land border; no emigration statistics were collected.

Identities: Many Cultures and Canadian Firsters

At Confederation in 1867, the question arose whether Canada was to remain a conglomerate of disparate regions, a federation of economic units strung along a railway line or a nation with a common identity. The question of national culture was being raised in much of the Western world in the nineteenth century. France, Britain, Spain, Portugal, and the Netherlands had emerged from their own multiple regionalisms into states by the time of the Age of Democratic Revolution, 1760s to 1815. Their national legal systems, administrative procedures, and institutions provided the frame for internally differentiated regional cultures. East Europeans, chafing under the reactionary dynastic rule of the Romanov, Habsburg, and Hohenzollern empires that were re-established by the Congress of Vienna in 1815, developed a national consciousness, an awareness of distinct cultures, languages, and economic interests in the "springtime of peoples." Similarly, on the other side of the Atlantic, the United States created a national identity: British English was Americanized, an economic regime called "the American system" was advocated, a "new man" was to emerge. Canada, Italy, and Germany, unified as states only in the 1860s and 1870s, developed their own national consciousness late.

The term "national consciousness" denotes an awareness of a distinct culture, political autonomy, and economic self-interest. Expressed aggressively and constructed as the highest culture in a hierarchy of nations, it becomes nationalism. It may also turn into dominion over peoples considered culturally less valuable. Territories are acquired by military aggression, by sale, and by bribery, or by promises of a better economic future. National consciousness as the construction of identity, and of a distinctive, recognizable culture, implies the drawing of multiple boundaries against the "Others." The distinctiveness to related cultures justifies separate institutions. Secondly, the homogenization of multiple regional cultures into the new national whole implies loss of particularities as well as tensions. One single culture does not fit equally well the multiple cultural traditions, economic pursuits, everyday ways of life of a fishing region, a mining area, an urban economy, or a farming territory. Thus national culture is always challenged by regional practices, and as a middle-class construct it is challenged from below.

From the 1870s to World War One, unification of Canada proceeded along several lines. An elitist and racist approach was taken by the Canada First movement, which believed in the superiority of English-speaking Celtic, Teutonic, and Scandinavian people over French speaking Métis and French Canadians. Thus its definition excluded large segments of the new state's population out of the cultural nation. Immigration politics favoured farming families as desirable "stock" but excluded unattached class-conscious craftsmen. Economic unity, achieved by a common banking system, was visibly related to railway construction. Canada's first transcontinental railway was completed in 1885, midway between the first US coast-to-coast connection and the trans-Siberian Railway. Culturally, a Royal Society promoting arts and sciences, and literature began to aim at a national readership provided unity from the top down.

But how did native-born urban lower-middle class employees, urban and rural workers, and farmers experience national unity? How did immigrants come to terms with it? Immigrant settlers often did not speak the language of the Canada Firsters. Immigrant labourers and artisans worked, paid local taxes, contributed to the national economy, but saw themselves labelled "shiftless slackers" by some spokespersons of the "preferred nation." When a sufficient number of nation-building preferred "Northmen" – who needed "Northwomen" to do the national cooking and washing – could not be recruited to people the new promising territories, non-preferred cultural groups were ideologically elevated to cultivators; the East European men "in sheep-skin coats" were invited to come.

Clifford Sifton's reflection on that invitation, years after his term as minister of the interior ended, is revealing:

> I think a stalwart peasant in a sheep-skin coat, born on the soil, whose forefathers have been farmers for ten generations, with a stout wife and a half-dozen children, is good quality. [1897]

> A Trades Union artisan who will not work more than eight hours a day and will not work that long if he can help it, will not work on a farm at all, and has to be fed by the public when his work is slack is, in my judgment, quantity and very bad quantity. I am indifferent as to whether or not he is British-born. It matters not what his nationality is; such men are not wanted in Canada, and the more of them we get the more trouble we shall have. [1922][3]

First, Sifton did not want merely men, but family working units with women and children. Secondly, he assumed that farming people form families while urban craftsmen do not. Thirdly, he excluded self-confident and organized working-class people. Gatekeepers like Sifton never included all inhabitants of their state into the nation; rather, they propounded a special role for their own culture and class. If Sifton's ideology had prevailed, Canada's economy would have been restricted to producing agricultural raw materials. Instead, the very decades from 1885 to 1914 on which he reflected, signalled the "triumph of industrialism." By 1920 less than a quarter of Canada's net domestic income was produced in agriculture, forestry, fishing, and hunting or trapping. Capital was steering a different course, accepting workers regardless of ethnicity as long as wages remained low; it did not want families but mobile, single young men.[4]

The emergence of national consciousness is reflected quite differently in immigrant life-writings. Whether agriculturists or urban dwellers, newcomers immediately had to establish an economic foothold: there was no governmental social security or ethnic mutual aid that would tide them over. First and foremost they needed land or a wage-paying job: land to till from spring to fall, lumbering or other jobs to earn cash over winter. Immigrant family men left their farms and tramped to jobs when the frost came. Immigrants wanted roads (and were happy to work off their taxes by doing road repair since they had time but no cash on hand) and railways to move to jobs and transport their agricultural produce to markets. Secondly, they were interested in only one government service, the post office. Through it they remained in contact with families in the home country; communication prevented cultural breakdown and isolation. Thirdly, once they had some money, they were interested in obtaining consumer goods, first via local shopkeepers then through that national economic institution, Eaton's mail-order catalogue. This provided the opportunity to allocate their cash, to get a glimpse of better implements to help their work and increase production, and to consume what they desired – within their means.

Once an immigrant's economic survival had been secured, once family relationships had been re-established after migration, the fourth goal concerned the future of the children. Immigrants petitioned for school districts, built schools, and hired teachers. Thus they built the institutions they needed from the bottom up, an experience quite opposite to their previous lives, where institutions had either existed or had been created from the top down by the lord of the manor, the institutionalized church, or state bureaucrats. Thus the Canada Firsters' rhetoric postulating a privileged English class reminded them only too clearly of their experiences in the Old World.

In most immigrant experience, the national polity, policies, and politicking, or, in a word, "Ottawa," and the urban elites of Montreal and Toronto, were distant; they are almost never mentioned in life-writings. The immigrants' everyday world consisted of the global and the local. Worldwide economic trends, a war far away – but in the British Empire – increased grain prices and the family income. A recession in the Western world deprived them of jobs and food. Their local world that made subsistence possible consisted of roads, schools, postmen, and markets. The national level provided a framework that permitted immigration and homesteading. In urban environments, the role of the federal and provincial governments was not only less benign, it was outright hostile to the labouring classes.

The self-righteous nationalism from the top down and the pocket-lining national economic policies of capitalists and party politicians, were countered from the bottom up by a moral economy of self-improvement: by hopes for family and intergenerational progress, for which Canada First rhetoric and national art had no meaning but a free school system was essential; and by practised local autonomy, which the elites accepted in the case of farmers, but which Métis and workers were denied. This moral economy of self-improvement provides the life-writings with a subtext of Canadianization. Few authors explicitly mention that they became Canadians, but most indicate a basic satisfaction with their lives in the framework provided by state and society.

Canada, like other states, thus has several histories; one of the political centre and many of the regions, one of capital and many of the producers – whether rural labouring and farming families, small-town craftsmen, jack-of-all-trades, female domestics or clerks, whether urban workingmen or workingwomen; one of publicly enunciated morals and family values and many of daily reproduction – child birth, food preparation, care for the elderly. Some of the many traditions are reflected in immigrant life-writings, but not all equally.[5]

CHAPTER TWO

Sources

The images of immigrant lives that we find in life-writings depend on the intended audience – relatives and friends in the case of letters, an anonymous readership in the case of autobiographies written for publication. They depend on the structure of memory and the psychology of a particular author. They reflect a perceived society and a specific social space within it, not an objective one. But men and women act on the basis of their perceptions and they shape and reshape their identities on the basis of their emotional reactions to an "objective" event. These subjective processes are as important as detached scholarly analysis that, intended objectivity notwithstanding, reflects scholars' own perceptions of both the society they live in and the society they study. Scholars are part of a discourse interpreting their society and shaping the collective national or regional identity.

Ethnic Studies Approaches to Private Lives

Immigrant experiences have been studied with increasing sophistication. Self-congratulatory group histories by bards from the respective ethnicities and the immigrant-as-a-problem approach of educators and social workers in the 1910s and 1920s was replaced in the 1930s by McGill sociologists and economists and by Watson Kirkconnell's attention to immigrant literatures. This scholarship provided a basis for the interdisciplinary approaches of social sciences, ethnology, and the humanities that have been applied since the mid-1960s to everyday culture, family life, and the world of work, to community building, institutional completeness, and retention of facets of the culture of origin. To this social history of the peopling of Canada and the emergence of a multicultural society can be added the views of the immigrants themselves, which reflect hardships and joy, loneliness and community, and a gradual weaning from old-culture habits. The resulting Canadianization was not an exuberant step into a pre-existing new world, it was the construction of new social relations, and, in the process, of changed identities.[1]

Ideally, studies of migration and acculturation deal with whole lives, mental and physical. Do they capture the expectations of a newcomer who looked at the port of Halifax after an ocean crossing? Do they capture the desolation of those who, barely arrived, had to be buried on Grosse Isle, who froze to death in a prairie blizzard, who had to abandon their homestead? Do they capture the feelings of parents watching their children venture into the new culture? Men and women coveting land found themselves in the middle of nowhere. Villagers in search of a job faced the frightening bustle of large cities, the despair of lasting unemployment. The novels of Ilya Kiriak about Pavlo and Kalina Dub from the Ukraine, and of Gabrielle Roy about the Toussaignat family, deal with whole lives of individuals with whom readers can identify. Are such fictional characters representative?

A gap exists between the literary rendering of immigrant lives that capture readers' imagination, and scholarly works that give a balanced and complex analysis but lack vividness. Borderlines were crossed by nineteenth-century literary history and well-researched twentieth-century historical novels and through oral history. The use of modern media, from open-air folk museums to television, conveys aspects of material life. In Sweden, where only a few centimetres of tillable soil cover solid rock, a museum exhibits ploughs with horizontal blades. What did a peasant family from such soils feel when looking at the fertile prairies and selecting a new place to live?

If we switch the scene to the 1990s, television shows Somalians, Rwandans, and others deluged with weaponry by the industrialized world, hungry refugee women and children, and gun-toting young men. It also shows the abundance, even glut, of food in wealthy countries. What do refugees feel, who struggled to come to Canada or were cast into it by the vagaries of international refugee politicking? They are confronted with supermarket shelves full of pet food more nourishing than what they could ever hope to offer their children. A pre-World War One Italian, asked why he uprooted his family to head for America, answered that it would not have been honest to stay put and leave them in poverty. Such feelings are expressed in autobiographical writings but not necessarily in social science analyses and averages.

Types and Functions of Life-Writings

Our main sources for understanding immigrant lives are autobiographical or self-life-writings. They include diaries, letters, autobiographies, and memoirs by migrants who came temporarily or stayed permanently. Observers' accounts were written by visitors, often with a specific goal in mind. No biographies or life-writings by one person about another will be used as sources here. But even the life stories sometimes needed an intermediary. Illiterate persons asked a friend to write for them or hired a public scribe. Some autobiographies were told to a family member or acquaintance and written down by this third person or edited from a voluminous manuscript by an editor.[2]

Diaries are essentially private, self-communication, while letters and autobiographies are shaped by the interpersonal need to communicate to another person and by the writer's perception of the addressee. A letter to parents is different from one to siblings or friends, a letter from one woman to another is different from one between men or across gender lines.[3] Autobiographies vary in emphasis, nuances, and tone according to whether they were intended to be read by children and grandchildren or by an anonymous reading public. The writer takes into account his or her audience and encodes the communication in such a way that recipients are able to decode the message. The circumstances of the writer – defined by life-cycle, class, and gender – influence perspectives. The autobiographical views of children, for example, revolve around a common, protective family sphere rather than around separate gendered lives.

Diaries, logbooks, or chronicles are, in the ideal case, written with an immediacy. Memory and later experiences do not yet colour the impression of the day's occurrences in the author's mind, nor do they impact on the transfer from mind to written text. In fact, however, entries may be highly irregular rather than on-the-spot records. They reflect "facts" as perceived by the particular author; other participants would offer different versions. Reflections of events or actions in eyewitness accounts are only "correct" when they remain recognizable to other participants in the same situations.

It is the function of a diary to include, first, a factual record. Among farmers, men keep a record of dates of sowing or amounts harvested, women of dates of the birth of children, of childhood illnesses, or market days and income from the sale of eggs or vegetables. This record may be used as a reference when later experiences have added new layers of memory onto the original event. A different, second, function is a writer's desire to set down his or her feelings, motives, or faith, or engage in a self-searching inquiry. Puritan and Herrnhuter diaries or those of working-class men or women in a conscious process of self-improvement ask: Did I live up to my faith-culture or class-culture? How should I act towards other members of the family, the parish, the labour union? Thirdly, a diary may be a repository of the writer's experiences that he or she may not dare share with others – a first love, ambitious hopes, insecurities. Diaries represent "a room of one's own," an intimate space into which others cannot intrude. Rather than being monologues, diaries may be dialogues with oneself, reflecting complexities of a person, multiple identities, "je suis un(e) autre," "je est un(e) autre."[4]

To social historians, who often have to reconstruct patterns of thinking and feeling from patterns of action, a diary may open a window into the innermost thoughts of the writer.[5] Ebe Koeppen, whom we will meet later, in old age told his life story in terms of hard work and minimal success, yet he had a consistently positive attitude. In contrast, his diary reflected despair and dismal loneliness. However, after a long period of no entries, he noted that he had always reached for the diary when in a bad mood. In a way, he had used his diary to unburden himself.[6]

Letters function as a communication between several persons across distance, between family members and friends close in emotions but spread over continents. A series of letters may reflect events related as they happen over a period of time, with an intervening temporal distance, in contrast to the immediate diary entry or an autobiography's long-term retrospect. Letters may also be action-oriented: they demand responses, an answer, money, information from the recipients. While the diary is immediate self-communication and the autobiography delayed communication with a public, letters are dialogues with intervening time lags before responses. Most letter collections provide one side of a story only: in an age of handwriting, few writers made copies of their own letters but kept those received.

In literary criticism, the accuracy of diaries has hardly been questioned since nobody except the writer could be misinformed, but the factual content of letters is viewed ambiguously. Juliana Ewing's letters "shade the truth in a loving attempt to protect her family from worry." A contextual approach does not support the hypothesis that immigrant letters paint a rosy picture of post-migration life. In the case of chain migration, letters provide clues as to whether prospective migrants should venture out or stay put. They include information on larger economic and societal forces, upswings and downswings in the economy, attitudes of the host society to newcomers; on the local ethnic community, job options in segmented labour markets; on the writer's achievement of a precarious economic foothold or success. Those beguiled into migration by a success story would expect the sender of an optimistic letter to provide a roof, food, advice on finding a job. Since success carried obligations with it, letter writers would pause to consider the consequences of their reports.[7]

Although these letters were not intended for publication, they were not necessarily private either. The immigrant Italian community circulated writing manuals with examples of letters, telegrams, circulars, and formal speeches, with facsimiles even of family and love letters. In the old country, letters might be passed from hand to hand among neighbours in a village, shtetl, or urban neighbourhood; they might be read to the neighbours in a local tavern. The audience was not anonymous, it was people the writer knew. "Public letters" written by men from the immigrant intelligentsia, such as priests or teachers, for newspapers back home resemble information brochures and guidebooks more than personal communications.[8]

Autobiographies written for the family or for publication and an anonymous audience remained marginal to a literary criticism that restricted itself to "high" literature. The new focus of the 1960s on "trivial" or everyday literature centred on European working-class autobiographies and on English-Canadian frontier women's somewhat genteel version of "clearing the bush."[9] Since the 1970s, in the increased attention given to the personal account and new theories of discourse, autobiographies have moved centre-stage. Questions about truthfulness, strategies of authors, cultural themes, and modes of expression have been debated. Autobiographers develop stratagems to make their story interesting, to catch the attention of prospective readers. The Icelandic-Canadian Laura Salverson, when searching for a publisher, was advised to write about illicit love rather than immigrant lives. While diaries are self-dialogues, while letters request responses, autobiographies are self-presentations to which no direct answers will be received. They reflect an author's view of his or her own life and the way he or she wants the reader to perceive the life. Autobiographies may present rationalizations of ambiguous experiences and actions, or continuities in disjointed life-courses. People remember the way they mastered problems and unexpected crises more than the jolt of a drought or unemployment, marital crisis or the death of a child.

The newcomers to Canada who wrote their life stories did not consciously follow models. No autobiographical tradition resembled, for example, that of New York intellectuals who measured their style and story against previous writings and who anticipated critics' responses. Such patterns of societally established *topoi* turn life-writings into culturally determined artifacts with but limited individual personal content.[10]

In a different category, we find the memoirs of *participant* observers – women and men visiting Canada for a limited period. Women explored opportunities for British nurses or domestics. Male observers of the hunter-and-traveller type, often with an inflated sense of their own importance, presented stories of the exoticism and roughness of colonial life. Some astute observers provided a wealth of information that supplements immigrant life-writings. In distinction to immigrants, they were detached from everyday toil; their economic base and permanent emotional relationships were located elsewhere, and their outside perspective illuminated issues in novel ways.[11]

Memoirs of specific events, reminiscences of the trivial and the tragic, unsorted memories of early settler families for commemorative local histories – a variant of the founding nation theme – usually consist of little more than anecdotal listings of the unusual. They do not reflect life-courses, but are merely disjointed accounts. Poems and literary autobiographical writings, on the other hand, reached larger audiences through oral traditions or publication. They may be considered personal reflections with a general meaning.

A more recent genre, the oral history elicited by an interviewer, changes the parameters. The intervention of another person, asking questions and setting a conceptual and chronological frame, and perhaps devoting only a few interview hours to a story of a whole life, imposes a structure on the autobiographer. Thus a German doctoral student asking questions about cultural retention and a Canadian researcher on multiculturalism interviewing the same postwar German immigrants will get different answers. Interviews of East European immigrants in the Prairies in the early 1970s resulted in accounts of hard lives and heavy workloads; yet another researcher's questions less than a decade later brought forth accounts of achievement and happiness. Such discrepancies may reflect multiple facets of the same lives.[12]

Life-writings reach readers through the intermediary of editors and publishers. Ideally, introductions provide the local context, explain family history and kinship relations, and check the particular story against other sources. All too often, this contextual information is absent. Family members bring to public attention a story and community historians publish a self-laudatory narrative. Critical comment on a person's narrative may hurt feelings and destroy rationalizations. Self-censorship may interfere, as when a Finnish immigrant woman recounted her family life in vivid colour, but omitted her communist political life. Because of the dominant Canadian culture's inability to deal with radicalism, she feared negative consequences for her children. Since the life-writings of common people used in this study are not part of larger collections of papers or of complex research designs, much personal context cannot be reconstructed.

To place the individual experiences in perspective, census data, local statistics, analytical studies, and descriptive community histories will be used. In recent historiography, reliance on "soft" data, narrative source has been critically contrasted to "hard" data, statistics. This is not a valid distinction. Census data, for example, are collected within set frameworks, by men and women with their own predilections and culturally determined forms of acting. Did they enter the back alleys in immigrant wards or walk to isolated homesteads to list each and every person? Or do we deal with "curbstone" data made up when census takers sat down on curbstones, not daring to enter what they were told were unsafe neighbourhoods? If they pried information from recent immigrants, did they understand their languages and their meanings? One Dominion statistician of the 1930s used census data to support exclusionist policies.[13] Did his opinion influence the data-gathering methods? Turning to economic statistics, what meaning do statistics of tons of steel produced have for local people? Do rails of steel improve local means of travel or do they facilitate penetration of capitalist enterprise into hitherto secluded communities? The data of a quantifier are of no better quality than the writings of a diarist. The cultural discourses are similar for both.

Life-writings by definition are positivist. The dead do not write, few of the illiterate commit their life stories to posterity, and the unsuccessful are reluctant to go public. Life stories therefore need critical scrutiny as to economic marginality, illness, and death. To ensure a stable identity, memory tends to neglect, gloss over, and forget discrimination and hate, despair and loneliness, broken relationships and unexpected deaths. In this respect, fiction written as historical realism may be more representative of historical totality than the selectively forgetful memory.

Literary Theory and Autobiography

Deconstructionist and post-modern approaches brought forth a large body of writing about strategies and deceit in life stories, especially by French and US scholars, but by the late 1970s the debate had reached an impasse. Criticism has been concerned with the design of an author, with discourse structures and culturally determined ways of expression, with recurrent *topoi*. Autobiographical literature has its roots in St Augustine's *Confessions*, Rousseau's *Confessions*, or Benjamin Franklin's *Autobiography of a Selfmade Man*; later authors, it has been argued, modelled their own written lives on or in contrast to the classic texts.[14] This exclusively literary approach overlooks, for example, the ethnological autobiography pioneered in the 1910s by Thomas and Znaniecki, in the 1920s by Paul Radin, and in the 1930s by Polish anthropologists.[15]

In a paradigmatic essay, Spengemann and Lundquist considered American autobiographers as "cultural types." Fictional and autobiographical processes were similar. "As an author translates his [or her] life into language he creates for himself a symbolic identity and sees himself through the focussing glass of language." Language may reflect assumed values and cultural myths, an American "pilgrimage from imperfection to perfection." Most US literary critics and historians emphasize the "distinctiveness and continuities of the American autobiographical tradition."[16]

The US literary critics who dealt with immigrant and ethnic autobiography developed a similar argument. Jewish-American authors, for example, were said to struggle with "cultural ambiguity," with shadows cast by previous experiences in the shtetl on their identities. Archetypal notions of Jewish existence and an "engagement with the idea of America" structured their autobiographical selves. The "predicament of the contemporary minority autobiography," according to Couser, is reflected in "a more or less steady march away from a private identity defined by [for example] Spanish towards a public identity defined by English."[17] Such critics assume that ethnic autobiographers are familiar with national cultural paradigms. They overlook regionalized, class-based, and gendered cultures.[18]

Were the common Canadian men and women whose lives we will trace involved in a conscious mediation between cultures? Did they write "on stage," performing for an interested audience? Was an Irishman in Toronto's Cabbagetown aware of autobiographical traditions? Did a Dutch homesteading family consciously push back the frontier? Did Macedonian women in Hamilton struggle to fulfil Franklin's model of self-made man? And what models did Japanese immigrants emulate? Middle-class autobiographers, such as the Canadian authors Laura Salverson and Fredelle Maynard, may tap the stock of cultural symbols available, but most of our authors led their lives without reflecting about central myths and archetypes. They followed traditions of everyday culture and, unencumbered by Rousseaus's *Confessions*, forged their lives between cultures and raised children. The tradition of Christian faith and rituals, if in several ethnic, national, and denominational variants, may be reflected in Euro-Canadian non-Jewish life-writings, but not necessarily in Asian-Canadian ones.

Canadian writings do not present a "Canadian type." Immigrants from a diversity of regional cultures and social strata spoke different languages, all possessing a variety of cultural symbols and discourse patterns. When they changed to a pidgin English or a French *patois* they did not immerse themselves in discourses of Anglo- or Franco-Canada. Some immigrants expressed themselves in ways influenced by their own cultures. Icelandic-Canadian authors interspersed their autobiographies with saga-like digressions. Authors whose parents had been part of the Russo-Jewish tradition shared the traditional rituals but no longer understood all of their old-world meanings. In any case, many migrants had not been part of the conventions or central myths of old-country emerging bourgeois societies. Shared experiences after migration, the adjustment to and creation of new cultural patterns, did not result in one comprehensive autobiographical pattern.

Migrants arriving in Canada did not move into a homogeneous new set of cultural patterns. Societally created myths, forms of language and metaphors changed from the Maritimes to Quebec, to Ontario, to the Prairies, to British Columbia. Did English Canada's British-centredness and Quebec's self-centredness inhibit the invention of one distinctive mythology? Life-writings do often reflect a process of getting used to, of coming to terms with the new social sphere; they present an implicit trajectory of Canadianization.

The Multiple Pre-Confederation Literary Traditions

Canadian literary life-writings have their roots in the pre-Confederation period. Several trends of public discourse, parallel or sequential, contradictory or mutually reinforcing, may be discerned. Genteel writers of this period were the forerunners of those women and men who wrote about their experiences with less literary goals and little formal education.

A first category of writings includes travel accounts by sportsmen, hunters, explorers; informative reports by army officers and civilian visitors; accounts of emigrant life or guidebooks for prospective English, French, and American immigrant men and women.[19] A second group covers the writings of English immigrants with means, of the kinship and friendship cluster of Susanna Moodie, Catherine Parr Traill, Agnes Strickland, and others. Their self-conscious "roughing it in the bush" exuded a quality of genteel colonialism. Their lasting achievement was the creation the pioneer women as an idealized character type (Elizabeth Thompson) at a time when women played but minor roles in literary discourse. As regards literary ambitions but certainly not as regards politics, these authors may be compared to the early nineteenth-century women from among European enlightenment, reform, and revolutionary circles. Thomas McCulloch, from Nova Scotia, on the other hand, satirized frontier society. Contemporary settlers whose only capital was hope for a future and a will to labour hard could neither afford such gentility nor had they been socialized into it. The Canadian public of later periods lost interest in these pioneer women's writings until the coming of the women's movement of the 1960s, the conscious adoption of multicultural practices, and new reflections about Canadian identity.[20]

A third approach of writers was of a pan-national and often romanticizing bent. Thomas D'Arcy McGee (*Canadian Ballads*, 1858) and Alexander McLachlan (*The Emigrant and Other Poems*, 1861) attempted to foster a Canadian national spirit taking into account some of multiple cultural backgrounds. Mary Esther MacGregor, writing under the pseudonym of Marian Keith, in *The Silver Maple: A Tale of Upper Canada* (1906) described the insularity of the separate seven early collectivities – the Acadian and Lower Canada French, Irish and English, Ulster, Lowland, and Gaelic Highland Scots. American and other European immigrants and surviving Amerindians have to be added.[21] A totally separate French-language literature emerged, its writers limiting themselves to calls for French immigration or, in view of emigration from Quebec, to a radically different discourse of emigration as the scrouge of society. Thus Pan-Canadianism was limited.[22]

A fourth group of authors took a different approach. They began to discuss ethno-cultural and political boundaries. Distinctions between the United States and Canada as well as between Britain and its colonies were stressed. A Yankee pedlar made fun of British North American colonial life. North American democratic virtues and forthright honesty were contrasted with the shallow life of European aristocrats and *parvenus* in France.[23] Boundary construction, in addition to the neighbouring nations and Europe, also involved other ethnic groups. American anti-Catholic and anti-Irish nativism combined with the Canadas' Protestant-Catholic tensions among Irish. Lurid novels depicted convents, immoral nuns in particular and bigoted Irish in general. English immigrants and visitors considered the Irish uncouth, savages without common decency, given to drink, and committing other enormities. On the other hand, authors sympathetic to the Irish also had their say. Anne Sadlier provided a romantic version of Irish folk life.[24] Finally, the Native Peoples were depicted as savages but, depending on the author's preconceived notions, as barbaric or noble ones.

In a fifth trend since the early 1900s, writers set out to portray national types. Courageous men and virtuous, order-loving women in rugged early Ontario or in the natural beauty of the Rocky Mountains built communities and led heroic lives. Ralph Connor, the pen name of the Reverend Charles W. Gordon, elevated Scottish settlers, particularly those of his native Glengarry County, to quintessential Canadians. The enthusiasm of the English-Canadian public for such ethnic romance in the garb of nationalism increased phenomenally. Connor's novel *Black Rock* (1898) was printed in an unusually large edition of five thousand copies, his 1899 *Sky Pilot* sold two hundred and fifty thousand copies.[25] The broad range of attitudes to the new variety of cultures was reflected in three publications in 1909: Bryce's romantic account of pioneers in Lord Selkirk's colony, Woodsworth's sympathetic if, in retrospect, prejudiced report on East European and others, *Strangers Within Our Gates* (1909), and Ralph Connor's exclusionist *The Foreigner,* describing East European immigrants living on the edge of Winnipeg. There Ruthenians, Russians, Galicians, and other the alien Slavs inhabited grimy and overcrowded huts. Dirty, booze-consuming, and violent, they carried the germs of old-world tyranny and degradation. Not surprisingly, Connor devoted his next novel to the North-West Mounted Police, a pan-Canadian myth.[26]

Historiography, too, was concerned with nation-building. The dominant English-language variant adopted an almost colonial perspective and evidenced a strong British bias. The "Makers of Canada" series (1903–11) and, in Quebec, Lionel Groulx's work (after 1915) celebrated the achievements of each of the two solitudes without any reference to the other peoples involved. This image of two constituent groups narrowed the multiple French immigrant cultures to the Quebec French, and homogenized the several peoples of the British Isles into a single group. Contribution histories of the Irish and the Scots were published earlier than works on the English.[27] Historians of other cultural backgrounds writing in their own languages could not influence scholarship, since the dominant society, either English or French, lacked the language skills to incorporate them.[28]

Finally, the immigrant experience has found its place in English- and French-language belles lettres since the 1920s. Writings of pretended authenticity such as those of Philip Grove contrasted with a broad stream of realistic and reflexive writing, such as that of Mabel Dunham, Nellie McClung, Laura Salverson, and Augustus Bridle. French-language authors such as Maurice Constantin-Weyer, Magali Michelet, and Damase Potvin, who often published in France rather than in Quebec, wrote about Swiss and French immigrants in the West. These immigrant novels – mostly written by women while the nationalist writing was the domain of men – have found renewed attention since the late 1960s.

Fiction, in distinction to personal life-writings, denotes a stage of social development in which groups collectively reflect their positions, roles, and developments, reaffirm, redirect, or redefine identities and activities. Autobiographical novels by immigrants cross the border between individual memories and collective attempts to deal with a common past. The autobiographies of two immigrant authors, Fredelle Bruser Maynard and Laura Salverson, are the most literary productions included as sources in our study. As one author perceptively noted, "The literary form of writing is an elaboration 'on' the migration experience, while the popular one is expressed 'from the inside' of this experience, in a more genuine and transparent way, without literary artifices."[29]

Regionally, few life-writings are available from the Maritimes, where deindustrialization and economic stagnation began early. Life-writings from Quebec are restricted to Montreal, but French-Canadian emigrants and internal migrants developed an autobiographical mode of their own. For the territories from Ontario through the prairies and the mountains to the west coast a substantial number of life-writings permits the presentation of a variety of immigrant experiences.[30] These writings cover most European immigrant cultures, Asian newcomers, and United States and West Indian immigrants. As regards internal migration, writings by African-Canadians, by Ontarians migrating westward, and by French-Canadians leaving their homes are available. Writings of native-born Canadians are mainly written by prominent people, though some workers have left accounts. Women are well represented while urban workers receive short shrift. Homesteading bachelors and families and western itinerant workers provide more than their share of testimonies. Canadian society of the century from the 1850s to the 1940s was not multicultural in the modern sense but it was many-cultured.[31]

CHAPTER THREE

Transitions

The decision to emigrate and leave the country of your birth was a long process. It was often the result of the family's economic circumstances and the region's socio-economic systems. The leave-taking from loved ones was a wrenching experience. The trip began with a train journey across Europe followed by the ocean-crossing, often perceived as dangerous and regularly combined with sea sickness. Further travel lay ahead from the port of arrival to the final destination – a harrowing experience for people who had most likely never travelled before. Men and women from the southern provinces of China or the Punjab faced a similarly harrowing experience crossing the Pacific. It would not be until the end of the 1950s and into the 1960s that air travel replaced the sea voyage.

Departures: Individuals, Families, Societal Frameworks

Some migrants were jolted out of their old-world lives by unforeseen and unwanted events. David and Anna Leveridge and the Durieux family from France, for example, lost their possessions through financial reverses. Others experienced declining fortunes, but were still well off, like the Stewarts from Belfast. The Irish Carrothers brothers, sisters, and cousins weighed opportunities carefully and left in expectation of having no rent collectors "annoy us." Nathaniel C.'s only regret was that he had not left earlier. Vincenzo Mauro, on the other hand, an agricultural labourer in Italy who left because winters without work meant misery, felt treated "worse than a slave" when digging sewage canals in Canada. Japanese women arrived with hopes for a better life but were faced with poverty and a racist society.[1]

With the exception of a few adventurers, most migrants were peasants, urban artisans, rural or industrial workers who were discontented with the opportunities life at home could provide. Recent discussion of retention of pre-migration culture has tended to idealize old world society. In fact, people left because they did not support the socio-political structures or because the economy of the country could not support them. Once a community in some corner of Europe had connections to intra-European and transatlantic migration, it was only a question of who in a family would leave. The decision-making process did not pit courageous individuals braving the unknown against the faint-hearted, nor did abstract push and pull factors send anonymous millions across the oceans; there was always more than one choice[1]. Stanley Brzyski wavered between France and Canada, Wladislaw Chuchla was told that mining in Alberta provided more possibilities than Brazil. Sikhs arriving in Vancouver moved on to California.

Potential migrants came to terms with these factors according to the state of the regional economy in which they lived, the availability of jobs, or the local supply of land. Viewed from the bottom up, decisions to leave were usually not made solely by the individuals but within a network of family, kin, friends, and neighbours. Family economies, structured by power hierarchies between men and women and old and young, were intended to benefit, to some degree, all family members and thus all had an interest in the decision who should depart. Joseph Lang, from the Stanislawow province in Poland, realized that his labour was not needed on the family farm but by his uncles in Edmonton mining. Anna Baczynski, on the other hand, was simply "an adventurous spirit."[2]

Familial and larger social networks provided emotional security as much as economic support. Thus, departure was also assessed in terms of emotional impact and spiritual consequences. Would migrants stay true to their old faith? Would departing sons and daughters send money for aging parents? Would they regret that they could not personally care for them? Feelings of guilt on the part of the migrant women and men and of bitterness on the part of remaining elders, or those siblings who stayed behind to look after parents, were not uncommon. The death of parents cut migrants' last connections to the old society to which they halfheartedly had intended to return.

Families faced with the need to send out some members into distant worlds weighed the expected economic improvement against the loss of labour and cost of transportation; they discussed the departure in terms of food available – one mouth less to feed; they grappled with the emotional aspects of life – long separation and possible homesickness. But, on the positive side, they considered the possibility of decreasing tensions between young and old and leaving unsatisfactory relationships. "I decided then to terminate my obedience," a twenty-one year-old man noted after his parents had beaten him with "a two foot stick." Sometimes a refractory son or an unmarried pregnant daughter was ostracized. Others left after a break in family ties. "Things were not the same after the death of my mother. Home was no longer an anchor; I felt cut off from my family; work irritated me." Relationships in disarray, whether because of death, divorce, or remarriage, made decisions to depart easier. Once unbalanced labour markets and land supply sent young men migrating – and they were usually the first to leave – marriage markets became unbalanced too. Men sent for wives, young women left on their own. Not all departures severed family relations for ever. Some men returned because their wives and children did not want to leave; sometimes an immigrant was able to bring out a parent or a brother or sister. Families extended across continents.[3]

Travel across Continents and Ocean

Having left their home village or city, pioneer migrants had to cross spaces unknown to them, and grope through routes uncharted by anyone they knew who could provide information and advice. But once a route had been established, subsequent migrants were told what to do and where to be on guard. Migrants who went back and forth and emigrant visitors to their families of origin acted as guides on their return trip. Groups organized themselves to support each other; men came with neighbours and cousins, women with other women. And when railway and shipping companies realized that money was to be made from these migrants, they perfected systems of transport to encourage departures.[4]

After the repeal of the British Navigation Acts in 1849, which ended the exclusion of foreign ships from the St Lawrence, migrants came in whatever ships were available and cheap. Families from Norway, for example, came on Norwegian boats engaged in the timber trade between Canada and Britain. Rather than using ballast, on their empty return voyages, captains relied on immigrants: they walked on board and paid. Dutch men and women came from the ports of the Netherlands, French via Le Havre. The Irish came directly on small boats or on larger ones from Liverpool. Scottish migrants often embarked in Glasgow or Edinburgh. Agents would arrange the trip to the port, sometimes accompanying parties of several families. Captains on whose ships migrants decided to travel might be recommended by friends. Passages were cheap and migrants provisioned themselves; and, guided by their meagre resources, they often underestimated the duration of the trip and their appetite. Migrants from other parts of Europe who used the English route landed in Hull, crossed the island by rail and re-embarked in Liverpool. "Busy Liverpool! Smart folk and hurrying folk. The Black Negro, the yellow Chinee, the bright-eyed Hindoo, the flaxen-haired Scandinavian, and the greasy Polish Jew are all seen in its streets." This biased, stereotyping British observer travelled with English, French, Swedes, Finns, and Germans. Another traveller glimpsed larger worlds when he realized that on his English ship the steward was a Black man, the first and second mate had been in Smyrna and California, and both had voyaged on board Spanish ships.[5]

In times of sail the ocean crossing took at least six weeks, sometimes up to twelve. In 1847, when many Irish, weakened by hunger and illness, fled their homeland, death rates on board soared. Robert Whyte left Dublin as a cabin passenger in May on one of the "coffin ships." His food was prepared by the captain's wife who always travelled with her husband. The emigrants received rations and had to cook for themselves regardless of weather and waves. Many, sent by their landlords, travelled involuntarily, others came on their own volition, but almost none knew anything about Canada. They had heard that the trip would take three weeks; it lasted for more than eight. Knowing that they were westbound, they feared disaster when the ship, because of winds, steered a southeasterly course. At first young men and women got up dances, but stopped when ever more people lay mortally ill in the hold. Finally, at Grosse Île, in the St Lawrence, a doctor hurriedly inspected the ship, but could not alleviate suffering since the island's hospitals were filled far beyond capacity.[6]

When steamships replaced sailing boats in the 1870s and once railways connected European hinterlands to the Atlantic coast, travel was faster. In 1874 a British union representative explored opportunities for emigration. His report may well have been overly positive since the union wanted to encourage emigration to reduce poverty and unemployment in Ireland. Canadian agents who wanted to increase their country's labour supply did their best to provide him with favourable impressions. The Ontario emigration agent, he reported, on one trip had arranged rail transportation to the embarkation port of Londonderry, sent messages home for those who could not write, and checked whether luggage was properly tagged. In the port, emigrants were accommodated in a special lodging house for sixpence a night: "Everything was well managed, plenty of boiling water, clean beds, care taken of luggage, and every question answered with courtesy." The migrants travelled on the steamship *Scandinavian,* with a crew of 120 and 997 passengers. Seven hundred travelled steerage, as did eighty-one orphanage children. Single women had accommodation "partitioned off" and there was no "impropriety." Food was plentiful and rich; one labourer said that he had eaten more meat in the twelve days on board than in the six months before.[7]

From diaries and letters we learn how many passengers fared. Scottish passengers on one boat in 1844 collected twopence per adult passenger and engaged two men to light the fires for cooking every morning. Ulster migrants advised the family back home to plan to arrive in the spring, in time for planting. "[Come] by Quebec ... [It] is the cheapest way ... For sea store plenty of oaten bread well har[de]ned and plenty of mail [meal] to make gruel. Some bacon, butter and eggs, and a few herrings. And for cooking utensils you can buy them at any of the sea ports." Some disconcertedly noted that the provisioning left them with considerably "lighter purses." Others described how the many passengers arranged cooking on the few stoves, and how helping the ship's cook might bring benefits. Those with surplus food might try to sell it to others. As to tools and clothing, prospective migrants were advised to bring their tools, to buy clothing in Ireland, where it was cheaper than in Canada. Each bit of information, each letter; made the trip of others easier and reduced the fear of the unknown.

In the late 1890s and the 1900s the composition of immigration changed and new routes opened. Migrants from Italy came via the ports of Genoa and Naples, some Southeastern Europeans via Trieste. Most East Europeans, like Germans and Scandinavians, came via the ever-expanding rail network to the ports of Hamburg and Bremen, or to those of the Rhine in Belgium and the Netherlands. Bremen, in particular, depended on this business. As early as the 1830s, shippers and city authorities had begun to regulate the traffic with the intention of increasing Bremen's share of it, preventing costs to the city arising from impoverished migrants, and benefiting the migrants themselves. Immigrants were supplied with provisions on board rather than having to bring their own food. This increased fares, but drastically decreased starvation. From the 1850s onward, city authorities recommended hostels to transit migrants, inspected them regularly, and ordered hostel keepers to post schedules of charges and of food provided. Shipping companies were required to transport arriving migrants within three days. As a result, migrants wrote home reporting that they had been well treated and well fed and, as the shippers intended, subsequent emigrants chose the same route.

If we follow the voyage of a family from Ukraine to Canada, of a Jewish craftsman from Poland to Montreal, or of a woman going into domestic service in Winnipeg, a complex organization emerges. In his or her home town a prospective emigrant would notify the shipping company's agent, often a local teacher or priest, someone who was literate. For a small commission the agent advised the shipping offices in Bremen and received notification of the ship's departure date, a timetable for the train trip, and a voucher for a ticket, a *Schiffskarte*, a German word that entered many languages. When emigrants produced the voucher at rail stations, train crews knew the routes and sent them to the right connections. At the German border they had to undergo health inspection after 1892, a process disliked and feared because the migrants felt treated like cattle. A special emigrant train transported them either directly to the port city or to Berlin-Ruhleben, where agents of the shipping companies helped them change trains.

Once in the port town, they could rest for a few days. Villagers reported their surprise at the size of the buildings, the electric lights, the vastness of the railway stations. They did not realize that the poorer people did not live in the centre of the town and that many people did not have electric lights. For them the trip was the bridge to better living conditions and if the trip was agreeable, Canada would be even better. Few realized that the trip was probably a high point in their transition, not a first step in an upward movement. In Canada, they were no longer paying customers; they reverted to their previous status as unskilled labourers or peasants.

On board ship, passengers helped and comforted each other. They governed themselves by electing a committee to arbitrate conflicts and determine rules. Separation after arrival in Quebec or Montreal, Saint John or Halifax, was "like the first breach in the family now that we were among strange faces and strange tongues." This observation provides an insight into the differences of social relations between the home society and the immigration experience. At home, people were born into networks and through childhood became familiar with the local geographical, social, and occupational space. On board ship, separated from the known, new relations had to be established quickly. Those sharing food and fears became neighbours. "We looked upon ... [a fellow passenger] as a near relative," a traveller noted in 1844. Leah Rosenberg, in 1913, shared this feeling: "Ship sisters and brothers" gave each other "warmth and reassurance" and sometimes remained lifelong friends. Often support was limited to people of the same origin: Irish would be on one side of the ship, the Aberdeen emigrants on the other.[8]

Steamships needed only ten to twelve days for the crossing in the 1880s. The steerage was crowded, and permission to go on deck depended on the weather. Some ships went as far as Montreal. Later, Halifax's Pier 21 became the main landing point, but smaller ports – Saint John, New Brunswick, for example – were remembered by immigrants as their first contact with the new land. Customs officers were said to be courteous, to perform their duties quickly, and to check immigrant luggage perfunctorily. This was to change in the years before World War One and in the 1920s. The Irish Peter O'Leary immediately recognized the political meaning of customs: the people of Ireland had never been permitted to protect themselves by duties against English imports.[9]

Travel in Canada

The boat trip ended in Montreal or in Quebec City at Point Lévis on the south shore, where the Grand Trunk Railway ran. There friends and relatives waited, as did prospective employers. Those who moved on to the prairies travelled westward was by rail or steamer. Train passengers were divided between reception houses for Quebec, Ontario, and destinations elsewhere. This efficient organization had reasons other than the immediate welfare of the immigrants: it provided profit for the companies, publicity by emigrant letters, and transport for the men and women without impoverishing them and turning them into public charges.

Steamboats for upriver travel moored alongside the quays. Some immigrants were accosted by company agents, each trying to head them to his employer's boat with promises of immediate departure, particularly low fares, and the like. Immigrants received their first impression of fast reaction to economic demand if, for reasons of profit, when large numbers arrived extra ships were quickly sent. In contrast to Europe, schedules were adjusted to customer needs. On the boats, the newcomers met earlier immigrants, "old hands," and Canadians, such as raftsmen going back upstream, for example. From these they could inquire about opportunities, provided they spoke the language. At each landing a family or two would get off and local women and children would come on board to sell gingerbread, roasted fish, and boiled eggs. On the Quebec-Montreal haul, often done overnight, a single boat might transport as many as seven hundred passengers. The upstream route from Montreal to Kingston took another three days, less for people with "heavy purses and light luggage" who combined travel by steamer and stage coach. For those going by train, all luggage was labelled with brass tags. Despite all organization and control, however, luggage might still get lost or be stolen.

Montreal's station, called "Tanneries," was a mile and a half out of town. In the 1870s a large shed, with a cooking room, a dining room serving food for twenty-five cents, and lavatories with an ample supply "of water, soap, and towels," provided an opportunity to freshen up and eat. Those remaining in Montreal could lodge for a few days in the Emigrant Home which provided about thirty beds and an employment office.

Getting to Upper Canada was easy for some, full of problems for others. An Irish woman coming overland to southern Ontario in the 1840s was informed: "You have acquaintances in nearly all the towns you pass through in Canada who will give you free quarters for a night." For those without family or friends, countrymen and women often provided help, in particular if those in transit came from the same county. From Toronto to southwestern Ontario, "look out for the cheapest way of travelling as by stage [it] is very dear." Steamers connected the city along the shore of Lake Ontario with towns as far west as Hamilton. Once the Grand Trunk was finished in 1856, most migrants took the train. When, decades later, the Finnish Grönlund family arrived, unlike the Irish, they not only received no help from settlers along the tracks, but did not know enough English to ask for information. Mr Grönlund had preceded his family to northern Ontario and had merely told them to take the train. They packed one lunch basket; the father had neglected to tell them that the Halifax-to-Timmins trip would take three days and nights. The expensive lunch boxes, containing little but having to last long, were a topic of many an immigrant memoir.[10]

A decision to take a job along the route was sometimes made on the spot. "Henderson [a Scot] got a situation in Quebec – he did not intend to stop long but only to get up to the ways of the country. Watson has got a place a few miles from Montreal with an acquaintance that he happened to meet." The writer himself found accommodation in a Montreal lodging house kept by a woman who, years ago, had lived near his home town. Settling in and becoming acculturated were often advanced by help from acquaintances who had come earlier. Like the shipboard friendships, any man or woman from the home district, speaking the same dialect, became someone who could be called upon for help in the new and alien society. Some immigrants came on special demand. The Ottawa Valley Immigration Society collected requests for labourers (for example, "a ploughman from Yorkshire" or a dairymaid), and sent instructions to agents in England to select a suitable person. The society then paid the ticket on the employer's behalf.

By the 1870s, Toronto was "one of the principal emigration depots in the Dominion, more people going there than to any other station, simply because it is better known." The city had a large reception house, and its labour office sent agents of the provincial government across the province to inquire about labour needs. For travel to the prairies, in the 1890s "a special train is made up within an hour or two of arrival [of large vessels at Quebec], and all are forwarded to the Montreal Junction, were they are attached that evening to the Trans-Continental Mail" with sleeping cars to Manitoba.[11]

In Canada, no collective memory, no myth about the ports of arrival, developed in any way comparable to the Statue of Liberty–Ellis Island myth in the United States. Neither did a negative image, comparable to that of Angel Island in San Francisco harbour, inscribe itself on the minds of Asian immigrants arriving in Vancouver. Of the two quarantine stations, Grosse Île below Quebec City and Partridge Island at Saint John, the former is remembered because of the suffering of the famine Irish; recently steps have been taken to commemorate Pier 21 in Halifax.[12]

PART TWO

The Maritimes and the St Lawrence Valley

In immigrant experiences, the political boundaries of provinces had little meaning. The Atlantic region, first called Acadia, then Nova Scotia, is one historic unit, in which common patterns continued even after the division into three provinces. Newfoundland, separate from Canada till 1949, with its fishing economy and small French element, was similar. As regards English-speaking settlers, connections with the New England culture to the south were strong. For French-origin settlers, the Maritimes and the St Lawrence valley formed one region with two cultures. The early end of immigration from France and the early, mid-nineteenth-century onset of economic stagnation had a great impact on the whole Maritimes–St Lawrence Valley region.

The St Lawrence river also functioned as the gateway to the settlements of Scots, English, and Irish west of the Ottawa river. Compact French-Canadian settlements were bordered by English-language groups in the Gaspé and along the US border. A constant emigration of young men from French Canada into the fur trade slowed population growth in Quebec and resulted in new and distinct French-language cultures farther west. At the confluence of the St Lawrence and Ottawa rivers, the city of Montreal provided an arena of contact, competition, and conflict between French- and English-speaking Canadians. The urbanized central Canada, with common patterns of work and ways of living, extended from the French-settled areas along lakes Ontario and Erie to the Detroit and St Clair rivers.

To the north of the French St Lawrence valley agriculture, the genteel English settlers around Peterborough and the British and French settlers along the Ottawa River developed a different economy and culture: trapping, logging and lumbering, and mining. In this world, extending from Lake St Jean to Mattawa on the Ottawa river to Georgian Bay at the mouth of French River, Amerindians and newcomers from many cultures interacted.

Over time, distinctiveness increased and four regions emerged in the eastern and central Canada: the Maritimes, the French St Lawrence valley, English southern Ontario, and a northern frontier region from Labrador to James Bay and Lake Superior.

CHAPTER FOUR

Immigrants in a Settled Society: the Maritimes

Mid-nineteenth-century immigrants to the Maritime provinces came into a mature society with a population of more than three-quarters of a million in 1871. We will first look at the many-cultured people in a historical and Atlantic perspective. Next, we will turn to the experiences of a merchant of German origin in Lunenburg, a Scottish immigrant, and the wife of an English military officer in Fredericton. We will contrast their lives to the experience of a man whose failure reflected prevalent notions about scions of English families in the "colonies." We will finally supplement the immigration story with that of internal migration and emigration.

Peoples of the Maritimes in a Regional Context

The Algonquian-speaking Micmac and, in the upper St John River valley, the Maliseet, first came in contact with Basque, French, Portuguese, Spanish, and English fishermen, who reached to the southern shores of the Gulf of St Lawrence and Newfoundland's east coast coves and natural harbours. When the Spanish and Portuguese empires lost influence in the northern Atlantic after the destruction of the Spanish Armada in 1588, their presence in the fishery fleets waned and Basques and Spanish were prohibited from landing after 1713. Some fishermen wintered over, villages emerged, and women came to work in salting, drying, and preparing the catch.

In the early seventeenth century, the territories of Acadia (1604) and of New France (1608) were incorporated into the French Empire.[1] French settlers came first in small numbers; a mere hundred lived in New France in 1627. But by 1750 some ten thousand had arrived: one thousand were deported prisoners, thirty-five hundred transported soldiers, eleven hundred women from orphanages, and three thousand came voluntarily as indentured servants. The remaining fourteen hundred came as free migrants. The early settlement of the Americas, from the French in the north via the British and Pennsylvania Germans to the Portuguese in the south, was mainly by those who were forced or temporarily indentured; few came as a result of free migration. Settlement was not the exuberant claiming of a new continent as has been depicted in positivist historiography and popular lore.[2]

In Acadia, too, numbers of immigrants remained small: four hundred Acadians in 1671 and a few hundred Scots – hence "Nova Scotia." In the next decades, families from the Poitou region in France, south of the Loire, emigrated from the ports of Bordeaux and La Rochelle. Itinerant fishermen and a mere three hundred French colonists inhabited Île-Saint-Jean (Prince Edward Island) in 1720. In Newfoundland, English settlers established themselves in 1638, royalist refugees came in 1642, and French settlers founded Placentia Bay in 1663. During the European wars of religion in the sixteenth and seventeenth centuries, some quarter of a million Huguenots emigrated from France. But these skilled and often well-to-do refugees were refused settlement in France's colonies. Almost all European states, as well as British North American and Dutch South American colonies, profited from their talents. The goal – to keep the French colonies Catholic – was achieved at immense loss of economic development, a loss borne by the settlers. In 1713 France ceded most of Acadia and Newfoundland to Great Britain, and until 1763 the Maritimes became a battleground between the two empires. At that time the northern coast of Acadia, the islands, and New France came under British rule.

The Maritimes were connected culturally to the French St Lawrence valley and commercially to New England. After 1713 Nova Scotia received English and Scottish settlers, while internal migration took Acadians from the Minas Basin to the French-held Île-Royale (Cape Breton Island). Although the Acadians had taken an oath of neutrality, they had refused to take an oath of loyalty. So the British government ordered them deported and dispersed to colonies from Massachusetts to Louisiana. Some were transported to England and France; others settled in Prince Edward Island. When French troops were withdrawn for the defence of Quebec in 1759, the British deported those Acadians who had fled to the island. Of the total population of thirteen thousand in 1755, about three-quarters were deported. Numerous men and women died during the ordeal, others established new cultural centres afar. Louisiana culture, for example, even today shows the lasting impact of the Acadian presence.

Many of the deportees migrated back to the Maritimes over time. Those transported to England submitted to the oath of allegiance and returned, often relegated to marginal lands. Through high fertility and a small migratory input of Quebec French, the Acadian population increased to eighty-seven thousand at the time of Confederation, or about 12 percent of Canada's total population. Collective memory did not lament the past, but rather built a bicultural society.

To offset the preponderance of Catholic French-speaking population, the British government embarked on a policy of attracting Protestant settlers. When Halifax was founded in 1749 by about twenty-five hundred settlers from Britain under Edward Cornwallis, the population balance tipped in favour of English-speakers. Over the next three years, some fifteen hundred "foreign Protestants" came, mainly from British-ruled Hanover and Brunswick, but also from Switzerland and elsewhere. Most settled at Lunenburg. In the following decade, eight thousand New Englanders, hundreds of Ulster Scots, as well as Irish settled in Truro, Onslow, and Londonderry. About one thousand Yorkshire people migrated to Fort Beauséjour (Cumberland), and other New Englanders began to farm along the Saint John river and the western shore of the Bay of Fundy. While assumedly disloyal Acadian peasants had been deported, no punitive action was taken against the powerful English-speaking merchants of the Maritimes and New England who traded with the French during the several imperial wars. They may, in fact, have lobbied for expulsion of the Acadians for economic reasons.[3]

Decisive changes were wrought following the Revolutionary War, when about twenty-eight thousand Loyalist refugees came from the newly independent United States. They included Pennsylvania Germans, New York Dutch, free Blacks, and slaves. Many Loyalists settled in Cape Breton, while on the mainland, as a result of tensions between the newly arrived settlers and the small resident population, New Brunswick became a separate province in 1784. A thousand Blacks, free and unfree, formed a permanent community in Halifax, where small numbers had arrived earlier as sailors or with New England migrants. Jamaica Maroons came after 1796 and after the British-American War of 1812. However, the majority of the Afro-Jamaicans and some other Nova Scotia Blacks emigrated to Sierra Leone in the 1790s.[4]

Bourgeois Life in Mid-Nineteenth-Century Lunenburg and Fredericton

After the end of the Napoleonic wars in Europe in 1815 some fifty-five thousand Scots, Irish, English, and Welsh came to Nova Scotia, and large numbers of Scots and Irish to New Brunswick. But they were joined by other nationalities. For example, Adolphus Gaetz, born 1804 in southwestern German territory (Germany as a state did not exist at the time) came to Lunenburg in 1832 and established himself as a dry-goods merchant. The area's prosperity rested on the export of dried fish to the West Indies and delivering supplies to Halifax. Gaetz did not choose to play the role of foreign Protestant. He became a member of the Anglican Church and held numerous school, militia, town, and county offices.[5] From his diary he appears to have been a man confident of his capabilities. A year after his arrival, he married Lucy Zwicker, daughter of one of the largest merchants in town. Lucy and her family provided him with access to social networks and business connections. While fewer women than men migrated, local women helped to integrate immigrant men into receiving societies as marriage partners.[6]

To Gaetz, both, the private and business spheres of his life were so normal that he hardly ever mentioned them. He does permit occasional glimpses into the family's economic base – for example, the high prices of provisions and cordwood – and into the future of his three daughters and three sons. Otherwise, he wrote about family matters only when relationships changed. While he never mentioned births – they seem to have been solely Lucy's business – he did pay attention to marriages and deaths since they changed his patterns of interaction. He was particularly touched by the deaths of his mother, his mother-in-law, and his wife's sister. Each severed relations. Male relatives' deaths were not mentioned; were they peripheral to the intimate life in the family sphere and to relationships?

Four aspects of his world formed the bulk of the diary entries: imperial and provincial politics and events, the predominantly male life in the town's institutions, migration and ethnic differences, and community affairs organized by middle-class women. Gaetz's interest in affairs beyond the local received greater attention in his diary than in many other Canadian immigrant life-writings. Public ritual, thanksgiving days, for example, "in consequence of the success of the Allied Armies in the War with Russia" in 1855, and a public holiday because of the peace in 1856, made this German immigrant, like other Lunenburg people regardless of cultural background, part of an imperial entity.

Sometimes the distant and the local merged into one celebration: military victories afar and "the abundant harvest" at home. Distant worlds might have an impact on local society and family life. The war between Austria and France in 1859, for example, caused "a great rise in provisions and other articles"; the US Civil War resulted in a stagnation of trade. The passing of the famous steamer "Great Eastern" in August 1860 heralded changes to come. Global economic and power hierarchies influenced the lives of men and women like Adolphus and Lucy Gaetz and, half a century later, of homesteaders and farmers on the Canadian plains. They noted that they received better prices for their crops during wars elsewhere in the empire. Developments a continent away, such as the Crimean and American wars, had beneficial results for the local Maritimes' industrial development and peoples' living conditions. "Tutto il mondo e passe" – the whole world is the home town and is reflected in it – said Italian migrants. Much later scholars condensed their and Gaetz's experiences in world systems theory.

Gaetz showed interest in provincial elections and held explicit opinions: he comments on an "ignorant" candidate, who spoke no proper English but "Dutch," a politician with manners "as though he has been born and bred in the interior of Africa." This ethnicization of political differences stood in contrast to Gaetz's perception of Anglo-German community life. Neither business transactions nor community affairs were discussed in ethno-cultural terms. Lunenburg appeared as one whole Anglo-German society rather than as a bicultural one. People from other cultures were on the margins: an American arrived from New Orleans in 1865 because of the "confusion" there; an Italian farmer committed suicide; a poor itinerant froze to death; a vagabond caused a fire; German sailors were tried in court. The only clear biases shown concerned Black people: a "nigger" reluctant to work, an "Ethiopian concert," singers dressed as "negroes."

Gaetz lived in a stable community in motion and took note of in-, out-, and transit migration. Reasons for out-migration were personal: a boardinghouse keeper departed for Liverpool; one minister migrated to the United States and another to England to convert to Catholicism, leaving his family dejected and destitute. A woman, divorced for improper conduct, had "no alternative ... but to proceed to some foreign land [i.e., Boston], where she would be unknown, and earn herself a living." Return migrants included three young men from Australia, their fortune but "known to themselves." A few employment-seeking Germans arrived. A short-lived gold rush in 1862 brought hundreds of many backgrounds,[7] during which boom conditions caused instability, stores, restaurants, and shanties were built, machinery imported. Thus, migration and short-term population fluctuation was part of community life.

The Anglican Gaetz appeared as an observer of the German community rather than as a participant. He watched as, to the chagrin of some of the community, a marriage celebration at the Lutheran church in 1858 was not conducted "in the genuine old german style" but "in half german and half english." Three years later this parish hired a new minister to preach in English. When this newcomer also changed liturgical customs, the innovation split the congregation. By the mid-nineteenth century the German-origin group had undergone an acculturation process over three generations and was in the process of making its final adjustments to anglicization and maritimization.

Viewed through Gaetz's diary, women's social activities in the public sphere were clearly restricted. They organized bazaars, and proceeds of their sales always went to some "useful" purpose. Separation of roles was so deeply entrenched in his mind that he gave special mention to the mixed gathering of men and women when the Nova Scotia governor payed a visit to Lunenburg.

Class differences were not evident to Gaetz, but they did exist. Farmers as producers were part of the community; those who owned hardly any property ranked at least one step down the ladder; Blacks seemed to be intruders in a society that did not want them. Urban life in the larger towns, such as Quebec City or Montreal, was certainly divided into more communities and evidenced more stratification at this time. But perhaps a diary from among the poorer people of Lunenburg would also have indicated more tensions and social segregation.

William Thomas Baird, the child of a Scottish father and his Irish wife, arrived in New Brunswick with his parents in 1816 at the age of seven. This family, too, blended easily into the urban life of Fredericton, Woodstock, and Saint John. William's father came with the army, then stayed as a teacher and purchased land. The death of the mother, was a wrenching event for the whole family. Young William was apprenticed to a drugstore owner in Fredericton, and later opened a general store and circulating library in Woodstock. The male world of militia and colourful uniforms became an important aspect of his life. At about the time that Gaetz recorded the gold rush influx, Baird also watched newcomers in Woodstock, the railway navvies. These migrant harbingers of change were employed to link the maritime and central provinces by the Intercolonial Railway, completed in 1876.[8]

When Baird died in 1870, the last British troops had just left Fredericton. But from 1867 to 1869, the city's life had been recorded by Juliana Horatia Ewing, the wife of Alexander Ewing, a military officer. She would later became well-known on her own account as an author of prose and poetry. In Fredericton she never left her own circle of military officers, clerical officials, and British administrators. She looked down on the Irish and on country girls, both of whom she employed as servants. She despised Catholicism. Her attitude to "Yankees" was ambivalent; their "vulgarity" annoyed her but they "often progress where we stand still."[9] Indians were "picturesque," and "Niggers" were only mentioned in passing. Her letters to her family were full of "useful information" about plants and natural phenomena. In fact, much of the educated colonial elite, whether in government service, as military officers, or as merchants, collected such information, sent home reports, and thus created repositories of knowledge on which scientists would later build their theories. The nineteenth century was an age of exploding knowledge and many visitors to distant parts of the empire contributed to the information available in the centre.

While we learn nothing about town life from Ewing's letters, one aspect merits attention. Both Gaetz and Baird had shown their interest in militia drill and the "street theatre" – to use a modern term – of the parades in front of a female audience. Juliana Ewing was pleased by the "neatly uniformed [British] red-coats," as well as by the military music. We will observe later that many women in the west, in particular those of British background, took favourable note of the neatly uniformed men of the North-West Mounted Police. In other countries, popular songs with a tinge of longing and love celebrated well-dressed officers. Did the replacement of the customary somewhat sagging male garb by a well-fitting uniform and a corresponding, less slouching body language change relations between the sexes, or at least the perception of such relations? Was the colour important, at a time when men's dress was almost invariably drab grey, black, or brown?[10]

Both Gaetz and Baird saw opportunities, never cast their life stories in terms of dislocation or ethnic culture, and became part of local society.

A Scheming and Failing Emigrant

In clear contrast to Gaetz and Baird stands an Englishman, M.C.S. London, who considered himself an emigrant but fled his wilderness cabin in New Brunswick, after only two months. His self-confidence, not to say arrogance, his scheming, his self-styled "unusual" and "perilous" enterprise, suggests a drifter with sufficient means to afford such a lifestyle. This type of person was to become the cordially hated English remittance man. Usually a scion of a wealthy family, the low-achieving and lazy son sent out to the colonies was disliked by native-born and immigrant alike. London had spent seven years in Australia, then eleven weeks in England with his family, with whom relations seem to have deteriorated quickly. He left for New Brunswick to inquire about investment opportunities in iron ore, land company tracts, and business outlooks.[11]

On his trip in 1851 he was told about "the railway, which is ... a determined affair, and which it is believed will rapidly be carried on towards, ay, and to the Pacific" – a feat not to be accomplished for three and a half decades. Immigrants were lured by local hopes for railway construction, better access to markets, and consequent local economic growth. For many these hopes were never fulfilled. But railways, any vague plan for construction, even only the hope for future plans of construction, were a central theme in native-born and immigrant Canadians' future plans. In this respect, the Confederation government did not simply trick taxpayers into vast expenses; politicians took up a national theme that had emerged in advance of the establishment of a nation. One author, affiliated with the railway interests, saw individual and national interest as combined: "The ancient maxim had been, 'settle up the country and the people will build railways if they want them.' The new and better maxim is, 'build railways and the country will soon be settled.'"[12]

London's opinions of the people he met ranged from mild sarcasm of the "I guess"–Yankees and whiskey-drinking bucks from the southern United States, to condescension towards a simple-hearted Irish family and Irish servant girls dressed in finery, to brutal rejection regardless of colour of skin. He uses the words "grinning, ugly, monkified," "haggard, care-worn, pallid, ugly," simply "ugly," in referring to a Negro man, Massachusetts people in general, and an Amerindian woman in particular.

In Saint John, London was proud to see the English flag, showed around his letters of introduction, and flaunted his Australian experience. He moved to Fredericton, inspected iron deposits, land tracts, and conversed upon the prospects of the country. Interested in seeing "human nature in all its infinite variety," he visited an Indian village and had himself canoed up the Tobique by two Indian men to begin a solitary life of clearing land in the wilderness, the "outback." He did pay the skilful men to build a cabin, prepare a canoe, and do other chores before they left. But mid-October was not really a good choice of time to start a homestead. The cold became disconcerting, and two months later he cleared out. According to his own description, people in the "*salons* of Fredericton" were happy to see his return and hear him talk about a colonization scheme. Undaunted by what might have looked to others as an ignominious departure, he noted: "Many a time have I wished myself back in my little forest castle." Possibly he did not get the undertones when New Brunswickers considered him "a notorious character."

Was this just another story of a solitary man, the famous "orphan hero" of American literature conquering the West? A more modern approach would turn the orphan hero into a standard male without social skills, unable to assume responsibilities or establish ties. All migrants had hopes and dreams; the more realistic the dreams, the greater the possibilities for achieving modest success. We will meet more schemers such as London in other parts of Canada. While they built castles in the air or the wrong places in the wilderness, their Canadian hosts actually built endless miles of shining steel, crossing the continent from sea to sea, providing navvies from many lands with jobs, highly placed contractors with fabulous profits, and the public treasury with a solid debt.

Aftermath: From Prosperous Society to Emigration Region

Both Baird and Gaetz lived to see Confederation but were spared the experience of a society in process of marginalization. The Intercolonial Railway did link the Maritimes to the Central Provinces, but investment strategies passed the Atlantic coast by. Some of the economic changes were unrelated to political unification, but nevertheless Confederation coincided with the ending of the Atlantic provinces' traditional economic mainstays, lumbering and ship-building. Steam-driven and iron-hulled ships replaced the plank-hulled sailing ships for which the shipyards of the Maritimes and New England had been famous.

As collieries and an iron and steel industry began to develop, settlement patterns changed. Cape Breton mining and industry attracted migrants from the British Isles and continental Europe in the 1890s and later, but many stayed only temporarily, soon leaving for the Canadian West or cities in the United States. In this respect the stagnating Maritimes and the traditionally agricultural areas of the St Lawrence valley faced similar problems. There, the rapidly growing population could find neither land nor new industrial or other urban jobs. The diaries of native-born women, published in the somewhat mistitled *No Place Like Home*, show many women of the eighteenth and nineteenth century who had been driven to work in New England factories, or farms in Michigan, Wisconsin or California. Others travelled across Asia as missionaries or accompanied seafaring husbands to South America.[13]

The cultural make-up of the Maritimes continued to change. Only Prince Edward Island remained mainly English-speaking, with perhaps 12 percent Acadians, some Dutch, and some Micmacs at the beginning of the twentieth century. New Brunswick's population was increasingly divided between an urban English-speaking sector and a marginal rural economy of French-speakers. From one-sixth of the population in 1871, French-speakers increased to one-quarter in 1901.[14] The large natural population growth was more than offset by mass emigration to New England after 1891. The pulp and paper industries of the 1920s and 1930s could also not provide sufficient jobs. Would great-grandchildren of the self-confident Baird and Gaetz or other proud Maritimers have considered working in them or in the notoriously unsafe collieries? As a consequence, immigrants of British origin and their children were overrepresented among the emigrants to central and western Canada at the end of the nineteenth century.[15]

Instead, other immigrants were still coming. In 1929 the Dutch newspaper *Het Vaderland* published the story of a Dutch farmhand, who with a local family came to one of the Manan islands to recultivate what earlier settlers had abandoned. Poles and other East Europeans came to work in the factories. In 1906 Andrew and Agnieszka Wróblewski came to Sydney, Nova Scotia, from a town near Lwów. Andrew worked as bricklayer in the steel mills but died in 1911, leaving Agnieszka to care for their four children. She decided to return to Poland in 1912. However, she remarried and remigrated to Canada in 1927, choosing to live on an Alberta homestead.[16] What to emigrants of the first half of the nineteenth century had been an attractive society offering economic opportunities become a region of out-migration after mid-century, first to New England, then to Ontario, the Prairies, and British Columbia. Larger economic patterns changed the lives of the immigrants' descendants.

CHAPTER FIVE

French-Canadian Migrations

French-Canadian history in the St Lawrence Valley has been deeply influenced by demographic factors. In contradistinction to other European peoples, French women and men had stabilized birthrates early and by the seventeenth century few emigrated. In consequence, North America's population by the 1750s consisted of about 65,000 French and about 1 million British.[1] When France ceded the economically unrewarding French-settled areas to Britain in 1763 in order to keep its lucrative Caribbean islands, the Quebec Act granted protection to the French language and the Catholic religion and assigned many of the province's administrative roles to the seigneurs and the clergy. This self-administration contrasted sharply with the coercion employed against the Acadians. By the nineteenth century, French Canadians, both Acadians and Québéçois, had developed a distinct pattern of extremely high birthrates. As a result of this continuous population growth, many felt obliged to search for their livelihoods elsewhere. At the same time, as immigration into the colony dropped, the French-language group did not face the challenge of having to accommodate a constant influx of newcomers from France – a pattern common to all other cultural groups of European origin, which kept them in touch with the ever-changing home societies.

Lord Durham's Report of 1839 emphasized the division into French and English and recommended British immigration as well as a union of the colonies under responsible government, based on the assumption that assimilation would reduce the division. Within the French-language group, two patterns of response to the increasing presence of English-speakers emerged. Acadians integrated more easily with other groups, often in a hierarchical rural-urban dichotomy. The French Canadians of the St Lawrence Valley, on the other hand, remained ensconced in a traditional Catholic village culture and urbanization processes became a battleground between advocates of cultural retention and those in favour of change. At the same time, French-Canadian culture, due to lack of European-French immigrants, became ever more distinct from France's society and culture.

The village culture of the French Québécois has been described merely as an economic regime of subsistence farming. However, farming families also engaged in commercial activities, such as selling lumber and their surplus crops. They opened saw mills and participated in the timber economy. Entrepreneurs established textile factories in the river towns, so that in time an urban proletariat emerged. While the exodus to the New England textile industry (forty thousand women and men left in the single decade from 1840 to 1850), has commanded most attention, internal migration has been neglected, as have the sometimes brutal working conditions imposed on Québécois workers by French-Canadian capitalists. Conditions, of course, were no better in English-owned factories.

In contrast to all other Canadian regional societies, no newcomers to the St Lawrence valley expressed themselves in life-writings. In bicultural Montreal, on the other hand, immigrants did reflect on their processes of acculturation and wrote about them. Different mentalities developed district literary discourses. Travel accounts and calls for immigrants from France were published. While the autobiographies of the men struggling for social change during the 1837-8 rebellion who had been deported to Australia had no impact on later French and English autobiographical writing,[2] the Métis uprisings and the execution of Louis Riel in 1885 were taken up with great intensity in public writing. But not so immigration; only a few internal migrants and emigrants from the mass migration to New England reflected on their departure and on Quebec's economic stagnation.

Calls for French Immigrants at a Time of French-Canadian Emigration

While the seigneurs remained silent, the early writing of the St Lawrence valley was in English: travel accounts, sportsman's reports, military officers' descriptions, a novel about Quebec garrison life by Frances Brooke. Nineteenth-century studies of economics and migration remained imperial in context. Hugh Gray assigned to the Maritimes and the St Lawrence valley the task of furnishing "the necessary supplies of lumber and provisions to our West-India Islands" (London, 1809); the Anglican missionary Charles Steward advocated immigration of Americans to the Eastern Townships. William Evans of the Agricultural Society in Montreal suggested local improvements (Montréal, 1835).

Only by the mid-nineteenth century did French-language authors insert themselves into the literary record. Reports of travels in Canada were published in Paris in 1855 and 1866. Stanislas Drapeau studied internal migration resulting from population increase (Quebec, 1863). In 1873 Joseph Tassé tried to attract French immigrants to the Ottawa valley and extolled "ses resources agricoles et industrielles, ses exploitations forestières, ses richesses minérales, ses avantages pour la colonisation et ses chemins de fer." The romantic back-to-the-land philosophy, which in some respects resembles both nineteenth-century European eulogies of peasant life and Russian social reformers' discovery of the peasants, brought forth a large number of publications. At the same time, the tenuous connections between France and French Canada were re-established by François-Edme Rameau de Saint-Père's *La France aux colonies* (Paris, 1859) and Sylva Clapin's *La France transatlantique: le Canada* (Paris, 1885). Frédéric Gerbié, after living in Quebec for five years, advocated French emigration to and investment in Quebec (*Le Canada et l'émigration française*, Quebec, 1884).[3] By this time, the prospective source of migrants, France, had its own urban manpower shortages which it met by attracting Italian labour and the St Lawrence valley was exporting labour to New England.

Two schools of thought about the relations of French Canadians to Great Britain and to English-speaking Canadians emerged in the second half of the nineteenth century. The first took pluralism for granted and did not intend to emphasize diversity. Attempts by each ethnic group to pursue its own nationalist agenda would be divisive (Gonzalve Doutre, 1864). French-origin people should insert themselves actively into the new national economic life rather than remain on its margins. Education should be secular, scholarship and philosophy free from religio-ideological impositions. The second school, headed by bishops Bourget and Laflèche, adhering to the medieval concept of states as defenders of the Catholic faith, saw French Canadians as a chosen people. In 1867 a French-Canadian crusading contingent, the Zouaves, embarked for Italy to defend the Papal States against the secular forces of Italian unification, and to oppose Garibaldi's program of freedom of speech, separation of church and state, and popular sovereignty. When Henri Bourassa became the political leader of the nationalist movement, his anti-British tones drowned out the early concepts of biculturalism. While Ralph Connor was developing the founding myth of the Scots, the Abbé Lionel Groulx constructed a French-Canadian mythology, more directly political and more explicitly racist.

In this climate of opinion, emigration from Quebec to New England and to the Canadian West became contested ground. Three serialized French-language novels dealt with the out-migration of farmers' sons as fur traders, as *coureurs de bois*, and as labourers to the United States. A theme of loss emerged.[4] In *Jeanne la fileuse: Épisode de l'émigration franco-canadienne aux États-Unis* (1878), Honoré Beaugrand argued that New England emigrants would be lost forever to Quebec.

In contrast, the ultranationalist Bishop Laflèche, unencumbered by economic and political analysis, in 1889 expected the emigrants to assume leadership in New England. New England and Quebec would then combine in a separate French North American state.[5]

The loss of French-Canadian culture, as in the forced migration of the Acadians, was a topic of a serialized historical novel by Napoléon Bourassa (*Jacques et Marie*, 1865–66; reprinted as a book, Montreal, 1866). Histories of Nova Scotia and American poems also dealt with the hardships of deportation.[6] Calls to end emigration by planned internal migration and settlement projects to the north of the St Lawrence valley brought little change. The opening of "new lands" in the Gaspé peninsula, in the Lac Saint-Jean region, and in the Laurentides caused internal migration but no agricultural take-off. The advocates of internal migration neglected to include the quality and location of the land into their calculations. When a colonization society attempted to attract settlers to the Témiscamingue area, a mere six hundred families installed themselves over a period of ten years.[7] Contrary to the literature in Upper Canada and the Maritimes, Quebec society devoted little attention to immigrants and few came; instead, a discourse of emigration and loss of culture predominated.[8]

The New England Migration

William Baird, on visiting Houlton, Maine, in the mid-nineteenth century, noted that he met many New Brunswick people, "driven hither by misfortune or choice."[9] In the 1840s, Britain's new policy of free trade deprived Canada of its privileged position within the Empire. What benefited the core did not necessarily benefit the periphery and British North America went into a crisis at a time when the effects of the depression of 1837 in the Atlantic world were still being felt. A reorientation of business, in particular towards the United States, resulted in new opportunities, diversification, and growth in the 1850s. Canada West (Ontario) massively increased its southbound agricultural exports, while in the St Lawrence valley agricultural land was exhausted.[10]

Six years after the beginning of the depression of 1837, Félix Albert was born some thirty kilometres northeast of Rivière-du-Loup into a family of eleven.[11] The family eked out a living, the children working part-time in lumbering. When Félix was fourteen, his father with two sons moved to farm a dozen kilometres farther east. There the family reunited, but the move, as so often, did not materially improve its economic situation. Neighbours or distant acquaintances offered to adopt Félix; but his father rejected the proposal, even though Félix, as well as his adoptive parents, would have benefited materially. Adoption or lending out of children resembled apprenticeship for boys and domestic placement of girls. It relieved one family of a mouth to feed, eased the ritual of transition during adolescence, provided another family with labour and day care for smaller children, and enabled childless couples to gain a heir. The placing of British orphans with families across the empire followed this practice, as had the French sending of *orphelines* to New France for purposes of marriage.[12]

At the age of twenty-three Félix Albert took stock of the family pool of labour and realized that his aging mother could no longer care for all of them. He decided to marry within a few weeks, checked his prospects with three young women, and was offered marriage to a fourth by her mother. Prospective parents-in-law looked over his farm to assess the economic basis of their daughter's future. In unusual speed, dictated by the labour needs of his parents' household, he married Desneiges Michaud, since her parents agreed to immediate nuptials. Over the next thirty-five years the couple had nineteen children. Family formation was an economic and social security project; religious, civil, sexual, affectionate aspects took second place. Productive and reproductive work followed gendered patterns and demanded labour input from two adults. In terms of generations, wife and husband took care of aging parents (social security aspect), and raised children as "hands" for farm labour (labour supply aspect). The latter were assessed by cost and benefit. Adolescent sons leaving the household meant the loss of their free labour. Parents could not retire as long as dependent children were still to be brought up. They had to negotiate their own care in old age with the sons.[13]

Like Baird and Gaetz, Albert took the presence of a woman in the household for granted and in his writings hardly mentioned her. However, when decisions had to made, he asked her advice or informed her about the issue. In a way, she was a partner, possibly because he considered himself "le petit Albert," a diminutive self-presentation found in many French-Canadian autobiographies, but not used by authors from any other cultural group. Once when the family was in bad straits, Desneiges took in washing with Albert's consent. However, when she showed him the dollar she had earned, he brusquely told her never to do this again. The daughters, if they entered his mind, did not enter his diary. They might have worked in the textile mills – he mentioned "children" working there – but he did not even mention their marriages. Most French-Canadian families dreaded separation. One of Albert's prospective fathers-in-law wondered whether the twenty-five-kilometre move would not be too much for his daughter. Albert, departing for the United States, was overwhelmed by "the thought of an absence of one or two months." He returned after seventeen days and "it seemed to me that I had been gone for five years." Perhaps men in this culture form closer relationships than those of other cultural groups. Upon departure and separation, men wept freely without loss of masculinity in the eyes of others, while young men and women of different cultural backgrounds expressed a desire for "independence".

Albert farmed for fifteen years before deciding to go to work in the Massachusetts factories in 1881. The family became part of the southbound migration of perhaps one million French Canadians in the century from 1840 to 1940, a high figure in view of the fact that the total French Quebec population amounted to but 1.3 million in 1900.[14] Farming was no rural idyll – it never has been anywhere. Agriculture meant hard work, long hours, and frequent worries. The Alberts were hit hard by bad harvests, early frosts, and wheat rust. When harvests were poor, sons temporarily looked for work for wages elsewhere.

Albert was also a bit of an entrepreneur, who changed money, imported a few baskets of fruit, bought wood lots to sell firewood, was always on the look-out for a profitable deal. He engaged in credit relations with pay in labour, barter, or cash. Being illiterate; he never kept written accounts. After migration to Lowell, Massachusetts, he took odd jobs, was soon working on his own account, and within a decade had accumulated substantial property. From his one-man wood yard he rose to ownership of several houses and stores. He liked to help others, doing business along the way. Styled "le Habitant," he met fellow-Canadians at the train station, found accommodation for them, and sold them furniture. His countrymen probably considered him a self-righteous busybody. He took credit risks and in the economic crisis of 1893 lost everything; many of his debtors seemed to enjoy his troubles. He, Desneiges, and the remaining children then returned to marginal farming in New Hampshire. Again pressed for money, he dictated his life story to an unknown scribe with the double goal of presenting himself as a model to others and making money from selling it. To use the terminology of literary criticism, it was a "hustling" type of autobiography. Similar to modern "two-for-one" sales, he promised four high masses to be sung for each buyer of his book.

According to the autobiography, the Albert family never came in contact with immigrants from other ethnic groups, although in the 1880s Lowell certainly was a community of many cultures. Neither parent spoke English. When Félix Albert had to deal with banks and institutions, a friend translated; for some of his business he hired English-speaking clerks, without ever mentioning their ethnicity. He and his wife easily found a community of French-speakers. Cultural differences were never mentioned; although he was reluctant to sell his

Canadian farm, he mentioned the Fourth of July but neither Quebec nor Canadian politics. Neither government nor factory owners seemed to play a part in his life the way he described it.

Except for their self-confinement to the French community in Lowell, the Alberts' life as immigrants was not substantially different from the lives of immigrants in Montreal or Ontario. The Maritimes and the St Lawrence valley, like Italian villages in Europe and the southern provinces of China, produced migrants for labour elsewhere. These men and women were not popular in the receiving community, a fact usually not mentioned in life-writings. The very year of the Alberts' arrival in Massachusetts, the official report of the state's Bureau of the Statistics of Labor called French Canadians "sordid and low," "the Chinese of the Eastern States." In Canada, while Albert was having his autobiography written down, the influx of Italian labourers to Montreal was being investigated by a government commission. Immigrant men and women were useful as cheap workers, but hardly ever received credit for their work, for the cities and national wealth they built. This did not take the dignity out of their lives, but they chafed under discrimination.[15]

Departures: Loss of a Lifestyle or New Beginning?

Three French-Canadian autobiographies deal with internal migration in the 1920s and 1930s in terms of displacement, loss of family, loss of culture, loss of *Heimat*, a sentimentalized home. This theme, however, was a discursive frame rather than a lived experience.[16]

Marie-Rose Girard, born in 1906, one of fifteen children, wanted to become a teacher. "Miemose," her affectionate diminutive name in the family, and one of her sisters remained behind when the family moved to Genier, Ontario, north of Cochrane. At the age of sixteen, Miemose followed, "devra s'arracher": "penchée à la portière [du train], le coeur brisé, je regardais fuir le paysage." In 1922 her parents worked a new farm, other French-speaking migrants lived in the neighbourhood, and she could borrow French books from a library "à secouer la mélancolie à s'adapter enfin à cette nouvelle province si différente." Within the family circle, however, she did not dwell on problems of acculturation but emphasized religiosity and happiness. Her parents permitted her to visit a sister, married in Williamstown in the United States, "to see different horizons." She married and by 1947 had given birth to ten children. Her story suggested a wonderful childhood, an uprooting to Ontario, and a difficult married life.

Lina Madore, too, started her story with a "je-me-souviens"-type introduction about her "petit coin perdu au ciel bleu et serein, qui n'apparaît qu'en un minuscule point sur la carte géographique, ignoré par le plus grand nombre des Canadiens. C'est là que se déroule ma plus tendre enfance. J'aime bien y retourner afin de me régénérer à cette source limpide." After this brief introduction, a familiar story developed: poverty, internal migration, a solid and supportive family life characterized by hard work. The one negative experience was an attempted date-rape with the connivance of a young couple she had considered friends. She was able to fight off the attack because of the strength she had gained in agricultural work. It was a life that symbolized the experiences of many families, French-Canadian or immigrant prairie homesteader. The "loss" was not evident in her experiences.[17]

Rémi Jodouin, born in 1912, insisted throughout his autobiography on calling himself "Loulou" or "le bébé," though he was the eighth of thirteen children. His parents farmed near Témiscamingue and sold dairy products, meat, and vegetables to Quebec and Ontario markets or worked in the forests. In 1914 young Québécois men from the village fled into the woods to escape conscription by the government in Ottawa. French immigrants in the prairies, with closer ties to France, voluntarily returned to defend their country. When lumberjacks came into the Jodouin's village to blow their pay – or have a good life, depending on the viewpoint – the farmers' sons could not keep up. They would have had to spend perhaps fifty dollars on a single weekend, money they and their families could not afford. In Rémi Jodouin's view, "[ces] mercenaires sans idéal ... [font ça] pour porter ombrage aux jeunes gens à l'idéal différent qui étaient restés attachés à l'agriculture." In 1923, when railway construction began and immigrant navvies arrived, Rémi and his brothers worked with their teams and earned good money. However, once the trains began to run, the local markets declined. When the crash came in 1929, Rémi migrated northward to the mines of Noranda-Rouyn.

The book's back cover summarizes his experience. "Comme des milliers de Québécois il a attendu la maîtresse d'école qui n'est pas venue, l'agriculture n'avait plus de place pour lui, il a dû s'exiler vers les mines d'Abitibi." He explained that teachers' pay was so low that many did not accept the positions offered. "Pour mes deux bons vieux [mon départ] fut le coup fatal à leur dernier espoir sur la ferme ... Dans mon coeur je porterais longtemps le deuil de cette rupture avec la bonne vielle ferme." He considered himself "Canadien errant," but, as we shall see later, built a house, married, and had several children.

Rémi Jodouin, like Marie-Rose Girard, lived a seemingly happy and successful life in the shadow of reminiscences of an idealized farming life. They evidenced a mentality that harkened back to the past and expressed sadness, while their daily lives involved adjustments, sometimes voluntarily and easily as in the case of earning money from railway construction. This "culture of grievance" was peculiar to some groups or sections of them.[18] Irish migrants developed the concept of "exile from Erin," in Jewish public memory the ever-repeated uprooting and persecutions played a special role. Loss was also the theme of writings of emigrants of other cultural backgrounds, but many were able to express sadness upon departure without establishing a lifelong discourse of grievance.

French-Canadian life-stories published from interviews, whether by the 1930s U.S. Federal Writers' Project or by scholars of the 1980s, do not echo this culture of grievance mentality. Neither did the life-writings of the 1837–8 deportees. They are matter-of-fact accounts of political and labour struggles, of family lives and problems. The protagonists of these stories, contrary to Albert, interacted with Greek, Portuguese, Italian, Polish, and German migrants, sometimes easily, sometimes against the wishes of their parents. They all learned English, though a number returned temporarily or permanently to Canada. All emphasized that, hardships of factory life notwithstanding, families and women in particular did not want to return to the land. They envisioned a different future for themselves and set about to build it.[19]

CHAPTER SIX

The Coming of the Irish

While the social space of French speakers extended from the Maritimes to the Ottawa river – and for the *coureurs de bois* farther west – that of the Irish extended from the Maritimes to the western end of Lake Erie. Irish came to French Canada because of military service in French armies, they came to Nova Scotia via the English connection, they came in the Loyalist migrations. Thus footholds for chain migration had been established early. The exploitation of the Irish peasants by English and Irish landlords and the rapid natural population increase had sent large numbers of Irish to Britain as seasonal agricultural workers and into the urban underclasses. A few went to Australia or other British colonies. After the end of the European wars in 1815, grain prices dropped and enclosure and cattle-raising advanced at a fast pace in Ireland. As a consequence, organized settlement in Upper Canada established colonies of Protestant and Catholic Irish between 1817 and 1825.[1]

About half a million Irish came to Canada from 1815 to 1855, with a peak in 1847, in the year of the "great hunger." The early immigrants to Canada contained a large proportion of Protestant settlers with means, but the bulk of the famine immigrants were Roman Catholics. After the mid-1850s, the vast majority of Irish emigrants chose to go to the United States and as a result the Irish community acculturated early. Like French Canadians, they were no longer connected to homeland culture by continuing migrations. In ethnic terms, many of the Irish from Ulster were descendants of Scottish immigrants, Ulster-Scots, or Scotch-Irish. In terms of religion, the Irish formed two distinct cultural groups, Protestants and Catholics. The Protestant Orange Order acerbated the religious split in Ulster while increasing acceptance of the Protestant immigrants among Scots and English in Canada. In terms of language, Gaelic-speakers were distinguished from the Anglicized English-speaking Irish.

An undetermined number of Irish left the Canadas for the United States. In this respect, too, the Irish were comparable to French Canadians. Migration was a class phenomenon, not only an ethnic experience. Those coming with means were comparable to the English. Less likely to move across "the line," they, too, developed a "genteel colonialism." Compared to other immigrant groups, a high percentage of the Irish newcomers remained in the cities as labourers: the famine Irish could not afford to establish themselves on land. Prejudices against the Irish abounded in contemporary English-Canadian society. In 1871, 845,000 Irish lived in Canada and one-third of Ontario's population was of Irish origin according to the first census.[2]

The traumatic experience of the years of the great famine, when potato blight acerbated the problems of exploitation and overpopulation, became part of the public memory of the Irish immigrants to Canadas. Famished men, women, and children died in large numbers of typhus, cholera, and other diseases both on board ship or later. Arrivals increased from about twenty-thousand in 1843 to some one hundred thousand in 1847, then fell first to about twenty-five thousand in the next years and then to ten thousand annually as the United States, which had refused to admit them in 1847, became open to them. Grosse Île's cemeteries and Celtic crosses serve as memorials to the human suffering. The famine created a new in-group hierarchy: at first the sufferings were "heartrending"; then the newcomers were viewed as carriers of typhoid fever; finally they were called "those wretched immigrants" by established Irish. They were not part of chain migrations in which families made decisions about sequential moves; theirs was rather a flight from starvation to the unknown and thus acculturation was more difficult.[3]

Irish-Canadian Life by Mid-Century

Life-writings provide a broad sample of the Irish experience: two family groups, the Stewarts from Belfast and the Carrothers from County Fermanagh, who became settlers in the Peterborough and London areas of Upper Canada; Jonathan E. Howard's family in Aston, south of Trois Rivières; and two urban dwellers, Jane White in Goderich, Ontario and Bessie Garland in Montreal. Some working-class immigrants, Wilson and Jemima Benson in particular, also left memoirs.[4]

The Stewart family and their friends, the Reids, arrived in 1822 "with their servants and all imaginable requisites in the way of tools and implements, household furniture, etc." Their Belfast manufacturing firm had failed, but in Quebec City, they were able to contact friends and well-placed persons with the help of letters of introduction. Frances (Browne) Stewart, born 1794, described the social and domestic life of her cultured Irish settler family from its immigration in 1822 to the early 1870s in Peterborough, Ontario, as neighbours of the

Traills. Even such well-to-do families oftentimes had to put a good face on a difficult life. The Stewarts lived for twenty years in their first board house in Douro. The roof leaked, the boards creaked, and they could barely reach their home by cart because of tree stumps in what was called a road. Their servant girl left to return to Ireland.[5]

In 1835 Nathaniel and Thomas Carrothers, whose ancestors had come from Scotland in 1602, reached Upper Canada. Over the next years, fifteen of their brothers, sisters, and cousins established themselves, some in Westminster, Ontario, others in the Ottawa valley, and a few in Ohio. The two brothers came well equipped since the empire provided the geographic space of migration. One of their sons departed for Australia, moved to California in 1870, but then returned to Australia.[6]

Family relationships can be reconstructed with difficulty. In eighteen letters from 1839 to 1870, the two brothers only mentioned their wives in passing. In his second letter, written sixteen years after his wife's arrival, Nathaniel described farm and garden, taxes, crops and livestock, and sent greetings to all his friends and family. Below his signature he added a postscript: "I forgot to mention that we had got six children, 3 boys and 3 girls. The two eldest are boys and the next are girls and the youngest is a girl. We have had none that died for none of them has had any sickness. We never lost an hour of sleep with them." Did his wife Margaret, upon reading his otherwise informative letter, tell him to add the children? Did she, too, never lose any sleep, did none of the babies ever have to be fed at night?[7]

The brothers were skilled carpenters. Nathaniel changed to farming after ten years, but Joseph remained in his craft all his life. Arriving at the age of fifty, he had to apprentice himself to a wagonmaker to learn this aspect of the trade. Some of his skills were no longer needed: factories planed boards, produced doors and sashes, and prepared fittings. Writing to William, their one brother remaining as a tenant farmer in Ireland, both men, like many immigrants regardless of ethnic origin, regularly pointed out that they did not have to pay rent, and wondered whether William would be able to make enough money to pay the annual amount. They added that they also had to pay but one tax, a small sum that was for building further roads. They were proudly "independent" while "you are all hard at work to make money for your landlords." William's two sons later joined Nathaniel in Westminster.

One aspect of their independence was the ability to produce on the farm everything the families needed: soap and candles, "sugar in abundance," all kinds of fruit and berries, vegetables, wheat and other cereals. They ate their own meat, and large quantities of it, emphasizing that they did not have to sell it to obtain cash for rent. Though the brothers may not have acknowledged it in their letters, obviously much of the labour that permitted this independence was that of wives, and of daughters and sons. Two groups of unmarried brothers from among the numerous Carrothers' cousins brought along one sister each to keep house for them. As in boardinghouses, the housework for several men was loaded onto the shoulders of one woman. The single addition by Margaret to her husband's letters pointed to limitations of the home economy: "If you come this spring I should like you to bring me some patterns of the newest fashion: capes and sleeves and coats and silk bonnet patterns. If you can, bring some straw plat with you."

In this note, Margaret pointed to a difference between the old world and new, again a theme echoed in many immigrant letters. "You would see more silks worn here in one day than you would see in Maguiresbridge in your lifetime." Furthermore, "[you] could not tell the difference between the lady and the servant girl," whose bonnet might be "ornamented with artificial flowers and veil." Wages for female domestics and male artisans were high. "Eating and drinking are very good in this country when compared to that of the farmers in Ireland." This seems to have been true for the Carrothers even when frosts destroyed much of the crops, as in 1860, or when business was slow, as in 1862 because of the American civil war. Such comments stood in marked contrast to the experience of French Canadians, whose landholdings were smaller.

One prerequisite for success was good health. If money was not always needed, labour was. Men and women who were strong, who had skills, and who could rely on the labour of sons and daughters prospered. Part of the family labour force might hire itself out to bring in cash. A carpenter could build an additional house and rent it for cash. Wood could be had for the cutting from someone who could not afford the labour. Once money was available, threshing machinery and crews could be hired and the farming family's own skilled labour might be allocated for more remunerative work. Under these circumstances an "industrious man," like an industrious woman, could make a good living and need not go to dig gold in California or Australia, as some settlers pointed out. The Carrothers's view was optimistic; after all, they were well established. Equally hardworking Highlanders, who were farther north and had only recently begun to cultivate their land, were reduced to dig roots in the bush when drought caused the harvest to fail.

Immigrant and native-born farmers alike were not shy to exhibit their successes. The fine produce of horticulture, agriculture, and cattle-raising was paraded at fairs. As in Europe, fairs served as markets and provided diversion and pleasure. However, the presence of merchants from afar was far less important than the input of the locals.

Fairs showed present achievements and suggested next year's prospects. They outlined a community's project for its future.[8] Fairs brought together kin and friends who lived in neigbouring townships but rarely got to see each other. The five-day provincial fair in London in 1865 attracted some forty-thousand visitors.

By the 1870s this rapidly evolving society could have been as stable and settled as Gaetz's in Nova Scotia. But families continued to grow and, like French Canada, the society remained mobile. Many of the Carrothers children took land eighty kilometres farther north, and the grandchildren joined the move to Manitoba and beyond, as did the sons of the Howard family. In 1858 a letter to William in Ireland noted that all Carrothers were well. "I must mention them by wholesale for they are a numerous progeny. In a few weeks they will come up to 90 in name and number." Some family members settled in the North-West Territories, but the land proved too distant from markets and they subsequently joined the rural-to-urban migrations.

The Stewarts's and Carrothers's neighbours were English, Irish, Scots, and Highland Scots, as well as Americans. "Indians" appeared only in accounts of "an attack some years ago" among Peterborough people, and as neighbours in a village of their own in Goderich. According to the Carrothers family, religious differences decreased, Catholic Irish joining the militia as loyal Canadians during the Fenian raids. Jane White, on the other hand, continued to look down on Irish Catholics and did not stoop to mention French Catholics. She rejected the English as "aristocratic" and exploitative. In Aston, Quebec, poor Irish and French settlers eked out a living; the local copper mine employed four hundred men and two hundred women. People of various cultural backgrounds were civil to each other, traded and helped, but did not usually mingle. Elections might pit the French-speaking against the English-speaking population.[9]

Well-to-do Irish families were well versed in British political structures and could afford to spend time on politics. From a conservative mould, they were against rebellion and supported politics that favoured landowners. They interpreted the arrival of "Americans from the old world" (that is, European immigrants from the United States), as a sign that they "are tired of their republican government." The Fenian activities in Ireland and in the United States were but meant to "rob and plunder." "The poor devils," said a wealthy Carrothers, are "putting their time and money to a bad use."[10]

As had been the case in the Maritimes and would be the case in the West, the coming of a railway changed economic life. When the Grand Trunk to Sarnia was completed in 1856 and the branch line to Goderich in 1858, it made the town a "Yankiefied place," according to Jane

White, who at age eighteen, had arrived from Belfast with her parents and a woman servant in 1849. Her father had invested in real estate in the bustling port on Lake Huron. She did not like Americans – "This proud mean aristocracy of money is very revolting" – though her investor-father pursued his financial interests just as keenly.[11] Expanding Goderich, like other small towns, attracted professions catering to the middle classes. When piano teachers were needed, in the late 1850s, word spread quickly and "a number ... all females" came.

Independence was more difficult to achieve in towns and cities. On farms, labour and home produce could substitute for income, but in towns cash was needed to buy provisions. "The mechanics and labourers are badly off," Jane noted when jobs decreased after the completion of the railway while food prices rose because of poor harvests.

Bessie Garland, the daughter of a gentleman farmer family near Enniskillen, belonged to the middle segment of society. She left Ireland after the death of her sister, her wish to go to "America" being fulfilled when a woman acquaintance took her to Montreal. The death of her father and the famine at home precluded her return. In Montreal she could have relied on a cousin, but was "too independent of spirit to be dependent even on relatives." She took a position as home help to an established family, but having been socialized into a mentality of sacrifice, she overworked herself and fell ill. Against warnings of friends, she soon accepted a another position as governess. When her brother, who had migrated to the United States, asked her to join him, her independence came to the fore again: she stayed in Montreal and never heard from him again. She was less independent when it came to expectations that women marry. A "forced and unexpected marriage" to an aging friend of her host family certainly gave her financial security as "an old man's darling," but she warned other women not to marry elderly men. When he died, Bessie Garland became a travelling book agent, content to earn her living and to regain her independence.[12]

While the Carrothers children were mobile geographically and the Stewarts and Whites were upwardly mobile, many skidded down the ladder. Those who became disabled or ill could not achieve independence or lost what little they had. A list of the Prescott, Upper Canada, Emigrant Aid Society, revealed the underside. Destitution forced many to apply for help: a widow, a "very old woman" with two grandchildren, an old man, "a discharged soldier," a labourer hurt in an accident, women without means on the way to join their husbands, children without parents, a young widower without hope carrying his infant daughter to a "brother," or, more probably, to the brother's wife.[13] While the Carrothers family was remarkably free of illness and death, Frances Stewart lost her husband in 1847. For a quarter of a century she had to manage on her own. Death was often followed by remarriage and such reaffirmation of life contributed to the myth of success.

Labourers: Multiple Moves and Assisted Emigration

The Carrothers, Whites, and Stewarts came to Canada in well-planned moves based on sufficient resources. Class as well as bad luck, both circumstances beyond an individual's control, could lead to quite different migration experiences. Typical of many immigrant experiences, Wilson Benson, born in 1821 in Belfast, described his migrations and his acculturation as a slow adjustment rather than the exuberant embrace of life in the new world. People "get used" to the new surroundings and come to value their independence. No US-style mythology of free land and free institutions developed, but an attachment to low taxes and little government interference emerged.

Benson lost his mother at the age of one. His father remarried and took the child to County Armagh, where the new family lived in penury on his stepmother's farm. By hard work they improved the farm but since they did not take out a deed in the father's name, they were helpless when the stepmother's sons from her previous marriage dispossessed them. Poverty forced the family to hire Wilson out at age twelve. This was the beginning of a decade and a half of unsteady but incessant work and dozens of moves. Whether his early loss of emotional attachment or a marginalized position in the family predisposed him to move from job to job we cannot tell. Class position would be sufficient to explain his mobility and modest circumstances, but class explains the framework of acting, not individual predispositions and decision-making.[14]

As an apprentice, Benson remembered that "labour is hard and treatment worse." When his father, to whom he returned at the age of fifteen, could not afford to send him to school, he left for Scotland, a "land of cakes" in the view of the Irish. So was England. The route was taken seasonally by masses of Irish workers, bound, for example, for jobs as hop pickers in Kent. Travel conditions were deplorable: "Women and children have to stow themselves away on deck among cows and pigs" and there were no female stewards for them. Benson joined a sister and her husband and the three moved to Glasgow to work in a cotton mill. Heading for harvest work in the Lothians, he met other tramping Irish and Highlander men and women. They slept in haystacks and food was always short. Hungry migrants sometimes carried a weak comrade to a well-to-do farmer on the roadside, threatening to leave him there to die. Usually they were fed, with a tacit understanding that no corpse would be left behind. Anthropologically speaking, the migrants' culture of poverty included ritual and rebellion as survival strategies. Benson's strategy, on the other hand, was to peddle goods along the route and thus make the days of migration, a time of expenses without income, to some small degree profitable.

At an unusually early age by Irish custom, Benson, aged eighteen, and sixteen-year-old Jemima Hewett married and decided to go to "America." The couple reached Brockville, Ontario, where Jemima's brother lived, in 1841. Jemima hired herself out for general housework, but for two years Benson could not find a steady job.[15] He worked at weaving wollen cloth, briefly and unsuccessfully as a ploughman, and as a porter in a hotel. He engaged with a Scottish baker, a shoemaker from Dublin, and finally worked in a factory for agricultural implements. He and his wife were able to rent a house and live together.

For the next six years Benson shipped out on lake steamers destined for the United States, and once he helped a runaway slave cross to Canada. His contacts with other cultures, including the ubiquitous French-Canadian raftmen, were much more varied than those of his more settled fellow Irish. His work was physically demanding, whether as weaver on a Jacquard frame, as cook for harvest workers which meant stirring kettles that hold perhaps a hundred gallons, or on the steamers.

Finally, the Bensons opened a store, first in Kingston, a few years later in Toronto. Jemima kept the store and provided the home base, while Wilson continued to move about. Jemima and Wilson wanted to establish themselves, but bad luck followed them. Time and again Wilson injured himself, had boxes stolen, or lost land because of faulty deeds. But notwithstanding all setbacks, the Bensons kept their goal in sight: a joint household and a secure economic basis. After each reversal they moved on with hardly a complaint.

Wilson remained conscious of his standing and ethnicity. After a fight between Cork and Connaught Irishmen, he showed concern about the "unenviable notoriety." The Scot James Thomson commented on Quebec City's lower town: "The Irish are just Irish," and transplanting did not improve them. The Bensons lived in Toronto's Irish neighbourhood, and when Benson travelled through the countryside, he followed Irish settlement patterns. But his steamboat contacts with native-born Canadians and their discussions on the prospects of the country "furnished food for reflection, and awakened in me a new and lively interest in the country and begat a feeling of identity in its welfare which supplanted the yearning desire I had hitherto entertained of returning to my native land." The death of his father ended such desires and his story might be subtitled: "The Canadianization of Wilson

Benson: A Hundred Different Ways on How to Settle Canada and What Not to Do."[16]

A conjunction of events changed the Bensons' life in 1849. A fire in their Toronto shop and an invitation from Jemima's brother to join him farming in Orangeville, Ontario, coincided. They decided that Jemima should go ahead to assess the possibilities. When she liked it, Wilson carefully planned the farming life, and, equally careful to cover the cost of the trip, made some money by selling whiskey along the way. After a year in Amaranth Township they bought a respectable farm in Artemesia Township. Then tragedy struck: Jemima and a child died in 1860. Wilson remarried; life had to go on. Almost twenty-five years later, an accident on a threshing machine left him a partial invalid. The family was again able to cope. They opened a store in Markdale. When Wilson died in 1911 at the age of ninety, the family had witnessed Ontario's phenomenal economic growth: "a market at our door," railway, mills, and factories in an area which "a few short years ago ... was overgrown by dense forest."

High mobility characterized Wilson and Jemima's early life. And such seasonal mobility year after year or permanent emigration without permanent re-establishment in the receiving country was the experience of millions of Irish and English. Over a ten-year period, only one-third to one-half of the people listed at the beginning of the decade still lived in the same place at the end of it. Such men and women stood between agricultural, industrial, and commercial life. Peasant cottages in Ireland, as in many other regions of Europe, contained but one large room for the family, an open hearth, and perhaps some animals. When subsistence farming no longer could feed the family, such cottages could easily be enlarged by an additional room. This "shop" could be part of the industrial world, male work for distant markets, or part of the commercial world, female retailing for the immediate neighbourhood. Women could divide their time between tending to customers, housework, and children. If a culture of migration existed, the cottage would be left altogether, a new life in the interstices of economic development be commenced afar.

Unionization and Emigration of Workers in the 1870s

Because of the miserable standard of living in Ireland and England in the mid-nineteenth century, the National Agricultural Labourers' Union in the 1870s "determined to organize a large emigration, and thus lower the supply and increase the demand" for labour in the home country. The union sent delegates to Ireland in 1873 to organize labourers and to report on living conditions. The "wretched conditions of a class" made men and women as well as their children "the worst fed, the worst-clad and worst housed probably in Europe." In Liverpool harbour, any observer could "see the agricultural labourer and his family, after years of unceasing toil, in a state of destitution leaving his country, and in the majority of cases the passage being paid for him, as he has scarcely money enough to purchase the necessary clothing."

Peter O'Leary went to Canada in 1874 to investigate emigration opportunities. An agricultural labourer, he had migrated to London at the age of twenty for "novelty and change" and for "more lucrative employment." He had learnt the trade of "street mason and paviour," and commented on the poor quality of the pavements in Canadian streets.[17] Emigrants in these years came from "nearly all the nationalities of Europe." There were large segments of English agricultural labourers chafing from a lock-out, Irish small farmers, and single young women intending to go into domestic service. The latter were usually provided with letters of introduction to Catholic clergymen in Canada who would place them. Children from the orphanages were also sent to Canada. O'Leary considered the English "the most industriously trained," the Irish "the most book learned" owing to the good education system, the Scots "the most calculating and practical."

O'Leary described the demand for labour from Quebec City to Niagara, including information on both wages and cost of food, rent, and clothing. Living standards cannot be measured merely by wages, which were often supplemented by home production. The consumption side, the allocation of resources, provided the other half of strategies to keep or reach certain living standards. Thus male-centred wage statistics reflected but part of family economies, and women's strategies to feed and clothe their families has to be factored in.

Quebec City, at that time, had shop fronts with "English, Irish, Scotch, German," and perhaps Jewish names. Many Irish were active in the lumber trade. Wages for labourers were good, cloth manufacture employed many, and even unskilled workers were well-clad. He saw only two beggars, old women, "none of them cringing, half-famished creatures with children hanging to their skirts so frequent in the streets of London." Along the St Lawrence, men, women, and children were getting land ready for crops, which they grew "for themselves" without fear of rent-day or the "land agent's frown." Servant girls could earn five to ten dollars a month, a piece of information repeated in many immigrant women's letters. A porter, like any other labourer, did not have to lower his dignity "by putting his hand to his cap, and in some cases taking it off altogether ... which leads the person receiving the homage to believe it is due to him through superior merits." This, too, was a theme echoed in emigrant letters of many ethnic groups.

O'Leary continued via Montreal and Toronto to Winnipeg, but as yet did not find the Manitoba capital an advisable location for labourers. Younger sons of Irish farmers, however, were already crossing the continent, by way of the Panama Canal, to reach the British Columbia goldfields. The settled world still ended at Georgian Bay, but prospects loomed across the continent.[18]

PART THREE

Urban Life, Farming, and Lumbering in Central Canada

Like cultural space, economic space is different from political space. Central Canada extends from Montreal, or perhaps even from Quebec City and the industrial towns along the St Lawrence, to southwestern Ontario and Georgian Bay. Montreal, "the real capital of Canada," became contested ground between French- and English-speakers as well as immigrants. In 1857 the government of the Province of Canada was shifted to Ottawa, then emerging out of the predominantly Irish Bytown.

Between Montreal and Toronto (until 1834 named York) numerous small industrial towns with lumber and related factories sprang up. Only in the 1960s did Toronto surpass Montreal. Since then Toronto has become the "meeting place," the possible Native meaning of its name, for more than a hundred cultures from across the world. But in the early part of the century it remained a British-dominated city.

Ontario, like the Maritimes and Quebec, experienced considerable out-migration in the second half of the nineteenth century. Farming families with sufficient funds to move to the West avoided the direct migration into industry that subsistence farmers had to undertake. Central Canada consisted and still consists of a farming and an industrial belt. To the north a world of lumbering, railway building, mining and smelting extended from Noranda-Rouyn to Thunder Bay. In the 1890s, a new centre arose in the West; Winnipeg became the gateway and distribution centre for immigrants.

CHAPTER SEVEN

Immigrants in Montreal

Thriving mid-nineteenth-century Montreal attracted newcomers in large numbers. William Weir, a young Scotsman, went to his uncle's family in Lachute in 1842, then became a teacher while learning French, moved back to Montreal in 1844, and in 1847 set up in business for himself. His retrospective is a political history of Montreal and Quebec rather than a life-story. James Thomson, a journeyman baker from Scotland, came in 1844; Richard Hemsley, an English watchmaker, lived there in the 1860s and 1870s.[1]

Without exception, these immigrants came in contact with both anglophone and French-Canadian native-born men and women. In Weir's view, the French were "gentle," the English "overbearing." Hemsley observed an *entente cordiale* between the two groups. Thomson, working under a French foreman, learned to communicate with him. According to his understanding, the French and only the French were called "Canadians" – an interesting comment on the delayed feeling of the English-speaking community that it was part of a new nation, and a reflection on its divided colonial and imperial mentality.

Other immigrants in Montreal were of Jewish and Scandinavian background. Native women sold embroidery and a Black community existed. During the American civil war, refugees from military service in the southern armies fled to Montreal. R.B. Nevitt, who was to be drafted at the age of fourteen in Savannah, Georgia, sought shelter in Canada, and in a letter home commented, "You have no idea how many Southerners there are here."[2] Montreal, with a population of 140,000 in 1873, grew massively at the turn of the century when Italian and other European workers came in large numbers and the Jewish community began to increase. By 1911, the city and its suburbs contained 528,000 inhabitants.

Labour and Social Mobility to the 1870s

James Thomson, journeyman baker and son of a blacksmith in Aboyne, Scotland, arrived in 1844. He was better off than Scots from the crofting areas which had suffered during the period of Highland clearances. Many potential emigrants from rural areas had to interrupt their passage through a port to earn money by casual work for the transatlantic trip. Thomson, with savings and a letter of introduction to a Scottish Presbyterian minister, contrary to his intention to "go West," stayed in Montreal. One of his first letters home concerned the abundant food in his lodging house. "We have always beef steak and potatoes to breakfast and also tea and roastbeef and potatoes to dinner besides a number of other dishes. The whole concludes with a glass of cold water there being no beer unless called for." Food habits changed: "The Scotch people all seem to turn English when they come here and to live on roast beef and white bread."

Thomson found a job at the bakery of two Scots, the mother of one of them keeping their house and tending the shop. Two French Canadians and an Irish immigrant worked there already. The foreman taught him some French, but he never learned Irish Gaelic. His experiences were as typical for skilled journeymen as those of Wilson and Jemima Benson were for itinerants. "The baking is harder work here than in Aberdeen but they are better paid and also better fed." To permit his friends in Scotland to judge for themselves, he sent precise reports: four journeymen fill the oven three times a day, with dough made of three barrels of flour. Wages ranged from ten to sixteen dollars per month. He started at a low rate since "baking is very different [here]" but he adapted quickly and a year later was earning seventeen dollars.

He kept ties to Scotland by reading Aberdeen newspapers, by attending the Scottish Presbyterian church, and by visiting a baker from Aberdeen in a nearby village. Initially he boarded with a man from his home district, then lived with his employers. The housekeeping mother had the help of a Scottish servant girl who earned about four dollars a month. "The girls dress almost as fine as their mistresses." He familiarized himself with the city while making deliveries.

To his correspondents he pointed out the differences to Scotland. As yet, there were no factories; food was cheap because south shore farmers came each day by ferry or by sled in winter; "all classes" of people dressed well, few had to go in rags. Only the farmers all looked alike "clad in stout gray homemade like clothes." He got along well with the French but remained prejudiced against the Irish. He took note of a synagogue – the 1851 census lists only 451 Jews in both Canadas – and of the few Amerindians in town. He described the timber and log rafts on the St Lawrence and the volume of shipping. His family and friends were thus informed about his worklife, his religious affiliations, and about anything that struck him as different.

A year after his arrival, Thomson wanted to move on, having the customary baker's complaints concerning nightwork and heat, but being content with wages and board. Once again, his move west did not happen. First, his employers persuaded him to stay until they found a replacement; then, when he was settling accounts with them, a "gentleman" entered the shop and offered to hire him as baker to supply Irish canal workers in Edwardsburgh (later Cardinal) in Ontario. Thomson accepted on the spot, happy that he was to work during the day and for only nine hours. He was able to speak French to the Natives who sold fish and observed the poor living conditions of the Irish. With others he collected money when news of the great famine reached the town.

Edwardsburgh, in contrast to backcountry regions, was economically well off, in his opinion, because money for business was available. When the canal was finished he supplied a shopkeeper with baked goods and gave up plans to leave for the West: "I dont care much as long as I can earn fifty pounds a year with a straight back and some leisure hours." Thomson did not advise his friends about emigration since he had not seen enough of the country. Two years later, in 1849, he changed his mind and left for the California goldfields via Chicago. He did well and upon return bought land in Edwardsburgh and visited Scotland in 1853. The following year, when he was thirty-one, he married Mary Armstrong. The Scottish baker had become an Ontario farmer who kept in close contact with his family, in Scotland. When his father lost his job as a blacksmith and his sister Helen had to work hard as a casual day labourer on farms, he and Mary decided to bring them out to Edwardsburgh. We will meet James and Mary Thomson again later.[3]

Richard Hemsley, a clock and watchmaker, did well in England. He was put in charge of a shop in Swinton even before his apprenticeship was over. His father offered to set him up in trade, "but the urge to travel was on me." Hemsley arrived in Montreal in July 1867, en route to Chicago, but a chance acquaintance, a jeweller, convinced him that the rapidly growing Montreal offered opportunities. Hemsley found himself a position as a watchmaker. He shared a room with a Scot recently returned from a South American sugar plantation and lived next door to an English ironmonger on a tour of the world. With Confederation, when the English troops left town, business lost its contracts for supplies and, according to Hemsley, the ladies their "scarlet fever," their attraction to men in colourful uniforms. In 1870 he set up his own shop. With no more than ninety dollars in savings, he asked his father for help but was refused and told to return. "Being determined to succeed," he cut all contact with his family as well as his Montreal "chums," who probably spent part of their wages on the pleasures of life. Having bought goods on credit but not finding customers, he turned itinerant and peddled his goods as far as Sherbrooke and Lennoxville. Ten years later, he employed eight watchmakers. Though at first disconcerted by the lack of skills among artisans, he soon lowered his own standards. He was no crusader but a businessman. He never mentioned marriage or childbirth but at one point vaccinated himself, family, and friends. His life and self-confidence resembled that of Gaetz. He may have written his autobiography to establish a model of thrift leading to success.[4]

While Hemsley successfully weathered his initial business crisis, the life of poor male, female, and child workers had fewer such success stories. According to O'Leary's 1874 report, "the hours are sixty per week, or ten per day, which are far too many, particularly for women and children, many of the latter being very young." Legislation to regulate labour-capital relationships was needed, "the time has arrived for Canadian politicians to consider the necessity of a Factory Act from a statesmanlike point of view, because if the people are permitted to degenerate through overwork the state is sure to suffer in proportion." Hopes for such statesmanlike vision was to remain futile for many decades. In Europe, reformers had as little impact, although the military establishment demanded protection of young workers since the health of the working class was so poor that armies could not fill their quotas of draftees.[5] To alleviate poverty in Montreal, societies to help the poor were organized by the different religious denominations. In O'Leary's opinion, they did their job much more efficiently than English poor law authorities, whose salaries gobbled up most of the funds allocated. Nevertheless, his outlook remained European: a framework for the activities of private charities should be enacted by the state.[6]

Italian and Other Immigrant Labourers

By the end of the century, working-class living conditions in Montreal had deteriorated. Factory owners exploited their human material mercilessly and housing conditions were often degrading. By 1891, of Canada's 0.3 million industrial workers, 20 percent were women and girls.[7] Ordinary working-class families no longer saw opportunities to set up for themselves, as we can see from testimony given by workers to the Royal Commission on Relations of Labour and Capital in 1889, and oral testimony of Italian immigrants collected in the 1970s.[8]

In Montreal, the commission interviewed both French- and English-speaking workers regardless of ethnicity, but none speaking other languages; thus both Irish and Belgian immigrants testified. According to labour market theory as well as empirical research, the native-born workers would be expected to hold the better-paying, more permanent jobs. Their working conditions would be superior to those of immigrants, who, at least at the beginning, lacked language skills and organizational experiences to fight back. While, according to their life-writings, mid-nineteenth-century immigrant labourers could rise, by the 1880s the commission's report appears to portray an era of social decline.

Cigarmaker Eli Massy explained that a skilled worker, even working year-round at seven dollars a week, could not provide for a family of four. Labour editor Arthur W. Short gave detailed information about the poor housing conditions that working-class families had to cope with. While the clergy preached the bliss of large families, some landlords refused to rent to families with children. Women who purchased a sewing machine on an instalment plan faced sellers who repossessed the machine for the slightest delay in payments without recompense for earlier payments. Edouard Miron, a young worker who did not show up for work one Saturday, was arrested by police upon demand of his employer and jailed for ten hours. The court dismissed the employer's complaint, but Miron received no recompense for the indignity and the time lost. Company police were paid by employers, registered with the police chief, and often wore badges of the municipal police.[9]

Children began apprenticeships early and employers coolly informed the commission that they had never heard of the province's laws against child labour. Working hours were arbitrary, "just as they wanted it." Patrick J. Dalton, a longshoreman, frequently had to work several shifts without a break, up to thirty-five hours in a stretch; refusal to work would have resulted in dismissal. Theophile Charron, as an apprentice, had often received a "crack across the head with the fist." Foremen beat children and adolescents considered refractory or just tired, or confined them in "blackholes." Some factory owners did the beating themselves. When Georgiana Loiselle, aged eighteen, was beaten by her notoriously brutal employer Fortier, a public debate ensued about a man placing a young women across his knees to spank her. Upon questioning, Fortier merely noted that, since the "girls and boys are bound to me," he could punish them the same way parents would. Bound labour, as has been pointed out by historians, throughout the nineteenth and early twentieth centuries existed parallel to free labour, and the borders were fluid.[10]

The somewhat disconcerted commission members called the city's recorder, Benjamin-Antoine Testard de Montigny, to hear his judicial opinion on employer violence, particularly against female workers. The highest judge of the city was not ready to take employers to task. Asked whether the law allowed chastisement of children, Montigny pontificated: "That is the interpretation that I put upon the law." He then proceeded to construct an interesting equation: "I consider it in accordance with common sense, which is the natural law, and conforms with positive Divine law, and the civil law."

Employers like the Hochelaga Cotton Factory encouraged internal migration. Families recruited from the Saguenay region who found after arrival that wages were considerably lower than promised were too poor to return. "Refractory" workers were sacked, blacklisted, and replaced by newly recruited Saguenay families, some of them too poor to buy shoes for their children. In response to the unholy alliance between municipal authorities, capitalists, and church, some workers emigrated to the United States. A woman from Sherbrooke noted that had her sisters "been able to earn their livelihood, I believe they would have remained."[11]

A recently arrived Belgian pressman, Leopold Lalieu, like others, had received letters on government stationery that encouraged him to immigrate and had been promised high wages. These Belgians had been sent to Winnipeg, where they found no high wages, not even jobs. The stationery had been forged. They had paid for their own trip and now were destitute. Fifteen years later, Italian immigrant workers faced a similar predicament. Antonio Cordasco, who in return for kickbacks held a monopoly for recruitment of workers for the Canadian Pacific Railway, used stationery he had printed himself using an emblem closely resembling the Italian crest. Prospective migrants understood the Italian government to back the recruitment drive.[12]

The CPR employed more than three thousand Italian labourers annually, shipping one-third of them to track work north of Montreal. Anticipating a larger demand for workers in 1904, Cordasco sent out circulars calling for ten thousand men to come. The circulars promised employment upon arrival at wages of $1.50 per day. They did not mention that Cordasco collected a "fee" of three dollars per worker and ten dollars per foreman. The workers, coming either from the United States or directly from Italy, paid their own travel expenses and Cordasco's commission, but neither Cordasco nor the CPR felt responsible for providing jobs. In 1904 the winter lasted long and by May an estimated six thousand Italians filled the parks and lined up in front of charities, several hundred of them totally destitute.[13] As late as July, men were still waiting for employment.[14]

According to Rodolphe Candori, clerk of the Italian Immigrant Aid Society, the vast majority of the migrants from Italy were agricultural labourers and "are fit for nothing else than pick and shovel." They were often hired by small farmers in the vicinity of Montreal at wages insufficient to feed a family and pay off the passage. A second group, skilled masons and stonecutters, numbered but about one hundred:

"Many of these are men who have traveled about the world and been in Germany, France and elsewhere. When they come here they are asked to join unions as a means of protecting labour. They join the unions and when they do so they find very little work – one or two days per week. Canadian workmen do not like to be supplanted by foreigners, so many of these masons are compelled to work as labourers." For example, Olinda Iuticone's father, a skilled stonecutter who had arrived in 1901, had not found a job in his trade and had to do casual work. A third group consisted of experienced railway navvies, some of whom had laid tracks on the Pisa-Genoa route, at higher altitudes and under more difficult circumstances than in the Canadian Rockies.[15]

Asked about labour competition and undercutting of wages, the secretary of the Charity Organization Society pointed out that seasonal Italian migrants took jobs that Canadian workers would not accept. The Dominion immigration agent described the workers as "a very competent lot of people, of strong, healthy figures, ... men in the very prime of life, and all they wanted was work." Montreal had a large "floating population," according to one labour agent, of Scandinavians, "Polanders," Russians, English, Scots, and Irish, most of them passing through on their way to the West. It also had a small Chinese community.[16] Italian migrants like Polish and Chinese ones formed a labour diaspora spanning continents, taking skilled and unskilled jobs worldwide. The Italian diaspora at first extended to Switzerland and France, then to other parts of Europe. Once steamship transport cut travel time and costs, they commuted across the Atlantic with Argentina as first the favoured destination, since its Spanish-Romance culture was more hospitable to Italians than the North American English cultures. However, by 1900, when unskilled jobs became more readily available in North America, the vast majority of the overseas migrants went to the United States. French-Romance Montreal, too, may have proved more hospitable to the Catholic Italians than English-speaking cultures.

Unwritten contracts bound many Italian workers to padrones, who acted as interpreters, bankers, and steamship agents. They were often bound to buy in company stores or pay commissions to the padrones. Only when workers could rely on their own networks were the middlemen excluded. Montreal's Antonio Cordasco controlled workers once they had paid his commission, since they could ill afford to pay again to another agent. His monopoly over CPR jobs forced applicants to pass through his office. He charged workers for travel provisions of dubious quality and insufficient quantity; in the camps, with connivance of the CPR, he supplied them with food at profits of up to 150 percent. These so-called free workers were kept almost like prisoners. The business was so lucrative that native-born agents attempted to cut into it.

Although the Alien Labour Act of 1897 had made importation of contract workers illegal, in 1905 James A. Smart, the former deputy minister responsible for immigration, convinced the department "to support a prepaid passage scheme whereby his agency would act simultaneously as immigrant bank, steamship agency, and labour bureau." Smart would receive two commissions, one paid by migrants on the ticket, one from the Dominion government. The immigrant Cordasco had exploited his fellow-countrymen; native-born Smart intended to exploit both the workers and his government.[17]

The oral life-stories of two women, Olinda Iuticone and Anna Pozza, and six men, Nicola Manzo, Raffaele Tarasco, Vincenzo Monaco, Constanzo D'Amico, Michele Marcogliese, and Antonio Funicelli, all except one from the central provinces of Abruzzi, Molise, and Campagna, provide a collective portrait of the Italian immigrant working-class in Montreal. They all arrived between 1910 and the early 1920s and describe a community in flux.[18] In contrast to the sojourning railway workers, for them mobility no longer implied instability. The community, including a hierarchy of small businessmen and *prominenti*, in 1911 consisted of seven thousand and would increase to fourteen thousand by 1921. Prior to 1900, only one-third of Quebec's Italians had been women; by 1918 their share had increased to 44 percent.

The eight individuals had relatives spread across Europe, South America, and the United States. In the far-flung diaspora, brothers and male cousins, sisters and female cousins helped each other, uncles brought in nephews, aunts supported nieces. Nicola Manzo and his father had worked in a West Virginia mine. When the father, along with thirty-six of his *paesani* was killed in an explosion, cousins helped Nicola, then aged fifteen, to return to his mother in Italy. He remained for five years and married, then left for Montreal with nine other men. After two years, he was able to bring over his wife.[19]

Raffaele Tarasco intended to go to relatives in Montreal, but by clerical error he received a visa for the United States. He tried to reach an uncle near Philadelphia, but mispronounced the town's name and was sent off in the wrong direction. His lack of English sent him searching for Italians and with their help he found the right towns and located the uncle. His subsequent strategy involved at first earning money at any wage offered, then taking better-paying jobs and moving to New York. There he was employed by the New York Central Railway and used his travel pass finally to reach Montreal. His strategy is typical. If lost during their travels, Italians would search first for other Italians, and with their help find men or women from the same region who would direct them to fellow townspeople, who knew the relatives in question. Mental maps were not geographical but relational.

For women remaining in Italy, the workload doubled. They had to take care of children and home and do the agricultural work usually performed by their menfolk. Whole villages consisted of women, the elderly and children. Some women never saw their husbands again, though letters and remittances continued. Death of the last relatives in Italy could make a stay in Canada that had originally been considered temporary become permanent, which had been the experience of Wilson Benson and Bessie Garland. Polish and Ukrainian immigrants in the West also mentioned the death of parents as ending their obligation to return.[20]

For Vincenzo Monaco, cultural interaction had been part of his life in Italy. He came from a village of Albanians who had fled Ottoman-Turkish rule centuries earlier. His father had migrated to Argentina and died there before he could bring over his family. His mother, at the age of thirty-two, was left to raise four children. Between 1914 and 1923 three brothers migrated to Montreal, where they could rely on their cousins' help.

At first, a major problem for Italian immigrants was language. Their compatriots could give directions but not provide jobs. "Si tu ne parles pas la langue, qu'est-ce que tu peux faire?" Nicola Manzo asked rhetorically. Raffaele Tarasco made an effort to learn English in order to be able to obtain work more easily. Vincenzo Monaco would have liked to talk back to abusive foremen but felt helpless without language skills: "On ne pouvait rien faire, même pas ouvrir la bouche." His dignity as a human being and his identity as a worker were at stake. The children learned French from their playmates in the streets and in school, so they had to take responsibility and become interpreters for their Italian-speaking parents.[21]

Many sojourning Italian men lived in boardinghouses. Entrepreneurially-minded women took in two or three boarders, others more than a dozen. The men did their own shopping, and they paid the women three dollars a month for cooking and washing. Labour agencies opened houses which accommodated up to one hundred men. Depending on the lodgers and the attention of the housekeeper, some places were dirty and full of vermin, others were neat and clean. Poor men had to share a bed, one sleeping during daytime and working night shifts, the other working in daytime and using the bed at night. Often a *paesana* became a surrogate mother, a person of authority and social control. She would insist on punctuality at dinner time; she would warn them not to frequent places of bad repute, perhaps out of solidarity with women left behind. "It was like a family." Men who did not fit in had to leave. A Sicilian who made nasty remarks about his boardinghouse-keeper was thrown out by her on the spot.

Once families formed, sojourners became permanent immigrants. They left boardinghouses and moved, usually to the Mile's End district, where they build shacks or even houses. As they had done in the village at home, they planted vegetable gardens and collected herbs in the open spaces. Food was fresh and expenses were reduced. Canadians wondered what the Italians were doing; the Italians wondered why Canadians knew so little about vegetables. Women raised chicken and rabbits, some even goats or lambs. Towards the centre of the city the keeping of animals and dairying, a traditional working-class way of supplementing meagre diets, had been outlawed. When a pig was slaughtered, a feast was held. Neighbours brought food, home-made wine, or beer. These neighbourhood activities ended when private slaughtering was prohibited and mass production of meats was left to big commercial slaughterhouses.[22]

The Italian groceries, "grosserias," became meeting places for women during the day and men in the evenings. Since the population was stable, local merchants gave credit over winter until work resumed in spring. When clothing workers went on strike, some restaurant owners offered free lunches. This relationship between the workers and the petty bourgeoisie has been overlooked in rigid class analyses. Merchants serving the daily needs of working-class families knew what a living wage was. A cut in wages not only impoverished these families but also the merchants provisioning them. Family economies relied on wages and on home labour, substituting one for the other in conscious allocation of scarce resources. Flexibility was important: "On économisait de toutes les façons possibles ... L'Italien ne crève pas de faim parce qu'il sait comment se débrouiller."

A sense of community, in addition to help for material needs and emotional support, also meant a sphere for spiritual needs. Having been part of Mont Carmel parish, in 1911 the Italian immigrants became the majority of the new Madonna della Difesa parish, with a larger church and more services. A school was built and the use of French in class eased the transition from Italian to French for the second generation. Parish schools began teaching in Italian, but then switched to French in second grade with some English. Education was limited, as the children's wages were needed as part of family incomes and there were few role models that would encourage the children to go on to higher education. Thus separated from native-born Canadians, Italians could act more independently, "personne ne leur disait rien."[23]

Nevertheless, the Montreal Italians had many inter-ethnic contacts. French Canadian, Italian, and Irish nuns taught in the parish schools. Children's street pals were French Canadian. When kids quarrelled, parents agreed that the French and Italians would each punish their own children for fighting to avoid inter-ethnic trouble. At work, textile operatives such as Olinda Iuticone shared the shopfloor with Jews and Canadians. Foremen, at first French Canadians, later included Italians, and finally Jews. Workers organized in one union, but the Amalgamated Clothing Workers of America subsequently opened separate French-Canadian and Italian sections. Jewish workers might come to the meetings of the Italians and join in dances. The musicians' union was multi-ethnic. On construction sites, Italian and Polish labourers worked side by side, "les travaux durs c'est toujours ces deux groupes qui les ont faits." English or pidgin English became the means of communication, though many also knew some French. Others associated with Greeks, Portuguese, and Sicilians, "on était mêlés à toutes les nationalités." Many foremen made no effort to remember names from other cultures, calling all workers "Joe." Only Michele Marcogliese remembered endless fights, "maudits Italiens, maudits Italiens."[24]

Workers showed solidarity on the job. Raffaele Tarasco presented himself as a skilled mechanic to a manufacturer of radiators, though he had no experience whatsoever. On the shopfloor he asked a Belgian fellow-worker to teach him. Questioned by the Canadian boss, the Belgian asserted that the Italian was "first class." The experience of solidarity on the job regardless of cultural background permeates immigrant industrial labourers' life-writings.

In 1911 Nicola Manzo still had to pay Cordasco a two-dollar fee to get a job. He thoroughly mistrusted all padrones and bankers. On the job, he felt like a slave. The labour agencies sent him, like thousands of others, to harvest work in the West with an English-speaking Italian as a guide. At railway construction sites Italians lived and worked next to Poles. One English boss, Armstrong, mistreated older and slower workers, seizing them, and throwing them on the ground. "Le travail forcé c'était toujours les Italiens qui le faisaient." Some workers resisted. A group from Calabria built a coffin-like box, forced Armstrong inside, and nailed it shut. He was rescued three days later but was taken off the job.

Discontented with this type of work, Nicola Manzo went to Toronto. There, workers with their own pick and shovel had to walk the streets until someone hired them for the day. This was like the old world: for seasonal agricultural work, "nous nous vendions comme si nous étions des chevaux." Agricultural workers repeated the image of human beings treated like work animals – or worse. Even when permanent work had been secured, the bottom line remained: "nous étions tous dans la misère." Some alluded to Christ's suffering when talking about work, the *via crucis*.[25]

The "Errand Runner": The Life of a Jewish Woman

Leah Rosenberg's life in Montreal takes us into a different world, a different kind of diaspora. From 1850 to 1900, an estimated fifteen thousand Jews reached Canada, largely from Western and West Central Europe. In the next twenty years, one hundred and twenty thousand Jewish immigrants came, mainly from Eastern Europe. They included those of Polish and Russian origins; those from Hasidic, Mitnaggedim, and Orthodox traditions; and Galitzianer and Litvak *landsmannschaftn* – that is, from Galician and Lithuanian regional groups. This diverse community remained separate from the life-worlds of native-born society and from other immigrants, since religion as interpreted by the rabbis prescribed everyday life in detail. Within urban communities Jews tried to retain their customs, just as Mennonites and Doukhobors did in their separate agrarian colonies. Though anti-semitism was expressed frequently, interaction and lack of persecution meant there was less need to construct closed communities. Thus compromises were negotiated, acculturation and Canadianization began.[26]

Leah had been born into a rabbi's family in Warsaw, Russian Poland, in 1907. As the youngest daughter of fourteen children, seven of whom lived, she "was rarely noticed and was thus better able to observe." In the 1880s, emigration was not yet an accepted step for Jews to take. Pogroms, often encouraged by tsarist authorities, multiplied, but the mythical America was a place of exile for misfits, not yet a haven for the righteous. "Next year in Jerusalem" was yet to become "Next year in America."[27]

Tied to the rabbinical and mystical Hasidic background, Leah learned slowly that "there existed another world than that of my immigrant parents." This delayed perception was common to most immigrants who came with neither English nor French as a language. It distinguished them from those who could verbally, if perhaps not conceptually, understand the receiving society upon arrival. Like all immigrants from ways of life in which religious or supernatural worlds had a close bearing on everyday practices, Leah was walled into a culture. Group coherence had been reinforced by persecutions across centuries, by the "pall of fear" that enveloped daily life. In addition, members of a rabbi's family were watched closely by the community. While James Thomson could "barter and exchange" his "heritage" with others without giving up his identity, Leah Rosenberg could not. Nevertheless, the Jewish community also offered strengths. It was highly literate and that literacy extended to women. Given men's preoccupation with Talmudic learning, it regarded breadwinning women as normal. Leah's parents had first migrated within Poland, then her father came to Canada in 1912, and her mother and the younger children followed in 1913. The family settled first in Toronto, then in Montreal, where early twentieth-century visitors commented on the "foreign Jewry."[28]

Leah's mother was well educated, "practical and down to earth," so she handled the business transactions of the family. She hoped that the children would stay true to the faith, which was more difficult than in Russian Poland. There "hoodlums humiliated old Jews," in Canada "change was around the corner." Where "Gentiles were not killers" but were "human, benevolent," acculturation was attractive.[29] It was "like a journey, to travel fast meant to forget where one had been," as one of Leah's sensitive teachers put it. On the other hand, to move slowly, like refusing to learn the new language, could cut grandparents off from communication with their grandchildren. Depending on their personalities and their relationships with their parents, some of Leah's sisters switched to English, others remained Yiddish-speaking. Life for the children became easier after the family had moved to cosmopolitan Montreal.

Leah cried in despair when her lack of French disqualified her from high school and her parents decided against further schooling. She then did full-time what had been her task all along – running errands for her father and doing small jobs and odd chores. In a typical intergenerational immigrant relationship, parents remain bound to their traditions and hardly adapt themselves and the children become messengers to, mediators with, and news-carriers from the new social world. This was Leah's role. She had to deal with institutions, get an American visa for her father, negotiate release from customs of her father's books typeset in Warsaw. At ceremonial functions she carried his bag and translated everything for him. He never learned to speak English, had no time for simple chores, and avoided going out because his Hasidic garb attracted unwelcome attention. In the process, she had to interpret Jewish culture and religion to those outside of it. Though she had to devote her life to him, she never lost her deep attachment to his loving and caring ways. Her mother, on the other hand, often appeared dictatorial to her, a reversal of standard roles that we will meet in the lives of other immigrant children.

Leah observed the whole gamut of male acculturation in Montreal, Jewish immigrants becoming rabbis or dealers in second-hand goods, becoming wealthy while cheating overworked poor women, going into the theatre or religious studies, marrying traditionally or negotiating a distance to the old cultural world. The small shops near Cadieux (later De Bullion) Street, "usually run by a married couple with occasional help from their children," were more than grocery stores, they were institutions of mutual help, emotional support, and interaction. "It was here that the welfare of neighbours was discussed, examined and sometimes solved. They were convenient places to trade recipes which were generously shared amongst customers and proprietors. Ingredients were described so eloquently that writing them down was unnecessary. Remedies for ailments were prescribed free of charge."[30] This was the women's sphere in which, in contrast to formal, male-dominated organizations, no minutes were kept. Historians thus only get one side of the story.

The people who talked so eloquently in the grocery stores have been called the inarticulate because they did not express themselves in writing. Independently of each other, our Jewish and Italian informants remembered the highly articulate discussions and exchanges of information, a feature that later immigrants remembered about stores in the prairies. Other workers, male and female, native-born and immigrant, as eloquently had informed the Commission on Relations of Labour and Capital about their plight and their lives.

CHAPTER EIGHT

Life on the Ontario Frontier

Settlement clusters in what was to become Upper Canada had first been established by English-speaking Loyalists of many ethnicities, who combined political flight from what they considered turbulent republicanism in the United States with economic gain through land grants at their destination. From the 1810s to the 1850s two distinct streams of immigrant settlers followed: genteel English and Anglo-Irish, and working-class English, Irish, Scottish, and Welsh. The first published their experiences and occupied public memory; the second, like the French Canadians, have to be reinserted into public memory by historians. We will look at the experiences of settlers with few or no means, first in a composite summary, then by meeting one family, and finally by looking at child immigrants.

Farming and Other Pursuits

In the fluid pre-1850s society, the Irish couple Jemima and Wilson Benson had to change occupation whenever circumstances forced them to. They had moved from Brockville to Toronto and finally began to farm in 1849. The securely established Carrothers families, who had farmed near London since the mid-1830s described the economic take-off in 1853: "London has become a large and fine place since we came to this country. There is a great many fine Churches, and merchant shops, and wholesale warehouses all of brick." Discovery of oil in southwestern Ontario in 1857 heralded change, "causing the greatest excitement ... [Oil] is going to become a source of wealth as great as the gold mines of California or Australia. There has been hundreds who has made a fortune of it in the last year."[1]

James Thomson, the Scottish journeymen baker from Montreal as we saw, bought a farm in Edwardsburgh on the St Lawrence River in 1854, but at the same time he and an acquaintance took a contract on the Grand Trunk Railway. He intended to lease part of the farmland or hire someone to do the ploughing and sowing, while he himself cut timber to fence the contracted railway section. Like Félix Albert near

Rivière-du-Loup, he seized opportunities. While Albert regarded farming as his primary interest, for Thomson it was subsidiary. He worked where he could make most money and hired others for less well-paying tasks. Thomson and his partner soon had fifty men and twenty horses at work. Local farmers seized the opportunity to get cash incomes. Thus no capital outlay for horses and wagons was needed, no workers had to be recruited from afar. The localization of railroad construction also saved on overhead in distant company headquarters. Thomson finished the railway section but it "will not pay very well, I have no money to spare this summer." So he next opened a store at a canal construction site to supply itinerant labourers, while his wife Mary improved a garden on the farm. When gold was found in the Cariboo, James Thomson, like other native and immigrant Ontarians, went west.[2]

Eastern Canadians began to be aware of options in the West. The grandchildren of the Carrothers families moved to the prairies as did the French-Canadian Bonneau family from Quebec. Some potential migrants had but vague notions of what awaited them. A minister in the Northwest once received a letter from Ethal, Huron County, farmers: "There is a lot of familyes [who] would imigrate there in the spring iff they could have the particulars of the country and in particular about the crops." Were there buffaloes and fish or but wolves and snakes? How about early frosts, climate, soil, crops, "the markets and the mode of living the people has?" The writer concluded with a query about "the best rout for going there and what it would cost a young single man to go there." At about the same time, a Norwegian gentleman farmer travelled through the Canadas to explore settlement opportunities, which, viewed from Scandinavia, still looked good. From 1836 to 1850, 240 Norwegians had arrived at Quebec. At the same time, the level of information about the West improved. One successful Ontarian, writing home about boom crops, added: "It would be a blessing to a Majority of struggling farmers" to come west "and be out of misery." Those interested should "go to the Toronto Exhibition this fall and there open their eyes and look at the Manitoba exhibit."[3]

Several Ontario immigrants left memoirs for the decades after the 1850s. John C. Geikie, with his five brothers and three sisters, came after his parents' death to settle on land selected by a sixth brother on the St Clair river. A widowed English "Emigrant Lady" arrived from France in 1871. Ann Hathaway's father tried to establish a farm in Muskoka.[4] A diary of an involuntary internal migrant, Hannah Kern, supplements the information.[5] Anna Leveridge with her children had to follow her husband from England in 1882 and left a complex picture of pioneer poverty and life.[6]

Hannah Kern, was torn out of a well-established life when her husband endorsed a note for a friend who then defaulted. At their residence in Dundas, Ontario, Hannah Kern had had servants, but like many other middle-class employers of household labour, she had trouble with their independence. Middle-class people of English origin could not accept the equality that lower-class men and women took for granted. After the financial disaster, the Kerns first took over a heavily indebted parental farm, but had to sell and move to a homestead. In 1873, at the age of fifty-three, she noted in her diary: "Instead of servants to come at my call, I am, and have long been, my own. Instead of using money already my own and spending my time in works of charity as well as of pleasure, I must now work hard for my living." Her husband was of a "naturally irritable temper," and disconcerted by the misfortune he was "at times almost ungovernable either by himself or anyone else." He was no help – an additional burden in fact.[7]

The "Emigrant Lady," also presented a life story of hard work and a rude downward slide from a comfortable position. As wife of an English military officer, "my wandering life in the army had rendered me very independent of extraneous help." After his death, she received a pension and settled in France. She lived her own life for fifteen years and took note of women's achievements. The Franco-Prussian War in 1870–1 uprooted her. She considered three options: join her eldest son in London, emigrate to a North American city and accept paid work, or stay with another son in Muskoka, near Utterson. This son had gone to New York in 1871 thinking it to be "an El Dorado" but had been unsuccessful. When she reached Muskoka, she found he was living on "hard salt pork, potatoes, oatmeal, molasses, rice and flour for bread." Little game was left in the area for enriching the table. His letters of introduction were of no value where skilful workmen were sought. From a "pretty drawingroom" the lady moved to a little loghouse. A corner was partitioned off for her by "scanty curtains" and she had to "slave and toil." She gave way to self-pity and constant crying.

The neighbours were a motley crowd of weavers from Scotland, English agricultural labourers, artisans and mechanics from everywhere, and an "old negro." The handyman was a ploughboy from Kent and Emigrant Lady had to reconcile herself to sitting at the same table with this "stranger ... from a class so different of my own." When she was not permitted to eat at the family table, the hired girl left.

Among the neighbouring families, the classic post-migration pattern of men tramping for work to the cities and women and children tending the land was prevalent. While Emigrant Lady, dependent on help from London in years of poor harvests, left the bush after four years, the eight Geikie siblings had sufficient labour reserves to get their farmland cleared quickly. While they complained about the bitter cold of the winters, the brothers also noted that in blistering hot summers their sisters still had to work over the fire to prepare meals.[8]

Anna Leveridge and Her Family

One day in July 1882, Anna Leveridge in Hochering, near Norwich, England, realized that the family's savings and credit had been wiped out by a defaulting friend and that her husband David was gone. A week later a letter informed her that he was off to Canada. Anna, pregnant and with six children, had to fend for herself and the family. She earned a little money as organist in the local church, and her brothers, friends, and neighbours helped. She began to give music lessons and took in sewing. Still, she had to begin to sell their possessions. "Not being able to pay my way bothers me very much."[9]

David Leveridge, arriving in Montreal, could not find work. When some minor gold deposits were found near Madoc, Ontario, he set out, dreaming of riches. But he had to take on odd jobs, fell sick, and used up the few dollars he had saved. After months of silence, he now looked to Anna for comfort, in hopes that she would contrive to find the necessary money to join him. It did not occur to him that she had already fed the children on borrowed money. He began a process of adaptation, built up his physique by hard work, and sent some money towards the fare. On the boat, other passengers helped Anna Leveridge with the children and a year after David's departure the family was reunited.

David, overseer of a farm in England, but without labouring experience, worked temporarily on a nearby railway extension. Some of the family lived in a tiny house in Millbridge, but since there was neither space nor enough food for all, the two oldest girls, nine and seven, were sent to neighbours as live-in help and company for the women, while the two eldest boys were sent to work. In this way, two boys brought in money and two girls did not have to be fed.

The residual family was far from church and school. Anna Leveridge, who did not see neighbouring women often, felt extremely lonely, always longed for letters from England, but had to tell her family that she could not afford to pay the 10 cent additional postage for an overweight letter. All correspondence was with her mother and her sisters. Her father was marginal but provided texture. When one letter smelled of his tobacco, Anna was reminded of home and asked that all letters be passed by his pipe. No more seemed to be required of him. When her mother died in 1891, two of her sisters joined her in Ontario.

While town women were dressed "very smart and in the height of fashion," the country women substituted homemade textiles for fashion, spun their own wool, and went barefoot. These families also made their own sugar and butchered their own meat. Such independence was the Leveridges' dream. Outside events might make their dreams come true: further gold strikes, a railway nearby, new mines, smelting furnaces, workers who would buy farm produce, additional settlers to construct a school. Instead, railway construction ended, and the mine that had provided David with a job closed down when the Mesabi Range in Michigan was opened up. The family was left to its own hard work and frugality. Reading from the *British Workwoman Out and at Home*, Anna knew that across the British possessions and dominions others faced similar challenges. The paper, issued since 1863 as companion paper to *The British Workman and Friend of the Sons of Toil* and addressed to working-class families, was "anxious to promote their welfare through ... the virtues of hard work, prudence, temperance, godliness."[10]

In 1883, without consulting Anna, David bought a farm on poor, rocky land. He was very different from James Thomson, who shared emotions and decisions with Mary, the children and his Scottish family. The farm meant renewed separation when David and the boys built "the house," a one-room shack. It was unheated when Anna and the children arrived in freezing weather. A kindly neighbouring family offered hospitality in their one-room shack for a week: "I shall be a long time getting used to such ways ... They did not mind it."

Coe Hill farm, according to Anna's description, was dull and one hundred kilometres from the nearest town and doctor. However, in Faraday, less than eight kilometres, a store was available, a school was opened, a church was being built. The girls could borrow books from a library, but the older ones remained with "foster-mothers." By 1885, the family owned some farm animals and expected to buy a yoke of oxen. With no alternatives in sight, Anna Leveridge came to terms with life: "I felt at home. I always feel so wherever I go." Her acquaintances remained English-speaking: Irish, English, Canadian, a Scottish-French couple. Farm labourers, in Anna's opinion, led as hard a life as in England.

Anna was a skilled housewife; like many women, she excelled in tasks that when done by men would have required an apprenticeship and brought good wages.[11] She did dairy work, made butter and cheese, kept chickens, and marketed eggs. She made the family's clothes, first by hand and later with a sewing machine; she crocheted and made quilts. When loggers camped nearby, she knitted socks and mittens for sale. She baked bread to sell to loggers, prepared fish and game, collected and dried berries. Her food production involved gardening and getting seeds from England.[12] It won her the admiration of neighbours and prizes at agricultural fairs. Anna expanded her multiple skills under the demands of frontier life. Not all women did so; indeed social workers criticized the neglect of children, and live-in farm help often complained about the poor food.

David Leveridge, on the other hand, like many immigrant men, had to take on odd jobs, copying what he saw others do, and working with second-hand tools that no self-respecting craftsman would use. The shack which he built for the family was made of freshly cut logs without even the bark stripped off. He became a jack-of-many trades and was quite flexible, but, like many immigrant men, underwent a process of deskilling.

Thus, in eight years of hard work, the Leveridges managed to re-establish themselves. If they did so far below their standard of living in England, they were sufficiently independent to accept it. Their capital was acquired by the itinerant work of the male family members, by Anna's home production, with the help of the older children, and by keeping a tight rein on expenses. No disaster struck the family, and Anna did not allow loneliness to push her over into depression. After the first few years the family seemed happy.

Child Immigrants

Florence and Gertie, the two daughters of Anna and David Leveridge who were placed with neighbours, were lucky. Their mother visited them, and they were taught house work and child care by their foster parents. In contrast, the unhappy early childhood years of British boys and girls placed in philanthropic "Homes" were caused by misfortunes besetting their families: illness or death of one or both parents, destitution or loss of jobs, work accidents or wartime mutilation, occasionally family violence by a drinking father or mother. Remarriage of a widowed parent and difficult relationships with a step-parent resulted in abandonment of children to a Home. A widowed working father tried his best to care for his children, but without surveillance they became truants. Contrary to the "orphan" or "Street Arab" image, most were placed in the Homes by a widowed parent or by aunts who had taken them in after death of the natural parents.[13] On the personal level, most children retrospectively held that the Homes provided them with a chance. In the societal level, child labour was still common and treatment of children in workhouses extremely harsh. On the imperial level, placement of surplus children in colonies rid Britain of expense and provided cheap labour where labour was scarce.[14]

The idea of coupling children's Homes and emigration originated with Maria Susan ("Miss") Rye who, in 1869, organized a reception house in Montreal and a Home in Niagara. In England Dr Thomas J. Barnardo helped to get many off the streets, and his Homes sent some sixty thousand boys and girls to Canada.[15] Two decades later, more than fifty agencies sent out children. Some 87,700 children, one-third of them girls, had arrived by the end of the 1920s when the Depression ended the demand.[16] In 1968 Phyllis Harrison asked surviving child migrants as their descendants to write short memoirs of their lives. Even then a few were still so troubled about shattering emotional experiences that they withheld their names.[17]

In Britain, these children had to develop a street-wise or Home-wise maturity. Some were asked whether they wanted to go to Canada as early as the age of eight and had to make a decision about their lives on the spot. To go to Canada, in their lore was to be given a chance. Those who came as sibling groups of two or three always desired to stay together, a wish that was hardly ever fulfilled. As adults, separated brothers and sisters would often search for each other. Some parents hoped to be able to follow their children to Canada, as did the father of Thomas Loach. George McDonald's mother, who had to place him in a Home when he was the age of three, managed to come to Toronto and to take him back twelve years later. Reunions after long separations were difficult. Jack W. remembered, "[I] worked my way on a cattle boat to Glasgow, and from there I rode trucks to London to see my relatives whom I hadn't seen for 25 years. This was the biggest mistake I ever made in my life. After living in Canada I couldn't live in England. My Canadian ideas of social classes weren't acceptable to even my family who were working people."[18]

The Homes intended to place children with families, who were paid five dollars per month when taking children aged six to ten. Children aged eleven to fourteen were expected to work for their keep and get some schooling. From the age of fourteen, they were to receive wages. The Homes quickly abandoned the plan to find adoptive parents. Indentured labour, – in other words, the economic nexus – was the relationship that interested to most "foster parents." According to several reminiscences, payment of wages was irregular at best. Contrary to the terms of the indentures, most children received little schooling. However, many farming families also kept their own children at home because their labour was needed.

In Ontario, children were distributed via the Peterborough and Toronto Homes, in the West through a training farm in Russell, Manitoba, and a Home in Winnipeg. A "Scotch" Home operated in Brockville. Catholic children were sent to Quebec. Other Homes existed in Nova Scotia and New Brunswick. When time for placement came, the children were either lined up in the Home so that interested parties could come to "view" them, or they were sent out singly upon request with a tag on the front of the coat, "like a bag of potatoes," Ellen Higgins felt. A farmer or a hired hand would pick them up when they forlornly remained the last on the train platform, "no kindly handshake, no enthusiasm ... It was just a matter-of-fact meeting." As in the case of the camaraderie of ship fellows, separation from their fellow Home children proved to be the decisive break with the past and with childhood for most of them.[19]

Placed overwhelmingly in farming families as child labour, the children's reminscences give us a glimpse of exploitation, withheld wages, lashings, sexual harassment. These children, torn out of their own families, did not feel the need to protect relatives, a reticence that so often veils intra-family violence. While philanthropists assumed a "natural" capability among foster-parents to rear children, these stories make clear that many adults lacked such competence.

The recurring theme of these children's life stories is loneliness and a hunger for love. Reared in the Home's Christian atmosphere, many were critical of the religiosity of their hosts: "I discovered that they did not practice what they preached." The girls and boys showed resilience, but the emotional scars stayed with them. The lack of attachment and their feeling of helplessness is underlined by recurring themes in their reminiscences: running away and cutting relationships was their only means of protest. For example, in 1914 an unusually large number of boys volunteered for the army to have an organization that took care. Girls who obediently married farm boys later put much emphasis on their writings on loving relationships with spouse and children.

When Harry Jeffery, as a ten-year-old boy, arrived tired at Reids Mill near Peterborough one afternoon, his foster-father/employer told him to change clothes and pitch hay for the rest of the day. The next morning at four the farmer "yanked" him out of bed with a whip and kicked him down the stairs. His next place was "just as bad. I never got any more schooling. I went to the bush and sawed wood and logs. The old man used to beat me for no reason at all." Finally, he ran away. "We were the cheapest slave labour the farmers ever had," (George Mackie, James Wilde). One foster-father, when asked, "Is that your son?" would answer "'No! He's only a Home boy we've got.' It's a wonder he didn't say 'We call him Fido'" (Jack W.). Inspectors from the Homes did not come often to check living conditions and the schooling of their wards.

Some had better lives and received a few years of schooling. W.B. Cartledge, in Charteris, Quebec, noted that food was "not the best," but that his employers' family was having the same. One young man, whose work was appreciated, was offered his foster-father's farm with no downpayment. With but one year's work on a farm he felt his experience to be insufficient and did not dare accept. Some farming families made boys and girls feel welcome. "Their home is my home," remembered Len Weston.

William R. Price, whose story can be taken as typical, came from the Rhondda valley in Wales from "unbelievably stifling coal dust," where poverty "was a condition of life." When he was four, his father was killed in colliery cave-in, and typhoid epidemic claimed the lives of two of his brothers. With no support for killed miners' dependants, "we were destitute." After a mental breakdown, his mother was placed in a workhouse and he and his little brother Hughie were bundled off to a Home where they were greeted by the "hungry eyes" of other suffering children. The cruelty and at times the "complete absence of any demonstrative kindness was unbearable." After the first World War Wales was in the depth of an economic crisis and "we were conditioned to a life of hunger at the home." William's one pleasure was singing in the Welsh Eisteddfod music festivals. A Welsh-speaker, he began to improve his English to become bilingual.

Sent to Canada, William liked the good food at the Belleville Home, but missed the affection. The first farmer, Ernest Huffman, had to teach much to the mining boy. He was unable to pay full wages and, probably never inquiring about Bill's childhood, punished misbehaviour by letting him go hungry. Bill ran away and was proud of it: "I would no longer sit back and wait for things to happen to me. I'd make them happen." The big problem, of course, was that children did not yet have the experience and skills to make things happen.[20]

One Home girl, who arrived in 1914, found a first foster-mother who fed her well, was kind, taught her how make maple sugar and look after lambs. For unknown reasons the Home demanded that she be sent back and assigned her to a new family. "Life there wasn't good. The wife often visited her mother and would be away for weeks at a time. I was put to work scrubbing floors, cleaning stables and milking cows. In September I started to school, but the farmer told me I had to work out in the fields." This time the Home took her away because she was alone in the house with the man. She was then placed with an elderly couple. While work was easy, the gruff old man took a dislike to her and hit her. Her next assignment was with a friendly Irish family, but "I was beginning to resent being sent from place to place. I was discouraged and homesick." After one more assignment her odyssey came to an end. An aunt of hers, who lived in Canada, learned of her presence, searched her out and took care of her.[21]

For most girls and young women, life was as difficult. Margaret Cleaves, sent to a farm and without education, "was afraid to go out anywhere. She remained on the farm working until she was 30 or 31 years old. She did not know that wages were due to her." Finally, a couple from Guelph hired her as servant, and there she married a bricklayer fresh from England. Agnes McFadden was sent around by her foster-family to relatives, wherever help was needed, and by age ten did the washing for whole families. Emily Boys trained herself to be able to work as butcher's help, seamstress, or midwife. For many of the young women, sexual harassment was a fact of life: "The lady was pleasant but the men were indecent." Sexual approaches came from mentally ill sons, grandfathers, men in general. Some fled back to the Home, some fought back, all tried to avoid being alone with men.

Under the British Homes and Empire ideology, most children were sent into British families in Canada. But children also lived with Germans and Mennonites, Pennsylvania Dutch and Amish. One boy in a German family, "damn near died of loneliness," because no English was spoken. J.L. Churcher lived with "Jewish people" in Toronto, whose locks surprised him, "but they were very fine people," he asserted, after coming to terms with the cultural difference. Occasionally, an English-speaking boy or girl would be placed with a French-speaking family. One such family was too poor to clothe their boy properly. When the grandmother knitted wristlets and cap for him, the farmer ordered the boy to return the gift: "I was considered an outsider – an immigré d'Angleterre." But cultural compromise was possible; when he married, his bride was half French and half Irish. Other cultural contacts were few: in the prairies a short meeting with Ukrainians, a friendship with Hungarian settlers (disliked by the English foster-father), a flirtation with a Swedish girl, work for Swedes, Norwegians, or Belgians. One runaway boy reached Halifax and "stole up the gangplank ... Then I ran into this big coloured man. He told me this ship wasn't headed for England but for the West Indies. He pointed out another ship loading for England, and sent me off with the biggest cheese sandwich I had ever seen in my life."

Many of the child immigrants suffered from a lifelong feeling of inferiority, but some could overcome this: "I have always been proud of being a Dr Barnardo Home Girl. Where would I have been without their kindness?" Most would probably have agreed with Jack W. "Looking back over my life, I believe no organization should have been allowed to ship out children under eighteen years of age. After that they have some chance to defend themselves against labour-hungry and dollar-hungry farmers." Care would have had to be taken to select new parents like "Old Mrs. Smith [who] was just like a mother to me."

Creating Canadian societies (and others, for that matter) involved child labour, abuse, as well as love from parents and foster-parents.[22]

Settlement of Ontario's rural regions involved families such as the Carrothers, who came with means and forged ahead with little or no difficulty. It involved downward adjustment of life projects, as for David and Anna Leveridge, who lived but modestly. It involved children for whom separation and exploitation meant emotional disaster, but whose resilience enabled them to refashion their lives as adults. Not only diversity of culture, but also diversity of class and family experience merged into regional societies. For the small people, human capital and social ties were the only assets with which to start. None of the men and women was engaged in a project of nation-building but they evaluated economic growth in terms of benefits to themselves and were ready to contribute. They did build their own lives and the sum of lives built and relationships established created a society.

CHAPTER NINE

Northward-Bound to the Lumbering and Mining Frontier

Urban workers left few life-writings – they did not have time to record their struggles – but long winters permitted reflection on the summer's adventures in the "Old" Northwest Territories, which would later be incorporated into the provinces of Ontario and Quebec. Northward migration from the densely settled St Lawrence Valley brought French-Canadian and other settlers to marginal farmlands, and into the mines or logging, where they mixed with Finns and other nationalities. The ubiquitous railway workers and engineers were among the first to penetrate northward, among them Italian labourers from Montreal. Around the CPR depot in Fort William, now part of Thunder Bay, a thriving Italian community emerged. Some of these immigrants and internal migrants recorded a particular trip or stint of work; they thought that their life included aspects of drama and excitement that would interest readers.

Railways and Lumber

To counter the image of all-male communities, we will first look at Florence R. Howey's years in the Northwest from 1883 to 1886. She came from Ontario's Norfolk County, her husband had graduated in medecine from McGill University in Montreal. Their northward move was a type of temporary internal migration. Because of the numerous medical practitioners already established, Mr Howey could not open a practice in southern Ontario as he had intended. So he got himself a job with the CPR to take care of the navvies. Florence Howey, though told "that women were not very desirable on construction," travelled to Sudbury to join him.[1]

Numerous other women lived in this frontier society. Most men lived in bunkhouses but married mechanics "put up a log hut and brought their families in." The women earned some money by sewing cotton sacks for the provisions to be sent in. Others came with technical training or as entrepreneurs. The telephone operator was a young woman; at Sturgeon Falls a woman owned and ran one of the hotels; another woman had established herself as a dressmaker. But when Florence Howey tried to find a woman among the French-Canadian CPR workers to do her washing, they declined; their status-conscious husbands would not want them to work. Because of her position as the doctor's wife, Florence could not develop close relations to other women. Concepts of social rank from the more structured societies arrived with the migrants. Florence met immigrants of vastly different backgrounds in the north. One of the engineers had worked for the city of Havana, Cuba, where his family had lived a genteel life. When warfare between Spain, the colonial power, and the reform and independence movement erupted in 1878, the family moved to Canada.[2]

The Scottish engineer F.C. Cooper observed ethnic hierarchies and ascriptions along the line from Selwood via Gowganda Junction to Port Arthur. He "deplored" the anti-English feeling but traced it "to the shipment to Canada ... of conceited ne'er-do-wells from the Old Country." In contrast, an English pastry-shop owner did well as a cook. To reach the camp in late May 1909, he remembered "scrambling over cut-down trees along the right-of-way, wading through streams, and picking one's way through the uncleared bush." Mosquitoes and heat added to the discomforts. Balancing on fallen trees with a heavy pack taxed any newcomer's abilities.

The company "shack" was divided into "a living-room, a kitchen, an office, the second engineer's room, and a common sleeping room for the rest of the party." In one camp only internal migrants – Canadians from Parry Sound – worked, in another Italians and Swedes. More often English, Swedes, Scots, Canadians, and Italians mixed. They spent years of hard, sometimes adventurous, often difficult work in the bush. Building a railway in the middle of nowhere required inventiveness and resourcefulness of all involved.[3]

Those lacking pluck and resourcefulness failed. Two young Finnish tool- and die-makers, intending to escape their work routine, decided on homesteading and lumbering. With the advice of an experienced logger, they bought supplies. Trudging in the direction of their land, their courage almost gave out. The swamps were deeper than their rubber boots were high, the packs too heavy, the Abitibi river difficult to cross. They built a raft and reached the other shore, but at night ominous howling of animals sent them fleeing back onto the raft. The next day they took shelter with a more experienced homesteader.

Many authors commented on the lumbermen. John Geikie noted that no English worker would be prepared to rough it as the men did on the Upper Ottawa. On larger rafts on the upper lakes, French-Canadian men took along wives and children. The skills involved in cutting a tree to fall exactly as intended, toploading a sleigh so that the logs would not shift, sliding logs down chutes, or building rafts of either logs or squared timber, impressed the Home boys who spent time in lumber camps. Some enjoyed seeing majestic pines, watching deer chased across the ice by wolves, breathing fresh air. Patrick Markham worked "where nobody could speak English, just French, but I got along fine." He, like Allan Slade, a Home boy from Sheffield, learned to speak, read, and write French. "It sure came in handy to me in later years."[4]

Some of the single men suffered from loneliness and lack of support in the bush. Mikko, arriving from Finland to a logging camp, could not get a single tree to come down cleanly. After five winters in the camps, a dream about sunny wheatfields sent him into a tailspin. Sinking into deep depression and refusing to talk, he trudged to a railway station and returned to Finland with no savings and, in his opinion, nothing to show but lost years. Reino intended to save his money, buy a farm in southern Ontario, and bring over his girlfriend from Finland. She, however, decided not to wait and married a local farmer's son. This sent Reino scampering to the next speakeasy. Like others, he collapsed when the relationships that supported him, or that he imagined, gave way.[5]

With experience and business acumen lumbering could be profitable. Henry had left Finland when his bride had died suddenly and he had felt lost and lonely. In Canada he saved his wages as a lumberjack. Returning from a winter's camp to Timmins, he never headed for a speakeasy, but, with a good Finnish education, got some books and read. After buying considerable tracts of land, he may have over-emphasized his success, but not his own good feeling when he called himself the "Rockefeller of the Canadian woods." Henry, who never fell in love again, often thought of women as he imagined them and in his craft-conscious frame of reference. His most important tool, the saw, "is more like a fiddle. It must be respected and pampered. It's as temperamental as a woman." With his nieces he was playful, but became uneasy when they turned into young women. "What is happening to my girls?" In this case the separate spheres that men and women often inhabit consisted of one space inhabited by lonely men and a second space, in their minds, peopled with female creatures of their imagination. This may have made real-world encounters difficult.

The North was culturally more diverse than rural Ontario or Quebec. Along the railway tracks and logging roads spread workers from many nations: Italian men from Montreal, Ukrainians from the prairies. Gus Romaniuk was sent to Cochrane in 1916 with no food for the trip. The company's cook fed him and his comrades, though by rule men were to receive food only after their first day of work. Gus and his friends, watching trains with excursion cars go by, asked themselves, why they, too, should not see something of the country. They sneaked off, had a good time, but upon return faced an exasperated foreman. They convinced him to let them stay on, worked extra hard, and by fishing in the evenings provided the gang with fresh fish. The foreman, pacified, let them have full pay. Their next move was to Fort William to dockwork. Men had to be mobile, while parents or wives kept the home base.[6]

A Finnish Family in Timmins

Aili Grönlund recounted the life of her immigrant family, or parts of it, late in her life. The editor noted that she wanted to tell an "exiting," perhaps embellished tale to rivet her readers' attention. Aili's perspective, like that of Home children and of Laura Salverson and Fredelle Bruser Maynard in Winnipeg, is that of a child and later an adolescent, who sees the family as a whole. In their eyes, the roles of mothers and fathers were not reduced to separate spheres, as in most of the adult life-writings. Roles were flexible: fathers might be more supportive than mothers; mothers, coping with recurring migration, relocation, and precariously little food on the table, assumed the role of stern manager of the family property.[7]

Aili had been born in Turku, Finland, in 1908. With her mother and two sisters she had lived in Helsinki, where apartment houses were comfortable, had central heating, and were kept clean by janitors. Aili's father Wäinö was the restless member of the family. He had crossed the Atlantic several times and had once owned a bakery in Fitchburg, Massachusetts. Whenever he had established himself, or thought he had, he called on his wife to follow. Her complaints about this "gypsy" style of life were unavailing: their money had been invested into the new enterprise and there was no turning back. Called to Timmins in 1922, the mother and the three daughters found the "American-style bakery" of his letters to be nothing but a "grey shack" in which he also slept.

Wäinö left the task of finding and furnishing a house to his wife. There were only two houses available and they had to settle on the cheaper one, which at least had an inside lavatory. This was deemed a luxury in frontier society, but the immigrant Finns remained baffled that people could stoop so low as to build houses without bathtubs. Before the Grönlunds arrived, the community had already established a sauna where families could rent a room to change and rest. Thus, contrary to the native-born and the English, the Finns could keep clean and cleanse their souls in the process.

Aili's life as a child in Timmins reflected a drab frontier town, far from the amenities of civilization. Immigrants nevertheless built communities where they not only worked hard, but enjoyed themselves as well. From a Finnish perspective, school in Timmins was "a hundred years behind the times." Thus the second generation's life would not be improved because of better education. Aili's mother came to understand that she had a civilizing mission to undertake in the bakery when she ate North American white bread for the first time. Finnish bread would certainly improve diets. The history of bread as food and social marker had taken an interesting twist. In many European societies peasants could afford only black bread and aspired to the white bread that the higher classes ate. Emigrants in their letters to family left behind would mention that white bread was on the table as a sign of improved status. Yet over time, this white bread came to epitomize food of no nourishing value.

Enclosed in the well-established Finnish community, Aili's mother never saw the need to learn English (or French). She had a large circle of friends, women from her generation, who admired her way of improving their modest home: "One can tell she comes from Helsinki." Her social space was the home, the shop that of Wäinö. He adamantly opposed painting the shop, both on principle and from craft-consciousness. The quality of the bread might suffer from the smell of paint, and anyway, they could not afford to close the shop and lose a day's income. Shrewdly, "mother said that men ... don't notice if things ... are done little by little." So she and Aili redecorated the bakery bit by bit, her father, according to her story, not noticing anything until a customer complimented him on how nice the store had shaped up.

The family judged expenses in cultural terms but differences of opinion arose between the generations. The admission fee to the sauna, including the "luxury" of renting a separate dressing-room for the family, elicited no discussions. But when the three girls demanded that a record-player be bought, the father sternly pointed out that its cost equalled that of six 100-pound bags of flour. Such spending would be frivolous. As in many other families, both native-born and immigrant, frugality and craft-consciousness were pitted against modernity and fun. The three girls, probably under the lead of Irma, the easy-going youngest who associated with Canadian friends in school, negotiated with perseverance and guile; they won.

The Timmins bakery business was almost a replica of the craftwork, over-the-counter sales, and distribution by horse-drawn wagon that had been practised by James Thomson or Vincenzo Monaco in Montreal decades earlier. But changes were in the air. Mr Grönlund replaced the horse with a truck. But when Aili complained of having to wrap and seal four hundred loaves of bread daily, her father refused to buy a recently marketed sealing machine: the family could not afford such an investment, it had to rely on her labour. Grönlund also assumed that another investment would soon be required – "someone was bound to invent something that would also wrap the bread." This scene took place in the early 1920s and caused the mother to label him "a dreamer." In fact, Josef Jodlbauer, an Austrian immigrant baker in Cleveland, Ohio, in the same years was able to convert from oven-baked hand-kneaded bread to machine-produced bread. Fortunately our Finns had not heard about this and in their lifetime their labour was not replaced by a machine.[8]

The Grönlunds, who had lived a comfortable life in Finland, had to make do with improvisations in Timmins like Montreal Italians. The Italians used second-hand timber to build their small houses. Aili's family used flour bags to make blinds for windows, clothing, and bed linen. Light-weight sugar bags were converted into summer dresses. In a society where everything was made for quick usage and decay, only the ugly print on the bags seemed to last forever. Flour-bag pillowcases boasted "colourful handwork, embroidered birds, flowers and butterflies." Later, when our story proceeds farther west, we will come across the multiple uses of flour bags again and again. The equivalent in the male sphere was haywire.

The Finnish community was sizable. While Finns never formed a worldwide diaspora, they settled in large numbers along the Canadian-US border and in Russia. There was a strong communist element among them, perhaps one-third of the group struggling for a better society. After the Russian October Revolution, several thousand Finns left the United States and Canada where, they felt, they could no longer realize their dreams, for the new Soviet workers' republic. Aili's mother was active in the communist movement but given the decades of repression in Canada from the 1920s to the 1950s, Aili chose to bypass the political life of her family.[9]

Much of the political activity intended to change society at large remained, however, internal to the Finnish community. "We knew very little about what was going on in our town, or the new country where we now had homes." Aili, who voiced this attitude, as oldest daughter was close to her parents and part of the family business. Her sisters, who went to Canadian schools, kept an eye on Toronto styles and wanted to change Finnish-Canadian peculiarities so as not to be ridiculed by their boyfriends. Like other immigrant children, they had to make choices.

Class and status among the Finns settled in the Timmins area became an issue when a small group of businessmen – or, more precisely, business-families developed out of the working-class community. When Aili's middle sister bought a fancy coat, others grumbled about shopkeepers getting rich. Ms Grönlund expressed the shopkeepers' disdain for community self-help. When the women prepared coffee, baked cookies, and brought cakes for festivities in the Finnish community hall, she grumbled: "They could give us the business, since we are good enough to bake their everyday bread." Innovations in community life not sanctioned by old-world customs caused intra-familial and intergenerational tensions. When the mother sternly noted that some of the innovative "foolishness" was not for her daughters, the father was more lenient and expected better business "if we took part in activities." Immigrants adapted and so did the mainstream business community. To attract Finns to their banks and stores they hired bilingual clerks from among the second-generation Finns.

Aili's mother was very concerned about propriety. Dating was one of the "un-Finnish" novelties. However, there was more to old-world Finnish society than she cared to know about. Matti, the bakery helper, at one point announced that he was going to marry a women from Finland, whom he had not met before, a mail-order bride. Helga Maki was arriving with her four-year-old son. "Mother said sweetly, 'A widow, I see.' ... 'She is not a widow,' Matti said. Heavy silence." However, once Helga had arrived the two women quickly took to each other. Ms Grönlund also thoroughly disapproved of Finnish speak-easy proprietresses. Uncle Henry, the lumberjack, was inclined to give them the benefit of doubt. His boys, forlorn in the new society, at least got the feeling that someone cared for them for a few hours, even if it was for payment. One of the women had had a Russian for a husband, a further fact against her, since tsarist Russia had annexed Finland. Another, from Helsinki, "kept a spotless house, and no fault could be found with her morals." Stories were invented to fit her into a respectable woman's role: she was working to buy a house in Helsinki for her aged mother; she was putting her two sons through university. She was highly educated and multilingual but fellow-countrywomen remained hostile.

While some of the Finns refused to learn the new language, technology, whether record-players or cars, inserted itself into their lives. Cultural change was imposed on them by economic changes and technical developments. What immigrant parents did not do to adapt would be left to the second generation to work out. Children came home with Canadian-born schoolfriends. In the Grönlund family Aili stuck to a recent Finnish immigrant as a boyfriend, but had dated an Estonian. Her sister was going out with a young Irish-French man. Finnish ethnic culture may have lost some of its old-country flavour, but was also enriched by these innovations. And when her daughters married in "a strange language," when her grandchildren were born, even Ms Grönlund regretted that she had not made any moves toward learning the English language, and so was unable to develop new relationships.

Miners in the North

William Gwilliam, a Home boy placed near Smith Falls, Ontario, in 1902 at the age of fourteen, received only four dollars a month and board. In winter there was no pay. Fed up with the way he was treated in the settled parts of Ontario, he hiked to the silver mines at Cobalt and to northern Ontario lumbering camps. At the age of sixteen, John Cameron came from Scotland. "With one suitcase, I headed for the mine at Kirkland Lake. No job there – moved to Noranda, trying all the mines en route, but no luck." On to Amos, Quebec; and down to the Lamacque Mines at Val d'Or, but again no job. He ended up "burning tree stumps on the side of the new road being opened." His wages consisted of what was called room and board, "a blanket in a tent and rabbit stew or goulash every day."

Cameron then backtracked to the Siscoe Gold Mine and "[I] managed to find a bunk in one of the bunkhouses. Eating was a problem ... [from] the mess hall I got kicked out twice, since the stewards knew that I was not an employee." Then ethnic solidarity helped; "a friendly miner captain of Scottish descent gave me a job and I stayed for a year." His next job was at the Noranda Mines. At first he failed the physical examination because of bad eyesight. Determined to work, he somehow got hold of the eye-testing chart, memorized it, and reapplied under different name and was hired. "I didn't enjoy my stay. The fumes from the smelter would drive you nuts." The dust and dirt made people look black all over. Next, he found a job in Timmins at McIntyre Mines, where, in the middle of the Depression "around two to three hundred men [were] at the gatehouse every day looking for work." Most of the time he worked underground in considerable heat. The Timmins he saw was quite different from what Aili had experienced. It "was a good place to work and there were lots of recreational activities: baseball, miniature golf, a large community centre with a curling rink, hockey rink, bowling alley, auditorium, ... game room." He married the daughter of the woman in whose boardinghouse he was staying.[10]

Rémi Jodouin, the French-Canadian farmer's son displaced by contracting markets and low incomes, moved northward by horse and wagon. Looking at families who lived in tents or in houses built of wet lumber, now full of cracks through which rain and snow passed, he admitted to himself that he arrived like "un seigneur roulant carosse." He and his friend Albert Pépin could stop over with a sister and settle in with his brother and sister-in-law in Arntfield. The two self-satisfied male guests condescended to accept their hostess: "La belle-soeur Antoinette faisait partie de notre compagnie à titre de cuisinière." The two men cut and sold wood and with the help of the brother soon had mine jobs, Pépin in the kitchen, Jodouin underground transporting cut rock. As to mine safety, Jodouin did not understand a word of English, the language of the foremen. His older and stronger co-worker, rather than providing training, tried to make life difficult for him. Jodouin had to learn by trial and error.

The mine was expanding and hiring new men, even in depression years. In 1932 his brother built a boardinghouse with a dozen rooms and a dining room. After his shift in the mine, Rémi helped at the boardinghouse in the evenings. In the vicinity two small French-Canadian agricultural colonies were being developed. The settler families had left their furniture and clothing in their villages of origin to build houses first. When the uncrated furniture arrived in the middle of winter, it was thrown out of the train into the snow and left unattended. The women, who a day later came to pick up their belongings, broke down crying; it was humiliating to be treated that way. Labouring men were not treated any better; during a strike at a Noranda mine, the bosses fired the workers and replaced them with "Frenchies." Bitter, Jodouin noted, "Ces grévistes ne demandaient pas de luxe, croyez-moi."

The bosses also played immigrants off against one another, depending on the composition of the labour force and labour demands. Jodouin did not understand English Canadians and Americans, who fired their own "sons" to hire "purs étrangers, les canadiens-français." He worked as helper of a Yugoslav miner, with Finns and, after the Second World War, with displaced persons. He was critical of economic power – "Dites-moi qui finance et je vous dirai qui gouverne" – and of low wages of workers. He did not begrudge the training given to immigrants in the later years, but noted that when the French Canadians had come they had not received any help in adjusting to and learning mine-work.[11]

The image of the North as one of hardy men and superhuman feats results from a male perspective. Gender ratios were unbalanced, but family shacks sprang up on the margins of railway camps and mine bunkhouses. Women came as independent small entrepreneurs. Northward moves were a way to make ends meet, not to strike it rich. For Aili Grönlund's family as well as for Gus Romaniuk's it was a downward move. For the Home boys it was a way to survive.

CHAPTER TEN

The Labouring and Lower Middle Classes in Toronto

The population of Toronto was less mixed in the 1890s than that of Montreal or Winnipeg. Just as Quebec City had a reputation of being predominantly French Canadian, so Toronto was regarded as the citadel of English Canadians. Both cities were "remarkably homogeneous, strong on church life, Sunday observance and morality," as the *Canadian Encyclopedia* put it, or, as others might say, a little drab. As late as the end of the 1920s, a German working-class immigrant was arrested on a Toronto beach for indecent exposure: he wore swimming trunks only, not a whole suit. Toronto nevertheless was a switchyard for many. Jemima Benson kept store in the 1840s; Peter O'Leary investigated labour conditions in the 1870s; Home children passed through the Peter Street or the Jarvis Street houses. Aili Grönlund's sister visited in the 1930s and regaled Timmins neighbours with reports about fashionable life and the stores, Eaton's in particular. As an administrative centre, Toronto attracted British immigrants. Protestant Ulster Irish came and during and after the famine a Catholic Irish colony developed.

After the 1880s, industrialization attracted workers from many cultures; Jewish, Italian, and Ukrainian communities sprang up. For the Jews and Italians, Montreal remained the most important cultural centre, whereas most Ukrainians went to the West. Wherever they settled, workers of all three groups participated in the labour movement and built their own trade unions and labour temples. In 1884 one proud author set out to produce a handbook on Toronto, "the brilliant capital of English-speaking Canada" whose edifices were "admirable specimens of that Parisian renaissance, which ... has been deservedly such a favourite with Toronto architects." His city was an historical one; a perusal of the handbook's pages gives absolutely no intimation of any recent arrivals.[1] Yet they were responsible for the city's growth from 1880 to 1900 by roughly 130 percent to 210,000.

Wage Labour and Small Business

To Ephraim Hathaway, Toronto in 1870 seemed "the most comfortable English-looking place he had struck yet." It was small and flat, "you could see over the whole city if you stood on an office stool in the street." A stonemason commented: "I thought the place very quiet and dull." The Geikie siblings saw "a straggling collection of wooden houses ... a few brick houses, but only a few. The streets were like a newly-ploughed field in rainy weather ... the pavements were both few and bad."[2] The immigrants never saw the fashionable parts of the town so eloquently described in the handbook, and to its author the immigrants remained invisible. According to the concepts of "invisible man [and women]," developed for Black Americans, and of "symbolic annihilation" of minorities and women, people of high status exclude from view and awareness what does not fit their interests, their concepts of society, their aesthetics. However, the views of newly arrived immigrants were also limited, if for different reasons. They saw only what they had access to.[3]

Ann Hathaway's family, arriving in 1871, had been spared the jarring experiences of the Home boys and girls from the poorer classes. When her father became seriously ill and had to leave his store in Stratford-upon-Avon, England, the family could afford to relocate to a North Wales farm, then to a larger one in Warwickshire. But expenses grew and Mr Hathaway sailed for Canada to look for a farm. The family, which included four girls and two sons, followed a year later, the girls bringing "pins, needles, buttons, tapes, cotton," imagining that they would never find such things in Canada. Upon arrival, no farm had been selected and the mother, Susan, rigorously opposed departure to "the backwoods," about which the children considered themselves well informed having read about "Indians" in the novels of James Fenimore Cooper.

The search for a boardinghouse proved difficult. "Just out from England, six in family," did not open any doors, to put it mildly, even though the official policy was to populate the country. One observer noted that in applying for a job there was no need for a meek "hang-dog kind of way," but for a brisk "can I speak to the boss?" They would also have to discard their English peculiarities of speech as fast as possible. Ms Hathaway succeeded "in coaxing a good-natured Irish woman, named Derrigan – who kept an untidy looking boarding house near Yonge Street – to take us in." The family quickly learned that farming in Muskoka was not a next-year hope but a distant dream.

Soon the older daughters had to think about getting jobs to contribute to the family income. Ann aspired to a position of governess. Bet and Sue found work in a millinery place, only to be told that their work was no good and that they would be paid wages only after a trial period of two or three months. The criticism, given their middle-class women's skills, may have been but a subterfuge to force them to work without wages for a time. They next worked in a sewing factory, but repeated accidents, as when a young woman's hair got caught in the machinery and a panic after a machinery breakdown, ended this episode.[4] Ann realized that there was no market for governesses but servants without high-flying English notions were in demand.

At this point, Ms Derrigan's troubles with her drinking husband came to a crisis. She left and Susan Hathaway, unconvinced by her husband's search for a farm, assumed command of the family and control over the boardinghouse. Her reasoning was sound: she knew there was a demand for rooms, had her own daughters for the housework, and could use the copious stores brought from England for redecoration. Susan rented to visiting English students, son Joe was sent to a farmer to learn agriculture, and Ann found a position in a store. Distribution of labour in the boardinghouse took an interesting twist. Bet and Sue quickly found admirers among the young boarders. Sue, the beauty of the family, "pulled the strings to make those manly puppets dance." They lit their own stoves, cleared the cinders, some even made their own beds, "all this in the hope of winning one smile or word of thanks from fair Sue." Sagely, Sue favoured none and kept all working. Bet, on the other hand, opened her heart to a young Englishman, a "fellow exile" endeared to her by "the tie of nationality."

Not all fellow-nationals were welcome. Once, when Susan Hathaway was away, the daughters banded together to end the stay of "Mr. Orlando Hawkins, with two fellow actors." Whenever acting in Toronto, Hawkins favoured the boardinghouse with his presence but never with any payment. Bet sent the trio packing. After marriage, Bet continued to help in the boardinghouse when needed. Ann, on the other hand, worked in the store day after day from eight in the morning till nine at night, longer on Saturdays. After six years she was granted her first holidays.[5]

A year after the family's arrival, Mr Hathaway acquired a farm on Lake Joseph, fondly called "Hathaway Bay." It was difficult to reach; travel on "the government road," recognizable by axe marks on the trees, involved clambering over rotten wood, jumping swampy places, ducking branches. Mosquitoes abounded but furniture was scarce, "a rusty cooking-stove, a rough table or two, and some chairs, ... a home-made bedstead and mattress." Food usually consisted of salt pork, self-baked bread, fish. With the boardinghouse revenues and Ann's wages, the family paid a local farmer to clear the woods. When Ben left school and Joe completed his agricultural training, they stayed full-time with their father in Muskoka.

After about ten years, Susan Hathaway decided to reunite the family. As a businesswoman, she recognized the vacation potential of

Muskoka; so the family pooled its resources, augmented by an inheritance from England, and opened a summer hotel. Ann used her second holiday in ten years to help furnish the house. The first guests arrived before mattresses had been brought up from Toronto. In many middle-class families, separation for a decade, the labour of all family members, and the capital infusion by inheritance were all necessary for success.[6]

Where family labour was insufficient, Home girls were hired. Lily E. Clapham, for example, came to Canada in 1912 at the age of thirteen. "The people I worked for [at a place sixteen kilometres from Peterborough] came from Toronto and were called gentlemen farmers. In the summer they ran a resort and we were very busy – up at 4.00 a.m. and working until 9.00 p.m. They had a small store and also ran the small post office." Lily was self-confident; had anybody ever punished her for mistakes, she would have hit back. She stayed for nine years but felt she had not learned very much.[7]

A year after the Hathaway family emigrated, an English stonemason arrived. His father had been a tradesman who had migrated to London for employment and had met his future wife, another in-migrant, there. Born in 1845, he became a Home child at the age of three when his widowed mother fell severely ill. Later he lived with relatives, worked on farms, and became a teacher's helper. When he was eighteen, he read Benjamin Franklin's autobiography and decided to become a bricklayer's helper in London. After three years on numerous construction sites, he graduated to skilled journeyman. In 1872 he decided to sail for America.[8]

In Liverpool, "I found a lot of all sorts ... bound for Canada and the States. Quickly chumming in with one or two," he went to buy mattress, tin plate and pot, knife and fork for the trip. He and his chums disembarked in Portland, Maine, and took the train to Toronto. Lodging with an English family on King Street, he saw poverty. His host had held a job only through summer and by winter only "the strenuous exertions of his wife" kept the family "from starvation." The stonemason realized, first, that he had come before the frost was over and, second, that most houses were built of wood. In spring, when he and his host searched for jobs, new emigrants "eager for work" crowded in and his unemployed host died "broken-hearted about three months after I landed."

One day the stonemason and two other unemployed workers, were accosted by the owner of a quarry west of Toronto, who needed men for producing lime and cutting stone. Only our stonemason accepted, the wages being too low for the two married man to feed their families and board out of town. Filling the lime kilns with raw stone "was labouring pure and simple, but I enjoyed the fresh air and the wholesome, plenteous food." He saved money but found "the want of a fixed hour for leaving work in the evening" disagreeable. A few weeks later, he was transferred back to Toronto, where the lime was sold from the railcars, to help oversee the unloading.

Work in Toronto was well paid, but the pace was faster than in England, an experience shared by James Thomson, the journeymen baker in Montreal. In Toronto the ten-hour day was still the rule in the early 1870s, but in this summer, a year after the great fire in Chicago, "tales of fabulous money being earned [there] by bricklayers and labourers" circulated. When workers departed, Toronto's building trades unions decided to use the shortage of labour to negotiate for a nine-hour day. The employers refused and a strike ensued. The stonemason was discharged for lack of work but with a promise to be rehired after the strike. In England, he would have waited for a settlement, but in Canada in view of the long winter months without employment, he could not afford this. Thus he left for Buffalo, once came back to Toronto, but under the impact of the 1873 depression he returned to Britain. Workers in Canada could earn better wages than in Europe, but in many crafts a summer's income had to get them and their families through five months of winter. Young fellows often proudly wrote home that they could take the fast pace of work, but over the years their strength would wear out faster.[9]

Unfortunately, no workers left diaries or reminiscences of strikes. Alice Chown, feminist and social reformer, came upon the Eaton's strike in February to May 1912. She and a friend were on their way "to get our new spring gowns" and watched a policeman driving people along. Angered "because of his roughness to the young girls who were evidently making their fight for liberty," she joined the picket line. She was bundled into a police wagon with working women mostly under twenty years of age. "I marvelled at the courage that made them face such an ordeal." About a thousand workers, one-third of them women, were on strike against Eaton's practice of forcing its workers and employees to agree to discharge without notice. Some of the women struck in support of discharged fathers, relatives, or fellow unionists in the International Ladies Garment Workers Union. Alice Chown knew from a "head official" at Eaton's that the grievance was justified. She talked to a Russian immigrant woman, in whose family books about labour and capital were read, who told her that women had "to go out" with the foreman to get a job, men had to give them "loans."

Alice Chown was asked by the women to help them reach the company's president, John C. Eaton, a philanthropist knighted for his benevolence. "They were sincere in their desire to treat their workers squarely, according to their proprietors' ideas, but in refusing to have committees of their workers they let in all sorts of abuses which they were impotent to know and curb." At the Labour Temple the striking women asked Alice Chown to use her social standing to influence the Toronto papers, "who were all afraid to publish any account of the strike, because the firm carried a large amount of advertising matter." She tried to involve various women's clubs, but they responded by offering charity only in cases of hardship: "The common, everyday longings for better conditions, for a life that would provide more than food, clothes and shelter, were not recognized as justifying a strike." The middle-class women did react to the fact that girls "had to sell themselves as well as their labour to get sufficient work to earn a living." The firms' managers had been instructed "first and foremost, to make profits," and John Eaton's welfare work was regarded as a "bulwark against the worker's case being judged dispassionately on its merits by the public."[10]

Other immigrants who left life-writings were Eric Smythies, an engineer, and Adam Tolmie, who came to Canada in 1911 and 1914 respectively.[11] Smythies's parents had lived in Argentina, where he had been born and raised, but had returned to England. A brother lived in Kenya. His decision to migrate was taken after gathering information from professional engineers whom he "met on ships in the various ports I had been in." They discussed the advantages and disadvantages of different countries and Smythies chose Canada. In the boom period from 1911 to 1913, his technical training was in demand. He moved through several jobs in quick succession, and then joined an English firm with worldwide connections as a specialist for their electrical equipment. He soon started his own business as distributor for an American manufacturer of electric motors. During the First World War he enlisted in the British army, to retain his self-respect as he said, and returned in 1919 with a wife, Ruth.

His firm was in trouble since his deceased partner's heir lacked technical training and financial acumen. Lack of income and the doubling of expenses in private life were summarized by Smythies in a classic formulation, reflected in many life experiences. "It was desirable to keep our living expenses on a modest scale for the time being, and Ruth was a very great help to me in this, while making a home for me much better than any I had when I was a bachelor." Smythies recognized that in order to get on a sound economic footing he could not just distribute American products but had to shift manufacture of them to Canada. The 1920s, for him, were a constant struggle to devise a strategy for his firm.[12]

Adam Tolmie's father, once a man of means, was a gambler who had neglected his family. In Canada, Tomie Sr became a police officer who was sent to search for French-Canadian draft resisters in the northern logging camps and for surveillance of construction workers, "foreigners, chiefly alien enemies." He made money on the side from illegal betting rackets. When his parents split up, Adam first moved around with his father but then ran away. During a stint as office boy, a supervisory officer, sporting the title "Colonel," made a sexual advance and he quit, feeling that a complaint by a recently hired office boy would have no chance against an established employee. Like the Home boy immigrants from broken families, he had difficulty getting his bearings. He moved illegally to Detroit where he earned twice as much as in Toronto and commented on the tensions between Black and White. Found by immigration officers, he cleared out, rejoined his father's illegal liquor trafficking activities, and was cheated out of his wages by his "charming parent." He befriended an Irish boardinghouse-owner, commented critically on her male friend, an English Jew "too good to do any work around the house or look for a job." In the depression years, Adam was sent to a government work camp in Winnipeg and then hopped the rails. As for immigrants in rural Ontario, life in urban settings involved struggle and hard work.[13]

English Immigrants among Canadians

The Hathaway family realized that their English ways were not at all esteemed, even in Toronto. "Stonemason" changed to Canadian terms quickly, for example by using railway "depot" not "station," to avoid being stared at. The British colonizers did not care if the peoples of India, Kenya, or Ceylon joked about their strange everyday customs; after all, they did not understand local languages. The Canadian colonials happened to speak English, or, more exactly, a North American variant of which they were quite proud (and which they were to keep distinctive from that of their southern neighbours).

As immigrants, the English had to undergo a process of acculturation. Just as there were Irish jokes and, later, Polish jokes, the English were also put down by Canadian-born subjects of the British crown, if for different reasons. Ann Hathaway put her pride aside and noted that many middle-class Englishmen or men from the gentry, who came "because they could not succeed at home," went about "growling and grunting" without ever spending a thought on fitting in. Few British immigrants did not have some story about conceited fellow-nationals. Ridiculous, scheming young men, unencumbered by knowledge or self-criticism, like M.C.S. London in New Brunswick, abounded. The Geikie siblings met "a stiff, conceited man, ... a relation to some admiral ... [who] carried his head higher" than anyone else but was exceptionally uneducated.

Respectable men with letters of introduction, expecting help from well-placed British-Canadian acquaintances, had to learn that letters were considered a sign that the bearers lacked work experience. Young men had been educated at private boarding schools "where they had an excellent education in the classics, also character training and discipline, but little or no training for any specific vocation." The British army, for which "they were first-class material," did not have enough commissions to go around. A number of them enlisted in the Royal North-West Mounted Police, believing that its "enviable reputation for devotion to duty ... was built up by the men of the 'Old School Tie' class from Britain." Many had been imbued with "some vague idea of learning to farm." So had German intellectuals, who had fled to the United States after the 1848 revolution. Their pitiful starts, combined with a developed sense of their importance, induced their more practical neighbours to dub them "Latin farmers" – men who spoke Latin but could not handle a pitchfork.[14]

British administrators and officers, whose tour of duty in the Mediterranean or India had ended and who could not afford life in England, came to Canada. They stood in stark contrast to immigrants. One immigrant farmer described their life, incredulous at the lack of social skill and adaptation:

> Captain L—'s ... house stood on a rising ground which was perfectly bare, all the trees having been cut down for many acres around. [In distinction to Anna Leveridge's little flower patch] There was not even the pretence of garden ... Mrs. L—, I found, was an elderly lady of elegant manners ... having been abroad with her husband's regiment in the Mediterranean and elsewhere. She had met Sir Walter Scott at Malta, and was full of gossip about him and society generally in England and elsewhere. Her dress ... had once been a superb satin, but that was very many years before. There was hardly anything to be called furniture in the house, a few old wooden chairs, supplemented by some blocks of wood, mere cuts of trees, serving for seats, a great deal table, and a "grand piano"! which, Mrs. L— told me, they bought at Vienna ... [a] forlorn look of emptiness was in the place; but the stateliness of language and manner on the part of the hostess was the same as if it had been a palace ...

The army supernumeraries without capital had no means to compel anyone to work for them. Such genteel, or perhaps more correctly pretentious, settlers complained about the "insolence" of the immigrant lower classes.[15]

British families who could not support all sons at home according to their standing or wanted to send off black sheep, continued to support them in the colonies at a lower rate of allowance. These were the so-called remittance men. Adam Tolmie, when unemployed, commented caustically: "a steady income, even if a remittance to keep one away from home, made life easier. No chance of being laid off there." The daughters of British families, on the other hand, were expected to earn their keep as governesses. Competent, but usually poorly remunerated, they were respected. For native-born Canadians considering themselves loyal subjects of the British crown it probably presented a challenge to reconcile notions of imperial grandeur with the sorry bunch of men coming from the imperial centre.[16]

Sons of Britain's middle classes were frequently brought out by Canadian banks as junior clerks. Their low pay necessitated "a supplementary allowance from home" but their families had rid themselves of one son to be provided for. Tolmie met one of these accountants, a perfect gentleman while sober. But "having to accept the wages he was getting [eleven dollars a week] didn't improve his disposition" and induced him to drink. Capital bought cheap labour wherever possible, even in the seat of the empire and from the middle-classes' supply of surplus sons.[17]

The position of the English may also have been undercut by the mingling with Scots, Irish, and Welsh, who after centuries still held grudges against the English or, to put it more positively, were still asserting their cultural distinctiveness. Great Britain, like Switzerland, consisted of at least four cultures, though the Gaelic Welsh, Irish, and Scottish languages had largely been replaced by English. Homogeneity was not part of any British nation-building process nor, for that matter, of any other nation state.

Finally, aspects of class, labour organization, and labour militancy contributed to the view of the English. Working-class English were "continually making the most trenchant criticism of the many things of which they did not approve." Imperial mentalities were not merely the domain of the better sort. In one respect, however, they had good reason not to adjust. Class-conscious English workers had resisted exploitation for long. Their union movement was strong and they were proud of it. Now employers posted signs saying "no Englishmen need apply," hired neither union men nor craftsmen unwilling to "make do" with products of lesser quality, nor self-respecting men insisting on breaks in the work day and regular hours. Thus craft-consciousness and labour militancy were transformed into an image of slacking English workers.

William Coleman came in 1927. "In England I was a trade union man and took my union ideas to Canada. I don't believe my Canadian boss had ever heard of a union." On the farm, he had to be up at five in the morning. One evening, he came to understand unregulated hours. A storm approached, but loads of hay had still to get under cover. By going all out, they saved the farmer's hay. Another boy, sent to a Manitoba farmer with "a contract and a letter of introduction," was greeted by a derisive laugh, refused any discussion of wages, and told "that Britain was merely unloading her unemployed on Canada." When he balked, the Canadian government intervened on the side of his employer, and "he was put down for deportation." One Home boy from England felt that "there was no law for an Englishman in Canada."[18]

The Canadian view of English immigrants was corroborated by many of the immigrants themselves, among them the Hathaways, Eric Smythies, and the Geikie brothers. Given the widespread equation of British-origin Canadians with founding peoples, we lack acculturation studies of English immigrants. The English newcomers expected to enter a society that was British, even if backward and colonial. While other immigrants knew from the beginning that they had to come to terms with a different society, the English did not. Many needed a considerable amount of time to understand that adjustment was expected of them. Others understood quickly and became part of Canadian society.

Black Workers

Black people, homogenized from their diverse African cultures of origin through slavery, were an internally heterogeneous group of early pioneers, Loyalist arrivals, refugee Blacks of 1812–16, and escaped slaves. While Britons expected to be observed and emulated, Black men and women had been trained by life in racist societies to observe all others and adjust quickly. As slaves or free but on the bottom of social hierarchy, they had to watch mainstream and elite society carefully to avoid punishment and bodily harm. Life-stories of refugees or "fugitives" were collected in 1856, when most had spent little time in Canada. Furthermore, like the Home boys and girls, their suffering in the past – the transition, the dangerous flight – dominated their thinking to such a degree that this part of the life-story had to be told first; indeed, that was what abolitionist authors wanted their audience to hear.[19]

The 1850 Fugitive Slave Act in the United States increased the number of Blacks who fled to Canada and the Civil War led to an exodus in the 1860s. Among European immigrants, slavery and flight to Canada was a topic deserving mention in life-writings. John Geikie recounted an incident, so did Wilson Benson. Was this an aspect of their Canadianization? Travelling from the St Clair river to Toronto, Geikie noted that in the hotels "most of the waiters, and a large proportion of the cooks, seem to be coloured," that in cities they also became whitewashers and barbers. Geikie failed to notice that Toronto also had a number of prosperous Black merchants, Black churches existed, and that public opinion held Afro-Canadians to be "a well-conducted set of people." The size of the Black community in Toronto peaked in the 1850s and numbered about five hundred persons in 1900. Parallel to the great migration of southern Afro-Americans northward into large urban communities, many Afro-Canadians moved to the United States in the 1920s. The Canadian communities recovered only with the new migration from the Caribbean, the pioneers arriving in the 1920s. Coming from "the islands" implied as many different backgrounds as coming from Europe: Barbadian, Bermudian, Jamaican, Trinidadian, Cuban.[20]

Afro-Canadian people, called "negroes" or "coloured" but hardly ever "niggers," were mentioned in many memoirs. Gaetz evidenced strong prejudices against the Nova Scotia Black community. Home boy Fred Sanders was helped by a Black sailor. "Stonemason" saw Black men in Toronto's streets. A mental screen obviously produced a rigorously gendered vision: all Black people were men.

The Toronto community had ancestors from many parts of the world and its members were highly mobile. Nine women, born between 1900 and 1919, had parents and grandparents from Dublin, Ireland, from among the Pennsylvania Dutch, from Spain or the Spanish colonies, from England. One ancestor, a foundling girl from Java, had been taken to Edinburgh by two Scotsmen and educated there. Another, brought as slave from Africa to Virginia after 1815, jumped overboard and swam for his life to a British ship. He lived as freedman in Halifax. Escaped slaves and free Blacks came from Ohio, Kentucky, Pennsylvania, Virginia, Baltimore, Cleveland. A French-speaking grandmother came from Montreal. Birthplaces in Ontario included Amherstburg, Hamilton, Shrewsbury, Barrie. The Barrie family would rent the upper storey of their house to White people from Gravenhurst. In other towns, Black people could shop and work but were told that they could not stay after dark. Such bylaws were often instigated by racist Whites. On the other hand, in Chatham a racist White repairman making "cracks" at the Black tenants was thrown out by the White landlord. Out-migration of Blacks from Ontario, partly as ministers or missionaries, occurred to Winnipeg, Halifax, and British Columbia.[21]

The ancestors of some Toronto Afro-Americans had lived in mixed marriages by choice, including marriages between Black men and White women. No sexual exploitation by slave-masters is remembered. Bee Allan's uncle was so white, "they didn't know he was Black," and he was hired as a streetcar motorman in 1924. Many worked as porters or cooks for the railways. "I knew I was blocked everywhere," remembered Harry Gairey, a skilled cigarmaker, after applying at a cigar factory on Front Street, "it was all white there." Some deliberately sought positions where they would not be called "boy." Black women in search of a job would call first to inquire whether Black people would be hired. A straightforward no saved the applicant the carfare to the factory. One foreman just grumbled, "What the hell do I care what colour they are as long as they do the work." Some whites hiring domestic servants wanted dark-looking people only. But who was "black"? Mixed marriages and shades from black to white were common. Bertha McAleer once went to visit Black friends. Realizing that she had forgotten the address she asked a little boy, "'You know where the coloured family is?' He said to me, 'What colour?'" At this age, the child was still colour blind.[22]

Addie Aylestock had relatives in Sarnia and Kitchener, her grandmother owned a farm in Peel Township. Depending on where work was available, her family lived in Glen Allan village, near the flax mill in Drayton, in Lebanon, and in Lucan, where "a cousin of mine had quite a big farm and quite a big business." Before she turned sixteen, Addie and three other girls went to Toronto: "Most of us left home pretty early because our parents were poor and weren't able to look after us." As a domestic she worked from breakfast till two in the afternoon: "I think they gave me enough for carfare."

Like some of the immigrants and Home children we have met, several of the Black Torontonians worked in the garment district. Viola Aylestock was active in the fur workers' union. "I really solicited for higher wages, better hours, all this stuff. There were a few other women that had signed up in the union, but on the executive it was strictly men, and myself as secretary."[23]

Violet Blackman, a pioneer immigrant from the Caribbean, came as a domestic servant, the work expected of Black women. But several women energetically told their daughters to get as much education as they could. Unlike slavery, education was no burden carry, and "the door is going to be open one day." One woman recounted how established local residents and recent immigrants from Jamaica, like the Reverend Stewart and Violet Blackman, got together to organize a chapter of the Universal Negro Improvement Association and to buy their own building on College Street. Black women domestics used their free afternoons to collect money among themselves and from their white employers. Once established in the building, "they had their own brass band, they had a choir, they used to put on plays ... It was wonderful, wonderful! This is why I put all my labour, all my time in it." Other organizations were founded: "We had a hard time, but we did obtain the charter and we formed the credit union." Domestics formed a Home Service Association, others were politically active in the Cooperative Commonwealth Federation.[24]

When the Toronto community learned that among Nova Scotian Blacks the economic situation was desperate, they held a collection for immediate relief, and lobbied Rosedale ladies "to send down and bring out girls to work in the homes, and while they were here, they sent back and helped their family to come out."[25] Among the early community activists was Don Moore, who had come from Barbados to New York in 1912 and moved via Montreal to Toronto in 1913. Trying to work in tailoring, he had to adjust to power-driven sewing machines, and to a Jewish employer. He worked on the CPR, then used his savings to go to Dalhousie University in Halifax. In Toronto in the 1920s he founded a debating club, the West Indian Progressive Association, a business club, the West Indian Trading Association, and participated in the UNIA activities. He associated with people from Jamaica, Barbados, Trinidad, Demerara, St Kitts, Antigua, and the United States. In 1954 he and others lobbied Ottawa to permit Black people to come as domestics, this time not from Halifax but from the Caribbean. From then on the Black community changed.[26]

Colour or regional origin, or in the case of the English bank clerks, class, did not matter to employers when demand for labour arose. Cultural attitudes could prevent hiring for long periods of time, but interest overcame principle or bias. Since Black women could not staff all Toronto households in search of cheap labour, women from many other groups came, too: Finns, English, Germans.[27]

PART FOUR

The Prairies: Labourers, Settlers, Entrepreneurs

First Nations' societies peopled the prairies when European fur traders began to explore what to them was new land. At the Red River basin the Métis developed a viable economy supplying the North West Company's lengthening fur trade routes into Athabasca and to the Pacific. From the north came the "Natives of the Hudson's Bay," the English- and Cree-speaking offspring of unions between HBC traders and Native women. In 1812 Lord Selkirk, who had settled displaced Highlanders on Prince Edward Island and in Upper Canada, established the Red River Colony with Gaelic-speaking Scottish Presbyterians and disbanded Swiss mercenaries. The settlement's neighbours included the Roman Catholic mission St Boniface and the HBC's Upper Fort Garry at the forks of the Red and Assiniboine rivers. Neither misgovernment nor pronouncements on "faulty stock" resulting from intermarriage prevented a multiracial society from emerging.

With Confederation and the transfer of Rupert's Land to the Canadian government, the territory was to be surveyed without regard to the established residents' holdings. The first governor, fearing food shortages, attempted to monopolize trade in provisions and by his "Pemmican Proclamation" provoked conflicts with the North West Company and the Métis settlers. Noisy newcomers, land speculators, and inept officials harassed the Métis, who in 1869–70 wanted to continue self-government and were labelled "rebels."[1] Like the Mexicans in the US Southwest after annexation in 1848, the Métis faced dispossession and many migrated westward. In 1873 the Red River settlements were incorporated into Winnipeg's many-cultured population.

The initiative of the railways, the CPR in particular, to bring in immigrants, was lauded, but railway posters diseminated false information, misleading prospective citizens even before they had set foot on Canadian soil. Up to the 1890s, railways had retarded settlement by not freeing up land from their government grants. The mass immigration after the mid-1890s, credited to the Liberals' new policies, came mainly in response to scientific advance, new strains of wheat and new dry-farming techniques, the exhaustion of the land supply in the United States, and higher wheat prices on world markets.

CHAPTER ELEVEN

Immigrant Crossroads at Winnipeg

Winnipeg became the gateway to the West when the transcontinental railway was completed in 1885.[1] French influence declined early. "Comment se fait-il que les capitaux français ne cherchent pas à s'assurer une part des richesses que l'achèvement du 'Canadian Pacific' a mis à la portée de tous? Pourquoi l'initiative privée ne viendrait-elle pas ici lutter, amicalement, sur le terrain économique avec celle des Anglais, des Allemands, voire même des Américains?" one French observer asked himself taking up a topic that was discussed in Quebec society at the same time.[2] As a distribution and manufacturing centre, Winnipeg attracted large numbers of immigrants, mainly from Eastern Europe. The population doubled between 1871 and 1881 to eight thousand and in the next decade more than tripled. St Boniface, as the cultural and religious centre of the French-speaking West, unsuccessfully opposed the abolition of French as an official language in the 1890s and of bilingual schools in 1916. The once thriving interracial community turned into a conglomerate of hostile ethnic segments under an English-speaking elite as prosperous as it was narrow-minded.[3]

English Meet the Many Cultures at the Forks and Beyond

In the 1870s the Hudson's Bay Company elite was still powerful in Winnipeg. When Peter O'Leary visited Montreal and advocated working-class immigration to the urban East, Harry Bullock-Webster was trained in the city for the unsettled West. While O'Leary travelled on meagre union funds, Harry's family in England had connections: "Out hunting one day, we met a friend of Dad's who was a big man in the City," and who suggested to put "the lad" into the HBC. "I could give you introductions ... though it's a pretty close corporation and they choose their employees mostly from Northern Scotland and Stornoway and other cold parts where they are brought up hard and more likely to stand the hardships of the North." Harry was accepted after a medical done by an uncle, another "big man," who knew that there was "no hereditary trouble" and simply pronounced Harry fit "to stand in Canada." His father was very pleased "to think that I should be drawing pay and be off his hands for some years." His training amounted to no more than having "been bred and brought up among horses" and having read James Fenimore Cooper. Thus he wanted to be sent to the Plains.

He began his "business education" at the Montreal company office in winter 1874, where he learned more in a few weeks than in his years of schooling. The voyageurs taught him how to handle furs in a French "patois mixed with Cree and English words." He became friends with them, but the "young fellows in the office" grumbled about his "messing about" with the wrong kind of people rather than going tobogganing with the English-Canadian girls. In the north he "would not see a white girl again for years." His part-Indian friend Jean Baptiste did not hold whiteness to be important: "By and by you see lovely Cree squaw that can ride a good horse, skin and cut up deer, and tan the hide and make the most beautiful leather shirts imaginable, with the embroidery in silks and beads." Once again the issue of women's skills, joint labour, and a family economy.[4]

While Harry Bullock-Webster looked for adventure, the missionary Alexander Sutherland toured the West in search of land for "prosperous millions" from the "overcrowded countries of the Old World" who would "work their way to a *manly* independence." In the imagination of many travellers and sons of the British gentry, the West became a place to experiment with routes to masculinity. The churches, in Sutherland's opinion, "have now before them one of those grand opportunities which may not occur again in the world's history – the opportunity of working out the problem of a Christian civilization on a purely virgin soil." The purity of the future was, however, clouded by imperfect men: an Amerindian village, "a miserable affair"; a German, heavily accented; a Black porter, impudent. Finally, an Irishman and his "very neat house of hewed logs" furnished him with "evidences of civilization." His hope rested on the Celtic and Anglo races rather than on Black "brothers." The churchman's masculinity seems to have been a composite of great projects, massive prejudices, and high self-esteem.[5]

William Bompas, appointed first bishop of Selkirk, Yukon, needed a wife on short notice before departure from England in 1874. He proposed to a cousin, Charlotte Selina, who had grown up near Naples, Italy, where her parents lived, and had returned to England as a writer. Her acceptance of the proposal transported her from cultivated society to utter loneliness. At Fort Simpson in the Yukon, no letters reached her for months at a time. She called these periods without relationships "a blank in one's life." The couple experienced food scarcities and the HBC monopoly prevented her from buying even a single fur from the "Indians" as a present for her sister. With her Cree servants cultural conflict erupted about the work ethic. She learnt the language of the neighbouring Native peoples to be able to talk during the sometimes year-long absences of her husband.[6]

In the North, the population was almost exclusively Native. In the Red River Settlement of 1870, it consisted of French Métis (48 percent), English Métis (34 percent), and Natives (5 percent), leaving 13 percent for Euro-Canadians – from the British Isles (3.5 percent), Eastern Canada (2.4 percent), the United States (1.4 percent), and other origins.[7] The coming of Eastern Canadians backed by military power resulted in an exodus of the Métis, who resettled in northern Saskatchewan and in the area that was to become Edmonton. The change from highly mobile occupations, such as trading and buffalo hunting, to settled agriculture was difficult. George William Sanderson, an English-speaking Métis, with his French-speaking friends had lived through annexation and the fight for self-determination. He left his apprenticeship to a skilled HBC craftsman to roam about as a trader. When he moved to Prince Albert to farm, he "found it hard to settle down, so when seeding would be finished, I would take a couple of teams and wagons, and go freighting until haying time came around." Only after the railway in 1890 deprived him of business did he settle permanently.[8]

Point of Arrival: The Immigrant Sheds

Two routes led to the Northwest from Toronto, one via the Great Lakes to Duluth or Port Arthur and onwards with the Northern Pacific Railway, the other by rail via Chicago and St Paul to Winnipeg. After 1885 the CPR's connection from Montreal via North Bay and Sudbury cut the time to travel from Montreal to Winnipeg from sixteen to four days on regular service. Immigrant trains moved more slowly. Once past Ottawa, immigrants crossed "through desolate, rocky country, studded with numerous lakes and covered with scrubby timber, uninhabited and ... largely uninhabitable." To a Welshman it looked worse than a "disused Rhondda pit." To settlers in search of fertile land, seeing nothing but bush and rocky waste for days was a sore trial. Then, some one hundred kilometres east of Winnipeg, the prairie burst into view. Travellers commented on the prairie "sky-scapes," "heavy clouds rolling eastward," "soft transparent hazes," at sunset "a mellow flood of golden splendour," as well as on the myriads of mosquitoes, making life a misery and rendering rest or sleep impossible.[9]

Crossing the continent by train meant wooden benches in box-like coaches on tracks laid quickly and without skill. The industrial catchword was "progress" and progress equalled speed. Contractors proudly announced that they had laid kilometres of tracks in a day: embankments were not allowed to settle, a process that takes years. Just as O'Leary had noticed the poor quality of the street pavement in the cities, no craft consciousness entered railway construction; the "shiny steel" became worse than a cobblestone road. Immigrants were crowded together in "musty, uncomfortable 'Colonist' cars, they slept leaning against one another on hard wooden benches. At the end of each was a kitchen, often dilapidated." Rapturous descriptions of these cars seem to have originated with "first-class sleeper lyricists," according to Frank Roe, whose family lay "on the bare slats for three nights as philosophically as we could." A French immigrant in 1906, however, remembered a "colonist car with ice water fountain and stove for hot water at each end, very clean wash rooms."

In Winnipeg, the railway station was "crowded day and night with people of all ages and backgrounds." Nobody was allowed into the segregated area of the Immigration Hall, but newsboys bribed the gatekeeper with a free paper and looked for friends from the old country. Joseph Wilder's father helped "people sort themselves out and find a place to stay." Those who had friends in town inquired among strangers of the same language and were shown the way. After the station had been rebuilt, a Ukrainian immigrant "felt as if I was in a grand palace, and I sat for some time admiring the magnificent surroundings." A traveller of 1906 remembered a "truly cosmopolitan crowd, in which the colour of skin ranged from the pale white of the Scandinavian to the deepest black of the African," with "Hindus" and Chinese in between.[10]

The immigrant sheds remained at the Forks, where the river boats and trains from St Paul had disembarked their human cargo. Three layers of bunks had been installed along the walls, but immigrants often had to sleep on the bare floors. In 1902 transient Doukhobors built old-style clay stoves to bake their own bread, since store-bought bread was too expensive. Pumps provided water and an opportunity to exchange information or discuss problems for those waiting to fill their buckets. Kyrylo Genyk helped Ukrainians, many of whom gratefully remembered him. He and his family came in 1896 after he had incurred the wrath of Russian authorities because of his socialist leanings, and his education secured him an appointment as an immigration officer. Processed immigrants would be sent on and be lodged temporarily in immigration halls in small prairie towns. Farmers would come up with their teams, offering for a price to transport the migrants to homesteads.

Help was not always available when needed. One Icelandic family, before moving northward to a homestead, left their fourteen-year-old daughter to be placed in Winnipeg as a domestic. In the confusion and bustle the immigration officials forget to give the girl's address to her parents and over time forgot about the incident. It took three years for the family to reunite.[11]

Laura Salverson, from Iceland, visited the sheds with her father, Lars Gudmundson. Known for his writings in Icelandic periodicals, he was often called upon for help. He guided newcomers, particularly those without relatives or friends, "through the ordeal of endless questionings, medical inspection, customs ritual." To the child, the shed seemed "a grimy, forbidding place, with dirty windows and battered doors." The hall was filled by Doukhobors, "a hundred human forms stretched out upon the dirty floor ... all wrapped in grayish, woolly, skin garments, that reeked with horrible odour." Women held bundles which might have contained a child or a tightly rolled feather bed.

> To my excited fancy, they seemed a race of hairy monsters, stewing in their own reek, like the animals in the circus. I could not skip through them fast enough. That is how I came to trip, sprawling on a huge fellow who lay spilled out in peace ... I lost my ... gift of flowers, and if I didn't scream, it was because the fright was shocked out of me when the huge bolster jacked-up like a spring, and the big bearded face ... crinkled with smiles. What was more, the surprising creature retrieved the bouquet of flowers, ... a woman beside him snatched them from his hand, and buried her hot grimy face in the sweet petals.[12]

Most newcomers stayed for a few days, some worked in Winnipeg for a few years. Mary Agnes FitzGibbon, a granddaughter of Susanna Moody, in 1877 met "immigrants of almost every nation." Their experiences, their hopes and anxieties, were intercultural. The tall, intelligent, and adept Natives impressed her. The Mennonites, in her opinion, were "excellent settlers," quaint-looking in their becoming dresses. The Irish were friendly, her Métis driver capable. Even the "lethargic-looking" Icelanders learned English quickly and become "teachable servants." A pretty and brave young Canadian woman "was worth ten men." Mary Agnes FitzGibbon's view of humanity was certainly more favourable than that of the stern Reverend Sutherland.[13]

Other immigrants included Michael Luchkovich from Pennsylvania, later the first Ukrainian-Canadian MP, Gus Romaniuk, and the Wachowicz parents as unskilled labourers in the 1890s and early 1900s. Homesteading families sent their daughters as domestics into English or Jewish households, where they learned the language and absorbed the culture. Boris Bruser, who had migrated from his Russian village to Odessa and on to Canada, headed for Vancouver, but his money ran out in Winnipeg. "If God choose Winnipeg, who was he to argue?" He settled, opened a photographer's store, brought his parents over, was betrothed by them to a woman he did not like, and broke the engagement when he met Ronachka. Married, they settled in one small town after another, returned to Winnipeg, moved on.[14]

What Halifax was for the Maritimes and Quebec City or Montreal for Eastern Canada, Winnipeg became for the Prairies. Here immigrants received first impressions of the world they had entered. While none of the seaboard towns developed an entry-gate myth, Winnipeg's immigration sheds were remembered by many. The modest accommodation matched their future modest lives of hard work. But placing the "gate" in the centre of the country is not only a contradiction in terms, it shapes public memory into a discourse that defines the East as settled Canada, the prairies as "immigration country," implies an established Anglo-Canada with a French cluster and a separate space for others ethnic groups. It also strengthens the myth that all immigrants were agriculturalists, though even during the settling of the West as many immigrants headed for towns in Central Canada as were going to the prairies.

Migrant Odysseys in Europe and Canada

Immigrants from Europe often had long wanderings behind them by the time they reached Canada. Others moved between Canada and the United States. For example, overpopulation, limited agricultural land, rule and exploitation by the three neighbouring empires sent Poles from the 1880s into internationalized labour markets and forced them to develop transnational cultures. Of Tomasz Opalinski's seven brothers and one sister, one brother moved to the United States, three to different cities in France, two to Canada – one via France and Tomasz himself directly. Tomasz worked for a Ukrainian and a Yankee farmer, at a railway job, in two different lumber camps, with an Italian mine-owner, on a harvest job, in a Polish-owned mine, and at half a dozen other jobs. Then he married a Polish girl from Lipnica and they settled in Edmonton. The places in the new society provided only jobs, the French cities were only postal addresses, but the Polish towns where his and his wife's families lived remained cultural spaces. For Tomasz Opalinski it took a long time before Edmonton became a new space filled with cultural meaning.[15]

The Duesterhoeft family migration began when Eduard's great-grandparents moved as agriculturalists from West Prussia to Poland in the 1830s and on to Volhynia in Russia. In 1913 Eduard Duesterhoeft returned to Hannover, Germany, to study for the ministry. Bilingual in Russian and the Russo-German dialect, he still he had to take language lessons. "If you are German but come from Russia, they would correct every word you would utter, saying it was wrong." During the First World War, the Russo-German students were interned as enemy aliens, but after the war, Duesterhoeft was able to come to Canada and two of his sisters followed. He ended up first among Russo-Germans in Saskatchewan, and then in Alberta, where "it was struggle for survival." Imperial rule, self-segregation into agricultural colonies, internationalized labour markets and wartime dislocation had forced men and women like him to move.[16]

Others, like Klaas DeJong, were forced into itinerancy by class position and poverty. The DeJong family, from Leeuwarden in the northern Netherlands, "moved in a gypsy-like manner to wherever Father was called to work" as a cabinet-maker and repairman for windmills. His mother helped on local farms, while at age fourteen Klaas's eldest sister wandered from farm to farm with her sewing machine, working for twenty cents a day. Once, Klaas earned a whole gulden and was sent by his mother to buy a luxury: some bacon. Icily the storekeeper, an established member of the local bourgeoisie, sent the boy off: "Your mother has no business squandering money on bacon!" He was fourteen years old when he got his first leather shoes. As an adolescent, he fell in love with Betje. Unjustly beaten by her teacher, she received another thrashing at home: "Never, never was the teacher wrong" in this society. When she became a washerwoman, her employer's son saw her taking a piece of bread and promised not to tell on her if she let him have sex. Once done, the son told on her nevertheless and Betje was first fined in court, then brutally beaten by her mother.

By assisted emigration – a scheme to get the poor out of the country – Klaas DeJong, came to Winnipeg in 1893. Along with other Dutch boys, he worked as an itinerant labourer in CPR yards, lumbering, and street repair in Winnipeg, tie-cutting in Ontario; Manitoba ice-fishing and ditch-digging, and harvest gangs; and jobs in the Rockies, Oregon, Montana, Spokane. His work mates included Dutch, Danes, English, Scots, Russians, and Swedes. In spite of the handships, DeJong found Canadian itinerancy an improvement over life among self-righteous Dutch burghers. He had meat to eat, his hours were limited to ten a day, and he could save part of his wages. But there was also hunger in winter, camps full of vermin but without "facilities to wash," contractors driving men "like beasts of burden." Accidents were commonplace; one Dutch emigrant had four fingers cut off his hand on his first lumbering job. Bosses cheated Klaas and his buddies out of their wages, clothes were stolen in bunkhouses. DeJong met little of the proverbial prairie hospitality, no ethnic networks supported him. Over the years, he sent money to bring over his parents, brothers, and sisters. In 1904 Klaas returned to Leeuwarden and realized that Betje had never received his letters – they had been kept by her employer. Being told that he had married an "Indian" women, she had finally married a tailor's son. But now she was a widow with a child to support. The two could finally marry, with Betje's parents arranging an expensive wedding and expecting the rich "American" groom to pay for it. After returning to Winnipeg, the couple turned to market gardening, hired "Galician" immigrant women, "some mighty fine women ... among them," and became successful.[17]

The Hardships and Delights of Schooling

If Winnipeg's population was of many cultures, so were its school children. Some parents needed their children to join the labour force or work on the family farm. In the bush or on the prairie, schools and teachers were not always available. But then, neither were they in parts of Quebec, as Rémi Jodouin knew. And Aili Grönlund did not attend school; first she wanted to help in the bakery, then the family took her participation in the family economy for granted. Though she regretted the decision ever after, the thought of school had "terrified" her. "I knew I would be sitting in the first grade until I could learn enough English to be promoted." She was fourteen and had attended an exclusive girls' school in Helsinki. Similarly, in a Toronto school about 1914, Leah Rosenberg felt "utterly humiliated." Florence Horne, a Home girl in Ontario, remembered: "I went to public school [in England] and had good marks in everything for a fourth grade scholar, but I knew no history or geography of Canada, so [at age thirteen] I was put in grade two. Many of the children teased me about my English words."[18]

An Icelandic girl began school at ten after a resolute aunt brushed her mother's objections aside: "Except for a few words and phrases picked up from my brother, [I] understood nothing of English." This Winnipeg girl, through the whims of her father, was temporarily deposited in Duluth. The "line" had little meaning for the people of the borderland. She badly wanted to go to school, but having been imprisoned not only in the family's Icelandic cultural traditions but by long illness, she felt profound confusion. In later life she could not even remember her first day in school. Enticed by her father with an exciting book, she knew how to read Icelandic, but was placed in grade one to learn reading in English. She found a friend, Katie Pepolenski. "Katie was a big Polish girl who had all the qualities which I lacked. She was pugnacious, cheerful, and completely satisfied with herself, although she was poor and almost an outcast in the school." The two girls, "awkward foreign creatures," "made an easy target for the cruel humour of our small companions." In her home, Katie proudly showed her friend the family icon which "occupied a place of honour above a little shelf that was dressed with a crocheted fringe." While this cultural heritage was kept intact, Katie had adjusted to life in the schoolyard. She once rescued her sickly friend from "a savage little mob" taunting her with ethnic epithets. She barged in "hitting right and left: 'Leave her alone, you devils! You skunks! you dirty Swedes! ... You filthy Cossacks, I'll spit in your eye! I'll spit in your eye and curse you to hell.' " This last threat probably reflected Polish religiosity, just as the ethnic references reflected a history of oppression. Sweden had ruled Poland in former times and Tsarist Russia ruled Poland with Cossack troops at the time of the Pepolenskis.[19]

Such support crossed ethnic boundaries. A Scottish immigrant boy in Winnipeg came to school on crutches. With his knee injuries he found it very difficult when snow fell. "A Polish boy and a Ukrainian boy came knocking at the house with a sleigh." They pulled him to school every day and brought him back home. Their families were neighbours but not close friends.[20]

Fredelle Bruser came to Winnipeg in 1931 from a Saskatchewan prairie town. Of Jewish background, she had done well in school and was proud of it. Winnipeg's Gladstone School was grey stone and asphalt surrounded by a steel mesh fence. The country girl happened to be a poor runner and short-sighted. Her schoolmates set upon her. "What nationality are you?" They did not take "I'm Canadian, from Saskatchewan," for an answer. Italian? French? In the small prairie towns everybody had known the Jewish storekeeper's family. With a public identity there was no need for identification. Fredelle blurted out "I'm Jewish." The reaction was immediate: "Ab-ra-ham ... don't eat ham." "Ask her if her father has a chopped-off dink." Girls filled her bonnet with horse paddies. "I learned at Gladstone School the many faces of defeat." Her prairie school knowledge did not measure up to the city school, so she was downgraded to Lower Four. The well-educated Fredelle corrected a teacher, Mrs Murphy, whose English was less than perfect, only to be strapped in view of the class.

Given the living conditions of many immigrants, children often came to school with lice. They were lined up in front of the class to be combed and cleaned. Natural aversion to lice and the public classroom display combined to cause an association of "Hunky" with "lice." Fredelle tried to hide her grief from the parents, but her father sensed her unhappiness. He could not change the school but he could comfort her. "A Jew is a wanderer ... It is not easy, a new school, new people. But what you are, in the heart and in the head, no one takes from you."

With no programs for teaching English as a second language in place, teachers solved the problem by seating children with some

English next to children with none. The system worked until a new compulsory school attendance law brought in so many immigrant children that the number of translators became insufficient. But, jointly with team sports and games in the schoolyard, English was bound to become the language of communication.[21]

Schoolchildren were indoctrinated and educated with the *Canadian Readers,* which, contrary to their title, were about the Empire and imperialism. Other stories also dealt with family life and the pleasures of childhood. In Winnipeg's Dufferin School, "with youngsters from many different nations," the motley crowd was unified by the Lord's Prayer and "Rule Britannia" or some similar song each morning. The British-centredness was also a drawback in other parts of the Empire, as an Australian autobiographer noted, who later came to Canada as an educator.[22]

Poor Immigrants: The Icelandic Gudmundson Family

Klaas and Betje DeJong had moved from poverty to modest security, whereas natural disaster catapulted Icelandic families from modest farming to poverty. Pioneer settlers from Iceland had come to Nova Scotia and Ontario. When a volcanic eruption in Iceland in 1875 sent hundreds fleeing, "New Iceland" was established in Manitoba by order-in-council with Gimli as its centre, a unique self-governing political entity. Within a year, nearly fifteen hundred arrived, some creating an urban nucleus in Winnipeg. In 1887 Lars and Ingiborg Gudmundson with their first children joined the community, where Lars's sister, "Aunt Haldora," awaited them. As the family's anchor, she assumed responsibility. "Because she wanted to learn the ways of this country, as well as its speech, she went out cleaning by the day." A trained nurse, she later transformed her house into a hospital, worked as midwife, and antagonized some community members by helping an unmarried mother.

Like many other immigrant families, the Gudmundsons faced immediate separation. The breadwinner had to leave in search of a job; thus began a Winnipeg-centred odyssey in which the family travelled jointly or separately to Minnesota, North Dakota, Mississippi, back to Winnipeg, on to Selkirk and back to Winnipeg. Laura, whose married name was to be Salverson, viewed her father as fettered to *wanderlust* and *vafurlogar,* the flickering flame of hope. When he announced that the family was going to move to Duluth, the news hit the family like a thunderbolt. He had sold the family cow before informing his wife or children. A further separation occurred when Laura's elder sister Anna was adopted by a relative after her father's lengthy illness led to "pyramiding debts" and lack of food.[23]

The emotional involvement of Laura's parents in family life counters standard concepts of gendered roles. Her mother Ingiborg was hard and bitter and had to make ends meet. By marriage she lost the ties to her own family; by trying to farm in Iceland she lost the few possessions she brought into her marriage; and she lost several children to illness and death. Ingiborg Gudmundson "rejected assimilation in any degree with a people whose sensibilities she doubted, and whose culture she therefore refused to admit." But she did have moments of cheerfulness and energetic action. Laura's father, Lars Gudmundson, was a warm, sheltering person. His dreams of country life idealized a rural Icelandic past and an organic, if hierarchical, family of parents, children, and servants under one roof. Between illness and feelings of "utter defeat," he maintained his interest in the lives of other people, his willingness to help, his readiness to give emotional support. Comforting new immigrants or writing poetry were his ways of expressing himself.[24]

Laura, Aili, and Fredelle, as well as the several immigrant boys who as adults wrote about their childhood, as children formed a close emotional unit with their parents. Children growing up in the poverty of the depression years, like Polish-Canadian Anna Kutera and Agatha Karpinski, shared these feelings. The Home children persistently questioned the need to be placed out. Agatha Karpinski and George Biedrawa were bitter when their parents proved harsh, took their wages.[25] In Laura's, Aili's, and Fredelle's childhood and adolescence, sisters played an important role; in other families sibling relationships were weak, friendships more intense. After marriage, the autobiographical retrospective of the three women reflects husbands as persons in separate spheres rather than as emotional partners, love notwithstanding.[26] Many adult men, though certainly not all of them, in their memoirs assigned only marginal roles to their wives. The child's view of family is that of a unit, the adult view that of separate but interrelated lives.

Lars Gudmundson, as a skilled saddle-maker, found a job; the difficulty "was to keep the family alive on the [piecework] wages." Ingiborg contributed to the family budget by selling her knitting. When Lars stayed home to look after the desperately ill Laura, he subsequently had to work long into the night to make up for lost wages and to pay the doctor's bills. His friends criticized "the sweatshop system under which men laboured in this land of publicized liberty." The sweatshop owner, a migrant from Ontario, was "ruthless." His workshop's windows admitted "inadequate light and no ventilation"; its roof, on the other hand, admitted rain and cold. The owner "killed every effort to unionize the shop." While he accumulated capital, his workers accumulated worries.

The family budget was tight. If healthy, Lars could make perhaps $24 a month. From this Ingiborg had to pay rent of five dollars, buy fuel and kerosene, costing between three and eight dollars depending on the coldness. She was thus left with about fifteen dollars to feed and clothe the family, pay doctor's bills and incidentals. Once the family was offered a small lot for a house at five dollars but the amount was far beyond their savings. They had to give up their rented house and move into three tiny rooms. Lars fell dangerously ill, so Ingiborg drove herself to even more work. A small Icelandic merchant granted credit and a fellow-worker took up a subscription – the classic working-class means of solidarity.[27]

For the family, but mainly for the children, acculturation began. Laura's brother and his friends participated in their school's band and rehearsed for Victoria Day. Laura and her friends found encouragement from a supportive librarian. Laura, keenly aware of her "queer made-over coat" which distinguished her from neighbours with style, badly wanted to be like the others. Even to communicate among themselves, the schoolchildren had to speak English – another means of acculturation. Noting that their mothers were in the process of producing "a new crop of babies," the circle of girls became aware that this ended all chances of financial assistance for their own education.[28]

During the 1907 depression the family once again could not make ends meet. Laura was deeply shocked when her father, under pressure of circumstances, averred that he counted on her to get married: a financially stable but unwelcome suitor had indeed proposed to her. "Anger that was nine-tenths pain" welled up in her, "papa disposing of my future in such terms as these ... papa, who should have understood." Laura declined the offer and set out to earn her living as salesgirl but was fired. As a domestic servant in a house "on the right side of town," the work was not bad. But one son tried to flirt with her, and the other accused her of stealing a cheque. She changed positions, worked with a Swedish woman, a Greek man, a Norwegian woman. She finally found a position in a tentmaker's company, sewing in a race against the "horrid clock." After falling ill and being dismissed as a result, she worked in a tailoring firm. But she also met companions that stimulated her intellectual life where, as yet unknown to her, her future lay.[29]

Life in Early Twentieth-Century Winnipeg

While Laura Salverson's autobiography provides a glimpse into the life of one family over time, other life-writings provide a composite picture of Winnipeg society and customs. Hugh Herklots, an English visitor in 1903, noted that the uniformed streetcar officials out from England were intolerably arrogant and that to Canadians "an Englishman is by his very nature incompetent." He watched immigrant labourers cutting ice, ate with Métis and Icelanders in the ubiquitous Chinese restaurant, saw the unemployed shovelling snow. In his view, the major cultural difference was shopping. In England, people buy when they need something, in Canada they buy when shops offer "specials." Women had other complaints about shopping: alcohol was cheaper than milk. Countrywomen coming to town to shop for the family often saw their husbands go into one of the many bars and then vanish with newly found drinking companions into the red-light district. Women "went home with their needs unfilled" and sometimes were beaten by the drunken men. Herklots reflected on interacting stages of economic development: "Nowhere so swiftly as in Western Canada can a man slip from the twentieth century to the simplicity of primitive times."[30]

For the well-to-do Jewish Wilder family in Romania with eight children, two developments changed their lives. Posters and bulletins advertised land and work in "America"[31] at a time when Romania's Jews faced drastic economic and political restrictions. One uncle, Beresh, liquidated his business and sailed for Winnipeg with his family of four and Joseph E. Wilder's elder brother Harry. In 1904 the other family members came and settled on Patrick Street, near Beresh's store. In the North End, the father helped to build the synagogue. The children's experiences in school were worse than those of Fredelle: volleys of stones, obscenities, bruises. Joseph quit school and began work as a newsboy. Depending on the news, he sold his papers in different parts of the town; sports events sold papers near the grain exchange, European news in the immigrant quarters. He became a participant observer in ethnic studies: "Slavs generally went into outdoor work, while Italians opened restaurants or fruit and vegetable stores, Scots went into the Police Department, Irish joined the Fire Department, and Jews went into the garment industry."[32]

Unlike the Gudmundson family, the Wilders settled in quickly. Unable to take a job that required English but knowledgable about wheat and flour, the father opened a bakery. Two New York merchants who resented his competition in the matzo business tricked him out of the shop. Next he opened a fruit shop on Logan Avenue; then, sensing the need for communication, he placed benches on the sidewalk and, with a sure sense of his potential clientele, added a gramophone playing European folk tunes. He never complained about lack of customers.

While many of newsboys were immigrants, there were native-born ones as well. James Gray, of English and Irish background, born in Winnipeg in 1906, in his childhood lived near destitution. His one-armed father was an alcoholic, and the boys had to move from school to school as the Grays' housing situation deteriorated. Their classmates included Jewish, Ukrainian, and Italian children. In 1916 James began his rounds as newspaper boy, a job which taught no skills but was the best-paying job on the child labour market. Just as in Toronto the quarters of the rich had been unknown to immigrants, James Gray learnt about a section of Winnipeg, Eastgate, that neither the poor nor the new immigrants could have imagined. "I entered into a world as new and as magnificent as any in the Arabian Nights." The lowly paper carrier was to remain invisible: "I was ordered around to the back door by a uniformed maid." One evening he took his family on a tour of the street, acting as guide, pointing out the marvels which existed only one long block away from where the Grays lived. James had better contacts with immigrants. While his mother held a prejudice against garlic and raw vegetables, his friends' food was more varied. "The Jews could do a dozen things with chicken or beef brisket that my mother never heard of." This was a niche new immigrants would discover a half century later when ethnic restaurants came to provide a change of fare.[33]

Another native-born Winnipeg child lived on the right side of the tracks; Dorothy Livesay was the over-protected child of an English journalist and his Canadian wife. The family could afford servants: "Katrina (from Austria), or it might be Marusia (from the Ukraine)" or "Polish Anna" who, to the disgust of the family, ran off to the "Indians." Later a girl from the countryside, Jenny, was taken in. She subsequently refused to marry her village sweetheart, since the one thing she wanted to avoid was going back into the rural world. Joseph Wilder remembered children like Dorothy. "I used to watch the rich kids being brought by carriage to Professor Zimmermann's Dance Studio ... They seemed like people from another world."[34]

Difficult Times and the General Strike

James Gray and Joseph Wilder were earning their few cents in 1913 when Winnipeg's real estate boom broke and the town entered a depression. A year earlier, the Douglas family had arrived from Scotland. The father, an iron-moulder, had preceded them in 1911, persuaded to emigrate by a brother who had been in Canada before. "There were always people in every family who felt that they should get away to the colonies [*sic*] to improve their lot." The depression reduced the father to three days of work a week. The family "worried about where the next dollar was coming from," but "compared with the unskilled workers or people who had had some misfortune, we were comparatively well off," noted Thomas C. ("Tommy") Douglas, the future socialist leader.

The Douglas family belonged to the class-conscious and unionized craft workers. The father wanted to be independent and had a "hatred of class distinction. The idea of taking off your cap to a squire and touching your cap to the doctor and preacher was foreign to him." The family made contacts regardless of ethnicity and one of the father's friends was a Chinese laundryman. Craft-consciousness, in the traditional sense, also meant "to give the boss a good day's work for a good day's pay." But in 1913, "a man would go down and stand around maybe even half a day, to find out if he was going to get work, and finally at noon be told there was nothing." Tommy Douglas went to the All People's Mission of the Reverend J.S. Woodsworth. The mission's small library "and the fact that somebody was interested enough to come and live amongst these people, and provide some type of social centre for the boys and girls of our community, meant a great deal to us."[35]

In addition to class tensions, the First World War brought out ethnic tensions and released a wave of chauvinism and militarism. "Ladies from the battalion auxiliaries occasionally turned up on Portage Avenue to pin white chicken feathers on able-bodied civilians who were not in the army." "Victory Gardens" were planted to counter rising food prices. Schoolgirls had to knit scarfs, mitts, and socks for Canadian soldiers, the boys turning the skeins into balls of wool. Children told "spy" stories about German-Canadians. A friendly woman of German origin who offered a drink to children playing in the hot sun became "Mrs Spy" – in the children's dramatic imaginations the water was surely poisoned. Some attitudes were gendered; "while the patriotic pew-holders were demanding the deportation of aliens at their church and lodge meetings, their wives were down in the North End succouring the alien women and children." Many immigrant families still held the dirty jobs that Canadian men and women did not want, but an "agitation started to have all 'enemy aliens' fired and their cleaning jobs turned over to the wives of overseas soldiers." Loss of jobs by the adults meant increased need for immigrant child labour to supplement family income. Immigrants from the enemy empires were suspected of disaffection and Poles and Slovaks, for example, hoping for independence for their countries, saw themselves lumped together with Germans and Austrians.[36]

In 1919 skyrocketing food prices, "shoddiness of wartime clothing and shoes," and "profiteering in the war industries" made life almost unbearable for those at the bottom of society. These conditions led to the Winnipeg General Strike. It pitted "common decency" against "Anglo-Saxon racism," thought James Gray. His mother saw the labour stoppage differently. "Men make me sick!" she exploded. "What right does he [the union leader] have to take food out of your children's mouths, Harry Gray, just tell me ... From now on you just try doing the cooking for this family and see how you like it trying to stretch things the way I have to stretch them." The tense atmosphere in the family resulted in more strappings than ever before for James and his brothers. Thus James felt compelled to scab. He carried the *Free Press* in spite of the strike and his disagreement with the paper's position in blaming "alien Reds" as instigators of the trouble. He did not get far. First a housewife doused him with dishwater, then a group of young men beat him up.

James watched special police start a riot and the so-called Citizens' Committee of 1000 support what to them was law and order and to others was poverty and malnutrition. The labour-sponsored Strike Committee took the worries of housewives and mothers into account. It asked the bread and milk drivers to go back to work for the sake of women and children. Ice wagons, however, did not run and in the heat milk turned bad easily. So the ice companies opened their storage rooms for people to "pick up their own ice." James Gray, unsuccessful with his-news carrying venture, went to get ice. Hardly out of the storage room, he was stopped by a woman who needed it. She gave him a few cents and he returned for more loads – no complaints about scabbing were raised.[37]

Again, the look from the bottom up may be supplemented by a look from the top down. Dorothy Livesay's experiences of the war and the General Strike were diametrically opposed to those of James Gray and Joseph Wilder. In the war, she remembered "young men with bright faces" and her father writing home about the "fun" from his assignment as war correspondent in Europe. This fun was followed by the bad news of the General Strike which was dangerous and warranted immediate evacuation, according to the father, who sent his wife and children with a servant to the countryside.[38]

The Winnipeg General Strike tore families apart and its memory lasted for generations. The survival of hungry working-class families was at issue. An American saying, "foreigners, come to take the bread out of people's mouths," had once been applied to the British colonial power and sparked the initial incidents of the American Revolution. In Winnipeg, a class alien to the needs of the common people sparked rebellion. This class, like its predecessor in 1869-70 and in 1885, could muster sufficient clubs and guns to quell the struggle for more equality. The royal commission that investigated the strike and its bloody suppression found most of the demands of the strikers to be justified. The gateway to the West did not lead to unlimited opportunities but to urban class struggle and rural hard labour to break the prairie soil.

CHAPTER TWELVE

The Opening of the West

Until the railways fanned out in the West, settlers from Winnipeg trekked out by cart. Collections of shacks, called towns, sprang up. The haphazard character and profit-making aspects of urban growth are reflected in many accounts. One real estate agent, selling lots in a distant western city, had a map "which showed the City Hall, then a little gap, and then came the property he was trying to dispose of." When customers asked about the distance between city hall and the lots, the agent asserted: "Not far," but cautiously added, "Really, I don't know the exact distance." A better-informed customer pointed out that the distance was twenty-five kilometres. "The agent was a little taken aback. 'We are trying to build up a town out there,' he said apologetically."[1]

Settlement was encouraged by the Dominion government and the CPR. In 1872 Sandford Fleming, engineer-in-chief of the Canadian Pacific and Intercolonial Railways, had travelled across Canada with the Reverend George M. Grant as secretary. The report, intended to attract settlers and published in both London and Toronto, was probably received with more trust as it was written by a man of God.[2] Two issues were addressed in particular – the prospective settlers' fear of "Indians" and the question of government "support," the contemporary term for handouts to the CPR. The report, mixing paternalism, religion, and economic interests, assured potential settlers that Native peoples were peaceful. Treaties should govern relations with the "Indians," these "big children" often "rude and noisy." It was taken for granted that the Dominion government would honour treaty provisions and Native peoples would "sacredly" do so if ceremonies conformed to their "ideas of solemnity." Economic interest was an added incentive, since without cooperation "they could not get tea or tobacco, guns or powder, blankets or trinkets." If churches and government were to provide missions, land for farms, and schools, Indians would soon live in "well-built houses and well-tilled fields."

As to government support, the report cast the topic in terms of nationalism and international competition. "Had the [US] State held aloof, maintaining that any interference or expenditure on its part in connection with emigration was inconsistent with political economy, that the tide of population must be left to flow at its own sweet will, and railways be built only where there was a demand for them, the great west of the United States would not have been filled up for many years to come." With some exaggeration Grant added: "We are now able to offer better land, and on easier terms, to immigrants than the United States or any of its railway companies offer, but they will continue to attract them if we fold our arms while they work." Nation-building not only justified government subsidies to the railway companies, it made them absolutely necessary. The national mission netted the privately owned CPR twenty-five million dollars, twenty-five million acres of land, and tax breaks.[3]

Storekeepers, like the Ontarian immigrant John Alexander McDougall, or railway entrepreneurs, like Mr Bonneau from Quebec and the Italian Giovanni Veltri, worker-contractors like the Swede Edwin Alm, navvies like the Ukrainian Gus Romaniuk, and British missionaries and observers of the bunkhouse scene often moved ahead of settlers. Those who left life-writings were men or families who came with capital or who were able through their personal capabilities to rise from worker to contractor. Those who levelled grades, hauled lumber, and cut ties either moved between bunkhouses only or visited towns occasionally to have a good time, but did not write and thus we cannot share their perspective. Seasonally employed farmer-navvies, on the other hand, did leave accounts.

Shacks into Cities

When Marie Bonneau arrived at Regina, Saskatchewan, from Quebec in 1882, it was a tent city without a railway connection. In 1887, Maryanne Caswell's family from Ontario reached an assembly of fourteen log and sod houses and, to their bewilderment, learned that this was Saskatoon. "What disillusioned, dejected girls we were … Why did we ever imagine it to be a city?" Many cities existed but as names on surveyors' maps. Similarly, the team of horses that a local family wanted to buy existed but in the future, "when they got rich": till then oxen had to do. But shacks could turn into cities quickly. Saskatoon counted 113 inhabitants in 1900, though the nearby Temperance Colony settlement had more. It counted 12,000 in 1911, 25,700 in 1921.[4]

Edmonton had two hundred inhabitants when Lovisa and John Alexander McDougall made it their home and base for business in 1878. About 1910 J.B. Bickersteth, an Anglican missionary in Alberta, called it "a great city," with fifty-five thousand inhabitants, large railway yards, and excellent tram service. On the streets, "rough railway men, miners, and odd customers of every kind jostle well-dressed women and smart businessmen." Bickersteth saw "the successful man" of the West as being of "new and venturesome optimism," "self-confident, insatiable, ... buoyant, swift-minded, gay, but often ruthless to the incompetent." Of untiring "devotion to the pursuit of money (not so much devotion to money itself)"; and in contrast to the subsidy-dependent railway capitalist, the Westerner lived in "an atmosphere permeated with the ideas of the market-place." This spirit extended to immigrants. The man of the church admitted that optimism was frequently shattered, that deprivation in overcrowded bunkhouses and undersupplied homesteads was the reality.[5]

Storekeepers and hotel-owners, though living in tent colonies or on a false-front "Main Street" that was also the only street, often had imperial pretensions. Lonely places on mud roads established their connections to royalty and empire, "could nearly all boast a 'Windsor' or 'King Edward Hotel.'" Chinese restaurants and pool rooms occupied shacks. Another observer noted in 1912 that people were acting and thinking in terms "of what the country *will* be."[6]

Early merchants often followed government commissioners who disbursed treaty payments to Native Canadians, hoping to sell as much as possible and realize a quick profit. Alexander McDougall did so from Edmonton and T.H.P. Lamb from Moose Lake, Manitoba. The McDougalls' fortune grew rapidly until an American firm joined the treaty "fairs" and undercut the Hudson's Bay Company and Canadians' prices.[7]

In Edmonton village in the 1880s, Lovisa McDougall felt lonely. Local Edmonton women did not suit her, they were "not much" and, worse, had children before marriage. Such complaints notwithstanding, she enjoyed the advantages of travelling and being independent. She hired Native and Métis women as servants, and had an immigrant from Kentucky as a handyman. She usually liked the women but switched to European-origin servants when they became available. But servant girls were few and quickly got married. Facetiously Lovisa hoped to engage one with "some deformity that would keep the fellows away." With an increasing white population, her attitudes changed. She summarily dismissed the Métis as "dirty." Ministers now "make the people in the east believe they have evengolized [*sic*] this country but every person that comes out here fails to see any good they have done, only to get a hold of all the property they can for themselves." Newspapers still came from afar; like Anna Leveridge in Ontario, Lovisa and her friends read the *British Workman* and *British Workwoman*. Their new store would give Edmonton, with a population still below five hundred "quite a metropolitan appearance," she thought in 1881.[8]

In the spring of 1906, when James G. MacGregor came with his Scottish and English parents, daily immigrant arrivals in Edmonton, according to the Dominion immigration agent, "averaged between three hundred and five hundred. The immigration building was crowded and the hotels were full. New immigration quarters were opened at the Exhibition Grounds, and a new immigration hall north of the CNR tracks was finished that summer." Day after day people lined up from the early morning hours before the Land Office.[9]

The internal migrants usually brought their farm equipment from Quebec or Ontario in special "stock and settler's effects" cars. Thus, compared to overseas immigrants, their start was relatively easy. Transport of stock and equipment from the station to the homestead, however, could present formidable problems. Muddy tracks, wet mire, rickety wheels, broken axles: "What a lot of unloading and reloading in those 200 lonely, uninhabited miles," the Caswells remembered; they had to bring in the lumber for their house from Moose Jaw. The Bonneaus in Regina, on the other hand, as railway contractors, erected "considerable store premises," selling to the numerous French-Canadian settlers and offering hospitality to the visiting Bishop Taché from St Boniface. They witnessed the second Métis rebellion and, like other early settlers, sympathized with Métis demands for security of property and for political participation.[10]

Internal migrants and immigrants shared many experiences. For both, life began in a tent or a sod house. Men went back east to find a wife, immigrants sent home for a "helpmeet." Daughters were lent out to neighbouring women for company, or to help nurse a baby and care for children when men were out earning money by freighting. In their teens, girls might be sent as domestics into urban households. They could achieve upward mobility through acquiring education and becoming teachers. But, as many life-stories report, young teachers were coveted as homemakers by local bachelors and usually left their poorly paid jobs quickly. To learn farming, Ontarians or English-speaking immigrants with means and time could attend the Ontario Agricultural College in Guelph, as did Edward Ffolkes from Norfolk, England. Others hired themselves out for a summer or two to an Ontario or Manitoba farmer, to acquire a rudimentary knowledge of agriculture. Farmers received advice from the Dominion Experimental Farms after 1886.[11]

By 1900 Marie Bonneau, married to Calgary newspaper editor Zachary Hamilton, could afford the services of a "China boy" and a German girl. Once they tried to engage a woman who seemed to be looking for work but the "splendid looking creature dressed in foreign raiment" turned out to be a prostitute. The Hamiltons moved in the English-speaking segment of society. To them "foreign settlements" on the outskirts of Calgary seemed to be a problem zone, full of Hungarians with diphtheria and Galicians in need of religious and social facilities, a "Home Mission" in the terms of the times. In the early 1900s the Regina railway yard received special emigrant trains almost daily and "was a perfect babel of tongues." While these outlandish communities were marginal, the Hamiltons enthusiastically participated in the rituals of Empire, such as Queen Victoria's Diamond Jubilee in 1897 and the festivities on occasion of the 1901 royal visit. One other ethnic group attracted their attention – the Americans. Some came as settlers and neighbours, others were cattle rustlers, horse thieves, and whisky smuggler. American capitalists came by special train to buy land, the cheques being collecting in a large waste-paper basket.[12]

While mercantile families built what local society called fancy stores, while capitalists shoved money across the table, roads had to be built, tracks had to be laid, chores had to be done. It would be instructive to have a diary from one of Lovisa McDougall's maids – but alas, none exists. A few workers' memoirs have, however, been collected. In Edmonton, Janis Jankovskis arrived with his family in 1905 from Latvia, then part of Russia. For two years he worked as a bricklayer, then bought land one hundred kilometres to the east and left the city. Kaspar Halwa and his family from Galicia reached Strathcona in 1898, and he took odd jobs in the small-scale coal mines opening to the river bluffs. He was eager for an education and with others paid a teacher for private English lessons. His educational investment and the school years among German-speakers paid off: with Polish, German, and English, he became an interpreter at an employment office and organized groups of men for mine work.[13]

In 1901, Peter Svarich (Petro Zvarych), a highschool student from Galicia, reached Edmonton with clear goals: he wanted to obtain a store clerk's position, to improve his English, and to set up for himself. But not even odd jobs were available. Finally, as a helping boy in a semi-finished printing shop he turned the crank of the press and cleaned the type. Of his wages of six dollars a week, half went for room and board. Next, he took a contract to build a house, then landed a better-paying job at a lumberyard and sublet the house-building contract. Better-paying did not mean more skilled; it could be unloading freight cars or wherever a temporary labour shortage required high wages to attract workers. Sometimes he did carpentry work, occasionally even helped design house-building plans. At the same time, he set about organizing a night school for Ukrainian boys and girls working in the city.

During a railway strike in 1901 for better wages and fewer deductions, Italian and Slovak workers with "long-time" experience – , that is, a year or more – organized themselves and headed for other jobs.

Recently arrived Ukrainians were stuck when the CPR did not board them, provide return transportation, or pay outstanding wages. Begging for bread along the road, they trudged back to Edmonton and milled around the streets "without work and without food." Peter Svarich, with help from city authorities, found them a job clearing a few acres of land on the riverbank. The work was soon finished and he "went around knocking at doors in search of any kind of employment." A self-organized soup kitchen and occupation of an abandoned shack tided the men over until harvest jobs became available. The Ukrainian men intending to farm were forced into itinerancy to kilns, mines, or sawmills.[14]

Railway Construction: An Italian Entrepreneur

Strikes and poor pay are not part of railway mythology. Settlers hoped for an economic impetus from railways and for larger markets, just as Maritimers, the Leveridge and Carrothers families, and many others had done. Plans to connect the Prairies by rail to Hudson Bay, thus shortening the trip to England by some sixteen hundred kilometres, were discussed in hopes of attracting large numbers of Britishers. Such imperial dreams conveniently overlooked the inaccessibility of the bay in winter. At this time of increased manpower demand in the West, Britishers were slow to move, emigration from Italy was on the increase, and mass emigration began from Austria-Hungary, in particular from the Galician territories.

From the mid-1870s on, Italian seasonal labourers in ever larger numbers first crossed the Alps into France and the southern German territories; then migrated into colonies in North Africa; next continued to South America; and finally arrived in North America. From Montreal outward, Italian communities sprang up along the railway lines. Communities separated by oceans – or the Canadian Shield – were held together by personal ties. Small villages and localized neighbourhoods became integrated into a world system of investments, labour migrations, and agricultural expansion. Commercial grain crops were harvested by migrants in the United States, Argentina, Australia, or South Russia. Railways built by migrant navvies transported grain to ports and thus to world markets. The resulting worldwide drop in prices caused an agrarian crisis in the migrants' areas of origin, including Italy. Better trade and transport systems also placed North Italian producers in competition with Chinese and Japanese producers of silks and rice. Within four decades, fourteen million Italians had migrated, some in transatlantic seasonal migrations, others permanently. About a decade later, smallholding peasants in Austrian Galicia were hit by the same world market forces.[15]

Giovanni Veltri, born in 1867 in Grimaldi, Calabria, was one of the Italian movers. Thunder Bay, Ontario, became the most important settlement of Grimaldesi. Veltri first went to North Africa and for two years worked in railway construction. "The Veltris and their friends" began the process of 'globalizing the village' by working on the frontiers of European capitalism."[16] Then his brother invited Giovanni to North America while his mother counselled return to Italy. America won and jointly with fellow-townsmen (*paesani*), he travelled via France and Belgium to Montana in the fall of 1885. His brother, head foreman and later independent contractor, sent Giovanni to nine different places in Montana, Oregon, and Washington until, in the winter of 1889, Giovanni returned to Grimaldi. He hardly ever mentioned his family, but we learn that in addition to his brother he had four sisters. He was drafted into the army, returning home to marry Rosa Anselmo in May 1893. His family was sufficiently important to him that he applied for leave from the army when their first child was to be born, a son named Raffaele.

In 1895 Giovanni returned to Canada, leaving his pregnant wife and child behind for over seven years. Probably in reaction to racism and ethnocentrism, he called himself John Welch. (Janis Jankovskis, the Edmonton bricklayer, changed his name to John Jones: it made life easier for his children in school.) His brother and partner offered him a job as foreman on a railway construction project in British Columbia. Whenever business was slow, particularly over the winter, Giovanni found himself other jobs. In the winter of 1895–6 he tried to improve his English; one winter later, he opened a bar. On the CPR contract at the Crowsnest Pass, Giovanni advanced to camp supervisor and soon leased short sections on his own account. He and his brother formed the J.V. Welch Company, but in the winter of 1899-1900, which they spent in Winnipeg, "few of us had even $100 in our pockets." He once more returned to his family in Grimaldi, leaving behind a well-equipped camp with forty-two horses, dump-carts and drag-boats. For the next two years he worked on the land in Calabria. But when, just after the grape harvest in 1905, news came that his brother Vincenco had developed a mental illness, he left for Winnipeg, taking with him his eleven-year-old son, Raffaele.

In his memoirs Giovanni expressed compassion for his brother's affliction. His marriage, seemingly harmonious and mostly divided by an ocean, was never mentioned in connection with his departures. Neither did he mention the births of three daughters, although he did remember all the names of the ever-changing male Italian-Canadian business partners, Canadian contractors, and relatives who worked closely with him or died on the job. Reports about the work, new contracts, discovery of a gold vein, and an explosion were all reported in the same matter-of-fact tone. Most of his partners were Italians, most of the larger contractors Canadians, but his workers included crews of Norwegians, Croatians, and Swedes. Only once did a work crew cause problems. When English "rock construction" workers arrived, he almost had a fit: at the isolated construction site "we saw several gentlemen [descend from the train] well-dressed and carrying suitcases. They all asked where they could find a place to eat." Angrily he labelled them "veritable loafers gathered from the streets of London." Only four of them, a family group, stayed with him: father, son, and two nephews. A Frenchman worked for him as carter, an Englishman as coach driver. He met Jews, one of them Italian-speaking, and an Irishman living with a "very kind and pleasant" Black woman. Thus the working community, Italian or even Grimaldesi at the core, was multi-ethnic on the fringes. Women seem hardly to have been present in his world.

His family contacts receded ever further into the background. During his third return to Grimaldi in 1909–10, he did "a lot of work in the countryside" but never mentioned wife and daughters. From 1910 on, he stayed in Canada for a stretch of more than twenty-one years. After fourteen years of continuous separation, thirty-one years after his marriage, the family came over, living at first in Winnipeg, then, with other Grimaldesi, in Thunder Bay. In his memoir, seven years of family life were condensed into less than one page. In 1931 his wife, daughters, and second son convinced Veltri to return to Italy with them. For him, this was "voluntary exile to my homeland, ... it certainly was not pleasant to be confined to my primitive native village." "Captured by my old passion for agriculture," he worked the fields, but also built a two-kilometre aqueduct to pipe in water. Mentally he remained suspended between Grimaldi and the prairies.[17] The one-time villager had become cosmopolitan without ever leaving Grimaldesi communities. He moved between his family and his world of male cooperation. Living in two cultures and many locations never hindered his efficient functioning. He worked or organized work wherever he happened to be. He was at home wherever he was in geographical space.

George Bielesh, a railway employee in Poland, also decided to go to Canada in 1906. When he returned to bring over his wife with their child, "she could not be persuaded." He departed alone in 1909. A second visit in 1911 ended with the same results. However, in 1913, Mary finally decided to join her husband with their three children and her brother John. The whole family went back "home" in 1922, as Mary had always intended. But European politics had moved a border, and their village was now in Czechoslovakia. George returned to Canada in 1924, and Mary and the seven children joined him in 1927. Mary took in boarders. The "farm and new house," their dream at the time of his first departure, never materialized.

While most railway navvies were unskilled, Italians had gained some expertise by blasting tracks into Italian mountains. George Bielesh also came with experience, and Jan Plachner, another Polish worker, had learned tunnel-building during his labour migration to Germany. In the late 1890s, "he got a job doing just that in the Rocky Mountains." Thus skilled workers came. The cost of training them had been borne by their society of origin, the advantages accrued to a Canadian region, a business corporation, to the national economy.[18]

Itinerants and Bunkhouse Men

The West has often been described as a land of opportunities: farmland to be cultivated, seams of coal to be mined, stands of timber to be cut. The life-writings reflect a different perspective. First, human beings are most important and resources take a secondary place. Secondly, resources that appear abundant in continental perspective are scarce in the vicinity of settler families. Opportunities did not grow like tumbleweed; men and women worked hard to survive and, if lucky, get ahead. If human labour could not turn rocky soils into productive farms, the working families had to move on. The willingness to move to wherever labour was needed explains the take-off of the prairie economy. Multiple temporary internal migrations turned a homestead into an empty shack for much of the year in the case of single homesteaders, a shack inhabited by a woman and children in the case of married couples. The so-called opportunities were few and far between. Obstacles studded life-courses, rocks the fields.

Edwin Alm, twenty years younger than Veltri, came to Canada in 1912, like Veltri after several years in the American West. Contractors, railway workers, and many settlers moved in the West as if no border between the United States and Canada existed. Alm came from a small Swedish village. His father had been a professional soldier and the family had moved frequently. He remembered poverty, coldness, and religiosity. For his education the family had to go into debt. Schoolbooks for seven kronor (about $1.40) were beyond its means. In the end, Edwin began work as a hired boy on a farm, keenly aware of rigorous class distinctions. At the age of sixteen, as a driver at a travellers' hostel, he slept in an unheated garret in the stable. He was on call twenty-four hours a day, seven days a week, and earned about fifty dollars a year. Many men and women emigrated, so in 1907, Edwin decided to go to America. No relative or acquaintance was willing to lend him the money for the ticket, but he was lucky: a visiting emigrant presented him with the necessary sum.

Countrymen on the boat directed him to the Swedish colony in Seattle. Once a drunken and broke compatriot took him and others to saloons and brothels with "girls of all nationalities." The women, however, wanted business and the penniless young men had to leave. Edwin realized that his options were either to seek quick amusement or to defer gratification and save his money. He took any job available: turnip-pulling on the farm of a Swede, road work for a logging company, farm work again. A Swedish foreman, a "slave driver," mistreated the road workers. After a pay cut, the Finns walked off. But the economic crisis in 1907 forced them to come back and work for nothing but food. A Swedish farming family invited Edwin and two others for Christmas, even though it could ill afford to feed them. Odd jobs and a diet of bread and canned tomatoes lasted for months. When for some misdiagnosed rash he was locked into the "pest-house," he lost "some faith in the highly touted American democracy" and made his way to Canada in 1912. Contrary to his class experience in Sweden, he was accepted as equal by townspeople, though but a worker: "This was a revelation to me."

He found friends from his home town, worked with Norwegians, Irishmen, Americans, and Italians, bought tools from a Jewish storekeeper, danced with a German girl. Lining railway tunnels, paving streets, building trestles, men faced frightfully high accident rates. One of his jobs was considered the "suicide gang," as he subsequently learned. Though involved in several bad accidents he was never dangerously hurt and remained carefree and of an "adventurous spirit." Retrospectively he noted that this lifestyle "still gives me a shudder." He was of rebellious bent, roughing up a city inspector, supporting the free speech fights. However, he considered himself "far away" from the theories of the Industrial Workers of the World – in fact, he was unable to get their name correct. For him and his friends it was a "sport" to go on the soapbox and be washed down by fire hoses.[19]

In his relationships to women, Edwin avoided any permanent commitments. He mentioned brothels and watched prostitutes, "streetwalkers," when working on roads or tracks. Many of the sex workers joined the entrepreneurs. As one worker recalled,

> some of them ladies carried their trade right out along the line. They'd come to the end of steel and set up a dance hall there. Just a rough floor, not even with planed lumber, with a couple of big tents over it. There'd be a piano player and they'd sell whiskey and other drinks. Each of the girls would have their own little tent. It'd be three or five dollars or up to eight dollars [in the 1910s] to go and visit them there. And every few weeks when the main camp moved that dance hall set-up would pack up and move right along with them.

These entrepreneurs made large sums of money and often had to go to town to cash stacks of cheques. Talking about the town "in its heyday when it was a bustling mining camp," one casually mentioned that she had six girls working for her in the good times. The Dominion government seems to have been seriously concerned. The Immigration Act of 1906 excluded prostitutes and pimps, persons of "moral turpitude." The exclusion was repeated in the 1910 law, which barred women or girls "coming to Canada for any immoral purpose." Neither sex workers nor customers would have considered themselves immoral. What was angrily mentioned by women was sexual harassment.[20]

Edwin Alm, as a "result of sheer loneliness," married in early 1913. The marriage was "doomed to failure from the start," and he never mentioned his wife again. They probably divorced, since he remarried thirty years later. His comrade, visiting Sweden, found a girlfriend who, just before his return to Canada, told him that she was pregnant. He neither wanted to desert her nor marry her on such short acquaintance. Edwin, concerned about the woman's predicament, arranged for a ticket to be sent to her to come to Saskatoon and have an abortion. A day later his partner, closer to him than any of his three brothers, died in a work accident. While deeply saddened, Edwin kept his head clear and cabled the young women to cash the ticket and do whatever she thought best with the money. He later visited her and was content to see her happily married.

In 1912 Edwin landed a job as foreman and, within a few weeks had set up his own business. The Swedish chore boy had become a Canadian owner of a horse and buggy. But within a few months, he lost his money to the beginning depression. Then a CPR contract in Saskatoon for an underpass "marked the beginning of a reasonably successful career." He was astute in calculating the cost of labour and reducing it by hiring machinery and thus gaining a competitive advantage. He held CPR contracts for the next eight years. Once he hired a crew of some seventy Russians; the cook and helpers were Chinese. During the labour shortage of 1918 a woman hired on as cook for a construction camp. Hoping for a contract in early winter, he had farmers cover the ground of the proposed construction site with straw to protect it from freezing. His innovative approaches gained him contracts and profits. In 1921 Edwin moved to Vancouver and became a real-estate dealer for the rest of his life. His was a modest success story.[21]

Gus Romaniuk arrived in 1912 in Winnipeg as one of four children travelling with their mother. The father met them and took them more than one hundred and fifty kilometres north to the homestead. Upon seeing the shack, the whole family felt cheated. Mother and Gus started to cry, but hunger forced them to set to work in order to live. In the same year a gust of wind blew a small fire into large flames and their shack burned down. Tears again, and again the pressure to return to outside labour to struggle for survival. Even though the family came with some money, the repeated mishaps, frosts, and illnesses forced the father and Gus and his brothers into itinerant labour. The 1913–14 economic crisis was beginning, but the men were forced to search for jobs nevertheless, as early frosts had destroyed their crops.

Gus, at the age of fourteen, began to cut railway ties and carry food to his father on distant work contracts. Two years later he went to Winnipeg; there he hired on with a railway crew, worked exposed to the elements, and slept in a boardinghouse with eighty beds. An acquaintance got him inside work – a hotel job polishing cutlery. Two young second-generation Ukrainian women who did the dishwashing lent him money so that he could buy some urban-type clothing. The next year, with friends, he went to Ontario: railway work in the north, logging in winter, in spring dock work in Fort William, doing double and triple shifts when ships were loaded, enduring lay-offs when no ships were in port. Gus and a friend also hired on with winter fishing crews on Lake Winnipeg, but by 1919 they still had not earned enough money to pay for food on the way back home. "We were happy to be home again. I stayed home till the end of winter, helping father in the woods and enjoying visits with my friends, neighbourhood dancing parties, and an occasional home talent stage play."[22]

Gus Romaniuk married but had to continue his migratory life. "I could see no future," he noted in 1925. "To be cut off from Church, school, social intercourse of every kind," meant "complete disillusionment." The attractive emigration booklets often misled: "For the settler who has little capital, the first few years on the homestead are years of continual struggle. Receipts are few – expenses many," according to one observer. Gus and his wife Emily built a house in Riverton and kept a store. They survived the hardships and were content. But he also mentioned a neighbouring couple, the Lisowyks. In a mud-hole their wagon upset and Ms Lisowyk was pinned down by the overturned wagon. She died before help came, "drowned in the quagmire."[23]

In June 1912 the missionary J. Burgon Bickersteth was sent out along the Grand Trunk Pacific Railway to a construction camp 225 kilometres west of Edmonton. During the crossing of the Atlantic he had already met an Italian who was returning from a visit at home to a railway job in the West. Looking out of the train he watched the "extra gangs" permanently on the move "ballasting up the track wherever it has sagged." Track-laying remained makeshift, grades needed constant repair. Bickersteth described Marlboro, "more of a camp than a town," consisting of "a straight row of hideous lumber buildings. The first is a store, the next a pool room, next to that again an hotel, then come a couple of bunkhouses, a large stable, and finally, on some rising ground, our shack and the church." As in any frontier town, "a number of shacks of various size and shapes" housed families. A more permanent element among the single men, in groups of three or four, also lived in their own shacks. Some hundred and fifty men occupied the bunkhouses. Two were filled mainly with English workers, the others with "every nationality and class – Canadians, Americans, English, Scotch, and Irish, Poles, Russians, Germans, French, Swedes, and numbers of Galicians." Some workers were "coarse and degraded," others had seen better days and found bunkhouse life hard to take; some were life-long migrant labourers, others were homesteaders working for a few months to make "a grubstake."

Bickersteth, like almost all autobiographers, touched on a theme that has been neglected by researchers on ethnic groups and bloc settlements: the many-cultured interaction, the mixed work crews of homesteaders and labourers, as well as on the presence of women and children in frontier towns. At Fitzhugh, west of Hinton, he saw "great fair-haired Swedes, sallow-faced Italians and Galicians, black swarthy-looking Russians, keen-featured Yankees and Canadians, ... strong-looking fellows" from England. Elsewhere he met a Bulgarian, an Austrian, a Spaniard, and a Bessarabian Russian of Orthodox faith. In the racial terms of the times, only West Europeans were white, with the position of the Irish unclear; all "dark-visaged" people were lumped together as "dagoes." Most of the latter, said Bickersteth, were dirty, which Englishmen seem not to have been. However, he admitted that no one could wash, "there are no facilities for it" in the camps "on the front" as he called the "head of the steel."

The foreigners, according to Bickersteth who did not understand their languages, jabbered continuously, were excited about nothing, turned into animals after a few drinks, and had no eating manners. They might earn good money but worked extremely hard for it. Labour relations were poor, "there was a good deal of ill-feeling between the contractors and the men." Bickersteth assigned part of the blame to the bad treatment of the men by the contractors. Men would walk off the job when conditions did not suit them. Thus, few strikes occurred but many departed in protest.[24]

The long, low bunkhouses were made "of lumber, covered with black tar paper." Inside Bickersteth noted "an atmosphere reeking with coal oil, bad tobacco, and wet socks." Along the walls two tiers of wooden bunks, with two bunks side by side, packed the men closely. A bench, boxes, and tree stumps was all the men had to sit on. For workers, even from impoverished European villages, such housing was a downward move. The contractors overcharged the men in company stores and paid in cheques which, so far from any bank, could only by cashed at a discount. "When you see the conditions under which these men live, you could hardly be surprised if the outlook which many of them have on life is little better than a beast's. They work like horses, eat like pigs, and sleep like logs." Immigrant workers often complained of being treated like draft animals. Some of the men, particularly those who earned "straight money" – that is, those who were paid year-round – saved their wages. The majority of workers were paid by the day, each day's wage having to cover living expenses for one summer day and one of unemployment in winter ("crooked wages"?). It was the bunkhouse segment of frontier society in which women were not present and which therefore made them great topics of conversation.[25]

In conclusion, we will quote Bickersteth's description of the process of the laying of steel:

> First there is the grade, which is left ready and comparatively level by the contractors, although a great deal of ballasting and levelling up is necessary after the steel is laid. The important thing is to get the rails down, no matter how, so that the supplies can be forwarded by train to the nearest point to the camps. About half a mile ahead of the ... [train and track-laying crew] come the surveyors, who stake out the line, putting in centre stakes, which are the only guide the steel-layers have to go by ... [At the head of the train, is] the pioneer itself, which looks ... like a large crane placed on a truck.

On either side of the train, the ties "fairly hurtle off the tram," each one caught by two men, until there are "enough for one or two lengths of rail." Then the tiemen stand aside. From the pioneer's "two long steel arms, placed at an angle of about 45 degrees, hang steel ropes which catch the rails as they come off the tram. Men rush forward, bear them down into place, and join them up to the last two already laid – the exact breadth of the gauge is given by a man with a properly measured rod. No spikes are driven until later." Two short hoots indicate to the locomotive to advance the train by some six or ten metres. Behind the train "comes the gang of spikers ... The protruding head of the spike, as it is driven in, catches the edge of the rail and clamps the whole thing down fast to the tie."[26]

Once the rails were laid, settlers could move in more easily, but land became more expensive. The settlers often had to claim a homestead or buy a partially improved farm and then join the contractor's crews and track-laying gangs. Thus, as in late nineteenth-century Russia, peasants became temporary urban workers, remained in jobs as peasant-workers for an increasing length of time, and in this way changed their mentality to paid work, becoming worker-peasants returning to the farm but occasionally. Finally they or their children would be urban workers. In North America, transatlantic migration filled rural and urban labour demand. Rural-urban migration from peasant plot, homestead, family farm to cities assumed larger proportions in Canada only in the 1920s.[27]

CHAPTER THIRTEEN

Community-Building: Homesteading and Bloc Farming

The prairies captured the imagination of many. Life was dynamic, with a better standard of living but a short time off in "next-year" country. The image of free land and the outdoor life led visitors to produce numerous factographic or opinionated accounts.[1] Educated Britishers travelled across the "Great Northwest" on self-assigned fact-finding missions. Osyp Oleskiv addressed his "About Free Lands and About Immigration" to Ukrainian peasants in 1895. A multitude of life-writings[2] reflects cultural origins, especially the experiences of Mennonites,[3] Russian-Germans,[4] Ukrainians (or Ruthenians),[5] Poles,[6] Askenazi Jews,[7] Germans,[8] Swiss, Dutch,[9] Danish, Swedes, Norwegians,[10] Finns, French[11] and Belgians, Italians, and the four British nationalities,[12] as well as from the other America, the United States.

After the worldwide depression from the 1870s to the mid-1890s had retarded immigration, from 1901 to 1911 some one million settlers arrived. They came singly or in family groups, reached fertile soils, rock-strewn lands, or ranching areas. Larger groups attempted to form bloc settlements to preserve their customs and language. Some had agricultural experience, others had none; some came with only a willingness to work hard, others with capital, still others with a supply of labour in the form of sons and daughters. Their experiences depended on location: close to a railway where land was more expensive, on good soil but distant from even small-town connections, or in marginal locations.

English visitors were often hostile to the newcomers or outright racist. Basil Stewart pointed out "the danger to the Empire arising from the indiscriminate immigration into Canada of Russians and Galician Jews, Greeks, Germans, Dutch, Poles, Hungarians, Italians, and even Syrians and Turks, and other people who, estimable as they may be in the land of their birth, are *not* the kind of material from which the British Empire has been made in the past, nor of which it should be built in the future." Such "hordes" usurped what was to be breathing space for the "teeming millions" leaving "overcrowded England." Others did not cling to a constructed Britishness; Canada's mixed people was "of her own race, her own aspirations, her own language; brought up to acknowledge the same law, same King, and the same flag."[13]

Settlers in Sod Huts and Beyond

Life in the new world often began in a hut no more than three metres by four and built of sods, the so-called government brick, or in a tent purchased from Eaton's. When a log-house could be built, lumber was often not seasoned and settlers were unskilled in carpentry. Pioneering in the West meant deprivation and back-breaking labour. Melting snow seeped through sod roofs in winter, mosquitoes drove humans and animals to distraction in summer. Immigrants and internal migrants remember the constant fear of prairie fires, the hardships of poor crops, swollen rivers, washed-out bridges. To one Catholic immigrant rain meant "'dollars falling from heaven.' It is Holy Water! This beneficial rain has just come in time to make the seed germinate." The sod house dweller's perspective was different. "Once the sod is saturated with water, it rains as abundantly inside as out." Beds mouldered, provisions spoiled. Under these circumstances women gave birth and raised children, men lived and died, children played and laboured.[14]

The move beyond the sod house, intended to be upward, instead could mean destitution or the grave. Frosts and locusts, illness and mental breakdown, sheer incapability or lack of physical stamina forced families to abandon their plots. People were called "bushed" when isolation and overwork had driven them out of their minds. A deranged Belgian woman wandered across the land. The family had recently been burnt out and had lost everything, including their seed grain." The neighbours "all chipped in to help them get started again." A year later, the woman became very agitated over a prairie fire and told neighbours that her husband was brutal, that "her son was an ingrate, and his wife a dissolute character, ... [all] abused her children." Did she consider emigration an abuse to the family? Did she project sorrow into physical violence? All we know is that she was afflicted by "prairie madness."[15]

Maurice and Maggie Destrubé, in 1918, enjoyed the "awakening of spring, bringing new life," particularly since Maggie was due to give birth shortly. When her time came, Maggie was seized by convulsions. The doctor, delayed by the spring mud, took hours to arrive. By then, mother and infant were dead. Maurice "was left too stunned to know what was going on around me." In similar circumstances, James Sadler found his wife Ellen dead one morning from an illness neither of them had taken seriously: "the shock stayed with me a long time; a kind of numbness." Neighbours and sisters kept house for him and his little daughter. He had recorded his life story in detail, but "the years that followed have kind of run together and the happenings don't relate themselves in my mind according to years." Whether this was from the "mental upset" of his wife's death or "the increasing worries" of the Depression years, he could not make out.[16]

Some settlers, cheated by land agents, lost their money and had nervous breakdowns into the bargain. A hailstorm of a few minutes might destroy the labour of a year; it meant no food for the family, no fodder for animals, no seed grain for the next year. Blizzards spelled disaster. Frank Roe's father died shortly after being lost in a snowstorm in 1894. Billy Clark visited his sister in Saskatchewan in 1907: "Sixty-four below and there was a wire to go out to the toilet and a wire to go out to the chicken house and a wire to go out to the barn. If you ever let go you were lost in a blizzard." In this terrible winter even the circumspect Frank Roe came close to suicide. Next-year country was no longer a future; even to "quit decently" the Roe family "needed a good season."[17]

A Frenchman, "stark, staring mad," drove three homesteaders out of their shack at 30 degrees below, over two hundred kilometres from the next store. After two days, they lured him out and shot him. A Scot with a hand frozen off continued to farm. One immigrant, "who had acquired a homestead but who couldn't face the prospect of living on it," sold his team of oxen. "Purgatory Lodge," scrawled on a deserted shack, indicated "the torments of isolation experienced by some wretched man." Another man "blew out his brains with a gun." Suicides became less frequent with denser settlement and less loneliness. Many never achieved improved living conditions and in retrospect only remembered that "life must go on" whenever another material or emotional disaster hit. This underside of settlement and nation-building never entered national lore.[18]

Those who survived moved from dugout and sod walls into a log cabin, perhaps within a year or as late as after a decade. Folklore holds log houses to be a quintessential hallmark of North American pioneer life. In fact, the building patterns were transferred from different parts of Europe. Frank Roe, a self-educated Alberta homesteader and railway worker, described two types, Scandinavian and East European. His iconoclastic account began: "I have often suspected that the famous Hudson's Bay style of log construction originated as the result of ignorance and inexperience which crystallized into a custom and then into rigid convention. This method consisted of sinking pairs of huge posts or piles at intervals and dropping the short length of logs between them." Experienced Scandinavian and Finnish settlers hewed top and bottom faces of a log, dovetailed the ends. On top of each log they spread a layer of moss. The next log bedded the moss tight and hard. The inside might be hewed or unhewed depending on time and preference. A bachelor from Quebec had built himself a beautiful specimen. The only nails were in the door and even the hinges were made of bulging knots and spruce rods. People from Ukraine built differently, with big straight green poles four or five inches thick. "They were peeled in June (when such things must be done to make a good job) and built up with sufficient space between them to admit one's hand. A long unbroken span of wall would be stiffened once, perhaps twice, with pegs driven into auger-holes above and below." This structure was left to dry for a year. Then women mixed mud with coarse grass to plaster the whole house and a thatched roof was added. Building thus combined the skilled work of both men and women.[19]

The best time to arrive was spring, in time to sow and reap food for the next winter. The later in the year migrants came, the longer they would have to buy provisions. Many remembered long months with nothing but potatoes or rabbit stew for food. Timely arrival meant a triple workload: building a shelter, breaking the land, and seeding. In the first years, men and women often stayed in urban wage work or hired themselves out as farm help. During periods of unemployment men looked for a homestead – women by law could not register for one. They needed a fee of ten dollars, or capital for a partly improved farm. Observers in the 1880s estimated that farmers initially needed between five and seven hundred dollars to buy implements, seed, and provisions. If a wet summer or early frost reduced yield, more money was needed to restock provisions and seed. Incapable men, like the Dutch banker's son Willem DeGelder, could sink one thousand dollars annually into their plots and still achieve few results. Experienced men like Joseph Monkman, a Métis from Winnipeg, described his abundant harvests. He knew the soil, the frosts, and ways to keep cattle under local climatic conditions. No newly arrived immigrant could match his knowledge and many paid dearly. Advice from earlier settlers often helped newcomers; railway information and government posters, on the other hand, more often than not were misleading.[20]

Some families came with enough resources to get information. Elisabeth and John Kurtenbach, who in the 1890s had left Germany for the Dakotas, moved their family to farms near Leofeld, Saskatchewan, in 1906. The price differential of land permitted the family to acquire larger holdings. A starting capital of eighteen thousand dollars and a labour force of several sons permitted them to take four homesteads among German-Catholics, Americans, English, and "the whole world." Since the family had sent ahead its eldest son to collect information about living conditions and quality of land, its assimilation into the community was quick. A few months after their arrival, Mr Kurtenbach donated land for a church, worked on building a Catholic school, and was so involved in community affairs that he asked his wife to finish a letter to the family in Germany. The sons were meanwhile breaking the prairie.[21]

Arriving also in 1906 but with no farming experience, the Durieux family from France had to make do. The parents had suffered financial reverses and came unwillingly after struggling for five years with the decision whether to emigrate. The two sons hired themselves out to "poor" French farmers to learn agriculture. After an accident, Henry was sent to St Boniface College as kitchen help. Marcel and another hired boy slept in a farm's attic, separated only by a blanket strung up on a wire from the daughter of the family, Marie. No other space was available. Marie questioned him about the life young girls like herself would lead in France. Her next-year world, it seems, was not the ever-elusive bumper crop, but a life with some refinement and a few pleasures.

When Mr Durieux selected land near Stettler, Alberta, it turned out to be of poor quality. The family continuously felt pinched by lack of money for the amenities of daily life. They needed their small capital to invest in a frame house, implements, and stock. The night after they erected the frame of their house, a violent storm destroyed it and blew away their tent. Their first load of lumber was wasted and they had to begin all over again. The house's insulation was meagre, no firewood had been cut, and the winter ahead of them was the brutally cold one of 1906-7. French, English, and Norwegian neighbours helped with food. They lived "in a sort of stupor."

Madame Durieux, who had spent the winter in town and was known as "the French lady," planted a garden in spring but with her urban background she found it hard to adapt. She was very supportive other family, telling husband and sons that everything was "superb and marvellous." When a track-laying crew passed by, new technology and larger investments meant that no men were hired with their teams, no women asked to supply vegetables. Large scrapers levelled the grade and then tent towns and blacksmiths' shops moved on. Giovanni Veltri and his Grimaldesi could have been part of the crews. Madame Durieux spoke English well, became the organist of the church, and social relations improved. Too late the family realized that prairie life, completely opposite to "her education," overtaxed her. Her "great need for spiritual comfort" ended when the emaciated priest, homesteading himself since the congregation could not support him, died. She contemplated his last resting place with "something like envy" and a year later she was laid to permanent rest too. Her husband had no desire to live on, and he soon followed her. The sons had to carry on alone.[22]

The Durieux family could afford a frame house and implements. Their life, callous as it sounds, was easy compared to that of families coming without means and knowledge of English or French. Frank and Maria Andreychuk had come with their five young children from Austrian Poland in 1903. As a poor cobbler, he had grazed their few animals "on the landowner's property," and had earned a little money by playing his hand-carved violin at weddings. Near what was to be Mundare, they lived in a hillside dugout with dirt floors and a straw roof. Here, Maria, who had travelled while pregnant, gave birth to a sixth child, a daughter.

Then followed "hardships too numerous to mention": little to eat, miles to walk to buy flour, barley for coffee, feet wrapped in rags, "patch upon patch for outerwear," no jobs. Occasionally, at a social "we played at a few dances." In spring, they walked for two days to get to the Edmonton land office to register a homestead. "Then came the hard years": a seasonal railway job at seventeen cents an hour; tough going, whatever they tried. Father and son John moved across Alberta in search of jobs. The baby died of the flu. They sold out and moved back to Edmonton. They divided resources, the parents undertaking another attempt at homesteading, the sons going into wage work to earn money for taxes and implements. "We finally had a small house of logs and clay." Son John married Pearl Romaniuk in 1916. "I tried to help my parents as much as possible. So did my brother, Michael, on his days off. My wife worked on our land while I helped my parents." She worked like the men "brushing, haying, and stooking." In between, she gave birth to several children, cooked and sewed, picked blueberries and cranberries to sell in Edmonton. When Maria Andreychuk died in 1939, the family could not afford to buy a coffin. Frank made a box, a granddaughter "earned a few dollars to buy satin material to cover the box." An old proverb about migration, known to the Russian-German immigrants, "death to the first generation, need to the second, bread to the third," reflects the immigrant experience better than all myths about opportunities, the lore of the great "Great Northwest" or of nation-building.[23]

Group Settlement and the Construction of Ethnicity

The Kurtenbach family settled near other German immigrants, the Durieuxs were neighbours to French-speaking settlers, and the Andreychuks moved to relatives and friends. Some groups sought to settle on compact blocs of land. Thus reserves were set aside for Mennonites. Other Mennonites stayed temporarily among co-religionists in Ontario, still others chose the Dakotas. From 1874 on, about eighteen thousand came, one-third of the Russian-Mennonite population, as well as an additional number from Prussia and the United States. The double ties, ethnic and religious, explain this group's cohesion, and that of the Doukhobor colonies and Jewish agrarian settlements in the West. Ukrainians and Poles crossed the Atlantic because of land shortages and Russian overlordship, Russian-Germans because they too lost their special status.

Separating themselves from their European societies of origin, Mennonites, through intermarriage over generations, had formed an ethnocultural amalgam of Dutch, German, Alsatian, and Swiss believers. Mennonite and German-origin families from West Central Europe, in search of cheap land and religious freedom, had been invited by tsarist authorities to ethnically Polish, Russian, or Ukrainian territories in the 1760s. They had settled in colonies to retain their culture and religion. When reform legislation in the 1880s and anti-foreigner feelings deprived them of their special status, many moved to the Dakotas and the Canadian Prairies. Others stayed until the 1920s, when freedom of religion was curtailed by the Soviet government. One small group of Mennonites, which had settled near Fargo, North Dakota, had to send its children to a predominantly Swedish school. The parents, apprehensive about cultural adaptation, decided to migrate once again, this time to relatives and friends on the Manitoba West Reserve.[24] At the time the Mennonites began to leave, Askenazi Jews fled the pogroms beginning in the 1880s in the Russian Empire. Many moved to the cities of Western Europe, more to New York and other American cities, and to Canada. Of those who came to Canada, some settled in small but distinct agricultural colonies in Saskatchewan such as Hoffer, Hirsch, Estevan.

Many Russian-Germans and Ukrainians, too, planned to live in cohesive settlement blocs. German-origin Arthur Stelter from Volhynia, whose family reached Dunmore, Saskatchewan, in the 1880s, remembered that "the farmers around us for twenty-five miles were Germans." These Russian-Germans were internally heterogeneous, coming from Volga, Black Sea, Volhynia, and other colonies, as well as from Polish lands. In the Tsarist Empire there had been little contact between colonies because of the large distances. Borderlines between groups were also fuzzy. Polish Czeslaw H. Chrzanowski married Lilian Drager, "of German descent," but in modern terms of multiple origin: her mother came from the Warsaw region, her father from Byelorussia.

"My wife attended Polish school and spoke both German and Polish at home ... [In Canada,] they started speaking English at home." His "German" mother-in-law was happy that she could talk to him "in Polish about her childhood days in Poland." In such families, German and Polish biculturalism had become a common hyphenated culture, which by migration to Canada entered a further process of change.

Most of these immigrants spoke several languages because they had interacted with neighbouring ethnic cultures in the old world. When Ludwig Nehring arrived in Leduc in 1928, "I spoke Hebrew, Yiddish, High German, Low German, Russian, Polish and Ukrainian and who did I meet first but an Englishman." Erdman Rosenau's father spoke Russian and learnt Ukrainian easily. Most immigrants acquired a rudimentary English, those who moved around more and those with social aspirations learning faster.[25]

Neighbourly contacts with families of different ethnicity but from the same region as well as interaction with English-speaking people in the marketplace precluded emergence of monocultural blocs. The German families in Nisku, Alberta, according to Julius Oswald, came from one and the same area in Russia but in Canada settled interspersed with Ukrainians. Bloc settlement could thus be regionally homogenous but ethnically diverse. At Fort Saskatchewan, English and German-speaking children played together. "At first the groups kept very much apart ... but later they began to mix a little." Elsewhere, too, Russian-Germans, Poles, and Ukrainians mixed. "There was a mixture of people but everyone got along fine together."[26]

The Galicians came from an area of tiny landholdings in the Austro-Hungarian dual monarchy and southern Russia, where Poles and Ukrainians lived interspersed with descendants of German and Jewish immigrants. From southern Russia Ukrainians also moved eastward to agricultural areas in southern Siberia with climatic conditions similar to those along the 49th parallel. Unable to differentiate between cultures, authorities and neighbours often used the term Galicians as a wholesale designation for East European newcomers which, like the equally undifferentiated designation "Orientals," had distinctly negative connotations. Contrary to later constructions of monocultural ethnic groups, life-writings indicate that a shared culture in the old world and neighbourly support in the new was typical for the Galician cultural group, whose rudimentary multilingualism helped communication and whose multiple interaction led to intermarriage. During the 1913 Alberta school controversy, in which the Department of Education fired provincially certified teachers of Ukrainian origin, the Ukrainians vigorously asserted their identity. The censuses of 1931 and 1941 listed more Ukrainian-speakers than ethnics (112 and 102 percent respectively) because of the linguistic integration of Polish, Slovak, and Belorussian speakers into this largest group.[27]

Some in this group tried to avoid home-sickness by staying among co-ethnics. Two Poles, George Biedrawa and a friend, reached Alberta in 1927 and worked together "on every job." Their first employer, of German origin, spoke Polish, while in Edmonton they associated with "hundreds of Polish immigrants." By prepaid ticket, George brought over a neighbour who was also hired by a Pole. George, along with three Polish friends, inspected homesteads southwest of Edmonton and with yet another Pole he went to the Peace River district. But they soon gave up and George, back in Edmonton, found a packing-plant job, probably among fellow Polish workers. He married a Polish woman.[28]

Settlement patterns, market participation, and workforce composition influenced the direction of acculturation. A Polish colony was mixed with Swedes, Germans, Scottish, and Norwegians. Russian-Germans entered a process of group construction but their contacts remained many-cultured, including Irish, English, Romanians and Chinese.[29]

In view of the dearth of places of worship and clerics, even spiritual needs were satisfied by inter-ethnic and inter-denominational contacts. Roman Catholic Poles invited priests regardless of the latters' ethnicity. The first church near the Halwa family's farm "was built by Greek Catholics about 1905. They were Ukrainians, but all the Poles who were there contributed their time, and work, and a few dollars too." When a few years later, "the Poles got together and built their own chapel," it was consecrated by a procession from the Greek to the Roman church. A Scottish immigrant served as a minister in Presbyterian or Baptist congregations wherever need arose. The Ukrainian Reverend Nestor Dmytriw, on the other hand, complained that a Polish priest had explicitly warned his co-ethnics not to go to a Ruthenian for confession. Settlers not only had to raise money to build their church, they also had to pay their priest. Dissension meant additional expenses or, alternatively, no services. For priests and ministers it meant lower incomes. In 1925 the United Church of Canada was founded, self-consciously Canadian and open to all ethnic groups.[30]

In the marketplace, storekeepers often were English or spoke that language. Jews were welcomed as merchants because owing to their middlemen position in the old world, they usually spoke several languages. Postmasters and mistresses also were English or had acquired some knowledge of the language. International market contacts were not specific to the new world; Julius Oswald remembered a Belgian-owned factory in his hometown in Russia. Millers of one language dealt with farmers of many. Any economic pursuit that was market-oriented implied interaction with other groups and mainstream society. Alternatively – as was the case on other cultures – a group of middlemen would serve as brokers to protect separatist-minded economic actors from direct dealings with business partners of a different culture.[31]

Inter-ethnic contacts were the rule among the prairie's part-time proletarians; both the "settled elements" and the "foot-loose" ones. Farm labourers hired on with whoever would offer a job; threshing crews and railway gangs brought together cash-strapped homesteaders and farmers regardless of ethnicity. The need for jobs precluded a search for co-ethnics: moves would be made after springtime sowing to farmwork in the neighbourhood; with the first news of railway jobs, there would be an exodus from the poverty of the farmer-employer to the wages of the contractor; in fall, came a change to the better-paying short-term harvest gangs and threshing crews, and in winter to lumber camp or odd jobs in towns. The "international homesteaders of the world" resembled the Industrial Workers of the World.

From the 1880s to the 1920s, the established classes in Canada voiced concern about an international working class of highly mobile unattached men, but prairie farmers were considered solid and land-bound settlers. They were, in fact, a multi-origin community practising solidarity and mutual help for survival and progress. Communication was multilingual, by translation, and pidgin English, and their children came to speak English. Neither homesteaders nor bloc farmers in the initial years were settled peasants. They commuted between farmwork and wagework, between peasant and proletarian lifestyles. Young women migrated to the cities for domestic jobs and often stayed. The agrarian families' migratory lifestyles and poverty in the Canadian prairies are comparable to those of Russian or Italian marginal farmers who migrated seasonally or multi-annually within Europe to industries and mines, leaving families behind. On both continents, wives and children tended the land until the men returned. Single homesteaders' land was tended by neighbours or left uncultivated. European peasant-workers often ended up in permanent urban work, though they had intended to enlarge their landholdings into a viable agrarian base. Canadian homesteading families shared the goal of making their land the mainstay of their existence, but they, too, often had to give up and join the urban working class.[32]

The life-writings show that separation into ethnic groups was, to some degree, distinctively Canadian. It usually occurred when groups became sufficiently large and sufficiently concentrated to support their own institutions and when a social layer of intellectuals emerged. Even if groups had been antagonistic in areas of mixed ethnic settlement in the old world, in their new life they chose not to replicate the society of origin. Borders between groups remained fluid and could be crossed.

Itinerancy and Skills in Gendered Perspective

Migrant peasant-workers and farm women from Europe faced similar lifestyles in North America. Like Home children cast about a community-bound Mennonite from Russia, many migrants found themselves part of a threshing crew the day after arrival. Families were separated much of the time, allocating some of their members to wage labour, others to domestic work, still others to stay on the land.

Farm labourers experienced year-long penury but an abundance of food at harvest time. Albert Kolber cleared bush and went hungry; others' complaints about treatment, exploitation, and food were similar to those of the Home boys. When Kolber joined a threshing crew, work was hard, but food was good. "A steam engine, fired with wood, was used. Eight pairs of horses were needed; six pairs to bring the wheat sheaves to the machine, one team to collect the grain and one team to bring the water to the engine. Two teams [of men] fed the threshing machine, one on each side." "The farmers' wives kept us well fed with plenty of good food. I especially remember their pies." In peasant economies, harvest time often was celebrated. It ended the pre-harvest food scarcity. While old-world lords or capitalist landowners relied on the judicial and police apparatus to control workers and to extort labour at peaks of demand, in Canada and other new societies incentives such as high wages and good food had to be offered. This market regulation of wages at times of high demand, from which Peter Svarich had benefited, had its reverse side in the quick lay-offs, as experienced by Gus Romaniuk in Fort William. No protective state or labour union helped. In contrast to almost any other time of the year, it was only at harvest time that no farmer could afford to offend his labourers.[33]

Ethnic hierarchies separated people in labour markets. Many East and South European workers, peasant workers, and itinerant homesteaders felt that English-speakers were hired in preference to them. Ruefully Antanas Rudinskas from Lithuania remembered that the small daughter of his English employer considered him crazy, since he could not talk to her. An English immigrant on a railway gang recalled that when a departing English foreman was replaced by a Hungarian, several English workers quit. "The gang was composed more and more of people from Central Europe, who conversed amongst themselves in their own language – good fellows and good workers, but I felt the need for company of my own kind, someone who I could understand at least." In hierarchies among East European immigrants, some Russian-Germans considered themselves above Ukrainians or Jews.[34]

In Canada class differences were less pronounced than in Europe. The Swede, Edwin Alm, was surprised to be accepted as equal. Czech and Slovak settlers thought they were treated as equals by immigrant American neighbours. But within the English group, the "better sort" agreed unanimously that in Canada the servant classes behaved without due deference and were "insolent," that tavernkeepers did not keep their place, and that maids dressed up "ridiculously." They felt odd when dealing with these classes on equal terms: "There was a dance down the creek the other day; the woman who does my washing, or rather her daughter, gave it. I went to it. It sounds rather funny going to a dance at your wash woman's but that cuts no figure out here." Only one English visitor viewed the new class relations in a positive light, stressing the sense of independence and self-assurance among settlers and workers, but adding that such developments should not be driven to extremes.[35]

For men, the frequent changes of jobs implied an absence of craft-consciousness; they had to be capable to take on any job available. Some were totally out of place, like the man who began to chop down a tree and, asked by increasingly uneasy fellow workers in which direction he intended the trunk to fall, replied that he was no prophet. Lumber was used without being properly dried, houses were draughty. "Any old thing will do" became a standard expression. Haywire was used for each and every repair, most of which did not last long. Low quality of workmanship on the one hand meant flexibility on the other. Farmers without mechanical training could achieve extraordinary feats in machine repair. The make-do mentality became a proud male I-can-do-it culture.[36]

For women, on the other hand, life on the frontier meant development of additional skills, the repeatedly mentioned poor housekeepers excepted. At home and in the farmyard, they prepared high-quality food, unless poverty forced them into makeshift meals. Many men could judge the quality of food, as the harvest crews' comments attest. Shopkeepers who accepted dairy products in lieu of cash had to be able to distinguish the quality of the butter. Dressmaking based on flour sacks was as challenging as it was ubiquitous. Carrie Bratsberg's mother "sewed me a dress for school by hand (as there was no sewing machine) out of flour sacks that she had dyed green." Flour-sack clothes continued to be worn into the 1930s. Women expanded their skills from a sound base into adjoining areas.[37]

Some women, such as Anna Baczynski and her girlfriend, set out by themselves for Canada. One settler noted that women who did not know how to ride were quickly taught by neighbouring women. Women came as teachers and nurses and as homesteaders. When necessary they worked in the fields as hard as men, as many attested. This new position of women demanded adjustments from men. In John Grossmann's opinion, nurses and schoolmistresses had no difficulty in finding homesteaders as marriage partners. But for a man to marry a woman homesteader was a risky business, since she would have "too many male hormones." There obviously were differences in intellect, too, since such marriages worked out – still according to Grossmann – if the partners divided spheres, the woman doing the management and financial calculations, the man the outdoor work. Women homesteaders were few; they had to buy land since by law women could not file for a homestead. Outspoken women demanded that the law be changed. Furthermore, many hired men were not willing to take orders from a woman even when she was clearly the better farmer.[38]

Multi-ethnic Culture: Interaction and Conflict

In settlements and at work, individuals and groups faced stereotypes. They had to react to bias and discrimination. Members of six groups had to deal with particularly strong ascriptions. The English and the Ukrainians evoked negative stereotypes. French and French-Canadians as well as Jewish people, thinly spread across the prairies, were represented in life-writings without predetermined characteristics. As regards African-Canadians, usually called "Negro" or coloured, and Asian-origin immigrants, almost invariably reduced to "the Chinaman," expressed racism was not as uniform as structural ethnic and colour hierarchies suggested. While Métis and Amerindians were not simply stereoptyped, immigrant Americans were often associated with illegal activities.

English men, in all their peculiarities, often provoked ascriptions, from which those intending to blend in suffered. In pre-1914 times, young men from families able to pay the trip hired on with surveyor's crews for summer "adventures." Their initiation to hardship was no sugar for tea, a shock for some. A young Englishman began to cut lumber for a stable, then wrote home to inquire about the breaking strain of logs. When nothing happened at his place, his Norwegian neighbours finished the stable, assuming that he was too "bushed" to look after himself. All observers agreed that the presence of remittance men was fatal; they brought the whole group into disrepute. Winnipeg, the terminus for honest people from many nations, should not be disgraced by such black sheep who blandly asserted "that the reason they do not work is that they cannot find work that a gentleman could do, and could not think of taking other work, as they have the family name in their keeping." Their version of "next-year country" was a "next-cheque-to-arrive-world." Genteel British women usually did better. They kept house for brothers, married, or remained independent. If single, they had to work since the gentry would send out sons on remittances but expected daughters to find husbands or to support themselves. English settlers who worked as hard as others were accepted, but felt they should actively try to get rid of their English accent and vocabulary. What to remittance men was but an unsophisticated colony, was an option for an independent life for many English women.[39]

Many Ukrainians, as part of the Galician group, were accepted as settlers. Others remained visibly different and negative comment came from within the group. The Reverend Nestor Dmytriw argued that "our people" from the Borschiw area "bring only disgrace upon our nation." They arrived penniless after having been cheated by agents. Miscalculating their arrival, they came in the middle of winter, "ill-clad, half-naked, barefoot, dirty, destitute." Afraid of losing their faith, they continued to "wear old-country clothes and their long hair." They did not want to change. Unemployed Ukrainian peasant workers, a countryman said, were "as helpless as children." Was it "blind obedience to foreign [Russian] masters" from the serfdom of the old world that had robbed some of initiative? Others were "able to be independent in ... thoughts and actions." Resulting discrimination as well as racist attitudes induced Pennsylvania-born Michael Luchkovich, who had come to Manitoba in 1907 and was elected to Parliament in 1926, to deliver a rousing speech against "widespread calumnies against the 'dirty, ignorant, non-preferred, garlic-smelling continentals.'" Asked how he could deliver "so brilliant a speech without any notes," he retorted: "My whole life was a preparation for that speech."[40]

French-speakers had made up half of the population of the only major settlement west of the Great Lakes, St Boniface–Fort Garry–Red River in 1870. Recruitment of further settlers by western priests was opposed by Quebec clergy, who instead directed migrants to marginal land within Quebec. Thus the number of Manitoba francophones declined while that of English-speaking Ontarians, who seized the opportunities in the West, increased. Father Labelle attracted French and Belgian settlers in 1885 before the worldwide agricultural depression reduced emigration. By 1896 francophones accounted for less than one-tenth of the prairie population. Another attempt to recruit French settlers, financially supported by the Dominion government, failed because of the opposition of Quebec's clerical-political elites and apprehension about loss of population in France. In 1914 French settlers left to help defend France against German aggression. The Manitoba English leadership dealt a further blow to the group by abolishing French as an official language.

In prewar years, the main acquaintances of the Destrubé and Durieux families were other French-speakers. The Durieux family's circle of communication grew when their parish became bilingual; the Destrubés, as storekeepers, had no feeling of isolation. The francophone group was internally as heterogeneous as any other: French Canadians, Métis, French immigrants, Belgians, and Swiss; accents differed by region and social status, immigrants from Burgundy and Brussels, weavers from Roubaix. Their Catholic faith cut across ethnic lines. Stettler's church was attended by Ireland-Irish and American-Irish, Czechoslovakians, Hungarians, and Poles, in addition to the French-speakers. "By singing in Latin, all of this blended fairly well; in English, it grinded a little, but, for the French hymns, it was unbelievable." Stettler francophones dealt with Swiss, Belgian, and American storekeepers, with Scots, Chinese, Irish, Finns, an Englishman, and a German.[41]

Jewish immigrants in the prairies were few and widely dispersed. Like other East Europeans, they were not considered "white." Most life-writings of the West do not mention prejudices. Prospective farmers such as Abe Plotkin and Harry Henig moved across a many-cultured space, while Michael Usiskin and Israel Hoffer lived in the Saskatchewan Jewish farmers' colonies. Ukrainians welcomed the arrival of a Jewish storekeeper, "with a Jew we could always speak in our own language." The Bruser family, on the other hand remembered antagonism from Polish customers, perhaps carried over from the old world. An English man rented a room from a Jewish family in Calgary; domestics working in Jewish homes in Winnipeg; Jewish storekeepers lived in German bloc settlements. In contrast, schoolchildren in prairie cities remembered being mercilessly taunted by classmates. Leah Rosenberg's experiences in Toronto and Montreal also attested to antisemitism.[42]

Afro-Canadians and Chinese-Canadians appear in prairie life-writings only through the eyes of Others. Immigrants usually met their first Black Canadians as railway porters. Some had seen Negroes in Liverpool, which had an African community of long standing: Tomasz Opalinski remembered having paid ten cents for seeing a Negro. In the West, Black people were mentioned occasionally as co-workers. Meeting "negro children" or being housed at a stopover by "a full-blooded negress" or by an Irish-African couple deserved mention in memoirs. The undertone was surprise and the "negro-but-nice" reaction.[43]

John Ware, a regional hero, attracted the attention of three autobiographers. Born into slavery, he reached Canada on a cattle drive in

1882, worked on a ranch, and then became an independent rancher in southern Alberta: "Although as black as the ace of spades," he proved "himself a good man in many a tight corner." Marie Bonneau Hamilton met John in Calgary, where a new proprietor of the Royal Hotel, about 1900, refused to serve the "coloured" man. Frank Roe, unhappy that cattlemen viewed the homesteader "with measureless contempt," explicitly excepted Ware as the only level-headed ranchman. Ware hired two English brothers, who remembered him as "a full-blooded negro, but one of the 'whitest' men" they had ever known. He died in 1905.[44]

Chinese had joined the gold rushes in 1860s British Columbia and migrated into prairie towns as restaurant keepers and laundry owners. They were much more frequently mentioned in reminiscences than Black people. With irony, Fredelle Bruser noted, "I had never seen a real Chinaman, but of course I knew all about them." So did most other Canadians and immigrants, so they thought. Better-off families hired Chinese cooks. By 1917, a Chinese community had started a truck-farming business in Medicine Hat through which a Russian-German woman gained access to markets for her produce. In mid-1920s Calgary, James Sadler lived near a sizable Chinese neighbourhood. One Jewish and two Scandinavian school girls in a Saskatchewan town went to "the Chink store" and pestered the old man. That he "was scared" of them permits a glimpse on a life characterized by racist exclusion. In their youthful cruelty, the girls hurt him and came off feeling strong. W.K. Yuen, owner of the general store in Shamrock, Saskatchewan, "was just 'Slim' or 'The Chink' – one of us, yet never one of us," Robert Collins recalled. Storekeeping in the prairies

> was a wretched occupation. Every family needed groceries but few could pay regularly so they cajoled or bullied Slim to spin out their credit. He survived by living alone on the knife-edge of poverty, shaving prices and tolerantly letting customers' bills pile up until they sold a side of beef or a load of wheat or a dozen eggs and, he hoped, paid off.

The store was a meeting places, "women could spin an hour's worth of gossip out of a sixty-cent grocery list," men issued "one-syllable weather reports," kids enjoyed five cents' worth of orange crush. "Slim seemed to enjoy the company, contributing smiles but little conversation."

In retrospect, Collins reflected on the hardships of this man's life. "How lonely he must have been." No one ever invited him, and when he did come to village socials he seemed to feel uneasy. When he could afford the gas, he drove to his friends in Moose Jaw. The community did take a stand when Slim was excluded from relief in the 1930s. Two men drove to the agency and saw to it that W.K. Yuen received a cheque too. When he finally decided to leave, the community organized a farewell party.[45]

Of many other groups, few receive special mention. Immigrants from the United States as neighbouring farmers were considered as helpful and friendly as all others. But a considerable number of criminals crossed the border. No other group, whether labelled by colour of skin, cultural background, or religion was as often mentioned in connection with criminal behaviour as the Americans.[46]

Contacts with Amerindians were reported less often than contacts with European immigrants. Native men and women were generally described as friendly, capable, helpful in providing food and shelter. John Henry Thomas, a Home boy who had lifelong difficulties in forming lasting attachments, was adopted by a Saulteaux Indian family in Manitoba. Upon their advice, he married a Saulteaux women twice his age. Both did trapping, John sometimes being off for a year or more. Except for the early British travellers, few autobiographers expressed racism. But the cultures remained separate.[47]

Canadians as internal migrants positioned themselves at the top of the ethnic hierarchy. An Ontario man in Manitoba, the "Wheat King," was an avid proponent of settlement of Norwegians and like Europeans, but he bitterly complained when the Dominion government asked Canadians to vacate land for a Doukhobor colony. It "was an injustice to ask a British subject to move out to make room for a foreigner." Over seven thousand of these religious refugees arrived in 1898 and 1899 and later he employed some of them.[48]

Few incidents of brutal racism are remembered. Memory expunges bad experiences to protect self-respect and identity. Ms Kohl from Mankota described how English-speakers, gentlemen in their own eyes, hoodlums by general standards, ran a Polish homesteader, George Muzury, out of town.

> [To] force George to leave ... some men beat him up in a very unfair fight. George was coming home from the badlands with a load of brush for fuel. They rode up beside him and whipped him with their riding quirts, then threw his entire load of brush off the wagon and scattered it to the four winds. Later [one of] my father's bulls was missing. One of the fellows that had whipped George ... told my father that he had found the bull near Muzury's place ... [with a leg broken intentionally] (My father was Justice of the Peace at this time, and this fellow thought this would be a good way to get rid of George.) Dad and a neighbor ... were quite sure that it's leg had been broken intentionally, but not by George ... [The men who disliked George had been in the area.]

George lived alone for a while and later his wife joined him. She was a little dark girl, and quite nice looking. Because of the hardships of homesteading, and the misery and discomfort caused him by some of his neighbors, George and his wife moved away.[49]

While many grumbled about the non-white East and South Europeans, male observers did take note of the "beautiful dark South European girls." Cohabitation, as the French call it, cooperation when need arose, and intermarriage brought about differentiated attitudes to other ethnic groups, at least in the retrospective of the life-writings. Intermarriage occurred not only between men and women of different Galician backgrounds, but also between a Finn and a Swede, an English printer and a Ukrainian woman. A Chinese man lived with an English girl. In neighbourly relations, "we" were the hard-working settlers regardless of cultural background, "they" were those ethnics who did not want to fit in. To avoid such intermingling, racists of all stripes and all countries united to press the government to restrict immigration.[50]

Community Socializing, Gendered Lives, Childhood Experiences

Anne Pieronek was born in 1915, the oldest of eight children. Her father, Martin, had come to Alberta in 1907, sponsored by an uncle. Her mother Frances had been the "little girl next door" in Martin's Polish home village. When Frances's father brought her over in 1914, at the age of fifteen, she and Martin married in the same year in the mining community of Coleman. Like other peasant mine workers, and the Montreal Italians, they built a small house, cleared a garden, and raised chickens, cows, and pigs. Martin, a farmer's son, wanted to go back to the land and had saved a small amount of money by 1919. Anne remembered that her mother wept during the trip to the land. A memorable trip it was: not in a Conestoga wagon or a settler's effects car or even a modest ox cart. "Dad packed all of our belongings on the wagon pulled by a dog," like those used by pedlars in Europe. The three children were wrapped in blankets and in a feather bed, the symbol of a woman's dowry in the old world. But the Pieroneks had only one feather bed, so the children slept on hay later.

The farm, twenty-five kilometres from Coleman, had been bought from an aging bachelor. The shack had dirt floors, "the only furniture was an old belly stove." Martin Pieronek patched up the buildings and helped plant the garden. Then the children and Frances, whose next baby was due in summer, were left alone, as Martin returned to the mine to earn money. Anne, the oldest child, even at four had to help wherever she could. She first washed the dishes and fed the chicken, later did the cooking and fed the pigs, then milked cows and helped burning stumps. In her "spare time" she picked berries and flowers and waited for the weekend, when her father and grandfather would be home. Anne got schooling to grade eight and worked for two years in a restaurant before she married, at the age of sixteen, in August of 1931.[51]

Anna Lang, at that time, had just been born to Polish immigrants in Rabbit Hill. Her parents, too, moved to homestead. The shack was dilapidated, the mother's first task "was to cut with a sickle, chop into small pieces, and, using her feet, mix with mud, the dry grass ... to seal the spaces between the logs, to keep the cold out." The Langs prepared their own feather bedding; it took months of collecting and stripping down before a few pillows and comforters could be made. The mother "sang to us all day long," gave religious instruction, and gave birth. Because there were other babies in the neighbourhood, a priest was "ordered" from Edmonton, but he spoke only Russian and the birth certificates were wrong. For lack of cash the families paid in farm produce, which the priest's assistant sold at the market. For Anna and Anne Pieronek, Christmas and Easter were great feasts, bringing treats, special foods, and neighbourly visits. The neighbourhood was Polish, Ukrainian, Russian, Czech and Slovakian, German and English. "We became, for a short time, somewhat multi-lingual." The family remained on the homestead for only three years, as the mother and children disliked the separation, and the father disliked farming. "I'm a coal miner."[52]

Family economies as part of the settling of the Great Northwest included child labour. Arthur Stelter attended school up to grade seven in winter, "in summer I helped full time on the farm. From the time I was about twelve years old I worked teams of horses, mostly disking, but also ploughing." He collected birds' eggs and "did some trapping for weasels and muskrats." His parents sent the pelts to a Chicago firm, which paid better than local buyers. Stanley Wachowicz and his brother once were sent to town, a walk of several hours, to buy potatoes. On their return it rained and a small stream had risen. They could neither jump it with their load nor throw the heavy sacks across. Finally, the brother jumped, "caught the potatoes thrown by me [one by one]," then Stanley jumped. "We were wet, but our farm was only a few miles away."[53]

Children usually reported positively on their childhood and adolescent family experiences and accepted their work in the family economy. Outside of family relationships, the endless sequence of tasks was viewed as exploitation, as the reaction of the Home children demonstrated. Some parents did exploit their children. For example,

Agatha Karpinski's family, after four years of separation, joined the father in Canada. They arrived in March, "a dream came true and we were a family again." But the dream ended in the middle of April. "My father made arrangements with the landlord for me to work for him for a period of three years. My pay was to be five dollars a months. But instead of money my father took a team of horses complete with harness and plow." Agatha had to work the debt off. In her family, interests were not negotiated for the benefit of all but were imposed on the children.[54]

Men were often unable to turn a shack into a home. A standard pattern of family reunification emerges from the life-writings: the shack prepared by the man would elicit a horrified look from the arriving wife, who immediately set to work to provide some feeling of comfort. Bachelors and families baked their own bread but in winter it was difficult to keep the temperature at a level so that the dough would rise. The fire had to be kept burning over night or the container with the dough was taken to bed. But, after the first trials, families were usually content with the results.[55]

To the social aspect of turning a shelter into a living space, the economic aspect has to be added. In terms of working hours, two persons were needed to do the field or wage work and keep the cabin in order. Many observers commented on how fast women were "snatched up" by men. Bertha Knull's husband bought his father's farm when the mother died. Bertha had to raise his four younger siblings and care for her father-in-law. "Lots of times the kids had to look after themselves because I was outside. When I came home at noon and at night I had to make the bread and do the cooking. I had to work like a man, too."[56]

Given the dearth of women, "long-distance" marriage was often arranged by correspondence (European "mail-order," Asian "picture" brides) or instant courtship during a man's short visit to his former homeland. Misunderstandings were compounded when prospective wives and their families had high expectations of Canada. They did not understand that a "farmer" might own an unimproved plot rather than a farm, that while European peasants lived in above-ground dwellings, a Canadian farmer might live in a dugout with leaking sods for a roof. A "short-distance" bride from the neighbourhood would have known what to expect.

Some women never overcame the letdown of a move from a comfortable house to a shack. Evan Davies's brother married during a visit in Wales. He misrepresented his homestead and folks in Wales wanted to believe that one of them had struck it rich. Arriving at the shack, his wife was aghast. "It destroyed at once those elements in her character that might have made her into a happy woman. She complained everlastingly of some ailment or other, and always told us that she was bound to be worse tomorrow. She developed a mental attitude that never moved very far from her ill-health and disappointment." This marriage migration destroyed a life.

Ms Mills, on the other hand, who had come west from Ontario, dealt forcefully with deception. She married a widower with two children and a well-equipped homestead. He did not tell her that he had bought machinery far beyond his means. The implement company, realizing that she had savings, demanded payment, and when she refused, foreclosed. According to her words, she accosted her husband in "what you might call a heart-to-heart talk," in consequence of which he left and was never seen again. She opened a boardinghouse and brought up his two children. She also would have liked to see the political position of women change, giving them a say in family investments; male "machinery duns," easily beguiled by company "drummers," should be restrained by law. "If we ever get votes for women in this country, I'll bet my bottom dollar that there'll be a law made so that men can't buy machinery without their wives agree to it."[57]

The CPR had early recognized the importance of women in decision-making. In 1885 the company sent questionnaires to an unstated number of immigrant women in Manitoba, asking them about their experiences. Extracts from the answers were published as a pamphlet in Britain in 1886: *What Women Say of the Canadian North-West.* The editor, obviously aware of a certain mistrust of the CPR, informed the readers that critical comments had not been omitted; interested parties might study the originals at the CPR's London office.[58]

Women did organize; Women's Institutes, for example began in 1897 and by 1913 existed in all provinces. One bachelor's housekeeper "invited the women of the district" for a gathering at which a local Women's Institute was formed. The Extension Service of the University of Saskatchewan began to open Homemakers's Clubs in 1911. The Women's Canadian Club of Regina organized competitions for pioneer stories in 1923 and 1924. Since the language was English, only internal migrants from Ontario, immigrants from England, and local women participated.[59]

Women writers of the West countered the imagery of male-dominated settler societies, which in Canada never assumed dimensions similar to those in the United States. Nellie L. McClung, whose family came from Ontario in 1880, as feminist and writer joined the Winnipeg Political Equality League and supported voting rights for women. Suffrage legislation was passed in Manitoba in January 1916. Alberta, Saskatchewan, and British Columbia did so in the same year, Ontario, the Maritime provinces and the Dominion followed suit by

1922. In Alberta, the single objection to woman's suffrage came from a French-Canadian MLA.[60]

Emily Murphy, born in 1868 to well-to-do parents in Ontario, migrated westward when her husband was advised by his doctors to pursue an outdoor life. Many English immigrants had come to the prairies on this same advice. Seemingly English doctors had not realized that the times of genteel hunters supported by family fortunes were gone and farming involved strenuous exertion. In 1903 the Murphys settled in "multiracial" Swan River, Manitoba. Inspired by Jack Canuck, a popular cartoon figure, Emily created Janey Canuck as a female counterpart. Both were optimistic nationalists, not far from the proud Westerners. Janey's opinions were "penetrating and frank," she proudly "rode astride," and became representative of many Western women.

Both Nellie McClung and Emily Murphy were part of a large movement of educated women westward as teachers, nurses, and doctors. For monolingual English-speaking teachers it was often difficult to induce children, who spoke anything but English, to learn; few were willing to immerse themselves in the children's languages. Some acquitted themselves masterfully, others failed. It was difficult, for the children too. A few left accounts, adoring teachers who opened new vistas, hating teachers whose main tool was a strap, bitter about teachers who let them down. The few female doctors received a considerable amount of respect from their patients. But the all-male North-West Territories College of Physicians and Surgeons refused to register Elizabeth (Scott) Matheson, who practised medicine in Saskatchewan from 1898 to 1918.[61]

A much-publicized aspect of life in the West is the struggle against the elements. However, most life-writings offer little drama, crises are met matter-of-factly. Laura Salverson's great-uncle, who lived near Gimli in the middle of winter, injured a foot badly, infection set in, fever turned to delirium. Great-aunt Steinun bundled him into a sleigh, harnessed herself to it and set out for Winnipeg, about eighty kilometres away. Her major problem was that she had never travelled the route, except when being conveyed to the homestead. She lost her way in a snowstorm, but a Native man found them and took them home. His wife massaged her feet back to life, fed the couple, and dressed her with deerskin leggings and moccasins before the man sent her off on the right trail.[62]

The theme that it was like one big family, present in life-writings from densely settled areas by people with a culture of close relations, is absent from prairie writing. Isolation, work patterns, resulting mental stress, seemingly prevented this feeling. On the other hand, neighbourly support and hospitality were a recurrent theme. The possibility of stopping over – wherever a person got overtaken by nightfall or bad weather – with the next homesteader, farm family, or Amerindian people, was as much a necessity as it was understood. "Anybody settling within a radius of thirty miles was a neighbour." Neighbourhood dances "aroused vast enthusiasm," and people would far, even in subzero temperatures and open sleighs, to enjoy the occasion. The limiting factor was the question of stabling horses and of opportunities "to bunk down" for the night. Guests did not overstay – they had to milk their cows the next morning. "It is difficult to give you any idea of the kindness and hospitality of the people," wrote one observer, Canada is "the land of open doors."[63]

As regards socializing, we will first look at a specific group in the prairies, the bachelor, perhaps the Canadian counterpart to the American cowboy, but embellished with considerably less masculinity.[64] The lack of women in frontier communities was illustrated by one priest who explained that he ministered to six ethno-cultural groups, but that the major division was between twenty-eight families to 131 bachelors. Generally, bachelors were considered somewhat cranky because of loneliness, but proved as helpful as any other neighbours, some even willing to babysit. In 1909 one Welsh bachelor, to celebrate his good harvest – the first one with his newly bought binder – invited twelve other bachelors to share two bottles of whiskey. Since "no bachelor was considered a fully-fledged cook until he could toss a flapjack on a frying pan without accident, and without touching it," the men decided to have a competition for best flapjack tosser: the first "whisked straight into Charlie McKenzie's face," the second landed on the floor. Then Joe Macey "did a beautiful toss which we all knew couldn't be beaten." Next, Jack Churchman got his stuck on the ceiling. Then one man, more skilled in drinking whiskey than in pancake-making, decided to "crown" the winner by pouring the rest of the dough over his head. In a wild mêlée, both had to be tied up because they were ready to beat hell out of each other and destroy half of the shack on the process. Thus ended an all-male "social."[65]

A very different image emerges of mixed socials. These were usually cooperative ventures, a welcome break in the never-ending routine of work. To a wedding, women would bring the food; then after dinner "there was a call for the bachelors, who were to wash up the dirty things!" They did. When a man lost his few worldly possession in a fire, "the settlement got up a dance for him – twenty-five cents entrance, and the food supplied gratis by the ladies." Whenever money had to be raised for a school or a church, a dance was organized, "the ladies of the settlement bring cake and pastries, and any and everybody from far and near is welcome. The men generally pay twenty-five cents entrance." A variant, the box social, was used to increase mingling for purposes of marriage. Lunch boxes prepared by girls were auctioned off among the men, whose purchase included the right to share lunch with the cook. "Of course the authorship of each box is supposed to be an absolute secret, but it soon leaks out who has made this with the blue ribbons, or that with the purple bows."[66]

Many communities set up drama clubs and staged theatrical productions. Performances for Christmas shows and plays were attended by audiences from linguistically related ethnicities. Theatre as an oral art had a long European village tradition among illiterate agrarian populations. Less often youth clubs, gymnastic societies, and simple ethnic associations like a Polish club were mentioned. However all community construction activity, whether by a municipality (school), a religious group (church), or an ethnic group (hall) was done in common.[67]

Not all communities were intact. Dorothea Bublitz described how an itinerant salesman "got fresh" with her. She grabbed her gun and sent the children to call for help. The neighbours "got a big laugh out of it" and told her that the same man had been caught before, delivered by his intended victim to the police. A girl, sent by her parents to accompany the town's doctor, realized that he was often on drugs and at the age of ten had to fend off an attempt to rape her. Children could also became pawns in tensions between their parents. One mother saw her husband gamble away the household money and sent a daughter along as "watchdog." The father bought her off with a quarter, a lot of money in a family of small income. She did not tell on him, but the memory stayed with her.[68]

In conclusion, we will return to Agatha Karpinski, who had been hired out by her father for three years because the family needed a team and a plough. Her brothers, too, worked for farmers "in exchange for feed, seed, chickens, cows and whatever else the farmers could spare for us." Her employer, the Armstrong family spoke only English, Agatha only Polish. "[My days] were sad ones ... I was only sixteen years old but I worked from sunrise to sunset ... I couldn't understand English yet and it was like being deaf and dumb. No one knew if you were sick, or lonely, or tired." The Armstrongs were, in fact, considerate. When Agatha saved a cow from perishing in a mud-hole she was given the cow and calf in reward. For a picnic Ms Armstrong gave Agatha "a fifty cent piece – which I treasured for about ten years, because it was the first cash I had received in Canada." The exciting day almost ended in disaster: none of the many young men danced with her. Dejected and lonely, Agatha got herself a rope to hang herself. While on her knees for her last prayer, the Armstrongs' calves, stampeded by two wild dogs, surrounded her for protection. With a task to be done she stopped thinking about ending her own life.

When harvest approached, Agatha found herself cooking for fourteen men. As cold set in, the hired man was dismissed and Agatha took on his work on top of being chore girl. When she left the Armstrongs, her father found a new position for her. This family was friendly and Agatha, who now spoke English, was happy. But "when the end of the first month came around my dad came too. He took my ten dollars and left me only some change he had in his pocket. I was disappointed." Her next position, with a supportive widow, was interrupted when Dad reappeared.

All of a sudden he came out with the idea that I should be thinking of becoming someone's wife. He already had in mind the lucky bachelor. He was only forty years old. If I wouldn't like him, he had an older brother. Their mother died some time ago and my Dad thought that if I became a wife to one of them I would have a house, a farm, and only two men to cook for. Best of all, according to him, I'd be only a mile from home.

The two men, whom she met for dinner, looked like her grandfathers. She "cried half the way home" – home had become the widow's house. Her employer, Ms Scott, acted quickly. She took Agatha to Calgary and asked friends to find her a job. As housekeeper with a Jewish family and now becoming part of the Polish community, Agatha set out for herself. She had discreetly informed her mother about the departure, but not her father.[69]

In the decades in which these immigrants settled the prairies, the territories became provinces, governmental structures were established. None of this was mentioned in the life-writings. These little people were busy with their own lives and their everyday problems. Without them, there would have been no need for governments.

CHAPTER FOURTEEN

Storekeepers and Small Entrepreneurs

Farming families and homesteaders, spread over large distances, had to buy provisions, clothing, and shoes. Men, who badly needed their time for clearing land and doing the chores, had to hitch up their teams or even walk for many kilometres to reach a store. In 1909, "the country was all wilderness, the nearest store was Oak Point, about thirty miles distance from our farm, which Dad did walk for groceries at times." Thus the arrival of a pedlar was a pleasure and the opening of a new store nearby even more so. Children viewed the choices with delight, women welcomed the opportunity to meet other women. Prairie stores performed the same function as the Jewish shops and Italian *grosserias* in Montreal.[1]

Small storekeepers were part of an entrepreneurial world that included railway contractors, women keeping boardinghouses, and many others trying to set up independently. All were part of a market economy still ruled by a moral economy of trust and relationships. Entrepreneurs were often intermediaries and did not accumulate capital. They were in pursuit of deals, of economic exchange, often without much profit. Like the railway contractors who employed several dozen men in summer but were barely able to survive in winter, they did not experience upward mobility. They were able to use their capabilities, their human capital, to build up a social capital consisting of business connections and a reputation for honesty. They considered themselves no higher in status than their customers, but were considered higher by customers and employees because of their ability to move about, to keep stocks, and to provide others with necessities.

Pedlars: "The Democratic Incense of Coloured Soaps"

A "little Italian woman" peddled in those Winnipeg streets in which the Gudmundsons had their home. Small, alert, beautiful, and formerly married to "a good-for-nothing," she had to earn her own living. Her "ingenious pack," made of oilcloth, was held together by curtain rings and a stout cord. "When she threw the pack to the floor, all the rings jingled gaily, and put one in an expectant mood." She "never made the mistake of opening the pack at once." She hovered above it, discussed the weather, illness, the mud in the streets, invoked the blessing of "the Holy Mother of God." When the "tantalizing" pack was finally opened by a quick pull on the string,

> ... a delectable perfume assailed your nostrils. That perfume of the pack was something to remember. It was the democratic incense of coloured soaps, sachet bags, bottles of toilet water, hair tonic, and those now forgotten scented hearts, which the knowing maidens of the day wore in their bosoms ... Silk handkerchiefs, embroidered with butterflies ... work[wo]manship such as one rarely sees today ... There were cheap ones, to be sure. Five- and ten-cent scraps of silk with gaudy cabbage roses ... [Sometimes, she had] a square of ivory-coloured silk, beautiful as the petals of a rose, sewn with hair-like silks in the most delicate shades, which some skilled Chinese lady must have worked long hours to execute.

Shawls, cards of lace, mending wool, aprons, mitts, comforters for the baby, and strings of rosaries completed the pack. Though the Gudmundson family rarely had money to buy these treasures, the house was never bypassed. A coffee and a chat provided the Italian woman with rest and the children always received a little gift. Jessie Beattie and Nellie Hislop, too, remembered peddling "lace ladies" and "tinkers." In Jessie's memory, Akra, originating from a Greek island and olive-skinned with dark eyes, would also begin by telling stories. The children listened and "our interest increased and our impatience with it."[2] James Gray, the Winnipeg newsboy, commiserated with the pedlars and junk dealers when their runaway horses and carts meant "a double disaster. Their wares would be strewn all over the streets, ... their rigs and harness would be severely damaged and the cost of repairs was an expense they could ill afford."[3]

These reminiscences are not merely vignettes of little importance in the larger context of family life and social affairs. Laura Salverson, née Gudmundson, called the smells emanating from the bag "democratic incense," a form of acculturation in marketplace societies. The poor might share in the wealth produced by society, if they could afford only a few fabrics. Viewed merely within the context of Canadian society, such small purchases do not indicate any substantial social rise. But immigrants, in the first years after arrival, compared the goods offered for purchase to the old world, where consumption was stratified by social convention. In Italy, the small people living in the backyard of a house did not even know what the "rich" in the front part of the same house would consume; bright colours, ornaments, and bonnets were for women higher up in the social scale. Emigrant Slovene peasants wrote home that they could afford to polish their boots. To the recipients of the letters in Slovenia it meant social ascent beyond imagination; only the lords of the manor wore boots, everyone else went barefoot. Those who had migrated savoured their small advances as large steps ahead, until they changed their yardstick to the incomes of their peers in the new society. The ability to select goods for consumption regardless of class, even if only in one's wishes, was a democratizing experience. In the old worlds, social convention and self-censorship did not permit men and women to aspire to something not sanctioned by class and social position.[4]

Prairie-Town Stores

For homesteading families, the opening of a store close by was a big event. When a new railway line arrived, towns mushroomed at the stopping points. Small-scale entrepreneurs opened shops, hotels, livery barns. A Slovak carpenter, Daniel Svanda, built half a town one summer. D.E. Macintyre, from Montreal, opened a store in what looked like the middle of nowhere which immediately became a centre for shopping homesteaders. The Russian-Jewish Bruser family, on the other hand, moved from town to town chasing the dream of a successful store.

As a child, Daniel Svanda saw his father migrate to work in the mines in the Tatra mountains. He himself worked in a saw mill, then, like many Slovaks and Romanians, migrated to Budapest, the Hungarian capital, where labour union announcements were published in five languages. As the upper classes of German and Jewish backgrounds underwent a Magyarization process, the labouring classes consisted of a multi-ethnic conglomerate of factory operatives from the peripheral regions of historic Hungary. In 1925 Daniel moved on to Canada, leaving his pregnant wife and their four children behind. One of his neighbours had been in the United States twice, in Argentina once, and had then settled in Canada permanently. Daniel took odd jobs, until a new "track was built from Ashmont to Grand Centre ... [In future Mallaig] there was only bush and farm land. I got the job of building one store. I slept in one shed that had been pulled there. I built two stores, a hotel, a garage, and a blacksmith shop. I gave the town its start." His savings then permitted him to bring his family over and buy farmland.[5]

D.E. Macintyre from Montreal moved west in 1904. Aged twenty-two, he "enjoyed unlimited confidence in himself and an abounding faith in our new and invigorating West, where hundreds of thousands of hopeful newcomers arriving every year needed nearly all the equipment" for homes, farms, or business. After operating the CPR's stores department on the Regina-Arcola Line for two years, he quit with fifteen hundred dollars in savings to open his own store. Selection of location was accidental but nevertheless well informed. Running into a CPR engineer in Moose Jaw he learned about plans for a branch line south from Wolseley and Macintyre and immediately checked the location out. Soon there were no more roads and after another fifty kilometres, he reached a shack "in this lonely land." However, the nearest homesteader in one single week had fed thirty-five people looking for land. Back in Wolseley, another accidental acquaintance, a commercial traveller, suggested a store location in the Qu'Appelle Valley, where the CPR had the grading done for a new line. "They're hoping to get the rails down before winter to move some of this year's crop."

The so-called new townsite was easy to find "because of two abandoned buildings." Otherwise there was nothing; a "thick cover of tumbleweed" hid the survey stakes. Macintyre decided to buy a corner lot on Main Street and Railway Avenue and arranged to be put up by farming family a kilometre away. His hosts, who used to walk twenty-two kilometres to Moose Jaw to buy necessities, were pleased about the prospect.[6] In Moose Jaw, a young French-Canadian carpenter, Noel Landry, was recommended to Macintyre. With his expert advice, he quickly decided upon the size and structure of the store. The next day, Mr Otto, his farmer host, started hauling the lumber and Macintyre set out for Winnipeg to buy his stock.

> Two days later Landry and his crew of four carpenters arrived and put up a tent. He had an empty water barrel and he arranged with some farmer to fill it. I moved in with the Ottos. In two weeks the store was up. On a Saturday Landry came to me and said, "If you want to have a dance you'll have to have it Monday night because I want to start putting in the counters and shelves on Tuesday morning." "Do I have to have a dance?" I asked. "Certainly. Every new building that goes up is opened with a dance. Anyway, it will be a good chance for you to meet your future customers." ... Landry explained the form. "Some of my men come from around here. They will spread the news tomorrow after church, and you'll have lots of people here."

Macintyre, the city man, remained uneasy. Music? "A fiddler or two will come along." Food? "The women will bring more than we'll eat." The advice of the experienced Landry prevailed. On Monday the carpenters cleared the sawdust and put up their nailkegs and planks for seats. By 9 p.m. a party was in full swing, with music, a caller for the dances, and a tempting array of sandwiches and pies.

Macintyre told his neighbours that he would be opening on Saturday. His stock, already in Moose Jaw, was hauled out on Thursday. "I hired Mrs. Taylor, the widow at the Ottos, whose qualification was that she had once worked for Eaton's in Toronto." That left Friday to unpack, price, and shelve the goods. However,

> I never got a chance. The word had spread and customers swarmed all over the merchandise, helping me unpack, and picking out what they wanted as they went along. They tried on boots and shoes, sheepskin-lined coats, gloves and mitts and overalls ... They were all so good-natured and eager to help that I could not turn them out. I had little idea what to charge and had to depend on Mrs. Taylor's knowledge of Moose Jaw retail prices or the buyer's honesty.

Everything worked out well. Even though the lot on Main Street and Railway Avenue in the middle of nothing but tumbleweed was less than Potemkin's villages in the South Russian plains, dreams of a prosperous future came true with a good crop in 1906. The village expanded rapidly even though the railway did not come until a year later – a year that also brought a depression. The briefly deferred dream gave business to elevator companies which provided for storage until spring.[7]

Macintyre had his clothing washed at the Chinese laundry in Moose Jaw. "It has been my experience that there are no more honest people in the world than the Chinese." Just as the young French-Canadian oldtimer had advised him, so Macintyre, a year later an oldtimer himself, advised "a young Chinaman" where to locate a laundry and how to build. The farming population consisted of "native Canadians from Ontario" to the south and west, of "Canadians mixed with Americans of Scandinavian stock" to the northwest, and a few families from the Jersey Islands. Many farming women traded eggs and butter for their purchases.

One day a railway agent appeared in the village, saying that it had been built in the wrong place due to a surveyor's error. The correct townsite was staked out, a contractor jacked up the buildings, the false-front stores, and the barns and hired "all the horses for miles around." A procession of houses followed by people carrying "their china and glassware" moved across the prairie.[8]

The Bruser storekeeper family, less successful than Macintyre, involuntarily did its own cross-prairie procession. "Neville, Foam Lake, Humboldt, Birch Hills, Winnipeg ... Altona, Gretna, Plum Coulee ... The towns rolled by ... they marked the rise and fall of stores ... the eternal idea of The O-Kay Store. And that is what I remember most strongly of all those years of defeat – my father's joyous conviction that *next* time we would prevail." Fredelle Bruser had a deep affection for her dreaming father. The mother, more stern and realistic, still made the kitchen the heart and centre of family life. With no other Jews in town, cultural and religious life was fraught with problems from a child's point of view. Others had Christmas trees, but "being Jewish was mostly not doing things other people did." While the parents, like the Grönlunds in Timmins, contributed to church-sponsored activities as "some sort of communal life," they were reluctant to have their daughters move away from tradition. The cultural roots grew outward horizontally "to other Jewish families in other lonely prairie towns."

Language in Fredelle's home varied from street and school language. Furthermore, in the father's Jewish stories set in Russia, "the landscape was unfamiliar, a world peopled by rabbis, starving *melameds* (teachers), matchmakers, grandfathers with earlocks and long caftans." The Canadian-born second generation lacked experience of "the life patterns which alone could have made these tales comprehensible." The neighbours, Norwegian in one community, Polish in another, multi-ethnic in Winnipeg and French in St Boniface, sprinkled with Gypsies, Negroes, Japanese, and Natives, made the children aware of their difference.

The father's store was kept open for endless hours, the hard work lasted late into the night. Poor harvests meant poor business; each bankruptcy was followed by another move and new demands for adjustment. "Our furniture was insubstantial" – her mother created a home out of next to nothing – but, Fredelle felt, "without money, we lived rich." In Grandview, Polish settlers and their leader, Steve Worchuk, patronized the store. Old-world anti-semitism and new-world racism lurked under boisterous behaviour. Worchuk threateningly remarked that the previous store owner had "tried to jew me down." Boris Bruser helped the Worchuk family after a son died, was called "a real white man," and became respected community adviser – until a cheaper and more modern store opened in their small town. Worchuk returned a hat he had charged and demanded his money back, calling the storekeeper a "kike." The father's humiliation was a humiliation of the family. After less than a year they moved again. Similarly, when Mr Bruser sold goods to an English-speaking woman who had not paid her bills for a long time, she commented: "You're a real white man, Bruser." But this did not help the family collect the outstanding debt. The Bruser parents lived a life in between cultures, full of defeat, but supportive of their children. Life in Russia had been an impoverished one, life in Canada involved never-ending threats to their identity. School friends opened new vistas, anti-semitism reinforced separation. An identity-preserving course to gradual acculturation was difficult to chart.[9]

From Fisherman to Interregional Merchant

Helgi Einarsson came to Manitoba with his parents and brothers in 1887. His Icelandic background was reflected in his writing, as broad-ranging as the sagas. He had premonitions of future events and felt he shared this with Native people. His education in Iceland had been limited to what occasional itinerant teachers could achieve. The family left after exceptionally cold winters, with the guidance of a visiting emigrant. Near Kenora, countrymen boarded their train to accompany the newcomers on the last leg of the trip. West central Manitoba meant wealth to the Icelanders: "We had never seen grass so lush. We were well pleased with everything and expected to get along well in this new land." The Einarssons bought two cows and an ox and had their house ready before winter. As a seventeen-year-old, Helgi lived at the Swan River settlement, then at the Narrows and Fairford. At the age of twenty-two he took a contract for a mail route – his father was a postmaster. He became captain of an Indian Treaty boat, with a Scottish agent, an English cook, a Native pilot, and an engineer of unspecified ethnicity. A year later he embarked on a decade-long business expansion. But although he had many far-flung business contracts, he did not get rich. His ethnic world was mainly Icelandic, Native and English-Canadian, but also included Syrians. In Hazenmore, Saskatchewan, Syrians homesteaded, relatives kept a store in Gouvernor, and further relatives moved out as pedlars.[10] Even as a trader, Helgi's social standing remained modest. While ice-fishing, Helgi met William Sifton, the brother of Clifford Sifton, the Dominion minister of the interior. He and a Sifton daughter fell in love but knew that the social gap was insurmountable. The Sifton family "regarded themselves too highly for me … I was only a poor Icelander." She hid her sadness, while to forget her, Helgi bought a gas engine and concentrated on learning how to work it.

Helgi and his friends left railway work quickly because of low wages and a high-handed foreman. He improved his English and became the group's translator. At the saw mill Helgi worked with three Norwegians, two Icelanders, and one man each from England, Scotland, Ireland, America, Canada, Austria, Hungary, and, occasionally, Natives. When the timberstands were exhausted, the mill was disassembled and moved. The Swan River settlement no longer satisfied the Icelanders: by 1889 it was "too thickly populated" and too far from winter fishing. The wages from the saw mill covered the cost of a new house.

Ice-fishing became Helgi's main occupation. From 1890 on, each winter's catch was more than the men needed for their families and Helgi trekked to Winnipeg to sell frozen fish. Just as railway work was not "straight money" because it paid only in summer, ice-fishing did not supply income beyond the winter. Helgi began to dry fish to market it in summer. Once the procedure was established, he hardly mentioned fishing any longer – only the unusual was noted, such as harvest work in the Portage plains, social gatherings on long winter evenings, the building of his own boat. His language skills and perhaps his readiness to venture out placed him in a position of mediator/businessman between his fellow fishermen and the English merchants. He bought nets on credit, took fish to town, returned with provisions. In passing he mentioned that in addition to hiring a man he owned two horses and four oxen. In this respect, too, the Icelander resembled the Swede Alm and the Italian Veltri. As small or even medium-level entrepreneurs they remembered what they did, not what they acquired. Since accumulation was not their goal, they did not fret when they lost. This may also be the major difference between Helgi's mentality and that of the Siftons and the Winnipeg-based American fish merchant Armstrong with whom Helgi dealt most of the time. They accumulated and, while helpful and friendly to others, exploited every opportunity they had to their own advantage.

Helgi sold large loads of fish to a Winnipeg wholesaler and tackled the monopoly the Hudson's Bay Company claimed to have on trade with the Natives. When he could not dispose of his frozen fish by lot, he sold it on the market by the piece, wholesaler and pedlar in one person. In Winnipeg winters, no cost for cold storage was involved. He got through the depression of 1893 but was aware of the suffering of others. Men sawed wood and earned perhaps thirty-five cents a day. One enterprising man installed a small steam-engine saw on his sleigh to make more money, but his fellow unemployed threatened to destroy the machine. His new-fangled ideas would have reduced their meagre earnings. Groups of men trudged to the city council "to demand food or work" and were sent to haul gravel for city streets.

Helgi's wholesale dealer expanded, bought a steam boat and brought in twelve men from Ontario to do his fishing. Competition was low-key: the experienced Ontarians explained to Helgi which nets were best, while he shifted his business to Fargo, Grand Forks, and Casselton in North Dakota and continued to experiment with whatever looked profitable. He sailed a two-men transport boat single-handedly, he used one of the first boats with a gasoline engine. But he remained prudent, shooting rapids in a flatboat first, to get the knack of it, before taking the engine-powered boat across. From captain of the Indian Treaty boat, still one of his sidelines, he advanced to trader with Native peoples. His relationship with the fishermen who worked for him or with him – this is not quite clear – remained fraught with tensions arising from different views of his position. He felt that he was helping others while having to shoulder the risk and getting little out of it. Though he occasionally permitted himself to travel first class, he was in debt repeatedly. The others "took for granted that I was extremely rich," envied him and showed "ingratitude." "I was operating six trading posts at the time and had a steamboat on the lake to transport my merchandise, but the truth was I never owned anything. My entire stock was the property of others."

During the next business crash, probably that of 1907, his wholesaler refused to buy at the old and expected prices. Again he sold boxcar loads of fish by himself. This episode revealed two aspects of his "Canadianization." First, he learned that in order to sell directly he needed a $250 licence. He argued that as a Canadian citizen and a British subject, he should not have to get a licence when an American concern was selling fish at high prices to Winnipeg people who "were unemployed and had little money." He was selling for lower prices. In the city council, the mayor supported him and he finally paid twenty-five dollars for a temporary licence to peddle fish from door to door. Secondly, he became aware of his larger reputation when a man from Ontario approached him to buy a whole box car of fish. Thus his well-known trustworthiness permitted him to reach ever more distant markets. But business continued to be transacted on a personal, face-to-face basis, on previous acquaintance, or on vouched-for honesty. Under depression constraints, he discussed his debts with his creditors on the same personal basis and a mutually satisfactory solution was agreed upon.

Helgi enlarged his market transactions to New York without entering the world of finance and profits. Business remained one of relationships, of verbal agreements that were honoured, or, if necessary, renegotiated in the interest of both sides. Competition was normal for Helgi, but he demanded fairness. In 1917, he decided to meet distant business partners and see parts of the United States. Though considered rich, he bought a cheap excursion ticket. In Duluth and St Paul he met acquaintances, in Chicago, Pittsburgh, and Philadelphia he visited corresponding merchants and fishing-gear manufacturers. In Cincinnati, where he had no acquaintances, he stayed in the sleeping car to save on hotel expenses. In New York, "a girl from the Narrows" showed him around. He picked up information that was new, from wartime international alliances to patterns of fish sales. There were other new experiences. In Chicago he saw with disapproval swimmers in the lake who were "half naked, men and women together, all in one great mass." In New York he was dumbfounded by the alienation of people from their neighbours and neighbourhood. People worked without knowledge, without skills, without contact to others. When he lost his way and asked a subway employee for directions, the man answered that "all he did was open and close doors when the train stopped and that he knew nothing at all about streets and street numbers." In Winnipeg or in the social landscape in which Macintyre located his store, such mentalities would have boded economic disaster. To Helgi the urbanites must have seemed more thoroughly "bushed" than any isolated homesteader.

Along with his far-flung connections, Helgi also had a local family. After his disappointment with the Sifton daughter, he was taciturn about his emotional life. Buying muskrat skins from a Native, he met the man's daughter Sara, who kept the house, milked the cows, chopped firewood, and fished in summer to provide for the family because age had debiliated the mother. Once, when he took her home, they got stuck in the snow and had to spend the night in the sleigh. "I must have been casting glances at her," for she told him she would not "do that." He respected her wishes. After three more years of once-annual trading contacts, she asked, "Why don't you marry me?" He answered: "I didn't expect to marry, but that if I did, I wanted a wife of my own race." A year later they became closer; working for the Census Board, Helgi had to stay at her home for a few days. Passing by six months later, he noticed that she was pregnant but they did not even get a chance to talk to each other. She had not told her own family who the father was. He came back in time for the birth, promised to take his part of the responsibility, and allayed her fears of having committed a sin. He did not believe in God and wanted to live with her unmarried, "the Indian way." She had been brought up Catholic and wanted to marry the Euro-Canadian way.

Over a period of eleven years Sara and Helgi had three boys and a daughter, who died in infancy. Contrary to Sara's wishes, they did not marry. In his opinion they were happy – married couples often fought. Sara, who continued to take care of relatives, fell ill after nursing a sister with tuberculosis. When she knew that she would die, she arranged for the children to be placed with her sisters and brothers. She and Helgi were married on her deathbed. When the boys had grown older, Helgi took them one after another on his boat for fishing and was proud of them.[11]

Moral Economies versus Capitalist Profiteering

Helgi, well-established by 1910, shipped twenty-five thousand pounds of whitefish to St Paul that year. He found a German concern, Freedmann Brothers, and sold to them for thirty years. Such independent business contacts secured his survival when big companies fought him in the 1920s. His modest approach to business continued; no sale was too small. Entering a "little Jewish shop" in St Paul, he met an elderly man selling fish and hens. Culture interfered with sales; the women bought hens only when the rabbi was in town to kill them. Puzzled, Helgi learned that "Orthodox Jews are permitted to eat only meat that has been killed by a rabbi." He asked the shopkeeper to purchase fish from him. The man declined, explaining that he was so poor that each morning he bought a single day's supply with the previous day's earnings. Helgi saw no problem in supplying him on credit and take payment when the consignment had been sold. When the old man went bankrupt, "he owed me about sixty-five dollars, which was next to nothing after having done business with him over twenty years." The Jewish man, too old to look after his business properly, "expressed his dismay at not having been able to pay." To keep Einarsson in business he suggested the local rabbi as consignee and Helgi continued to ship.[12]

In 1920s Riverton, Manitoba, Gus and Emily Romaniuk opened a store. Gus had worked with Icelandic ice-fishing crews on Lake Winnipeg. Like Helgi, he had to learn about cultural habits. The naked swimmers that raised Helgi's concern for decency in Chicago had their equivalent in a naked Icelander in the snow. Gus wondered whether this man had gone mad. He turned out to be sound and sober, snow-bathing according his people's customs. The Ukrainian recalled his many Icelandic neighbours as "a warm, open-hearted people, always generous and hospitable to travellers."

Gus's moral economy and work ethos were similar to Helgi's. He, too, was ready of find work or trade wherever possible. He always relied on trust with his Native customers. Like Helgi, he began new lines of business, furs or cattle for example, because some neighbour or Native needed cash and wanted to sell. Only then did he inquire about marketing possibilities. These men, intermediaries rather than businessmen, provided services to producers unable to reach markets directly. They often had no notion whether a profit could be made or even the break-even point reached. But they did need to make a living; so with each additional debt incurred, Gus's worries grew. Like the fishermen, he "had known nothing of the falling market." Though active and respected in the many-cultured community, "I no longer reckoned time by holidays and happy events on the calendar, but by dates due for installment payments."[13]

In the world of capital, different principles reigned. When prices declined in the supra-regional market about which the fishermen and Helgi knew little, Helgi's wholesaler Armstrong informed them of the stock market crash of 1907 in New York and refused to pay the prices agreed upon. In a breach of ethics, he reneged on the customary oral agreement to take Helgi's fish, offering to buy at a price so low that

Helgi could not have satisfied any of his creditors. In the course of their trading relationship, Armstrong had changed from the world of trust and negotiated interests to the world of finance, where only profit counted, regardless of business partners and honesty, regardless of customers and the impoverishment of small people. Originally acting on behalf of the American-owned Buffalo Fish Company, Armstrong later represented the Chicago-based Armstrong Trading Company. At this point of his trajectory from business partner to profit-oriented capitalist, Armstrong still gave Helgi a chance to sell elsewhere, even helping him to find customers. His creditors offered Helgi double the price of Armstrong per pound for whitefish, triple the price for pike, and thus nobody went under.

Next, Armstrong set out to acquire a monopoly on all frozen fish in Manitoba and Saskatchewan. He was successful, except for Lake Manitoba, where Helgi and others fought back. Armstrong at first tried to make Helgi his employee at whatever salary Helgi would ask. Helgi refused to give up his independence. Thereupon Armstrong threatened to cut Helgi's credit for nets and other fishing gear unless he would give a mortgage on all his possessions, an unusual procedure in this moral economy. Helgi had to accede but explicitly exempted the homestead where Sara and their sons lived. When Armstrong's lawyer asked him to sign the papers, Helgi scrutinized them. Just when he was ready to sign, the lawyer suggested that they have lunch first. Upon return, Helgi signed without realizing that the papers had been altered, now covering the family home as well. Armstrong, with this stranglehold over the home and subsistence basis of Helgi's family, immediately tightened the noose, ordering suppliers not to trade with Helgi unless they wanted to forfeit his business. Helgi, unsuspecting, in the next winter accepted twice the amount of loans from Armstrong than had been agreed upon. The sale of the catch next spring left Helgi in debt, if only by $350 of $10,000. Armstrong, refusing to extend credit, sent the lawyer to prowl the family homestead. Helgi, furious, accosted Armstrong in his office. The office of the wholesale Armstrong Trading Company was now also that of the provincial treasurer and finance minister: Armstrong had joined the Roblin government. Another business partner lent Helgi the sum needed.

Armstrong next induced Helgi to agree to a cartel. In the coming season, both were to pay the same price for fish on Lake Manitoba. In a moral economy even of regulated prices, the fishermen, if exploited, would have had recourse: they would have ostracized extortionate buyers from the community. This they could not do with Armstrong who belonged to a different community and a different economic world. Thus, at Lake Winnipegosis, with Armstrong's prices for fish, people "could no longer make a living as fishermen and had to give up that occupation." People had to resettle elsewhere. Cut-throat Armstrong, still in the government, cheated Helgi again. When Helgi wanted to accost Armstrong, he realized that the face-to-face pattern of doing business had been ended, that he could only talk to Armstrong's representative. In Armstrong's world, any compromise was but a ruse to continue making profits regardless of the cost to others and the local or, for that matter, national, economy.

Helgi's world had changed too, perhaps imperceptibly to himself. At the beginning of his trading career, he was close to the other fishermen. But when they envied what they considered his success, while the partners at the selling end of his operation trusted him, he shifted his relations to their side. The suppliers of fish were hardly mentioned any more in his memoir.

Changes of the moral economy in a world of mutuality were also experienced by the Destrubé brothers and their wives when they decided to open a store on their homestead, north of Edmonton, to supply their neighbours. The men and women who previously had to make a week-long ox-cart trip to get flour and other provisions patronized the store and made it a success. "Business picked up faster than we could cope with." However, "a sinister looking American" settled nearby, announced plans to open a store, and bragged that he "would soon put the Destrubé Bros. out of business." His approach, too, was cut-throat in nature, but he had no capital. He attempted to ruin the Destrubés by destroying their homestead and forcing them out of business. His criminal dealings included poisoning of dogs, killing of horses, store break-ins, and burning of haystacks. Police found goods stolen from the store in the American's house. Armstrong's and the American's goal was to destroy a community's moral economy, in the latter case for the gain of an individual, in the former in the name of a new economy order.[14]

Storekeepers and interregional merchants doing business based on trust and on mutual interests were the mainstay of the Prairie economy. The entrepreneurs needed neither venture capital nor large-scale business connections. Instead, they relied on their human capital, on their ability to identify and seize opportunities, and to absorb losses by negotiating compromises between the interests of seller, middleman, and buyer. Their social capital consisted of their relationship with customers and suppliers. A breach of trust would squander this capital. Excluded from this moral economy were men and women denied social access because of ethnicity and race, such as W.K. Yuen and Boris Bruser, a Chinese and a Jew. When wealthy merchants departed from the customs of the moral economy to exploit others, the exploited organized politically on the provincial and national level, to remedy the situation, or at least to prevent a collusion between government and capital. One large-scale businessman decided to operate on trust and thus tap the moral economy for his purposes. Timothy Eaton's mail-order department store become an institution encompassing the Prairies. His moral economy, however was consumer-oriented and excluded the producers.

CHAPTER FIFTEEN

Building and Imagining Western Society

Once immigrants had set up their homesteads and the question of provisions and stores was solved, communities had to be organized formally if only because children needed a school. People proceeded parsimoniously, since taxes might drive them back into poverty. The local was part of larger worlds. Two organizations, the Hudson's Bay Company and the North-West Mounted Police, spanning the prairies and beyond, mediated between the local and the national and worldwide markets. A third larger connection was in the immigrants' minds – old world politics and families. A fourth connection, the pomp and circumstance of the British Empire, remained marginal to their interests and perceptions unless they came from its core. Once farming families entered staple production, in particular wheat, family incomes depended on connections to and prices in world markets. New mediators, railways and wholesale companies, became a necessity but were profit-oriented and distant from communities. Their employees stood on the line between profit maximization and face-to-face everyday dealings with customers. When rates became exorbitant, local communities turned to national courts and to political action. Consumption became related to the outside world via Eaton's catalogues. Most of the men and women did not separate these spheres: politics meant political economy and political economy meant society and social relations.

Pillars of Order: The Hudson's Bay Company and the Mounties

Before the advent of regular governmental institutions, the HBC trading posts served as relay stations and hostels and sold provisions. Knowledgeable factors ruled and gave advice, their presence gave comfort. This alone would account for the many positive reports. In addition, the factors built a reputation for being well-informed, judicious, and fair. Relations of trust developed in a hierarchical structure. It has been suggested that British fair-play traditions were transported to Canada. But fair play had not entered into relations between lords and tenants either at the time of the Highland clearances or the enclosure of common land in

England. Honesty and fairness paid off; no armies, police forces, or courts had to be maintained as long as the exchange of goods was based on mutual trust. Enlightened self-interest guided the HBC's British Columbia factors when they discreetly stored gold they occasionally received from Natives, in order neither to disrupt the fur business nor the Native economies. When the company finally did ship gold to San Francisco, the Cariboo gold rush ended the old ways immediately and forever. After the end of the monopoly, storekeepers, faced with Native customers paying in furs, could rely on the latter's own sense of fair dealing. "Indians" knew the quality of their furs in relation to the prices in the store and did not take advantage of "green" merchants.

When the HBC sold Rupert's Land to the new Dominion government in 1870 but retained control of its posts and adjacent lands, it was reduced from being a government to becoming only a trading and real-estate company. Yet old mechanisms continued to function. When Claude Gardiner, in 1894, planned to invest in a ranch, his father wrote to an old acquaintance, the HBC's Winnipeg chief commissioner. The latter first placed Claude with a rancher to learn the business and a year later advised him on how to invest profitably without taking undue risks. Later the company could still provide a Scottish immigrant with a job, but only as store clerk in some city. Towards the end of the century, the company was replaced by the more modern Eaton's.[1]

The second pillar of order was the North-West Mounted Police, established in 1873. An early plan to recruit half of the force from among the Métis was shelved after their struggle for self-government. Rather, the protection of Natives from American whiskey smugglers became an important task, supplemented later by the protection of settlers from American horse and cattle thieves. Policing followed a policy of administering order in keeping with earlier customs. The Mounties became a myth.[2]

The "scarlet fever" of women caused by the uniforms of British soldiers ended in 1867, but uniforms remained attractive, as independent sources from both sexes at different times and from different cultures affirm. During a visit after the First World War, the Prince of Wales "was quite a sight in his military uniform and many stories were circulated as to his escapades with the local ladies during his stay" in Toronto. A French-Canadian woman, pestered by soldiers in 1940s Edmundston, New Brunswick, rejected their advances, but noted, "il y en avait bien assez d'autres filles pour tomber à genoux devant un uniforme 'kaki.'" Polish pilots stationed in Alberta for training in 1943 received considerable attention from local young Polish immigrant women.[3] As to the Mounties, the force consisted of "nice, polite Englishmen" with "dashing" looks, of "handsome fellows." At issue were not only looks and comportment, but also hospitality – one of the engaging feature of the HBC factors, too. Regina society spent a lively winter in 1899 due to the dances organized by NWMP men waiting to go to the South African War. The somewhat inflated self-esteem of the force did not escape notice of more critical observers: "Some members of this organization quite manifestly supposed their official advent to be the beginning of all things in the Canadian West previous to which the earth was without form and void."

The Mounties, as a force or as individuals, assumed tasks which would later become the responsibility of social service agencies. In the winter of 1881–2 the men saved part of their rations to relieve starvation among the Sioux and looked after isolated settlers, bringing food if necessary. For newcomers, this conduct was the opposite of the police-controlled class societies of the old world. While myth describes the Mounties as solitary, quick-acting, stern but compassionate men, reality saw many of them married, with wives as helpmates.[4]

Like the HBC factors, Mounties were part of a British-Canadian genteel society. They could help individuals and apprehend criminals but could not mediate class differences. No striking workers could see fairness in their support of big capital and small employers. As early as 1874, officer Nevitt was on active duty against what he considered to be rioting workmen. In the 1910s, a boy from Fernie, British Columbia, remembered Mounties escorting strikebreakers to work. Miners' wives lined the streets throwing "rocks over and under the mounties' horses." In its Security Bulletins, the Reverend J.S. Woodsworth of Winnipeg was accused of preaching revolutionary doctrines. In 1918, contrary to politicians' rhetoric, the Mounties noted that no widespread labour radicalism existed. But it remained watchful: "particular attention must be paid to different labour unions" and farmers in the "foreign settlements" because "this class ... is particularly susceptible to Bolshevik teaching."[5]

As regards the early years of European penetration of the West, one further aspect, sexual symbolism, merits attention. Male forays into the wilderness were regarded as "exploration," adventurousness, sportsmanship, or colonization of the land. Men struggled with the elements, subdued the land. When female migrants joined them, the first-white-woman theme appeared, an implicit reference to sexual attraction, to women courageous but out of their sphere. Marie Bonneau and her girlfriend were the "only two white girls" the young Mounties had seen for months. Harry Bullock-Webster had been told to carouse with white girls in Montreal since he would see only "squaws" in the West. Sometimes pluck and endurance received its due, as when the first white woman crossed the Yellowhead pass "and did so with six children." This concern may have been specific to English and Canadian culture. It was never mentioned in autobiographies of Ukrainians or Russian-Germans. French-Canadian authors acknowledged the role of women by emphasizing family life. Later the theme of sex ratios, devoid of racial connotation, merely referred to the scarcity of women and to the need for them to share in the labour and produce children to serve as family workers. The theme of sexuality only reappeared as a racist discourse when the "Orientals" mixed with "white" society.[6]

Old Worlds, Empire, World Markets

Upon arrival in this society, immigrants were still steeped in the politics, hierarchies, and absence of rights of their old worlds. They were neither required nor did they intend to insert themselves quickly into political life. Men and women came to improve their economic prospects. Whether itinerant or homestead-based, logger or domestic, they had to survive. With no family support or social security system, they had to function immediately in the new environment. No complex ethnic communities provided support, nor could earlier immigrants among their ethnic group help for more than a few days. This is best illustrated by single men or single families arriving on the barren prairie: a shelter had to be built, gardening and hunting for food had to commence without delay, all family members had to contribute their labour or go hungry. Men who entered the labour market, a less isolated experience, might receive help from co-workers, but finding a job in a foreign culture and language required immediate functioning too. The economics of survival determined everyday lives.

Many immigrants wanted to dissociate themselves from old-world politics. Immigrants from the Germanies in the 1870s wanted to leave a war-prone state and monarchical society. In the 1920s, Poles left because they considered the protection afforded Poland by the Treaty of Versailles insufficient. Regardless of origin, immigrants embarked on constructing their lives and local societies. They reacted to larger forces, when, for example, during the First World War some of them were suddenly labelled "enemy aliens." Poles and Ukrainians began to organize for political action. Their old-world co-ethnics were, in fact, seeking independence from the enemy empires. In contrast to the United States, where ethnic communities had reached institutional completeness and political strength earlier, old-world animosities between ethnicities seem not to have influenced multi-ethnic cooperation in the prairies. Does this indicate that common men and women had no stake in nationalisms propounded by the middle-class intelligentsia and political leadership?[7]

Political activities varied with interests and culture. Sojourners intending to stay for a few years only focused on their societies of origin. A few immigrants were unhappy about their limited knowledge of political life in Canada. English-speakers from Britain could enter politics, if they wished. Only one autobiographer, a woman, remembered a Dominion Day picnic and a few mentioned Fourth of July celebrations. Marie Bonneau from Quebec and her future mother-in-law attended a political meeting, aware that in 1900 "members of our sex did not usually go to political gatherings."[8]

Giovanni Veltri, greatly interested in national railway policy, never mentioned either politics or nationalism or his contribution to nation-building. He did meet one Manitoba premier, when buying a team of horses from him, and was proud to have met the Italian ambassador. He Canadianized his name to Welch and changed his political behaviour. On a visit to Italy, he talked back to a *carabinieri*, an unusually bold action for a villager. The dialectic of politics involved both old and new society. Visible self-assertion in the old world was paralleled by changes in the new that came gradually, sometimes unperceived by the immigrants themselves, sometimes considered insufficient by the host society. Veltri and George Bielesh, after their return to Europe proudly kept their Canadian passports. To Veltri, his final return to Italy meant exile from his chosen land. In his mind the politics and social conventions of the old world and the new had been fused into one whole.[9]

The ever independent Frank Roe argued that the Dominion government was of little concern because the CPR "was then popularly defined as being 'the Government.'" This comment on a specific form of nation-building also contained an analysis of the political economy of the times. The CPR connected farmers to markets across the globe. In 1891 less than one thousand rail cars left Moose Jaw filled with wheat, but the many small points of shipment, where individual farming families sold their crops, added up to more than twenty-thousand cars that left eastbound from Winnipeg. In Montreal A.M. Klein, glancing at the grain elevators, felt he saw "all the coloured faces of mankind."[10] Farmers noted their connection to world systems. The Empire of which Canada was a part was repeatedly involved in distant wars; so supply for armies afar had immediate consequences for grain prices on the prairies and food on a farming family's table as well as on machinery bought and credit-risks taken. The awareness of the impact of price fluctuations on the world markets and their relations to imperial wars is specific to immigrants to Canada; no comparable references have been found in a sample of US immigrant writings.[11]

While Canadianization occurred almost invisibly, the imperial context was highly visible through ritual, pageantry, and far-flung journeyings. Numerous British immigrant families had lived in Asia in the colonial service or had been separated when fathers or sons left for colonial duty. James Sadler's father had lived in Africa buying ivory for an English firm; Raymond Patterson never met his father who left for South Africa before his birth. Australians and New Zealanders coming to the West and the Rockies as prospectors or settlers indicated the Empire's reach. Imperial ritual helped inculcate affinities to Britain, by royal visits and Diamond Jubilee Day in 1897, mentioned in British and Canadian life-writings but hardly in those of other immigrants.[12]

British emigration was made easy by the imperial reach over much of the world. The English "can emigrate to any quarter of the globe without changing their flag, their allegiance, or their language. An Englishman ... has the choice over half-a-dozen splendid countries to live in, of every variety of climate; he may choose according to his fancy, and remain an Englishman always." At various times Canada meant different things to different classes. British philanthropic institutions sent the Home children to the Empire's "white" segments before the First World War; population planners dumped demobilized soldiers and "surplus women" under the concept of "Empire emigration" in the 1920s. Imperial racists aggressively voiced their attitudes towards non-British and non-Teutonic peoples. John Rowan considered the Dominion suitable for British "people of small fortune, whose means, though ample to enable them to live well in Canada are insufficient to meet the demands of rising expenses at home." The most vehement opponents of emigration "are those who are most actively employed in enriching themselves by means of cheap labour. The cheaper the labour market, the faster they can make money." This exploitation is reflected in the Canadianization of lower-class British emigrants. "Britishers who have been embittered by the hard conditions of their former life in the old country are sometimes rather contemptuous of the land of their birth."[13]

In the early 1910s one British observer gave a succinct summary of the sinking of roots by non-British immigrants and the dual loyalty of the British. According to J. Burgon Bickersteth, among the majority of the people, "this cosmopolitan collection," "one sentiment is noticeable ... after they have been living a few years in the country, and that is loyalty to Canada ... There is a very strong feeling of Canadian nationality, which is growing every year." Loyalty to the Empire, on the other hand, was strong only "among the British element." This reflects the experiences of the Irish Wilson Benson, the Italian Veltri, the Ukrainian Gus Romaniuk, and the Pole Walter Chuchla. Romaniuk, at first desolate about the poverty of homesteading, noted only a short time later – even if this may be a rationalizing retrospect – "To me my boyhood days in Myshkiv already were becoming indistinguishable from dreams."[14]

Local Self-Organization and the Irrelevance of the National

While the Empire and world markets were present in some immigrants' life-writings, national politics were almost completely absent. The exceptions were Helgi Einarsson and Lars Gudmundson who mentioned the Laurier government briefly and positively, probably because of the special political position granted to Icelanders in the Gimli region. Only merchant Einarsson and gentlewoman-farmer Georgina Binnie-Clarke attempted to influence national politics, as did Tommy Douglas. For most only the local counted in their memoirs.[15]

Community institutions were established from the bottom up by migrants who grew up in societies in which such activities came from the top down, were the exclusive domain of the upper classes, government officials, lords of the manor, clergy. Once the economics of survival had resulted in a foothold, or, better, a livelihood, outward links were institutionalized: a store to obtain provisions and consumer goods, a post office to connect to the family left behind, a church to link to the realm of the spiritual, schools to equip children for their future. National institutions, such as the immigration hall and the land office, remained brief stopovers. Creating local institutions permitted practical experience in political system and politics. It democratized immigrants from absolutist states more than any abstract notions of a free country and constitutional procedures. In local organizations immigrants could contribute prior experience in village self-government, or could become active when their interests demanded it and their means permitted. Even costs and resulting taxes could be integrated into family economies. Taxes might be converted into labour in road maintenance, costs for church or school be reduced by undertaking the building within the community. Had tax collectors been as ever-present and as haughty as in European societies, political involvement on the national level might have come faster. Letters to relatives and friends at home emphasized that no rents had to be paid to landlords and no tax collector would mercilessly confiscate the last cow. Because of these attitudes, the politics of protest often began against the one "national" but private institution – the railway corporations and their confiscatory rates.

The opening of a post office was important to immigrants because it provided the lifeline to family members remaining in the old country. Even though the postmaster or postmistress was an English-speaker, many emphasized that he or she belonged to their own group. In Ledwyn, Manitoba, postmaster Dmytro Zinkowsky's "home was the cultural centre of our district. He was an educated man, had attended public school at Sarto and could speak and write English." Elsewhere a homesteader brought out his sister "and by opening a Post Office in the place she did a lot towards civilizing it."[16]

In order to build churches, men and women were ready to invest time and to donate material. The one controversial issue was its location in the community. A comparatively wealthy family who could afford to donate land had the church and by implication the community's social centre at its front door, while others had to travel many kilometres for each service. At the same time the value of the adjoining farm lands increased. Once the decision had been made, men and women would get together to raise the new church's frame and combine this working bee with a dance or picnic, as was done for barn-raisings and other joint endeavours. Thereafter, depending on time, skills, and resources, they worked individually on finishing the building, or contributed a special skill – for example, forging an iron cross or gate. "All our social life was centred around the church. There were Sunday school picnics, and religious holidays."[17]

When children had to be sent to school, families, occasionally opposed by the bachelors, formed a school district, elected a board, fixed and collected school rates. The schoolhouse, built by the community itself, had to be as near to the centre of the district as possible. Provincial Departments of Education sent teachers and gave grants-in-aid towards the salary. To reduce cost, some communities boarded the teacher in family homes, not always to the liking of independent-minded women or men. Pupils might have to chair school board meetings if none of the parents spoke sufficient English. Ethnic or religious controversies could divide boards. In most schools, one pupil took the position of janitor. He or she had to keep the room clean and, in winter, fire the stove. Extended cold spells could induce a community to close the school altogether in winter and in fall harvest work reduced attendance. When immigrant parents demanded bilingual teachers since their children had no English to start with, they often found themselves opposed by English-speaking neighbours. Forbidding pupils to use any language but English was long remembered with bitterness – even if the reason was not cultural arrogance but to prevent students from acting behind the backs of teachers who understood only English.

Classes were multi-ethnic. At Lac la Nonne, Alberta, British, American, Canadian, French-Canadian, Métis, Scandinavian, and German children were among the twenty pupils in 1910. Lydia Kupsch from Bruderheim, Alberta, remembered: "I began to speak English only after starting school. It was pretty hard to understand. The teacher used a lot of pictures." For both adults and children, libraries would be organized on the initiative of the immigrants or the teachers. They might contain books in the old language for those unable to read English but "books on Canadian folklore became available." Often groups with related languages or dialects, like Czechs and Slovaks, agreed to establish a joint library.[18]

Self-help organizations had been a common feature of pre-migration agricultural communities and labour movements. After migration they assumed additional importance because the traditional help of kin and friends was not available. Communities and cultural groups formed clubs and rented halls for dances, theatrical productions, and educational meetings. In times of crisis in the society of origin, whether war or flood, such organizations coordinated relief efforts. In times of international tensions, such as the coming of wars or fascism, the organizations assumed political functions.

Since political opinions in all ethnic communities were divided, rival organizations sprang up and existing associations spawned splinter groups. Institutional life was pluralistic and sometimes acerbic. The Polish-Canadian Society in Edmonton, for example, was rife with dissensions. "A group of people who spoke good Polish and who had organizational ability" joined. They were "Byelorussians who tried to dominate the Society"; they also were "communists. We had to get rid of them at all costs. They made slanderous remarks about the Polish government, church and priests." The Polish majority restricted membership to Poles who were Catholics. The homogeneity ascribed to people of similar ethnic origin by the host society and postulated by self-appointed ethnic gatekeepers did not exist in times of continued migration. Men and women of one group professed allegiances to different denominations, political persuasions, and social strata. Over time, a reduction of the diversity by a process of constructing internally heterogeneous groups as ethnicities, as well as a process of homogenizing Canadianization, reduced ethnic cultures to an outward symbolic ethnicity and expanded the hegemonic culture to a pluralistic one.[19]

The Kurtenbach family of German origin and the Icelander Helgi Einarsson illustrate the ways in which the local and the old world, specific economic interests and national politics, were entangled. John and Elisabeth Kurtenbach, on their Saskatchewan farm, retained an interest in their society of origin. They read German-Canadian and German newspapers. For relatives and friends in the Rhineland, John described the Canadian political system, Elisabeth the economy: the 1907 depression made it "a hard time for poor workers." Two themes emerged, perennial ones in emigrant letters: self-determination, "We elect our own civil servants"; and economic advance through market connections and population growth, "The quicker the immigrants come, the quicker railways and businesses of all sorts will be established." As to ethnicity, "We Germans are well respected here and we play a great part in the political life and farming community of this country."[20]

Helgi Einarsson, fisherman and trader, intervened in politics when capitalist business attempted to use the national government to impose its interests locally. In the political economy of Canada, the stranglehold on small producers came from private corporations, not from hereditary nobles. During one of the several depressions, the supervisor of fisheries in Winnipeg used the NWMP, now an institution of class-based rule enforcement, to arrest Helgi for unlawful fishing. "Times were hard ... because no one had money to spend. The [big] fishing companies at Selkirk had their cold storage plants filled with fish they were unable to sell." They requested Ottawa "to ban all fishing on Lake Winnipeg the following summer." This would not only have thrown the small fishermen, whether Native, Icelandic, or other, out of business, but would also have prevented them from fishing for their own food. Secretively, public officials, in collusion with private capital, planned a hearing in Winnipeg with a representative from Ottawa. Getting wind of this, the small fishermen and traders organized, elected speakers, and came to the meeting en masse. Sveinn Thorvaldsson, a Riverton merchant, argued that, given the times, he had to reduce prices on his goods by half and take the losses. Neither he nor his customers saw any reason why the big companies should be protected from losses to the detriment of the consumers. He spoke as a community member, not as a capitalist looking to his profits. Helgi, living with a Native and informed about treaty rights, spoke up for Native fishing rights. The community won its case against the capitalist outsiders and their local political servants.[21]

Towards Larger Society: A Democracy of Consumption

Pedlars were said to carry "democratic incense" into homes where every penny was turned before being paid out. At the beginning of the twentieth century, Eaton's mail-order catalogue carried the world of consumption into these homes. An Eaton's mythology replaced that of the HBC and the Mounties at a time when genteel Britishers were outnumbered by independent-minded farmers and workers. Eaton's became an institution in the West, vastly more important than the Ottawa government, to judge by the reminiscences of immigrants. Its sales policy followed the principle of honesty of the HBC and the Mounties and, more importantly, of the cash-strapped settler families' moral economy.

In a society dependent on trust, Eaton's inspired confidence. Its return-and-refund guarantee reflected the needs and practices of a mutual-support society. Having even freight refunded, a Dutch homesteader noted, "All right Mr Eaton, if I ever need anything else, you can depend on my patronage!" The advice to do home sewing seemed to show that Mr Eaton was not out for profit, although Eaton's happened to sell sewing machines. "It was a personal thing, the bond between customers and Mr. Eaton. Although Timothy [who had arrived from Ireland in 1854] was already dead a dozen years, my parents and their neighbours invariably addressed him by name: 'Well, let's see what Timothy Eaton's got on sale this time.'" Across the prairies, the catalogue gave access to possibilities of consumption; it was "a book to dream over." Its illustrations overcame language and cultural barriers, its advice took the place of an encyclopedia. If a family had no money to spend, the catalogue and the dreams of what might be, perhaps next year, did not cost a cent. In the worlds from which the immigrants came, much of Eaton's merchandise would never have even been visible to small farmers, landless labourers, or urban workers.[22]

Timothy Eaton's Toronto store had been in business on the corner of Yonge and Queen since 1869. Eaton's arrived in Winnipeg in 1905, creating "quite a stir." Contradictory rumours, depending on economic interest, abounded. While some thought small businessmen would suffer, others claimed that "there would soon be jobs for everybody at Eaton's."[23] Economic space did change. "When Eaton's ... built the biggest store west of Toronto at Portage Avenue and Donald Street, the merchandising centre of gravity began shifting rapidly up Portage Avenue." Timothy Eaton and his son appeared in person and announced there would be "no dickering and no bargaining. Everything was to be sold at the price marked." This permitted trade over long distances without personal contact with sales personnel. Joseph Wilder, a newsboy, had the papers grabbed from him by people eager to see Eaton's ads. "I would not be surprised if some children learned the word Eaton's before any other."

Delivery of purchases in Winnipeg was carefully orchestrated to get maximum effect. One newsboy described the scene. The "stable-master managed the dispatch of his afternoon delivery with all the showmanship of a sergeant of the Royal Horse Guards ... [at] the trooping of the colour." When the wagons were lined up inside the building a policeman would

> halt traffic in all directions. Then the big door would fly up and the first rig in line would lunge onto the street ... The Eaton delivery rigs were such an attraction that people who were in the vicinity regularly gathered on the corners to wait for the show ... To us, Eaton's had the finest stable of delivery horses in the whole world and we would almost have rather been Eaton's drivers than locomotive engineers.

Newsboys and other delivery personnel who had to knock at the backdoor at the homes of the rich were impressed that an Eaton's driver with the parcel would step up to the front door at a fast pace "that would have got him expelled from any teamsters' union on earth ... There was none of this 'all deliveries at the rear' nonsense with any Eaton driver." Drivers, as highly placed personages, had to keep their distance from the lowly, too. "No Eaton driver was ever allowed to give a boy a ride."[24]

Those fortunate enough to live in the capitals of consumption, Toronto and Winnipeg, could roam the store. In a party of Galician women, one young woman with experience, but overdressed according to our English informant, acted as "as guide and interpreter." Sewing woman, farmer, or town dweller would find what he or she wanted, "anything from a safety pin to a threshing machine or a grand piano." A Black "expert dressmaker" in Toronto, Elma Gairey, told her Black customers that they could not afford her prices for a full dress: "Now you go down to Eaton's or Simpson's or some other store and you can get the dress cheaper. Bring it to me, then I will alter it for you." In summer, Eaton's, like other stores, arranged picnics, big affairs for children and adults alike.[25]

Eaton's catalogue, "the Prairie Bible," set styles across the country. Vera Lysenko, in *Westerly Wild,* recreated the impact: "'Your drapes are unusual,' said Julie, as she examined the crimson hangings at the window. 'They've caused considerable talk among the neighbours,' said Haugen drily, 'Since they've never seen anything like them in the mail order catalogues.'" Women wore dresses from "page 27 of the mail-order catalogue"; a man went to a dance "in my old snappy blue serge suit (Eaton's advertised everything as 'snappy')." When, after years of poor harvests, a good crop was expected, one farmer's wife "got out her catalogue first time in years." According to a disconcerted missionary, women used Sunday services to show off "their joy rags." Immigrant women no longer had to sew, dowries could be purchased. "Everything, even dusters and dishcloths, had to be monogrammed, embroidered and edged in handmade lace. This time the material was bought from the mail-order catalogue, no more flour bags." A Galician Jew remembered his Canadianization in 1927 Saskatchewan: "Leafing through the Eaton's catalogue, I had decided to look more like a Canadian and ordered knee high boots and other western style garments." Beyond turning immigrants into Canadians, Eaton's could do more. Sent out of the house because their mother was feeling unwell, Anna Kutera and her brothers and sisters upon return found a baby. "We were told that the babies came from Eaton's catalogue and were delivered by this nice visitor," the midwife – a delivery girl who did not have to come by the back door either.[26]

Lumberjacks expectantly waited for the catalogue, too. For them it was rather the lack of dresses that was interesting. "There is enough of a woman for me in those mail-order catalogues that come to the camp twice a year ... All of us ... leaf through those shiny new catalogues. In the winter ones, the ladies are in nice woollens, like our union suits. They are so pretty and curved. In the spring catalogues they are in flimsy and lacy what-do-you-call-'ems. We leaf through the fresh new books leisurely and discuss every smiling face. Then we do our picking. You write your name on her and she's yours until next season. You may look at her anytime, she never talks back or gets underfoot." When a man would change his choice and "decide he likes somebody else's girl better," fist fights could ensue. While these rough lumberjacks were sufficiently discreet to discuss smiling faces only, one boy remembered that his "sex education" came through the catalogue's corset section. When the young man fell in love for the first time, he remembered, "Other girls in my age group were still built like posts but this girl was a veritable Eaton's catalogue Junior Miss."[27]

National lore usually has an underside. In Winnipeg, during the General Strike, "Eaton's turned their fine horses over" to the committee of 1000, the businessmen's anti-strike front. In Toronto of the 1920s, Harry Gairey "couldn't go to Eaton's and ask for a job, or to the Bell Telephone." He was Black.[28]

Construction and Deconstruction of the West

The railway, wheat, and farm machinery all contributed to an image of the West that contained aspects of industrial mass production and national wealth. While agriculture did mean mass production, wheat pouring into elevators or into the hold of ships reflected the lives of the producers as little as cars at the end of an assembly line mirror the lives of industrial workers. Canadian authors who viewed the West in a national perspective were many. Other viewed it in ethnic terms.[29]

Nellie McClung shared the image of expanses of golden wheatfields. Her vision of Canada was "missionary; it was rural; it was assimilative." It was also feminist and embedded in temperance and other reform activities. She combined the national with the familial, including a mothering ideal, self-organized women's clubs, and educational opportunities for women. She joined the Winnipeg Political Equality League. When the Conservative Manitoba premier Roblin commented that voting rights were not for "nice ladies," she defiantly stated "I am not a nice woman." By 1921 the Roblin government was out and she sat in the legislature for the Liberal party. In her evangelical perception she decried poverty and deprivation but found working-class self-organization and direct action, like the General Strike, difficult to accept. She chose the side of "respectable" Canadians who saw their image of rural bliss, golden wheat, and orderly society rudely destroyed by the strikers and quickly united to break the labour movement by violence, slander, and deportation.[30] Janey Canuck, "the naive, youthful, self-confident, and brash" creation of Emily Murphy, shared the vision of independent women's lives. Emily Murphy was ready to accept massive immigration and was optimistic about the advantages settlers would find in Canada and Canada in them. Settlers' mass production of wheat would make Canada a strong nation. People wanted to hear the message; her *Open Trails* (1912) sold over sixty thousand copies. It was more attuned to the times than the backward-looking Glengarry-Scot books of Ralph Connor, which, however, sold even better.[31]

Frederick Niven, in his *Canada West*, written before but published after the onset of the Depression in 1929, remembered "the old days ... when the English speech was everywhere, indomitable settlers driving the first furrows, and the wild young men, the breakers of the prairie, going on their jocund way as though to the sound of bands." He presented several such Hollywood-type pictures of the settlers. But, he asked, will "Progress spell Problem?" In his opinion, recent settlers were no longer of the right type. The early settlers from the "preferred races" had "found their journey well requited, growing their two or three thousand bushels of wheat every year" and getting a good price from grain merchants. But newcomers from the same groups "cannot or will not ... tackle the job," were unwilling to wait long for telephones, electric light, and other amenities. The non-preferred East Europeans, on the other hand, with their "trivial" demands upon life, accepted the "dreary toil and spiritual stagnation." However, "should the [hardworking] non-preferred overbalance the [culturally superior] preferred," Niven envisioned problems. Their absorption would have to be carefully organized by government officials with no bloc settlements permitted. Niven probably had never observed the easy mixing of immigrant men and women from many backgrounds reflected in their life-writings. He also could not fathom the coldness of hearts and minds of government officials displayed in the deportation of workers in the 1920s and non-admission of Jewish refugees in the 1930s.

From the decline of the quality of the farming population, Niven turned to a second "problem," a recurrent theme among highly placed observers – the untrustworthiness of the lower classes of the preferred races. The Canadian railway companies did their best to facilitate the coming of "extra hands" for the harvests, but the immigrant human material did not do its best. "We find immigrants of the wrong type, not agriculturists, not adaptable, swelling the ranks of the unskilled labourers – or even creating a class of casual labourers – and flocking to the cities in winter clamouring for relief." Like policy-makers in Ottawa and British population planners, Niven did not understand that "extra hands" needed employment outside of harvest time and had heads to decide for themselves.[32]

In 1871 the Prairie population had numbered less than thirty thousand; by 1911 it had grown to 1.3 million. Isolated settlements had become larger social spaces that coalesced into one Prairie region as part of the nation. While political leaders had envisioned this process, it was the immigrant families who built the societies. Sifton, aware of the lack of Britishers, had elevated the East Europeans to families in "sheepskin coats." But when immigrants and native-born rebelled, as in the Winnipeg General Strike, a police magistrate who interned the strike leaders explained to a sympathetic prime minister that he had observed Ruthenians, Russians, and Poles to be "Bolsheviki." "It is absolutely necessary that an example should be made ... If the government persists in the [repressive] course that it is now adopting, the foreign element here will soon be as gentle and easily controlled as a lot of sheep." That had been the goal of old-world lords of the manor. Protests were to coalesce into a national movement only in the 1920s.[33]

PART FIVE

The Rockies and the Pacific Coast

The mountain ranges, the valleys, and the coastal fishing grounds of British Columbia had been unincorporated territory of the Hudson's Bay Company until the 1850s, when its mineral deposits attracted prospectors and miners. Gold had been the hope of many migrants, transoceanic or internal, and now also transpacific. In Gaetz's Nova Scotia a small gold rush sent people scampering for riches; David Leveridge was lured to Ontario by gold; the Dutch homesteader Willem DeGelder mailed off glittering pebbles for chemical analysis. The British Columbia gold rushes on the Fraser River in 1857, the Cariboo in 1860, and the Klondike in 1896, attracted tens of thousands. James Thomson, the Edwardsburgh farmer, set out, as did Alexander Robb from Ireland. From Canada East, the West was distant: early routes led through Panama or California. Prospecting "in a wild country," Alexander wrote home, meant loneliness in the midst of fortune-seekers from many cultures. During the first rush American, European, and Chinese men came, as well as a small number of women; in the Cariboo, seven thousand arrived within a short time. Most were disappointed, Alexander Robb and James Thomson among them. Both laboured in road construction and took odd jobs before returning, richer only by experience.[1]

A decade later, British Columbia became part of the Dominion of Canada, although it took another fifteen years to complete the railway connection to Eastern Canada. In this period the white population, native-born and immigrant, increased from twenty thousand in 1871 to twenty four thousand in 1881, but Native Peoples still were in the majority. In the construction of race in British Columbia, white included Métis, the offspring of Native women and HBC men. While across Canada dreams concerned railways, in the West it was trade with Asia that seemed to promise riches. Again dreams were not to be fulfilled for decades, but a surplus-producing labour force could be tapped: Chinese, Japanese, and "Hindoos" from India. After the 1820s, the Asian contract labour system supplemented the Atlantic migration system and the Russo-Siberian one. Vancouver became one of its destinations.

CHAPTER SIXTEEN

Mining in the Rockies

George M. Dawson of the Canadian Geological Survey explored the Crowsnest Pass area, the southernmost link between Alberta and British Columbia, in 1882 and 1883, and in 1898–9 the CPR built a line westward through the pass to tap its coal seams. Towns sprang up, and a memorial on the height of the pass credits two Italians as early pioneers in the construction work. When mountaineering became a hobby for the rich, alpine guides hired from Switzerland and Austria initiated a chain migration. Some Banff houses were constructed in the Swiss style, contrasting with the pagoda-style CPR stations. For the 1901 visit of the Prince of Wales, a Ukrainian railway worker who used to hike in the area of Lake Louise, not yet named, was ordered to blaze a trail to the lake. The next morning Mounties were brought in by freight train and drawn up on parade just before the prince and his retinue arrived. The multi-ethnic railway workers first cheered the prince. Whatever the feeling for British royalty, they next cheered the royal cooks to get some of the "dainties" brought in. The prairie custom of sharing had to be encouraged across social hierarchies and the men knew how to play the game.[2]

Investors, Workingmen, Marginal Men

Encouraged by a visiting Canadian politician, German financiers founded a "Deutsches Canada Syndikat." A mining engineer from Berlin, Martin Cohn, who had travelled for professional reasons to Ireland, England, and China, was sent to explore investment opportunities in 1906. He was wined and dined in Ottawa. In Sudbury, he expressed interest in the production of nickel, needed by Krupp to harden steel, but found the environmental damage of the sulphur fumes repulsive. So he continued his explorations.

During his travels Cohn observed Canadian society. He remarked that male Anglo-Canadian high society had problems in seeing women except as the focus of sexual phantasies. At a ball in Ottawa the debutante daughters and high-society ladies "rushed quickly through the lobby in apparent fear of the contaminating stare of the men." In Edmonton, a wealthy Frenchman scandalized the local society. "That man is always bringing a French girl over from Paris and lives with her." Socialites whispered that she wore "a transparent kimono." Cohn, who met the woman, found her to be well versed intellectually as well as a good cook.[3]

Cohn took note of "coloured" Pullman porters and Winnipeg's cosmopolitan crowds as well as of English immigrants' "very superior attitude" to "the Canadians as colonials." With his own countrymen his relations were mixed. A German-Canadian farmer's shack was "so dirty that I was ashamed of my countryman." Another, who "was aware that I happened to be a countryman, consequently charged double the usual price" for pulling his car out of a snowdrift. This was the opposite of the solidarity described in homesteaders' life-writings. Cohn took an immediate dislike to Count Alvo von Alvensleben. From his Vancouver residence, which "looked like a castle on the Rhine with turrets and bastions," Alvensleben cheated other German aristocrats out of funds for real estate schemes, paying the German consul to write references on official stationery. Edwin Alm, the Swedish farm boy turned real-estate dealer, dealt more honestly with his customers. On the other hand, Cohn took a liking to "Dutchie," who led a secluded, marginalized life in the wilderness. He was rumoured to be a murderer, but had invented the story to be left alone. "I was in the [German] army. My corporal scolded me because a button on my tunic was loose. I talked back to him, he swore at me, and I slapped his face. That was a crime. The same day I deserted and sailed as a stowaway to New York." While few German immigrants mention the army in their reminiscences, French and English observers and immigrants repeatedly ran into men from Germany who left because of the draft or war.[4]

Cohn engaged a surveying party and a capable geologist, and invested in the Alberta Bighorn and South Brazeau coal fields. He met G.M. Dawson, and was impressed by his knowledge. In fact, he was always ready to grant recognition to capable men, whether internationally renowned geologists, outfitters, head packers, or Native guides. He often travelled with Stony Indian men, whom he contrasted favourably to the fat cats in Alberta and the pompous investors who financed the Syndicate. Packers often had to deal with high-ranking Europeans, and quickly put them in their place. An English lord who on the first evening of his outing coldly informed the men, "I am not used to eating with my servants," was told that he could wait until they had finished. A Spanish prince who refused the simple food did not get any. A German officer who ordered the men around was regarded as a lunatic and told to shut up. Ability counted, not pretensions.[5]

At first, Cohn's Canadianization was radically different from that of other immigrants. Travelling about the country and meeting influential persons, he was impressed by men – immigrant, Native, or native-born – able to find coal seams and to mine them without expensive equipment. While for others a homestead or a job would do, he hoped to acquire a "monopoly." He worked closely with the specialists from the Canadian Geological Survey and respected their pragmatic attitudes. Returning to Berlin to report on investment opportunities, he entered a different world, unconnected to geological facts and the realities of mining. A French professor at the Mining Academy called him a swindler, because, according to the books, there were no coal seams in the Rockies. To convince the savant, an international conference was arranged at government expense in Canada. Cohn's financial backers lived in a world of bonuses and commissions for deals made. It was of no interest to them which coal field was opened up commercially, how the mining was to be done. Noting that "something must be radically wrong with the capitalist system," Cohn changed his name to Nordegg and, like homesteaders and farmers, drew closer to Canadian ways. "I had really now a stake in this great country."

Nordegg did business with the railway construction company of Mackenzie and Mann. He did not know that they had tried to cheat Giovanni Veltri's brother Vincenzo out of mining rights. The Italian immigrant had dared bring a suit against the powerful company, won it, but did not have the capital needed to invest in larger mining operations.[6] The company cheated Nordegg in 1914, using "the opportunity afforded them" by the war to try to enrich themselves. By that time, a railway line had been built from Red Deer to Rocky Mountain House by the Canadian Northern, paralleled by another built by the Canadian Pacific. Dumbfounded by such waste of capital, Nordegg convinced the two companies to agree on a joint bridge across the North Saskatchewan. Their august presidents, Sir William Mackenzie and Sir George Bury, at first were taken aback at the suggestion that they should talk to each other. Construction would have benefited from a pooling of investments earlier. The tracks over which Nordegg travelled were not yet ballasted. "After hard bumping, one car jumped off the rails." The engineer simply hooked a telephone to the line and asked for another engine. When none could be sent, the train's entire crew, with heavy bars, lifted the car back onto the rail. Another car jumped the rails one curve down the line; so after a few more jumping cars, the crew called it a day in the middle of nowhere and settled down to sleep in the box cars.

Nordegg's planned mining town started with two bunkhouses and a cooking shed, "filled to capacity" when he saw them for the first time.

"When I opened the door I got such a whiff of foul air that I quickly shut the door again." He slept in a tent at more than forty degrees below zero, warmed by a coal fire from the seam he had discovered. "I imagined the realization of my dream to see cottages arise to shelter families who would find work through my endeavours. The valley looked beautiful, with snow-covered mountains all around and the line of the high Bighorn range in the distance." On his next trip, he saw "a huge steamshovel cut a gash into the hillside" and "a small crowd watching it." Mule trains had been brought up from Texas and camps had been established. But life was not ideal. Some of the miners "considered life at the mine too dull and hard and ... missed the joys of civilization in the old mining towns. So they left and were on the way out."

In 1912 Nordegg began "to build a modern and pretty town," with a bath in every cottage. His engineers opposed "this unheard-of idea." With advice from medical specialists at the University of Toronto, he projected "the best-equipped hospital west of the Calgary-Edmonton railway line." He planned a community with public buildings in which the ugly water tower was hidden by colours of "various shades of green" that blended it into its background. In the log houses, according to Nordegg, "the men had excellent quarters, although [he added] their number increased now very quickly." Nordegg's friend Dutchie clung to his views of society. "The Collieries as a visible, and the absent Directors as an invisible, body had according to his view been formed only for the purpose of sucking the blood of the lesser employees and workmen." Nordegg himself admitted, "The contractors made the men work until nightfall."

At the mine, tunnels had been dug so far that ventilation was needed. Heavy machinery, lumber, and mine rails were still stacked at Rocky Mountain House because the railway bridge had not been completed. Should all of this be hauled over the frozen river? An early breakup of the ice ended this speculation. Soon temporary sleepers rested on the trestles and men could cross the river as on a tightrope. Twice a day construction trains brought in heavy machinery and hauled off large stockpiles of coal. Sir William Mackenzie congratulated Nordegg. "He said I was the first man in his experience to have kept his word in finishing construction work in time and well within the cost estimated, let alone to have the promised 100,000 tons of coal ready for shipment ... All that deserved a reward, ... he would name the town after me."

With the cottages finished, women came, including the assistant manager's wife with a baby. Need for a school arose and "young lady schoolteachers" were hired. Better housing had to be constructed for the officials, an "upper town" separated by the railway from the workers' "lower town." Nordegg's misgivings about this layout were justified. "It created a caste of superior men, and even more so of superior women. The ladies [from Eastern Canada] would not mix socially with the women living below the railway line, and all my attempts to level this separation failed utterly." He saw his chance when the town's movie theatre opened. The self-defined upper classes, who would not even talk to the schoolmistresses, had the first three rows roped off for themselves. Nordegg, accompanied by the four teachers, took seats up front. At the subsequent reception the "gentlemen of the upper town" were happy to ask the young women for dances. The teachers, but never the "others living in lower town," were "accepted into society."

Nordegg, who was happy to see others marry, never mentioned any loving attachments of his own. His silence may have been prompted by sadness. He had married a French woman, Berthe-Marie, in London, who because of poor health had to live in mild Mediterranean climates. Later she died. In 1912 Nordegg brought their fourteen-year-old daughter, Marcelle, to Canada and took her on an arduous but fascinating trip through the Rockies. For her, he wrote a loving, illustrated memoir of the trip. Marcelle was undergoing psychiatric treatment in Germany in the 1940s and died in January 1945, probably killed in the Nazi program to exterminate mental patients.[7]

In 1914 Nordegg was officially listed as an enemy alien. The Italian miners remained friendly to him, even though many of their Canadian relatives fought in the Allied forces. The Belgian engineer – Germany had invaded Belgium – and the mine's doctor, on the other hand, turned hostile. Nordegg went to the United States, into "exile," but returned later. He then divested himself of his ties to the finance companies and took out Canadian citizenship.

Others, too, came to invest. Gaston Giscard, from France, could afford to sail second-class in 1910. He had capital, but at first decided to accept a variety of jobs, homestead, and keep a store in order to learn about Canada. In 1912, with others, he founded the Société Immobilière Franco-Canadienne in Edmonton "to invest advantageously French and Belgian capital in the Canadian West." He took an interest in the Edmonton oil boom, but was not fully convinced that it would last. His plans, too, were cut short by the war. With hundreds of others he returned in August 1914.[8]

Immigrants or Aliens?

Nordegg, like Polish and Ukrainian immigrants from the Habsburg and Romanov empires, resented the impact of war in Europe on their private lives in Canada. Not all fears of Canadian authorities were unfounded. An Austrophile Ukrainian group supported the Habsburg monarchy. A German, Max Otto, who lived in Canada from 1912 to 1921, according to his own boastful account, collected information for the German secret service and operated a small propaganda outfit to oppose Victory Loan drives. He considered himself as belonging to an elite, a master race, far above Russian Germans, Jews, and all Germans who had acculturated to Canadian ways of life.[9] But most designated as enemy aliens had developed life-projects as Canadian citizens. Their life-courses were interupted by top-level politics and the European war.

The Polish immigrant, Waclaw Fridel, like other Austrian citizens, had to report to authorities once a month. Since in Wabamun, Alberta, there was no police for miles around, the so-called enemy aliens reported to the local post office. "Once I failed to report ... for three months. I was having some personal problems as well as difficulties at work." Walking home one night, he wondered if he should turn himself in to the police. He was also angry: "I am not guilty of anything, I do not owe anyone anything. Austria is not my country." The next day he went to the post office. "I knew the whole family who operated both the store and the post office. I explained my problem to the girl in the store. She took my papers and, without a word, set her seal to my papers three time with different dates each time." He never had to report again. The war ended.[10]

In 1918 Canadians were more concerned with the havoc and death caused by the flu epidemic than with the war. Many of the immigrants, though keenly interested in the fate of their relatives in Europe, had difficulties in following the course of the war. Gus Romaniuk noted "We were happy to hear that the war was over. But we didn't know who had won!"[11] The peace induced some hyphenated Canadians to return to their newly independent countries in Eastern and Southeastern Europe to help rebuild devastated farms and cities. Others left those stagnant economies for Canada.

Miners in the Crowsnest Pass

Walter (Wladyslaw) Chuchla was one of these postwar Polish immigrants. In his home town, armies, friendly or enemy, had foraged for food; none of the family's livestock was left and the two draft horses were gone. His father and a brother came home sick. The country's economy was in shambles. A war with the Soviet Union about Ukraine in 1921, and the coup of 1926, further diminished the chances for a stable life. So Walter sailed from Gdansk with other young men. For reasons of hygiene, the men's hair was shaved, a procedure they found degrading: "We looked like prisoners or convicts with our bare heads." In the spring of 1926 he reached Halifax.[12]

Walter's first job was with a Ukrainian widower whose sons were busy making moonshine. "I had to be cook, farmhelp and errand boy." After two weeks he left. Trudging through snow and mud, he felt exhausted and cold. A friendly Canadian-born Ukrainian took him in. Again he left. With friends he began to search for a homestead. After several harvest jobs, Walter reached Coleman where the Polish grocery-owner, Michalski, hired him and two other men to clear land. Half a year later the three were discharged and, after deductions for groceries and rent, ended up with thirty-six dollars each for six months' work.

Even though he had little money, Walter was becoming part of the Polish community, which had come together, – partly to defend itself against wartime slurs, and also to build a community hall. Working at a saw mill, Walter donated money and time. He and friends organized a Youth Society for young Canadian-born Poles and young immigrant bachelors. Unemployed once again, he no longer had to search for a job by himself: the Polish Society for Brotherly Aid helped him get a steady job with the International Coal & Coke Company. The Polish farm boy became a Canadian miner. Underground he began as helper, but then advanced to better-paid piecework with a "very good and experienced partner, a Slav man," who taught him how to work safely. None of the miners' memoirs contains information about the work experience, but frequent accidents induced the Poles to found an insurance association.

Experienced miners from the Krakow district and from south of the new Czechoslovakian border were now living in the numerous boardinghouses run by Polish women. They enjoyed company and organized "many parties with singing and dancing." As to the married men whose wives remained in Poland, "a lot of gossip and jealousy" resulted. Some, "smarter, observant and more influential in the English circles," became community leaders. The president of the Polish Society, re-elected again and again, was accused of a domineering attitude and ousted, but not before the society was involved in an expensive lawsuit. The Youth Society, on the other hand, did well: "drama group, library, entertainment, lectures, ... concerts." Plays were staged regularly. The library, which contained more than three thousand books and pamphlets, mostly donated by the community, exchanged books with Calgary, Edmonton, and Vancouver. Young people helped older residents to build their homes, mixing cement, doing carpentry without pay. Walter, with four others, organized a band, playing the saxophone.

Walter built himself a two-room house with a garden and was "eyed" by mothers and young women. He fell in love with one of the daughters of a farm family, sixteen-year-old Anne Pieronek, whom we have met earlier as a child going out in a dog-cart. "They were a typical Polish family with traditions observed during Christmas, Easter, or any other special days like birthday, namesday and others." A comparison of Walter's memoir with Anne's much shorter one confirms the adherence of her family to traditions. "The day before Christmas, there would be a big preparation of twelve meatless courses symbolizing the twelve apostles." Only two of the numerous Polish memoirs mentioned this festive meal. When she met Walter for the first time, she probably wore clothes made "from sugar and flour" sacks. "We did look funny in them but we were happy to have that much and did not complain." The wedding in August 1931 left the two in debt. "The coal mines worked for only 2–3 days per week, monies were scarce and we could not go out much anywhere, only to the farm to help with the crop." On the other side of the continent, Rémi Jodouin shared this Depression lifestyle between farming and mining.

In spring of 1932 the miners of Coleman, Blairmore, and Bellevue decided to strike. Anne was involved with demonstrations and picket line, Walter with the relief committee to help poorer families by distributing pork and beans. To raise money he played at dances at mines not on strike. Anne and he survived on produce from her parents' farm. The union lost and seventy-three men were blacklisted, Walter among them. With hundreds of others looking for work, he could not even find a job in road construction, so Anne worked as a waitress in Blairmore and he kept playing at dances.

Politically his life was difficult, too. Strikebreakers accused him of supporting the union's left wing. The social, political, and personal became inextricably mixed. A newly-wed man was not supposed to be out playing at dances. Some women resented his marriage since they had considered him a candidate for their own daughters. Families with drinking men felt, perhaps with justification, that Walter had bypassed them while distributing relief during the strike. The charge was ethnicized: he had given the food to "others, not Poles." He was accused of having kept some of the donations for his playing to himself rather than turning it over to the union.

Walter concerned himself with the task of getting his citizenship, while Anne worked and supported the family. His application for naturalization was rejected on grounds that he did not hold a permanent job. It would take twelve years and three applications before he was successful. Acculturation did not mean acquiescence. He was aware of demonstrations in Regina and Winnipeg. He rode freight trains in search of harvest work, even with wages down to fifty cents a day. Stopped by the RCMP in Camrose in 1934, the men told the officer that they were hungry. The RCMP procured bread, butter, and buttermilk, then barred them from proceeding eastward where thousands were demonstrating for relief and ordered them out of town.

Moving to Edmonton in winter 1932, he worked in a coal mine, Anne as a waitress. Walter continued his music, in an the orchestra that "consisted of two Poles, two Ukrainians and a Frenchman on the drum." They were paid in kind – bacon, chicken, sausages, sometimes a bottle of moonshine. In June 1934 Anne and Walter's only child, Alexandra, was born. A streak of luck arrived in the person of Anne's attractive younger sister looking for work. Young men began to visit bringing food. Several came, for Christmas, and with them a twenty-pound turkey and a gallon of wine. Anne and Walter divided the blessings with the poor Ukrainian family whose house and kitchen they shared and were in turn invited for Ukrainian Christmas, thirteen days later. Walter never mentioned what became of Anne's sister and the young men.

In 1935 Walter Chuchla was rehired at the Coleman mine for the night shift. His boss and superintendent seemed to be more supportive than some community members, and it was from them that he learned about the slanderous remarks made about his relief committee activities. Community life was full of tensions, most of them connected to old-world politics. Some Poles were accused of being fascists, some followed left-wing ideologies, and, in Walter's words, were "agitating against the Polish people." A spring flood and a cave-in nearly destroyed their house. Then Walter was injured in an accident and had to stop work. The family relocated to Calgary, where Anne worked in the Hudson's Bay store at the CPR station, and as a cook in St Joseph's parish. After different jobs, Walter settled into a janitor's position with the school board.[13]

The experiences of a miner from England, Bill Johnstone and his wife, Dorothy Riddoch, paralleled those of Walter and Anne in some respects. The economic framework and mining, as well as their enterprising natures, explain the similarities, different cultures notwithstanding. Bill came from a miner's family. In England also the pay was poor, but the family lived in a company house and owned a piano. Pedlars served the neighbourhood because working-class families could not afford to buy in large quantities. His mother "could neither read nor write, but she could account for every penny in the household spending." His first wages in the pit were less than what he consumed in food at home. The families were "subsidizing the coal companies and owners." He was a union man and remembered the failure of the strike of 1926: "The miners were starved back into the pits." In 1928, at the age of twenty, he left for Canada, "the cheapest place to get to in the Commonwealth."

Like many others, he had been promised a job, which did not materialize. The station agent took responsibility and after a few hours a farmer picked him up and drove directly to work with him. Bill had not eaten for more than a day because he ran out of money and was so weakened that the day almost ended with a work accident. In winter, he found a job at a prairie coal mine in Dinant, Alberta, and was taken by surprise that no machinery was used, every piece of coal being picked by hand. Earning more than in England, he was able to buy presents from Eaton's catalogue for his family. "I had never seen anything like it. Here was a huge department store at my fingertips." He worked with "twelve men of different countries, cultures and environments." When he fell sick, a pidgin-English-speaking German cured him. In the next year, his family from England came under a Hudson's Bay Company settlement scheme and was sent to marginal land, like other late migrants at that time; the company's legendary fairness had given way to shady land sales. A neighbour had but one piece of advice: "Get the hell out of here while you have a chance, because you'll never make it." The words proved prophetic. Bill helped the family, but by Christmas there were no presents and little food. The family lived of rabbits and other snared animals. Their borrowed old rifle went off accidentally killing Bill's brother Tommy. As in the case of Maria Andreychuk's death, "there was no money for a funeral."

Bill's sister Ethel joined the rural-to-urban migration to work in Edmonton. Bill had left his parents and younger siblings in order to work in a mine near Hinton until a cave-in pinned him down. Out of hospital and hungry, he got a three-course meal at a Chinese restaurant for a quarter. Farm work. Threshing. Mining. One winter, the miners sat and waited until a farmer came to buy coal, then sat and waited again. Employers sized him up "as if I were a horse on sale." After six years he could build himself a two-room shack in Wabamun, Alberta. This, he felt, gave him standing. From itinerant he advanced to "property owner" and as such was "part of the community." He married the housekeeper of a neighbour, a woman of Nova Scotia background, and was proud of "her spirit and grit." While Walter Chuchla advanced through the social assets of the Polish community, Bill advanced individually through studying for miner's certificates. He and Dorothy moved to Vancouver Island and became part of the rise and fall of the Cumberland and Union Bay Dunsmuir mines with their "Asian, African and European" working population. James Dunsmuir, the owner and lieutenant-governor, in 1906–7 had refused to sign legislation excluding "Orientals." On this occasion, capitalist interest merged with non-discrimination and bypassed federal rhetoric about the foot-loose working classes and about racial inferiority.

In the Vancouver Island mines Bill felt at home because he worked with a "traditional mining class," which he had missed in the prairie mines. His training, however, elevated him out of the class: the non-fraternization policy of class-conscious miners with managers and technical personnel left him without friends. Class was highly visible in Cumberland, and intentionally so. "In 1897, on a high piece of ground overlooking the city, James Dunsmuir had built Beaufort House as a residence for the general manager. It was far above any other building in the district in style and size." In the late 1930s miners unionized, the last occupant of Beaufort House, Lieutenant-Colonel Charles Villiers, died, and the extravagant establishment was boarded up. A few years later Bill Johnstone supervised its demolition while economic change devastated the mining community. In 1947 the Leduc, Alberta, oil discovery reduced the value of mines and of miners' skills.[14] Bill and Dorothy Johnstone, like Anne and Walter Chuchla, shaped their lives within the constraints of larger economic forces – depression, sectoral expansion, and decline.

CHAPTER SEVENTEEN

East and West Do Meet

From the perspective of the colonial powers, the northwest coast had been a shared as well as contested domain of the Spanish, Russian, and British empires. From the perspective the Native peoples, the newcomers represented threats as well as trading opportunities. Natives exchanged goods with the eighteenth-century transpacific vessels of the European powers and in the nineteenth century with Northwest Company and Hudson's Bay Company factors. European men and First Nation women lived together in keeping with "the customs of the country." Some men became "Indianized" and their children developed Métis cultures. Much of the British Columbia elite, including the governor and top officials, were of mixed race. Unlike the Red River Métis, the British Columbia Métis, owing to their status in the power hierarchy, could establish themselves as founders. The "British" character of British Columbia is a later construct.

With the gold rushes after 1857, a second Euro-immigrant society emerged interspersed with an Asian-immigrant one. This gold-diggers' culture disrupted traditional Native lifestyles and reduced game, which was a basis for their subsistence. At the same time, contagious diseases destroyed whole segments of the Native populations. A third stage was reached when a British settler society was to be superimposed on Métis culture and male camp life. Landowners of British origin, unwittingly copying the St Lawrence valley seigneurial structures, intended to establish a hierarchical British gentry society and missionaries began to preach racial purity. Unions between immigrant men and Native women became fewer; increasingly Native women were stereotyped as "squaws," and "dark Indian" women were portrayed as the depraved counterpart to virtuous and idealized white women and a threat to the morality of white men. The view of race and gender was brittle, however, and had to be reinforced by a pervasive hegemonic ideology of whiteness, by power relationships, and by class structures.[1]

As in the Prairies, life-writings mention Northwest Coast Native men and women with respect. Some immigrants realized that fears of "the Indians" based on European literature were unjustified. Contact between the distinct worlds occurred on a competent matter-of-fact basis. The Native people's trail-guiding, hunting, and fishing capabilities, their knowledge of the land without reference to survey stakes and women's sewing skills, were appreciated. In the initial phases, contact might mean destruction. Walter Moberly, who had hired Natives as packers, remembered "the dismal wailing of Indian women" after smallpox had killed family and kin. In 1884 a white Canadian law severely curtailed some of the social customs of Native Peoples.[2]

Perceptive if prejudiced Euro-Canadian observers had recognized the possibilities of Asia and "the Future of North-West Canada" early. William Newton called the impact of the Trans-Siberian Railway and Japan's rise to power an epochal event. He had commented on the economic and commercial potential of Asia, but warned of Japanese and Russian immigrant "hordes" that might invade the Northwest to the detriment of "the old British stock, and the old British virtue."[3] Immigrants from Asia came on commercial ships and with the British navy, as gold prospectors and workers, as merchants and domestics, and as contract labourers until racist legislation began to exclude Chinese by imposition of landing fees after 1885. For migrants from India, who were British citizens and thus could not be excluded, the Canadian government resorted to administrative subterfuge. Immigrants had to arrive by "continuous journey" from India – an impossibility in the days of coal-powered ships. Like Halifax and Quebec City for transatlantic migrants, Vancouver became the important entry port for transpacific migrants. Angel Island, the US receiving station, still evoke memories of suffering and detention; in Vancouver, little more than the *Komagata Maru* incident, in which Sikh immigrants unsuccessfully tested the continuous journey provisions, is now remembered.[4]

Establishing a Society

In 1843 the Hudson's Bay Company established Victoria as trading post; together with New Westminster and Vancouver it became the destination for men and women who had a broad range of prior migration experiences. Its early history is reflected in the reminiscences of John Sebastian Helmcken, whose grandparents had moved from German territories to London in a migration of skilled workers and entrepreneurs in the sugar-making trade. As a ship surgeon he reached the Hudson Bay's York Factory in 1847, sailed to Singapore in 1848, and accepted a position at Fort Victoria in 1850. Medical support was also available for the sizable French group which established the Société Française de Bienfaisance et Secours Mutuels in 1860, a precursor of modern health insurance plans.[5]

Other multiple migrations included gold miners and sailors from Australia, men and women from the British Isles via Cape Horn, and Eastern Canadians via Edmonton, the United States, or Panama. In the Prairies most internal migrants came from Ontario and some farmers from Quebec; many teachers and some homesteaders came from Nova Scotia. In the Lower Fraser valley Maritimers were labelled "fish-eaters." Migrants reflected imperial history: parents or grandparents had been in India or Ceylon, came with the Royal Engineers, or had lived in the Australian or Caribbean colonies. British Columbia's Catholic priests from Belgium, France, and Italy, on the other hand, reflected the imperial reach and recruitment of the church. Early settlers bought from pedlars of many cultures; one reminiscence of a generous Greek man parallels that of the Italian woman in Winnipeg. Among those driving the last spike near Craigellachie was the French-Canadian contractor, Amable Lagacé. The Lagacé family and many other French-Canadian families, as well as Italian Catholic immigrants, settled near St Mary's Mission and at Hatzic.[6]

Eric Duncan, arriving on Vancouver Island from the Shetlands in 1877, lived in a predominantly British neighbourhood in Nanaimo which also housed Norwegians, Indians, Japanese, the "colliery Chinamen," and an English-speaking Italian. The community's two leading merchants were a "generous" German Jew, Alexander Mayer, and a "skinflint" Englishman, John Hirst. Duncan also met a Black man, widely travelled in the Caribbean and South America.[7] Friendship and marriage patterns reached to Australia and New Zealand, as well as back to the old world. When the Irish-Australian Adam McKelvey was widowed, he returned to Ireland to marry. "The story of his opulence brought out a whole crowd of young Ulstermen." Eric Duncan married a Swedish woman, Anna. Her mother had migrated from northern Sweden to Stockholm, worked as a domestic and raised her children. Widowed, she joined her brother in Nanaimo as housekeeper, but because of his heavy drinking, she left to work again as a domestic. Eric and Anna Duncan, who had no children of their own, adopted a baby boy whose Ontario-born mother had died.[8]

John Johnson, a sailor from a Norwegian working-class family, in 1884 found British Columbia's labouring class to be very independent. John had had no difficulty in adventuring away from his home town of Frederikshald. Local ships sailed to the Maritimes in the timber trade; English capital opened quarries in Frederikshald and supplied construction sites as far as Japan. John sailed to ports from England to Spain, from New York to Savannah, and on the Pacific. He acted as guide to the daughter of a middle-class Frederikshald family going on a prepaid ticket to her sister in Chicago. The two took a liking to each other, but never even expressed it because of the class differences. From Victoria, he shipped on boats crossing the sound. Once, carrying Chinese labourers for a Vancouver contractor, the boat was met by a large crowd and had to cast off again. "Indignation meetings" of white citizens opposed "this importation of cheap labour," an attitude shared by John.[9]

In addition to Eric Duncan's many-cultured acquaintances and to John Johnson's Norwegian community, a genteel English male and female immigration reached British Columbia, one of decidedly declining means. The British pioneer woman as a type was not merely a phenomenon of early Upper Canada. Many of the women were single; most were resourceful and ready to adapt. One of them was Susan Allison.[10]

Susan Moir had been born in Ceylon into a Dutch-Scottish family with a tradition of colonial service. When she was four her father died and the administrators of the family's estate made little provision for the widow with her three children. Returning to England, Susan's mother became dependent on the hospitality of relatives and remarried to regain some kind of economic security. Susan's new stepfather aspired to the status of country squire. Reports that the Canadian northwest coast needed families of good British stock induced him to take the family there: first-class passage, in the baggage a rosewood piano, silver candelabra, and porcelain figurines. When the family reached Fort Hope in 1860, Susan was fifteen. They met contractor Walter Moberly, had credit with the HBC, and moved among people of upper-class background. The prospective squire, however, had more pretensions than capabilities. Within a year the family was broke and moved into a windowless shack; in the summer of 1864 the stepfather deserted them.[11]

Susan worked as a governess and moved in with her married sister in New Westminster. She saw no prospects in Hope because the Cariboo road to new "gold mountains" bypassed the town. To build an infrastructure to the town, the Royal Engineers had been called in but became a burden because of "the costliness of their provisions and of their transport," their parading and their consumption patterns. They did not even finish a survey and Governor Douglas contrasted them to the Natives, some of whom "shewed remarkable cleverness in sketching out a map of the route [to Similkameen], marking the rivers, mountain valleys, passes & buildings."[12]

Another immigrant in Hope, John Fall Allison, saw as few prospects as Susan. His father, a surgeon from Leeds, had settled his family in Utica, New York, but they could hardly make ends meet. John preempted land for ranching in Similkameen and developed a working relationship with the Natives. He broke even, but had no savings to help his struggling father. In 1868, forty-three-year-old John and twenty-three-year-old Susan married. At the ranch, John's partner, who did not want a woman around, left. In July 1869 Susan gave birth to a child, the first of fourteen. Four years later, the family moved to the Okanagan valley. Susan learned Chinook; she sewed shrouds when Natives succumbed to an epidemic; she met Métis "outlaws," perhaps rebels against an unfeeling society;[13] in the cold winter of 1879–80 she was sympathetic to the plight of the Indians. "Chief Joseph" of the Nez Percé "was really a good man, fighting ... for his people's rights." "The Indians are good to those of kin to them."

Twelve years later, in Princeton, John kept cattle and Susan kept store. For Christmas they invited local miners, including three Chinese men, who lived in an old cabin of theirs and helped by building fences and getting firewood. Most of the social contacts were with the local Natives. Once, the roof of their house caved in from the weight of snow. In another winter, when their house burned down, Natives alerted neighbours. All kitchen utensils had been burnt and one of the children suggested baking the Indian way, rolling the dough on flat stones. A year or two later, American cattle thieves stole their livestock, then a flood washed their house and ranch buildings away. "We made the big stable comfortable and even managed to entertain such of our friends as passed our way. Soon we had another garden started, though we missed our well established asparagus bed. But the currants and gooseberries flourished as well as ever." Susan Allison, who concluded her reminiscences at this point, seems to have remained a gentlewoman throughout her life. In contrast to her male relatives, she and John did not squander anything, never ran from losses. They rebuilt their lives, raised their children, received visitors, held public office.[14]

Chinese, Japanese, and East Indian Newcomers

The Allisons never judged by colour of skin. They could distinguish their neighbours by culture: Blackfeet, Chilcotin, Fountain, Lillooets, Similkameen, Flatheads, Okanagan, Shuswap, and others. They valued the work of their Chinese acquaintances. In general, however, sojourners and immigrants from Asia were lumped together as "Orientals" with clearly racist undertones. Contrary to the East European "Galicians," who had lived together and shared experiences, the arrivals from Asia came from different cultures and spoke distinct languages. No bonds united the several peoples, only ascribed traits and discrimination forced them into the single category of Oriental Others.[15]

Walter Moberly, civil engineer and contractor on the Cariboo road through the Fraser River valley, "could not get a sufficient number of white men" as workers. With government funds for wages overdue, he made a special effort to raise money to pay his white workers. However, "indebted for clothes and other necessities," they broke their contracts to join the gold rush. Like entrepreneurs, they had decided to work for their own profits. Moberly was obliged to contract one stretch "to a body of Chinese" and compelled "to employ, much against my wishes, a large force of Chinese laborers." In his words, "the bad faith and unscrupulous conduct of the white laborers was the cause of the employment of Chinese labor." He quickly formed a positive image; he found the Chinese "worked most industriously and faithfully." When they asked him to buy some pigs for a feast, he did so at his own expense, "I was so pleased with the way they did their work."[16]

About 1910 a British observer commented on the Asian immigrants in Vancouver. Chinatown stores displayed "weird-looking eatables" but perhaps served "wonderful dishes" inside.

> Celestials here belong to the lower classes, shopkeepers or labourers, but occasionally one sees a richly dressed lady walking along the street with a couple of children, all wearing beautifully worked silk coats and wide trousers; blue and black seem to be the favourite colours, and sometimes rich patterns are embroidered on them in brilliant hues, but always very tastefully.

Chinese men worked as cooks, domestic servants, gardeners and launderers (washing "excellently and very cheaply"). Japanese immigrants lived in a different quarter on Powell Street. A Hindu, "meek and inoffensive" but holding his head high, was treated "with silent contempt by most of the 'superior race.'" "Look at the medals on his waistcoat; he has rendered valiant service to the Empire of which he is a citizen as much as any of the others, and he finds it hard to be treated as an 'undesirable alien.'" The Punjabis, Sikhs, and Pathans had been told of high wages and a climate similar to their home regions. Neither was true and, worse, they were treated by Canadian authorities and Irish-Canadian labour leaders as the Irish had been treated by the English. "They must have had a severe shock as to the interpretation of British law and fair-play." High-handed authorities and underhanded white workers mistreated Orientals on the assumption that "they can make a living where a white man would starve." Sending their savings to China or Japan, they "spend next to nothing in this country." Employers welcomed "this influx of Oriental labour as being cheaper than white," and easier to exploit. This support for immigration had the same motive as employers' opposition to emigration in Britain – it "enables them to get rich quicker."[17]

For middle-class society "the servant problem is a very serious one out here, and in this respect the Chinese are a real boon." Rich families could afford to import British servants, but they would marry and leave, or prefer to work in stores. Even an elderly woman servant of a young immigrant couple, whose forebears had served in the family for generations, married three months after arrival in Canada and left without notice. Thus, "those who can afford it can get a Chinaman ... and most excellent servants they make." However, ordinary folks had to economize and took but "a share" in one servant, who "goes round a number of houses ... doing the 'chores.'" Another observer commented on the duplicity and clear-cut racism. "No Chinese or Japanese were to be employed in working the timber" on government leases, but the very same leases were sold "to vague 'American interests'." In a logging camp, the Chinese cook was sober while all loggers, of self-styled superiority, were drunk.[18]

In their life-writings, Japanese,[19] Chinese,[20] and Sikh[21] immigrants discussed the discrimination. Bill Hong, who came from southern China in 1912, and Masajiro Miyazaki, who came from Japan in 1913, were brought over in their teens by their fathers who had been in Canada before. Bill Hong, a railway worker, became a mining contractor, and by the late 1920s, he was an entrepreneur with a mine, two stores in Barkerville and Stanley, a cafe, and two trucks. He took care of his father and stepmother, probably through the labour of his wife, and after the death of the mother, paid for his father's visit to China. But he was often in debt; he and his wife Fay, "don't spend a nickel unless we have to." In winters – again like Veltri and Alm – he took odd jobs, such as sawing wood.[22]

Masajiro Miyazaki lived in Vancouver's Powell Street Japanese neighbourhood, where his father had experienced the 1907 riot. Leaving Masajiro in Vancouver, his father left for the Skeena to work in the canneries. The community was well equipped with stores, boarding-houses, restaurants, and a bath house. Masajiro went to school and became a janitor boy, like Ukrainian and Polish children in prairie schools. In summers he worked in saw mills, sometimes with his father. Japanese women would take in washing or do housework for the men. Masajiro remembered "Hindu" (probably Sikh) neighbours with their temple on First Avenue. An Anglican Japanese Mission offered child care. Sometimes he taught English to new immigrants.

He applied for naturalization in 1924 and as a student at the University of British Columbia, he had recommendations, but was denied on a technicality. He wanted to be a doctor but his career path was not easy. Queen's University "wrote to me that non-white students can't serve as interns at university hospitals so can't graduate." Accepted at a small college in Kirksville, Missouri, he lived with relatives and worked as waiter. Like James Gray in Winnipeg, he caught glimpses of the other side of society. "I saw social life of rich aristocratic Americans while working at the St. Louis Country Club" at debutante parties with "50 extra white coated Negro waiters." After graduation he found a job in a Los Angeles hospital, in the Mexican district. Back in Vancouver in 1930, Masajiro Miyazaki opened his own practice on Powell Street, working closely with Japanese immigrant midwives, one of whom also operated a rooming house for Japanese women. He helped organize a Japanese newspaper, the *New Canadian,* and acknowledged the openness of the Saskatchewan CCF government under Tommy Douglas towards Japanese-Canadians.

In response to discrimination, the Japanese community had early become "a complete unit." Japanese women had arrived independently, others came as "picture brides." Love letters were written by hired persons who knew how to write: "They wanted me to say good things about their life in Canada" so that fiancées would indeed come. Banks began to hire Japanese clerks to get the community's business, just as establishments in Timmins had hired Finnish clerks. The community was doing well until war was declared in 1941.[23]

A second Vancouver Japanese-Canadian centre was the fishing community of Steveston. Men on the boats and women in the canneries remembered very hard work. "When I came [in 1925] I was almost six months pregnant. It was in July, fishing season, so I started work in the cannery almost right away." Moto Suzuki did not mention the birth of her child, but she remembered that they received their wages only at the end of the season in November. Work varied between one hour and endless days depending on the amount of fish caught. Shifts were regulated by the tides, the whistle would call the women whenever the boats came in, day or night. "There was a *mori* house [day care] where the mothers would take turns looking after the kids when we went to work." In the 1920s "one bathhouse served many families and we each took turns getting the bath ready for everyone because it took such a long time to heat the water. Later, each family built their own bath."

Like Chinese road workers, Japanese fishermen recalled tensions with white men. After Japanese fishermen had formed a labour union, the white men's union was opened to them in 1900. But a strike lead to racial violence; the Japanese fishermen considered the white union's demands too high. More importantly, they could not afford to lose part of the season, since their families had to live the whole year from one season's income, while the striking white fishermen could work elsewhere in between seasons. The tensions may reflect the family situation as well as racism. Settled married families, in this case the Japanese, have different interests from mobile unmarried men. Japanese men and women who left their protective community in search of other jobs had to suffer the hostility of Euro-Canadians.[24]

A third way of life was to be found in the logging camps. Maki Fukushima, like British gentlewomen, came from a family whose fortunes were declining. She shared the dream of going "to America" and making money. Her future husband had emigrated from a neighbouring village a decade and a half earlier: "I didn't know what kind of man he was, but I was happy as long as I could get to America." What might sound materialistic in terms of modern notions of romantic courtship was normal in Japan, as in many European cultures, where marriages were arranged by parents, often without consultation of groom and bride.

Maki Fukushima's first shock came when, upon arrival in 1914, she learned that Canada was not America. Her husband met her in Victoria, bought her "an outfit of Western clothes," and the next day took her to his tie-making camp near New Westminster. There she had a second shock: "It was such a filthy place." The bunkhouse had cracks in the ceiling. "What a miserable place, there's nothing like this in Oshima, so how can there be one in America." No time for complaints, "there was work to do right away"; she had to cook for the whole crew. Her intense desire to return to Japan ended in "complete resignation." After a stint in Steveston, her husband moved her to Port Alberni, Vancouver Island, where he ran a logging camp with his brother. The two wives cooked for forty men – outside "in the rain and snow." The investor miscalculated and the two contractor couples and the workers were broke at the end of the season. "Every time I read those letters [from my family in Japan] I cried." In between, she began to raise two children and gave birth to a third. But during a visit to Japan she had to leave all three with her mother, as she had to have her hands free to work in the camps. Later, her husband worked as gardener, she as a housemaid. Their employer family was friendly inside the house, but outside in public view, distance was maintained. Then the employer campaigned for public office: "He asked my husband to stop gardening for him, just during the campaign. He must have thought it was a handicap if people saw that he had a Japanese working for him." Her husband never returned to work for the man. In 1927 Maki brought her children back to Canada. "I settled down and never thought of going back again." Acculturation had crept up on her imperceptibly.[25]

Billboards and Orchards: Orientals, Bohunks, Englishmen

For some women and men, like Maki, dreams about a materially secure life induced migration. For others "the lure of advertisements, skilfully done on ... [CPR-paid] billboards, was well-nigh irresistible": they presented productive mines, inland lakes and orchards, a New Canaan. Under the influence of the advertisements, C.L. Cowan, missionary-to-be for the Scottish Presbyterian Church of Canada, made his decision to cross the ocean in 1908: "Scotland was then agog over the novel [by Ralph Connor], *The Sky Pilot.*" A travel agency clerk in Switzerland "saw all the beautiful posters: grow apples and get rich." His money got him only to Hamburg, the North Sea emigration port. After a year's work he continued to British Columbia. During a visit home, his sisters "decided that he needed a wife and I was it," Ruth Beguin recalled, assuming she was selected as being young and strong. Farm chores began immediately for her. The straight road to a better future described by the CPR, sky pilots, and people winged by dreams was often hard to travel. Winnie Carson's parents reached the Lardeau-Duncan area in 1916 by paddle-wheeler. They were put on shore late one evening, and left there "with thousands of mosquitoes" for the night: father, mother, and three small children. Kootenay Lake people joked about big expectations and of hardy pioneers; in fact, people settled because they were too poor "to move on."[26]

Others came without billboard fairy tales into internationalized labour markets, like the "young Englishman from Cornwall, going to get work in salmon business at New Westminster." Arnt Arntzen, a sailor from Norway like John Johnson, jumped ship in New Orleans just after the 1907 depression, jobbed his way up the Mississippi, reached Winnipeg in 1912, and took a job in railway construction along the Upper Fraser. Two hundred men were dropped off near Jasper to be marched to bunkhouses in the wilderness. Arnt and a partner set out for themselves to a camp about sixteen kilometres below Tête Jaune Cache on the future route to Prince George, where thousands of men were working on the grade. "They had a sawmill there and a crew of carpenters who were building scows. They'd load those scows with thirty, forty tons of freight and four men would float them down the river with the current." The scowmen got "big wages."

Arnt Arntzen, who had been a sailor with an arctic skipper on an English seal-hunting cutter, on an ore boat plying the Narvik to Rotterdam route, on a German tramp freighter in the North and Baltic seas, and on an English transatlantic steamer, took the job as Fraser River scow captain. On each end the scows had "a big oar, with two men on each one" to keep them pointed down the current through rapids and chutes. "Green crews" would stay too close to the shore where big trees hung over "and quite a few men got brushed off." Scows shot towards rock walls at forty kilometres an hour. Either the men turned the scow in time or they smashed up. "There was no chance of swimming. Once you were in that water you'd had it." A lot of men drowned. "Of course, men were cheap. It was the freight that the company was worried about."

After two seasons, Arnt moved to Fort George which consisted of the HBC trading post, a big hotel-saloon, a few scattered houses, and a tent colony. "But in anticipation of this big boom that the railroad was supposed to bring ... real estate promoters were staking out hundreds of town lots. Some of the promotional literature had more railroads and industry coming into Prince George than Chicago." Prince George was "a tough place" because of graft: "the local politicians and judges were in cahoots with the saloon keepers." The police would arrest railway workers for drunkenness and gambling, "haul them into court, ... fine them thirty-five dollars and costs." Running into the arms of the law was certainly more costly and less satisfactory than ending up in the arms of "some of them ladies."

Railway camps "housed men worse than you'd keep cattle." When typhoid fever broke out in one camp, government inspectors and a doctor blamed it on impure water. "We had crystal clear water coming right off the mountain" but "filthy conditions" in camp. "The I.W.W. came up and their walking delegates tried to organize the camps." Arnt joined, "had a card and thought the I.W.W. was pretty good." But over time he realized "that there was no chance for a revolution."[27]

Dreams of a "productive and profitable fruit ranch" brought people from across Canada and Europe to the Lardeau-Duncan region. Their goals proved elusive, since the Okanagan valley where a few decades earlier life had been so difficult for the Allisons, was more fertile and closer to major markets. "My folks came here about 1910 from Alberta," said Steve Sawczuk. "They immigrated from the Ukraine in 1900 and their first stopping point was Ontario," then Alberta, then British Columbia where his father was cheated by a land agent. He had to pay a second time to begin fruit ranching in 1905. Winnie Carson's family, who could not make ends meet in Saskatchewan, settled in Argenta about 1916 among French-Swiss and Swedes. The father hired on in a lumber camp and was home only on weekends. When he contracted typhoid fever, the mother, in addition to caring for the children, cooked for the men in a logging camp. "Eventually Dad got hold of a piece of property and built a log house, dragging the logs from the bush with a harness on his own shoulders." In 1919 a school was set up.

"The children would do the janitor work and the men would cut the wood for heating. The community built the school." The fifteen children "were all nationalities, Polish, English, French."

Many men ended up in logging. Maitland Harrison came in 1908 and lived with his crew in a tarpaper cabin. Another outfit "went broke and had a terrific sale. They had dozens of teams of horses and all kinds of equipment. I got a team from them and quite a little bit of equipment ... One cutter was a Canadian from the East. He had an Italian partner and they cut together. Our teamster was a Swede. Our cook was a little Irishman." In 1928, when only cottonwood was left on their land, "a chap called Dvortz started the veneer works at Nelson" and sent a crew of six Swedes to get the trees out. Even during the Depression "everyone had a job. We were running our camp, paying our men." The small pole-cutting contractors in British Columbia remembered with some puzzlement the high demand for poles in the United States; it was the time of rural electrification and expansion of telephone lines.[28]

At this time, the Maglios, too, had reached modest success in the Italian community of Nelson. Domenico Maglio had left his village for America in 1890. He shovelled coal in New York, took odd jobs, made it to Canada as a navvy, then worked in a Nelson smelter. His fortune came through a lucky chance. He fell in love with a successful French woman who owned a local hotel. He became hotel manager and saloon owner, and he called her his wife to conform to norms during a visit to Catholic Italy. However, the relationship fell apart. In 1912 Domenico again visited his home village, Monto Fredino. At forty-seven he wanted to find a bride and, guided by a dream, the twenty-two-year-old Gioconda Bartolini consented to marry him. In Nelson, Domenico owned a hotel jointly with a Swede who, according to the Maglio view, held a jaundiced view of Italian friends who frequented the place. The Maglios sold out, opened a grocery store, and soon owned several rental properties. With Domenico's health and mental capacities declining, Gioconda took over the property management, though her old-fashioned husband had planned a purely domestic role for her. The Maglios never fell for the orchard propaganda, but ran a little gardening business as a sideline. Montreal's Mile End Italians would have felt right at home.[29]

The 1920s English element was represented by Edward Fitzgerald Fripp and Irene Shadwell. She was a trained nurse, he, slightly disabled in the war, had received the standard advice to try "open-air life." With the support of the Soldier Settlement Board, the two left for Canada in 1920. They expected to prosper, their families expected more. To their surprise, empire settlement was many-cultured; on the ship were

"Bohunks," a Belgian Jewish factory worker destined for Montreal, and a Dutch preacher who wanted to escape a Europe "going Bolshevist" and planned to grow peaches in southern Ontario. For Edward and Irene, the scheme meant an impoverished life. After a year's separation as waitress and farmer's help, they began to farm in the Okanagan valley but the harvest of 1922 was poor.

The discontented Fripp, like James Walker in Winnipeg, reflected on the sad state of the imperial economy, the British government, and on race and class. He considered English people superior to anyone else but, he had to admit, they were so arrogant that it would come as no surprise if Canada left the Empire. The uncaring imperial government had filled the fruit-growing areas with officers "axed" from the Indian army, provided them with shacks only, and forced them to compete for a livelihood with peoples "of alien speech and ideals," including "a bunch of Japs." Competition by New Zealand in the fruit market undercut his and Irene's labour. "Agriculture," he pontificated, "is an ancient and honourable profession." Yeomen farmers should be better rewarded than bricklayers, should command more respect than a bank clerk. It was wrong that a butcher could own a car while a rancher could not afford one. A gas-pump attendant instructed him in capitalism: "Old John D. Rockefeller has just endowed a new institution, so he's had to boost the price to get his money back." Irene and Edward were caught between classes. They brought their fine silverware and once ordered a dress for Irene from England while at the same time barely able to live off their casual labour. Similiarly, a former officer of the Dragon Guards had descended to brush salesman, and another from the army in India worked as garbage collector.

The social and economic contacts of the Empire's immigrants were decidedly non-English; Edward worked in a logging camp operated by a Finn with Poles and Swedes which made him "the only white man." The Finn, to Fripp's bafflement, "was both an exceedingly hard, conscientious worker and an ardent Communist." Irene had to do domestic work for Canadians. As farmers the Fripps received advice from their Chinese neighbours, and learned about financial arrangements from a labourer. The Chinese had caught "the democratic spirit" and refused to work more than ten hours a day. He recognized that their hired Chinese man was "a gentleman." English women, in contrast to Canadian women, worked in the fields, "endeavouring to fill the shoes of Chinamen whom their husbands could not afford to hire." Reversed gender roles, ethnic mixing, and couples from the imperial centre who ranked below colonials made it a complex world. Fashioning a new world view did not get easier when Fripp saw "Chinamen," unlike the yeoman agriculturalist, exploit and exhaust the soil but succeed. "You may make it, if you watch what those Chinks do. They're the guys that know."

Finally, like many "who had been on a farm at one time," Edward and Irene drifted to Vancouver to earn a "precarious livelihood, though always in the hope of something better eventuating." Irene took a florist's job, Edward was tricked by a man of "a rather Semitic cast of countenance" into paying for a correspondence course. He avoided a stock-peddling scheme and sold vacuum cleaners instead: "They're as good as a real flesh and blood maid, and, what's more, they don't talk back to you." He obviously lacked some of the sophistication of either pedlars or Eaton's. In Vancouver, the Fripps could have met the family of Chan Sam who faced similarly complex worlds between a Chinese and a Chinese-Canadian culture.[30]

Intercultural Lives: Families and Unions on the Skeena

The Wicks family at the North Pacific Cannery on the Skeena river was among the few immigrants of European origin in a community that was Native and Asian. Though not quite as lonely as the homesteaders, it was even more isolated. The story of this family is a strange case of ethnic ascription. A Frederick Wicks, first mate on a German ship headed for South America, died on board. To avoid legal and administrative entanglements, the dead man was buried on the high seas and the captain gave his position and papers to the second mate, the Polish Boyki, who remained Frederick Wicks for the rest of his life. He became a Northwest Coast tugboat captain, obtained a night watchman's position at a cannery after an accident, and briefly visited his place of origin, Danzig/Gdansk, in the mixed Polish and German ethnic territories on the Baltic coast. There he met a widow, seventeen years younger than he, with two boys. They fell in love, or – the way the reticent Fred would describe it – took a liking to each other. In 1900, a year after he returned to his solitary two-room framehouse on the Skeena, the future Mrs Wicks left her job at a sugar-beet factory and followed with her boys. The tears in her eyes upon arrival at the Skeena may have been less due to seeing the loved man than to the utter loneliness of the place.[31]

When the cannery workers came back to the Skeena in spring, a labouring and fishing community formed, in which "mother," the only name we have for Mrs Wicks, had to get along. She was a strong woman: in Danzig she had once knocked down a man who beat his wife. The two boys, the younger of whom wrote an autobiography, picked up English and taught the mother, using for reading material the Montreal *Family Herald*. The two brothers also learned words from Native languages to communicate with their school friends. Mother learned some Japanese to be able to talk with the only other couple who wintered at the cannery. Pidgin English or Chinook, a creole language combining Native languages with Spanish, French, and English, provided the main means of communication. Cultural misunderstandings did occur. The German boys, for example, were proud to be given a bow and arrows by their friends but lacked skills. On first trial they shot another boy in the face. The Canadian teacher lacked understanding. Oblivious to the cultural significance of bows to the Native pupils, she confiscated all of them, broke them, and burnt them in the classroom stove.

In summer, the cannery community consisted of whites and Japanese, among them, in 1913, the father of Masajiro Miyazaki, and, for several years, Ryuichi Yoshida. A Chinese crew did the can-making and crating under contract to the "China Boss," who took part of their wages. Native families came from Haida, Tlingit, and inland groups. Some were picked up by the company tugboat, others came down the Skeena in cottonwood canoes, the Haida in cedar ones. The men fished, the women washed and packed the salmon. Living and working with them, the Wicks family was able to get beyond the generic "Indian" and understand the different cultures involved. As in Nordegg, the community also contained marginal men, such as Doctor Bolton, his helper "stuttering Hans," and Brazilian "Portugee Tom," who was said to have left his home after his wife had died in childbirth.

As to cultural contact, Natives looked down on the hardworking Japanese, considering them greedy. The thirteen-year-old Walter shared a boat with a Japanese man when he had to begin to contribute to family income. Paul, the older brother, teamed up with a Chinese boy in the cannery. Ryuichi Yoshida organized a Japanese fishermen's union. Whatever the disagreements among the many-cultured men and women, they were united in their hatred of the cannery owners' exploitation. A 1993 exhibition concerning Native lifestyles confirmed this: "In the cannery, we became really good friends with everybody, like the Whites and the Japanese and everybody." Joint protests forced one company to take down signs indicating segregated restrooms for "White" and "Indian."[32]

From 1904 on, when railway construction to Prince Rupert began, the occupationally homogenous and ethnically heterogeneous community was filled with "foreigners": Swedish workers, French-Canadian and Finnish tie-cutters, Chinese cooks. The Wicks family moved to Prince Rupert, and the two boys married in 1913 and 1915. The family faced wartime anti-German measures. Walter lost his job and had to register with the police, but Paul, a telegraph operator, was protected by his boss. The brothers' English-origin wives were sneeringly asked why they had not married "Britishers."

Compared to homesteaders, the family was wealthy. During his years of solitary living Wicks had accumulated savings. He enlarged the house and the family even acquired a German-English dictionary from Vancouver. According to Walter's autobiography, from the moment of arrival the family settled in as smoothly as Adolphus Gaetz had done in Lunenburg, Nova Scotia. As a watchman in year-round employment, the father held an elevated position of trust in the multi-ethnic community and had a "straight" income.

Ryuichi Yoshida, Japanese immigrant and union organizer, had been born in 1887, in what is now Chiba Prefecture. He had studied law, but, failing the exam, decided to go "to America" in 1910. After brief stints as gardener, railway worker, and mill labourer, he began fishing in Steveston. Two fishermen worked in each open boat and lived for a week before returning to shore. They slept and cooked in the front, with only a canvas protection from the weather. In the back, they stored fishing gear and fish until the collector boat came for the catch. They lived by the tides, not by day or night. When Yoshida came to the Skeena, some twelve hundred Japanese and about the same number of Native fishermen worked there. Their yearly income was not much, being limited to the salmon runs, but their seasonal income was high, at least as measured by the low living expenses. The fishermen's Japanese bosses were considered "respectable," with wives who cooked as well for the crews as farm women did for threshing crews.

In the Depression years, Yoshida remembered, prices for fish did not go down much – they had always been low. He worked in lumber camps in winter, only once in a "white camp," since most camps were strictly segregated. Japanese fishermen repeatedly went on strike against cannery owners. Canadian authorities sometimes intervened by deporting strike leaders. A Japanese gambling-house owner, on the other hand, owing to ties to the Vancouver white civic leaders, did not have to face RCMP intervention.

To counter the anti-Oriental movement, to cut loose from the conservative Japanese Association directed by businessmen and the Japanese consul, and to fight the cannery owners, Ryuichi Yoshida and Etsu Suzuki organized the (Japanese) Labour Union among workers from many trades and published the *Daily People*. As union organizer, Yoshida criss-crossed British Columbia. He had married in 1922 and a daughter was born a year later. But his family life was quite different from that of the Wickses. The Yoshidas and Etsu Suzuki with his partner, the independent-minded, "modern" Japanese poetess Toshiko Tamura, temporarily formed a communal living arrangement. Both men earned little and as union activists had no prospects of being hired. To the distress of both women, union meetings involved considerable consumption of sake. Ryuichi did change his lifestyle when his wife fell seriously ill and he had to take care of their daughter. Toshiko Tamura formed a friendship with one of the Powell Street midwives, perhaps the same one with whom Masajiro Miyazaki worked.

Ryuichi felt that the Labour Union, whose strength lay in the Skeena fishermen, did not achieve much. Of about six thousand Japanese workers, only some sixteen hundred joined. The union faced the hostility of the Japanese Association and the Euro-Canadian labour unions in addition to that of employers. In the 1930s, the CCF broke ranks with "white solidarity" – as Yoshida pointedly noted – not because they liked the Japanese but because they were ideologically opposed to racism. Once Yoshida had decided to involve himself in the labour struggles, he took Canadian citizenship. He worked for cooperation with the white unions and wanted the Nisei, second-generation Japanese like his daughter, to decide their own lives without being indoctrinated either with Japanese culture (which he valued for his own generation) or with loyalty to an increasingly militaristic Japan. In this respect the Yoshida and Wicks families shared the same views.

Conflicting Cultures, Complex Lives

The trajectory of Chan Sam and his wives Huangbo and May-Ying Leong as well as their children reflected the complications of rigid Confucian prescripts for child-parent relations and of one man holding together a family in both China and Canada. Canadian exclusion laws, decisions about family economy and status in village society, and finally civil war and the advent the Communist government, truncated relationships. When Chan Sam left Chang Gar Bin village in Kwangtung province in 1913, his decision for the future seemed to be clear. Upon departure he wore Western-style rather than Chinese clothing. His link to the past was equally evident. He left behind a wife, Huangbo, and a daughter. In China he had cultivated his land "and prayed to the Gods that he could keep starvation from his doorstep." What for the Fripps had been the European civil war of 1914–18, for Chan Sam's family was the civil war in China after 1914. In Vancouver the Chinese peasant worked in a shingle mill and slept in a bunkhouse. Contrary to the Fripps, he had no imperial mentality but, like them, he had a status to lose. In accordance with Chinese customs he decided in 1924 to take a second wife and by negotiation, bride price, and papers of a Canadian-born Chinese woman, May-Ying came to Vancouver. Her husband treated her to a dinner and at its end told her that the restaurant owner was her new boss and for the next two years she would have to work off the cost of bringing her over.

As a waitress she "was considered to be almost one and the same as a prostitute"; men stared at her, but she learned to entertain customers without permitting them to take liberties. Each evening she returned to the shop that Chan Sam co-owned. She was torn between the tea-house role and the honour of being a shopkeeper's wife. Chan Sam was torn between expenses in Vancouver and in Chang Gar Bin village. He saved every tip that May-Ying received and carefully husbanded their incomes. Like the watchmaker Hemsley in Montreal, he lived in penury. The scarcity of women after the exclusion law of 1923 meant better wages for waitresses, who had to be young and beautiful since no tea-house could stay in business without them.[33]

To solve his problems at the Vancouver location, Chan Sam opened his own business and May-Ying began to work there. In 1926 and 1928 two daughters, Ping and Nan, were born to them. In business May-Ying was the better host and thus could talk back to her husband. At the village location in China, problems loomed. He had not told Number One Wife of May-Ying. When others did, he decided to return in style with his Vancouver family. Their work made him the richest man in the village. He introduced new ideas, including schooling for May-Ying. She, too, introduced new ideas, refusing the customary subservient position of a Number Two Wife. When she was pregnant again in 1930 she insisted on returning to Canada. Chan Sam assented but left both daughters with Huangbo. Under depression conditions they could not find a job and another daughter was born. So May-Ying left Chan Sam and went to Nanaimo to work as waitress again. Chan Sam pursued her and a new arrangement was negotiated. He took care of the baby and received all her wages, while she made her own decisions. Thus she supported both the Nanaimo and the Chinese village family segments. Then May-Ying went into gambling, particularly mah-jongg, and she felt ever closer to the men who paid her compliments. She suggested that Chan Sam return to China, where he was enraptured by the vision of a larger house. "As the house began to take shape [in 1935] villagers and workmen alike saw it as a testimonial to the man himself." May-Ying enjoyed her independence but remained tied to custom, sending her wages to Chan Sam in China. In 1937, the year Japan launched its attack on China, Chang Sam once again returned to Canada. Over the years, May-Ying continued to lead her own life, and Chan Sam quietly worked wherever he found a job. The stress led May-Ying to alcohol and ever more gambling, the revolution in China made Huangbo and the big house the target of communist cadres. The third daughter, Hing, in Canada, had to straddle the disconnected worlds of her parents and two sets of cultural norms. Winnie, as Hing called herself in school, became a successful nurse and married – another transition completed. While the Chinese Empire crashed, as did the British to which the Fripps had been attached, her daughter re-established connections to the family in China.[34] The migrants continued their lives in the local life-worlds that were so much more important for them.

PART SIX

Discrimination and Exclusion, 1920s–1950s

The breaking of the Winnipeg General Strike in 1919 and the War Measures Act of 1914 to limit freedoms of native-born and immigrant Canadians alike cast a shadow over society. Working-class immigrants feared deportation, labour organizations feared disruption. Colonization like that of the Peace River District was hailed as part of a frontier spirit, but settlers were reduced to ever more marginal lands on settlement "fringes" distant from market connections. Discontent with economic conditions in the 1920s and even more in the 1930s, as well as the feeling that neither provincial nor national governments acted in the interest of the people or even knew what was going on, resulted in an extension of local political involvement to the national level. The Canadianization that had almost imperceptibly grown upon people resulted in conscious self-organization and protest. Initiatives by agriculturalists had been hailed under "golden sheaves of wheat" rhetoric but initiatives by workers were branded "communist agitation."

Immigration came partly in response to industrialization. But ten years after the Royal Commission on Relations of Labour and Capital, Sifton in 1899 still had wanted to admit "None but agriculturalists, we do not recognize the labourer at all." Sifton's successor, Frank Oliver, added race as a factor for exclusion. None should be admitted that would "deteriorate ... the condition of our people." While the British-Canadian political elite pronounced racism to be their creed, capitalist employers were willing "to buck the nativist consensus when it advanced their own profits."[1] In the 1920s the government subsidized passage for those entering designated sectors which were suffering labour shortage, and these men and women were forced to go to their assigned destinations with no private initiative permitted, even though jobs were often not available.

Fabulous profits, on the other hand, were realized in stock-market speculation. In 1929 the stock market crashed and with it the hopes of millions of men, women, and children, twisting their life-courses into unrecognizable shapes. A few speculators took the easy way out, jumping out of Wall Street windows. But most women and men shouldered the responsibility for families, and struggled to restructure their lives. Some found niches and their initiative helped them survive. Social workers and nurses, clergymen, mothers, and local political activists had to tell men in government what to do.

In Europe, fascist and authoritarian regimes came to power. In Italy, Mussolini took over in 1922, in Poland, Pilsudski in 1926, and Germany, Hitler in 1933. When Europe's refugees, Jews in particular, began to arrive in Canada, the racist bureaucracy lacked any sense of compassion.[2] When the *state* of Japan entered the Second World War, *people* of Japanese descent in Canada were deported to internment camps. Hungry and desperate Canadian unemployed were sent to camps or clubbed by the once respected RCMP. Since few of the men, women, and children had anywhere else to go, they had to cope with the hostile host society.

CHAPTER EIGHTEEN

From Dislocation to Politics of Protest

In continental Europe, dislocation from the First World War, hunger, and postwar economic havoc sent many to North America. Prospects for life-courses remained in limbo, as for example, for the Dziuzynski family. In August 1914, Carolina Dziuzynski's father was drafted into the Austrian army. The family had to evacuate their home, leaving livestock and crops behind. In some places, officials would give them food, elsewhere they were reduced to begging. Even people willing to help "would tell us to move to a different place, as we were a burden to them." From the Lwów district they trekked to Nowy Sacz, already overcrowded with refugees; the residents, later to be refugees themselves, called them gypsies. Trains freighted them to Limanowa. There, among the mass of humanity Carolina's twelve-year-old brother was separated from the family. A year later, shunted to Nowy Sacz again, the grieving family found him in the care of an uncle. During further treks, a sister was lost. The Red Cross located her years later in Berlin. After the war, the family reassembled in the destroyed home village and two years later left for western Poland. In 1926, Carolina and friends used the domestic help immigration scheme to leave for Canada.[3]

At the same time, Great Britain tried to rid itself of demobilized, often disabled soldiers, "surplus women" without husbands or jobs, and labourers deemed superfluous. The Empire Settlement plan, which brought some one hundred thousand people to Canada, was used to keep the colonies British, the Anglo-Saxon and Celtic "races" dominant. Ex-soldiers were provided with land under the ever-repeated medical advice that outdoor work would invigorate them. Educated women were sent to civilize colonial society as governesses and nurses. Lower-class women were exploited as domestics. The importing of harvest labour was described as a scheme to fill CPR ships and trains. About 185,000 immigrants came under the Railways Agreement of 1925, lured by misleading posters and pushed by intolerable conditions at home.

The 1917 and 1924 exclusion laws of the United States directed migrants to Canada. Persecution of the religious and substantial farmers (kulakhs) in the new Soviet state sent people on the move. Dislocation reached as far as Syria, where the brutal French occupation caused villagers to emigrate. Push factors intensified, the trip to North America became more complicated, treatment on the receiving side more degrading. Distances to be travelled increased. Mennonites and Russian-Germans from the Soviet Union no longer booked their trip directly via the ports of Bremen and Hamburg. They travelled to Moscow first, then moved to Riga, then by Baltic liner to England. Poles travelled via Gdansk and Liverpool. A few fled eastward to Harbin in China and came via Shanghai.

Immigration from Asia continued, racism notwithstanding. Chinese migrants had to pay an entry fee or head tax, from 1885 on, which was raised to one hundred dollars in 1900 and five hundred dollars in 1903. Japanese immigration was restricted by "gentlemen's agreements" in 1907 and 1928. South Asian de facto exclusion came in 1908 by administrative provision. About sixty-six thousand men and women from Asia lived in British Columbia and other provinces by 1921.

The Chinese Immigration Act of 1923 effectively ended migration: it was an exclusion act or, as aging Chinese-Canadians came to call it, an extermination act, since the ethnic group would die out. While in everyday life Asian and European immigrants found ways to get along with each other, whether in cooperative or conflict-prone relationships, gatekeeper elites expressed racist positions ever more openly. For example, the Royal Commission on Chinese and Japanese Immigration in 1902 declared migrants from Asia "unfit for full citizenship," "obnoxious to a free community," and "dangerous to the state." The Asiatic Exclusion League, established in 1921, became the major racist propaganda league.

Postwar Dislocation and Canadian Immigration Controls

Nineteenth-century British immigrants described officials at the ports of entry as friendly. Scientific pronouncements on the low "racial" quality of the newcomers and germ-laden aliens changed attitudes. Poles on transit in England were singled out; as one said, I had "to be disinfected and most of my clothing was ruined by the disinfectant. All the men had to have their hair shaved off." In 1910 "ruthless immigration officials" did not even accord them a minimum of respect. They sent back migrants after health inspection: "wives separated from husbands and children from parents."[4] German John Grossmann, who had marked "no religion" on his form, was questioned by suspicious immigration officials.[5] Anna Baerg, travelling in 1924 from a Mennonite colony in southern Ukraine via Libau on the Baltic Sea to Antwerp, had her hair inspected for lice. During a "Canadian commission" examination, "We were herded like common criminals from one enclosure to the next." Of the approximately thirteen hundred people, sixty-four were held back "because of parasites or sickness." On board ship, second-class passengers had the crew restrict the deck space of the immigrants; below Quebec City a further inspection seemed like "an auction where we are items to be auctioned off." Dejectedly she commented: "As an immigrant one must make allowances."[6]

The Canadian government gave financial assistance to men who registered as farm labourers and women registered for domestic service. In the stagnant 1920s, many migrants did not want to take either occupation but had no other means to reach Canada. Police accompanied the migrants on westbound trains to see that they did not leave before reaching their assigned destination. Albert Kolber, in 1927, "was tempted to jump from the train in Montreal, then in Toronto and Winnipeg." He did reach Edmonton, where the newcomers were "accommodated overnight in barracks." Stanley Brzyski was sent to Saskatoon in 1926: "I had the address of my wife's uncle who lived in Winnipeg. When the train stopped there, my friend and I got off and hid from the police." When Carolina Dziuzynski and her friend Julia wanted to get off the train in Toronto, where Julia's aunt lived, police shoved them back on. "Rumours were, that Western Canada was shivering from the cold and lots of snow, similar to Siberia," to where czarist governments had sent Polish rebels. In Winnipeg, a Polish priest and a German woman advised the frightened domestics to acquiesce, continue westward, learn English, and work until their contracted time, usually six months or a year, was up. Carolina was placed with a shabby, disorderly family with ten children. She left, worked for a Polish family, left again, and worked in a Calgary hotel until she got her bearings again. She became active in community affairs and married a Polish man. The odyssey, which had been forced upon her by war in 1914, lasted for a decade and a half.[7]

Those who reached their destinations had to deal with conditions that were the opposite of what Irish immigrants in the 1840s and Scots in the 1870s had experienced. Tomasz Opalinski and a friend reached Mannville, Alberta, one evening in 1928: no bed, no washroom, thousands of flies. "We were very uncomfortable under these filthy conditions," and they spent the night on the sidewalk. George Biedrawa and a friend "did not have the courage to go and knock on a door, so we slept in an empty box car." They did receive help from the Edmonton immigration office. A CNR employee helped Frank Linkiewich to find "other people who could speak his language."[8] The government's attempt to manage migration, in order to overcome a shortage of labour in the worst-paying sectors of the economy with the worst working conditions, gave prospective migrants support to cross the Atlantic. But after their arrival it stifled personal initiative and help among their fellow ethnics. The selection policy at departure was not matched by a placement policy at arrival, the government support for employers not matched by equal support to workers.

Four decades later, when the White Paper of 1966 and the Immigration Act of 1967 were under debate, potential employers stressed their demands for unskilled mining and seasonal harvest labour. In the changed climate of opinion, the minister of manpower and immigration, Jean Marchand, categorically answered: "I am not prepared to enslave immigrant workers who have come to Canada ... If the working conditions are poor, or the wages too low, they will move to Toronto or Montreal ... We cannot enslave them." He adamantly opposed chaining immigrants by contract to a particular place of work.[9]

Empire Migration: Surplus Women and Demobilized Soldiers

Since the late nineteenth century, ideologues of Empire had intensified the drive to send out cultured women and strong men to provide the colonies with people assumed to be superior to immigrants from other cultures. Periodicals such as *The Imperial Colonist* and *United Empire: The Royal Colonial Institute Journal* were among the most outspoken advocates of the civilizing and empire-building role of women, or, more exactly, of "surplus women," those who could find no husbands in England and who could not contribute to national wealth at home, given traditional gendered spheres, roles, and wages or incomes.[10]

Marion Cran, in 1909, and Ella Constance Sykes, in 1911, toured Canada to gain first-hand experience of the demand for and the working conditions of servant women and independent farming women. Cran travelled on free railway passes, Sykes could afford to ride Pullman cars. Their ideological frame was the English people's "small but warm corner" of their hearts for the colonies and "pride of possession" – four decades after Canada had achieved Dominion status – coupled with rather "vague notions" of everyday life. Traversing Canada from Quebec to British Columbia, they reaffirmed their preconceived notions of class. Proletarian women were incapable; middle-class were fair or pretty or beautiful, "warm and proud," and talked eagerly about happy lives. They preferred "this healthy, busy land" to "the hectic life of Paris and London," where those who stayed would be "wearing their futile lives away on the social treadmill."

The Canadian domestic treadmill paid low wages: fifteen to thirty dollars a month plus board. Ella Sykes, who hired on as farm help, did not last long in any position. For fifty cents a day she would have to cook, wash, clean, and look after the children. Dairying work and feeding large harvest crews came in addition. A Miss Darlington, in the London *Morning Leader*, had noted a few years earlier: no English general servant "would stop a day in a situation where such work was required of her as the Canadian farmer requires of his wife." Young women worked on their parents' farms as "hired men" but without wages, "the call of the prairie" turned out to be "the call of the kitchen." One English family for whom Ella Sykes worked discussed whether she should be permitted to eat at the family table. She, in turn, did not like to sit at the same table as the hired men. Attitudes had not changed since "Emigrant Lady" in 1870s Ontario had been appalled to have to share her table with labourers and servants.

The issue of the emigration of women hinged on opportunities and independence, and neither Cran nor Sykes realized the inherent contradictions of their proposals. "Servants are hard to get in Canada, and when found very expensive, ill-trained and independent," they noted, but they wanted educated and independent women to emigrate. Nurses and doctors were needed, "sensible, skilled women," but Canadian physicians' organizations refused to license women. Women should become independent homesteaders and poultry farmers, but they did not advocate changes in the homestead law to give women the right to file for land. In practice, given the marriage market, most women would probably marry quickly rather than fill the positions assigned to them.[11]

Lower-class servants did come and Nellie O'Donnell, born 1907 in Tipperary, was one of them. As an illegitimate child, she had been a "surplus" person at an early age: sent to foster parents, returned to her mother, sexually abused by a shell-shocked and drunken stepfather after the war. Neither mother nor priest gave her any support. The parents used her as a maid and stopped her from going to school, so she ran away. A farmer treated her brutally. When she was twenty she left for Canada. On the boat a minister started to lecture her "about going to another country and about my church and about this and that." He shut up when told that she was Catholic. The young people on board became friends with each other and were sad to part at the end of the trip. Ella Sykes, from her perspective, had been "rather horrified to observe how free-and-easy became the relations of the men and maidens ... [in] what I imagine is the fashion of the servant's hall." Arriving in Toronto, Nellie O'Donnell was unexpectedly on her own. An aunt "wanted nothing to do with" after she heard of the illegitimate birth.

Nellie was critical of the Canadian government for "bringing boatloads of us out ... from Ireland or wherever" and "putting us in awful jobs." She, too, had seen inviting CPR posters but experienced hostility. As a maid in a big house with several servants, "I had to stand at the end of the table, wait while they ate, and serve the next course." One evening, after a fit of sneezing, she was dismissed on the spot with a remark about Irish people not understanding anything about Canadian germs. In her next job she had to answer a doctor's phone but was let go because of her Irish accent. In a third job her employer, a businessman, tried to assault her sexually when his wife was out. Though the Depression had come, she found a job in a laundry. "If you really wanted you could find jobs that the Canadian people didn't want." Her initiative was punished. Since she did not work as a domestic, the Department of Immigration asked her "to refund the difference between the reduced rate and the full third class fare." She was unable to pay.

For protection from deportation she married. Her husband, an Englishman, hit and abused her. Pregnant and working in a factory, she kept "well laced up" on advice of her forelady, who kept her on as long as possible. That the baby was not a boy infuriated her husband, who became even more abusive. She fled. A supportive woman placed her with the baby as housekeeper to a Kapuskasing businessman with three children in return for room and board. Drunk, her employer raped her; her husband abducted the baby daughter. Acquaintances rallied to help; she snatched the baby back and got a divorce. Still in Kapuskasing, a friend proposed to her. "He had a steady job and I had the feeling that I would have a home and security." But he did not want the child, so she refused him. Respecting her courage, he changed his mind. They married and moved to Timmins, where Aili Grönlund and John Cameron also lived and worked.[12]

Demobilized British soldiers like Edward F. Fripp, often somewhat disabled, were sent out to the Prairies or British Columbia to settle and support themselves. Some prewar emigrants had returned to Britain for military service and came back both wounded and married, like Harry Strange with his wife Kathleen in 1920. Peggy Holmes's husband, an emigrant of 1911, had served in France and returned in 1917 partially disabled. She joined him in the first contingent of war brides.[13]

Robert Collins's Irish father had come to the prairies in 1912. He could still afford to buy a prefabricated house from Eaton's when, at the age of thirty-seven, he married a much younger American woman. He served in the army, was gassed in the trenches, and came back to the farm 75 percent disabled. There, Robert was born in 1924. At the beginning of the Depression the family was reduced to haywire for repairs and flour sacks for clothing. Pinned down on their land, they considered the visit of an uncle "entertainment of the highest order."

The emigrant and soldier remained attached to the Empire. When King George VI and Queen Elizabeth passed through Moose Jaw, the family travelled the hundred kilometres and left their cows and chickens – "a vital part of our 1939 food and income strategy," – unattended. For fifteen-year-old Robert, Moose Jaw was "a glimpse of the world."[14]

Peggy Holmes was considered by her husband's friends to be as "green as grass. She don't know nothin'." Women noted: "She's one of them English war brides that's tooken our boys." Trying to help with the milking, she could not even distinguish one cow from another. She was city-bred, and had been educated in Hull, England, where, inspired by her suffragette grandmother, she had become the first female bank clerk. In Canada, her husband found work in the CPR freight yard. "By this time the glamour of the returning war hero had disappeared, and the ex-soldiers were left to struggle as best as they could." Engulfed by hostility, she found support where few would have looked for it. "My first friend was the Chinese cook, Wong. When I felt hopelessly down in the dumps he would comfort me, saying, 'Don't worry, missie. I fix you nice Chinese food. Me homesick, too!'" Similarly, the Scottish harvest worker James Walker, down and out in Portage-la-Prairie, received help only from a "Chinaman." This, he remembered, set him thinking.[15]

Peggy and Harry Holmes began to homestead in Alberta's Ashmont district in 1921 among Ukrainians, French Canadians, and Métis. The shack Harry had lived in before the war had been pilfered and burnt down and they used the shack of a homesteader who had given up. While trying to come to terms with reality, they watched discouraged homesteaders tramp by, leaving them their few belongings – a team of horses and a wagon-load of "junk and tools, bear traps, etc." – in return for a suit, a pair of shoes, and a few dollars. They planned a whole farm but earned a living by cooking for a harvest crew; they intended to build an English-inspired two-storey gabled house but when winter came, they lived in a tent inside the empty frame. When accidents occurred or when women were pregnant, the homesteaders could not afford a doctor. With a licensed midwife the situation would have improved quickly, but male doctors, supported by the government, had pushed women out of this role. The Powell Street Japanese-Canadian midwives were as bitter about this as were their English sisters. When Peggy Holmes became pregnant, the couple returned to town. She later became a successful broadcaster.

The experiences of Kathleen Strange, in Fenn, Alberta, were similar. She and her husband bought second-hand furniture from departing farmers. They wanted a California-style bungalow and were cheated by workmen who considered them rich. Kathleen was willing to tackle whatever had to be done, but lacked experience. Going to haul lumber for the bungalow, she did not know how to balance the load and how to direct her team uphill with the heavy wagon. Slowly and with setbacks, the couple made out well by going into seed grain. Although comparatively successful, they, too, after frosts or other mishaps hoped for "next year." The labourers and acquaintances of the Stranges formed a mixed group. Kathleen became friends with a Chinese restaurant owner – after, as she admitted, she got over her snobbishness. They employed English immigrants who fitted well into life on a Canadian farm. A Vancouver solicitor, on the other hand, who had lost a lot of money, came as harvest labourer "to lose his identity and to earn sufficient money to keep himself going." Kathleen observed the daughter of neighbours who, when taken back by her parents to Russia, realized that she had become Canadianized and returned to Alberta by herself. Kathleen shared the experience. Called back to England to care for her sick mother, she realized that she no longer liked the old society. At the onset of drought in 1927, her husband took a job in Winnipeg in agricultural research. She reluctantly supported the move, knowing that city life would reduce her sphere to homemaking.[16]

Immigrants from continental Europe had similarly discouraging experiences. John Grossmann, class-conscious and critical of German bureaucrats and politicians, had been discouraged by stagnation and unemployment. In 1929 homesteading was a philosophy made of hope, adventurousness, and a longing for independence. The odds were against the marginal homesteaders.[17] Grossmann, like other homesteaders, frequently worked for wages to accumulate a starting "capital." Homestead women would hire on as cooks with surveyors' crews, while they avoided the rough bunkhouse men of railways. One observer had commented: "It is self-evident that any place on land or sea that is unfit for women is equally unfit for men, either from a moral or sanitary point of view."[18] But no improvements were forthcoming.[19] British Empire Settlement migrants, like the dislocated from continental Europe, had to accept land in ever more marginal areas. Peggy Holmes and Kathleen Strange watched men give up, saw women "bushed," knew that doctors were far off. Migrants who settled the Peace River district of Alberta and British Columbia, in a worldwide perspective, were part of a "pioneer fringe," as contemporaries called it, which attracted Chinese to Manchuria and Mongolia, Russians and Ukrainians to Siberia and Transaralia, immigrants and internal migrants to Brazil's forests.[20]

Itinerant Labourers, "Communist" Wages, Hard Times

In addition the Empire migration projects, harvest labour was recruited. Marion Cran regretted that English urban workers were not fully equipped to labour on the soil, and other observers did not understand that this work would last for two, perhaps three months if weather permitted but that unemployment lurked in winter.[21]

James H. Walker in Scotland and Nellie O'Donnell in Ireland shared many experiences. Both saw the numerous CPR posters, both saw depressingly high unemployment, both felt that emigration might deplete their countries of young people. Walker and two friends, a clerk and an engineer, contrasted quota policies of the United States with the carefree CPR invitations to fifty thousand harvest hands at four dollars a day. The three young men left in August 1923 believing in a male-centred traditional emigration discourse: "Canada might make a man of me! So many people had used that phrase." On the ship they dreamed of their future in terms of the full four dollars *every day.* Passengers with more experience bluntly stated that they would not be able to stand harvest work and painted "a sombre picture of labour conditions in Montreal." In Quebec City, tenements and ramshackle houses caught their attention. "Was it possible that there were poor people?" Working-class housing figured neither in CPR brochures nor in the voluminous literature on Canada that James had devoured as a boy.

On the westbound train they fed themselves from the standard but expensive box lunches while being told by oldtimers, men out for the second time, that they had fallen for a CPR scheme to fill its boats and trains. In Winnipeg, James stayed with friends of his mother, who suggested that he look for a city job rather than go stooking for "lousy Doukhobors" and "Bohunks!" The pioneers on the prairies who were producing Canada's staples did not receive much recognition for their contribution to the national economy from those who considered themselves to be the elite of the nation. James was still unperturbed. Impressed by the number of automobiles and the manifold activities – a big difference to the slow life in Scotland – he and his friends continued on to Portage-la-Prairie.

There they encountered unexpected conditions: no "poster farmers" but "hard-faced real men," farm kitchens with electric light that compared to Scottish suburban villas but farm families' clothing that compared to that of the Scottish poor. Hired at $3.50 a day, they proved unable to keep up and were thrown out the first evening with only $2.50 each. The town overflowed with men fired from harvest jobs scurrying about for food. The next job paid $2.50 a day. Immigration officials magisterially stated that they had nothing to do with CPR promises, that the four-dollar wage was a "communist" demand and that strikers were "slackers" too lazy to work.

Walker nailed down a three-dollar railway job but had difficulties in getting along with the many-cultured "foreigners." He had no concept that, in Canada, he was a foreigner. He witnessed ethnic conflict: a Russian straw boss under a Welsh foreman fired an Englishman, where upon all the British workers went on strike. The Welshman then fired the Russian. Illness brought Walker back to Winnipeg and into contact with more Canadian "foreigners" – a Jewish doctor, a Lancashire Jew, a fat Jewess, a Scottish woman by the name of Slowacki, a Polish waitress, Chinese. "Bohunks," he finally conceded, were "perfectly harmless."

Walker discarded his hopes for high wages and avoided considering himself a failure by taking the side of imperial employers and turning on those "agitators" sticking up for four dollars. "Shipping the discontented population of Britain to the Colonies," he opined, did not solve social problems, since they brought their grievances and "extremist politics" with them. "Glasgow's troubles were now going to be Winnipeg's." Hearing a man tell how he set fire to his employer's haystacks after being cheated out of his wages, Walker commented: "These men were the raw material with which wars were fought and continents settled ... 'Survival of the fittest' – old Darwin was right." He felt that he was getting tough himself. "I was growing up and becoming a man!" After a stint in Montreal and a job in a rolling mill, he procured a job on a cattle boat with the help of a bribe and returned to Scotland. His was a brief and not very successful visit to Canada as a rite of passage to manhood.[22]

Three other men – Stjepan Bradica from Croatia, Iver Lassen Andersen from Denmark, and Albert Eskra from Poland – arriving in 1926 and 1927, did not have the option to return home, be supported there, and write a book about it.[23] Bradica was a labourer, Andersen wanted to get ahead, and Eskra planned to farm. Bradica, on a contract for a job in Winnipeg, found that he had been deceived – there was no work. After hanging around with friends at the railway station for two days, a policeman told them to get out and take a bath, but he did not tell them where. Stjepan wired relatives in the United States for help and they sent sixty dollars. Hungry and cold, the men walked eastward along those tracks that had carried them westward on an empty promise. At Fort William, they found no Croatians and lodged in a Ukrainian boardinghouse. The next day, in Port Arthur, countrymen "treated us nicely, fed us and put us up in a bedroom" – a change after sleeping on station floors or benches.

Such experiences – a fake contract by a Canadian railway and help by immigrant countrymen – made ethnic clustering rewarding and Canadianization difficult. The Petrone family who lived in Port Arthur at that time achieved both. The father's work life was Canadian, the children's education Italian. While Mrs Petrone could become an apartment-house owner, her daughter Penny Petrone could not enter the English-Canadian better classes.[24] Since Bradica spoke some English he was selected by the "unemployment office" to make up a gang for track work, while non-English speakers who had milled around for days didn't get this chance. On the train to the job, the Croatians were bullied by a conductor, who "menaced us with the fear of deportation to Europe."

A Ukrainian foreman placed the Croatians with experienced men "so that we could learn the nature of the work." For several weeks things worked out well. But with the cold season approaching, they daily watched trains full of transient workers – an internal eastbound migration. They, too, moved off. Approaching Sudbury, some jumped too late and ended up where police were waiting. They did not mind; to be locked up meant shelter and food. The others continued to Hamilton and Oshawa for factory jobs, which, in 1927, were still to be found. The internationalized segments of Canadian labour markets, particularly those for seasonal labour, were unable to provide steady jobs. Those who found work did so through ethnic networks or on their own initiative.[25]

Iver Andersen reached Alberta full of confidence. He went trapping and worked as a carpenter. Letters from his family and Danish newspapers helped ease the separation from homeland and kin. His belief in success survived his realization in 1927 that some hundred Danes in Edmonton "had no money, many were begging in the streets." Men starved to death, "there is no social assistance here." He moved between Edmonton and Vancouver Island in search of jobs, logging in places similar to those where Maki Fukushima had cooked for crews a decade earlier. At first he shared British racial attitudes. Russian and Polish workers were "dirty and thieving, ... even more despised here than Negroes and Chinese." The Vancouver "Chinese, Japanese or Hindus ... work for almost nothing." But Iver approached immigration and labour supply from a perspective diametrically opposed to that of the Briton, James Walker. According to the Dane, too many came "from England, and the English immigrants are everywhere considered first. They are good for nothing, but England tries to get them in all the important jobs, so that they can help to tie Canada to England, because [England] is afraid [Canada] will become independent, just as the States did earlier." In this perspective, men like Walker were not proving their masculinity but picking the plum jobs while holding forth about survival of the fittest. Andersen changed his attitudes, "I live with a Japanese, get my clothing washed and fixed by a Chinese, and eat in a Greek restaurant, that's Canada." He remained in an optimistic mood: "I haven't saved much but I haven't suffered either and now that I know the language and the conditions, now I am going to make money." But cracks began to appear in his beliefs. He advised countrymen not to come, saw wages decline, observed profit-hungry employers, and noted that work is "considerably harder than in Denmark." To save his view of society, he remained an individualist: the discontented did not want to work, "a man can do well here and save money if only he will work."

Some evidence supported his optimism. First, individual initiative was possible: any worker was free to quit whenever he found a better job. As contractors, workers became their own bosses. Secondly, class distinctions were fewer: "you don't have to stand with your hat in your hand for anybody." People in workman's overalls and finely dressed ladies and gentlemen ate in the same places and talked to each other. He shared Edwin Alm's experience: "It is the working-man who is somebody and counts for something." On roadwork in Toronto and Sudbury another migrant observed bosses actually working and considered this "practical socialism." Thirdly, rags-to-riches opportunities were still available. A Dane who had started from scratch now employed two hundred men. The abundant harvest of 1928 gave him hope to make enough money to buy himself a suit – his clothes had been stolen in the first winter and since then he had not been able to afford new ones.

Newspapers reported in 1929 that rioting workers in Edmonton were dispersed by police with "teargas bombs." In Toronto police fought protesters at the doors of the provincial legislature; according to another British observer, the confrontation was the fault of "communists" who held a meeting "against police orders." Work was almost impossible to find. At this point, Iver's courage, hope, and view of society broke. "It is terrible to have to be idle in the city [of Vancouver] ... I stay in bed and read ... You get depressed ... when you are forced to do nothing ... if only the work hadn't stopped I could have made good money." By 1931, after a sawmill accident, his mother sent money and asked him to return. "I am not coming unless I can pay for it myself." Opportunities? "If there is an accident [in saw mills] they don't stop at all, just push him aside, and another one can start." A country, where workmen count? "They threaten to send them back to where they came from." Canadians blamed the immigrants, did "not care for foreigners," sneeringly asked him whether he had learned to sign his name and whether all Danes ate raw fish. He blamed the big steamship and railway companies and the "huge swindles at the stock exchange" for industry's standstill. "The police is terribly brutal." The family in Denmark never heard of Iver again. He died, but not in a saw mill or other accident. He analysed societal conditions, joined the Communist party, supported the Vancouver strike against camp-confinement for the unemployed, and was active in the Ottawa march of 1935. After ten years in his chosen country, he volunteered to fight against fascism in Spain. There he was killed during the Ebro offensive on 17 August 1938.[26]

At that same time Albert Eskra, who had come from Poland to Alberta, lived through "the year of the worst crisis." He was very different from and yet in some respects similar to Andersen, who came with an education and dairying skills. Eskra came with little education but a blacksmith's training. Both young men were ready and able to work. While Iver's world view crumbled in Canada, that of Albert had been destroyed in the wartime Poland. Depending on who was in power, Albert had fought for the Austrian Empire, was a tsarist Russian prisoner of war, was told to fight the bourgeois Polish government, and was sent to fight against Soviet Russia. His siblings had joined the worldwide Polish diaspora: two brothers and a sister were in the United States, another brother in Prussia. The Polish government, like the German, offered marginal land for colonization but his application was rejected; too many applied for want of any other possibilities to earn a living. When Eskra reached Prince Albert, Saskatchewan, in 1928, he had no resources except one friend.

He and his chum did not find farmers who could afford to hire both. A cold spell ended his first job after two days; the Polish farmer could no longer feed him and sent him off with fifty cents for two days' work. The farmer's wife secretly added another dollar and food. The women in this family worked like men but were not as stingy. On Easter Sunday, at church nobody talked to him. The only soul who recognized his plight was a "Chinaman." By sign language he hired Albert for three days of dishwashing and paid cash. Next came stump-clearing with Russian-speaking Poles for a dollar a day plus board. He appreciated that "nobody is standing over him." He met English people, French Canadians, and Doukhobors. Most settlers in the Blaine Lake region were East Europeans, spoke Russian regardless of ethnicity, and went to the Polish or Ukrainian church. When Albert showed up for Sunday service again he was no longer a stranger. Farmers and their wives discussed their hired hands on the phone.

During harvest no farmer offered a four dollar wage. Over winter, he settled in with an unmarried young Polish farmer who cared for his elderly parents. With no wife to share his work, he hired Eskra at five dollars a month plus board but could not pay. Thus, at the end of his first year, Albert had survived but saved nothing to either start farming or open a blacksmith's shop. He was one of the many rural proletarians neither established in village crafts nor the urban working class. His life project was flexible: he would travel any path that local society and the regional economy would permit him to take.

From April to November 1929 Albert did well, clearing about $450. Using his economic and social capital, he set up as a blacksmith in a shop vacated by a Czech. The local Polish storekeeper and his French-Canadian wife, informed that Albert was "being looked over" by local women, acted as self-appointed matchmakers and arranged the marriage of Albert and Anastasia, a local widow's daughter of Ukrainian origin reputed to be a good housewife. Economically, disaster loomed when Albert lent his small capital to a farmer who defaulted and the customers at his smithy could not pay. Nevertheless, his and his wife's good reputations as workers helped them. She was skilled, judicious in making decisions, and ready to take on or learn jobs considered to be in men's domain. But even after harvest work for two French Canadian, taking in boarders, and blacksmith work, they had to spend the winter of 1931-2 on her family's farm. Albert was dejected; it seemed that the Depression economy offered no path forward. He, Anastasia, and their baby daughter survived, but only in the family economy of her relatives. It had been to avoid such dependence on his own family that he had left Poland.

Albert's brother-in-law recognized both the need for additional family income and the need for Albert to make himself useful. He suggested that Albert use his skills to make grain boxes, which he could sell for $25 when Eaton's charged $45. Anastasia and Albert, now with two small children, used their networks to move to a farm near Drydor in March 1933, the shack being raised in winter when neighbours who had free time were on hand to help. Anastasia cultivated a garden to make the family independent of store-bought food. Neighbouring women gave chicken and eggs, and later piglets. Albert worked on the farm buildings or did blacksmith's work for neighbours. Little or no money circulated. Time worked and machinery lent were the means of exchange. The only problem that Albert remembered was the priest in town. He asked for a $10 contribution to the parish, when Albert and Anastasia owned a total of $1.50 between them. When Albert explained the situation, the priest called him "a Communist and Bolshevik." Labelling, once ethnicized, now was also politicized. The wrong label or unemployment could mean deportation.

The Eskras' farm buildings expanded. Anastasia learned carpentry, and, could drive a nail like a man, as Albert respectfully noted. But there were now six children, and a bank loan which had not been repaid. For taxes, the government took labour in lieu of cash, but banks did not take time worked as instalments on loans. Like the Durieux or the Leveridge families, the Eskras never had any money, but always succeeded in improving their situation. Albert added the caretaker job of the neighbouring school to the chores he shared with Anastasia. Neighbours worked off relief cheques with road repair; Albert repaired the machinery, and soon had a balance due to him. The one area where they seemed to lack knowledge was in birth control. In a time of a surplus of labour and of machinery coming into usage, children's labour was no longer needed but they had to be fed. Family size forced – or induced – the Eskras to move again. They now needed two box cars for their effects, including an harvester and a sower. In the new place, they hired an Englishman with heavy machinery to do the stump clearing at fourteen dollars an hour, work for which Albert had been paid $1.50 a day. Anastasia as the agriculturalist and Albert as the blacksmith supplemented each other well. Between wage work paid in kind and toiling in the fields and with little money to spend, they accumulated property and credit with their neighbours.[27]

From the Regional to the National: The Politics of Protest

In the 1920s, poor living conditions resulted in the organization of province-wide and national political protest movements. Ethnic social clubs were adapted to defend a group's interest. Unions and the Winnipeg General Strike of 1919 brought workers together. In cities, where women could not grow food in gardens, where barter arrangements of payment were difficult or impossible, job programs or niches in the economy helped men and women to survive in times of crisis. Ukrainian unemployed workers organized themselves, others improved their assets on the labour market by their own efforts. But these immigrants found that neither mutual help nor local solidarity provided help against grain elevator companies, high railway rates, or the collusion of government and capital.

The oft-cited market forces were of no help to small people. Markets were global, access to them controlled by powerful corporations. The prophet of the invisible hand of the market, Adam Smith, however, had analysed the economy in terms of regional units, where entrepreneurs could react to each other, not in terms of distant capitalist interests, wars a continent off, or globalized markets. His was a world of producers and merchants, not of capital flows and commodity futures.

The life-writings of immigrants contain little information on larger markets or local labour struggles. Worker-contractors mentioned strikes as instigated by grumblers without cause. Edwin Alm joined the free-speech fights on a whim; Einarsson criticized unions as going "too far." He argued "that no one is obliged to work for lower wages than he considers his due, but I do not see that he has any right to forbid others, who have only a little, from working for lower wages." The immigrants were poor, had no craft consciousness to defend, but a survival to ensure. Their strength was the flexibility to take any job available. Starvation wages, however, were criticized repeatedly by contractors, labourers, and farm women alike, whether in the 1880s, in the 1907 depression, or in the 1930s.[28]

Willem DeGelder observed "juries" that arbitrated between farmers and hired men in case of wage disputes. Labourers, in his opinion, could get their rights. To the missionary Bickersteth, the mutual support of farmers indicated socialist leanings and he seemed surprised that neighbours helped when a local socialist was burned out. Farmers formed cooperatives, as did the four neighbours of Evan Davies who jointly bought a threshing outfit. Agriculturalists have been credited or charged with extreme individualism; as owners of their means of production, they are not usually considered part of the working class. But immigrant farmers often survived only by inter-ethnic solidarity.[29]

Problems beyond the local and regional demanded organization or use of the state apparatus. The railways had raised hopes and economic prospects at first in New Brunswick, then across Ontario, then they became a means for national unity in the 1860s. They had used up their credit by 1900. Like the elevator companies, they were unresponsive to local needs and could not be influenced by regional political action. Rural people voiced discontent about big business as early as the 1880s. The regulatory Manitoba Grain Act of 1900, and the Sintaluta trial after the mishandling of the 1901 bumper crop, were victories for organized farmers who formed regional grain growers' associations. Evan Davies, the Welsh homesteader, participated in establishing the Saskatchewan Grain Growers' Association "to demand a fair price for their crops." He served as delegate to the 1911 conference at Moose Jaw where it was decided to establish coop elevators. For Albert Eskra, it deserved no special mention that he sold through cooperative arrangements. Each farmer had a booklet in which his sales were entered; no bureaucracy was needed.

Two Norwegians, Ole Hjelt and his brother Andreas, reached the southern Saskatchewan prairies in 1908. As supervisor of a lumber company in Norway, Ole had come to realize that workers were exploited. He transferred his radicalism to Canada. In his fictionalized autobiography, he had several neighbours discuss life on the farm. The spokesman for religion, Reverend von Fabelberg (i.e., of fairy-tale hill), opposed education and free thought. Like so many other immigrants, Hjelt and his neighbours were happy that no nobility imposed hunting laws. Impositions, however, came from capital, land company agents, grain elevator companies, railways, and merchants. Banks, in particular, viciously exploited the farmers' need in years of poor harvests. In a down-to-earth way Hjelt described the economic interests and rivalries between men, the low attendance at church in times of pressing labour, the boasting of rich farmers. Education, free thought, and cooperation were his solutions.[30]

In 1924 Saskatchewan farmers formed the Wheat Pool, a cooperative marketing organization to give them some bargaining power in the marketplace that profit-oriented large private companies and the capitalist market economy could not and would not deliver. Farmers received an estimated initial payment after delivery of their crop; later total receipts were pooled and distributed among the members. The Pool added grain elevators to the marketing system in 1926. It published a newspaper, the *Western Producer*, from the press of which several farmer's autobiographies were issued. The Pool faced serious problems in the Depression years because its initial payments to farmers in 1929 and its purchases of supplies for the 1930 harvest had been too high.

Few of the farmers mentioned these activities in their life-writings. Many of those whose lives we have traced did not yet speak English and thus could not participate actively. Homesteaders on marginal lands remained in subsistence rather than market agriculture. For others, the daily struggles remained more important than any long-term strategies for improvement and control over marketing. The life-stories of Louise Lucas, a German-American immigrant to Saskatchewan in 1910, and of Tommy Douglas provide a glimpse of how the local became the national, the mutual aid a critique of the system.

Louise Lucas and her husband Henry wanted to be able to plan their future on their farm in Milestone, Saskatchewan, where they arrived with their two small children in 1910. The first crop looked good, until an early frost hit. The year 1915 produced a bumper crop and the war in Europe guaranteed high prices that farmers still talked about ten years later. In 1921 the postwar slump hit hard. A potential bumper crop in 1928 was destroyed by early frost. Thereafter it was literally dust rather than grain that the Lucas family had on its table. Next-year country became the-future-was-a-decade-ago country. Men and women who shared these experiences had begun to voice discontent by electing some sixty Progressives to Parliament in 1921. Since farm women were not reduced to homemaking, kitchen, and children, the grain-marketing cooperatives and producers' associations had women's lodges. Louise Lucas joined her local lodge and became known for speaking up when a Wheat Pool organizer at a public meeting used as his example a farming family consisting of "a man who had raised four sons." She was elected delegate for her district to the March 1927 convention in Moose Jaw, where the inequities of the capitalist banking system and the brotherhood of [wo]men were discussed, among other topics. Thereafter she became a featured speaker at many rallies.

Banks, railway companies, big business, and government "did things to men and women. Could men and women do things to politics" and the economic system? The self-help cooperatives decided to add political action to their agenda in 1931. Since provincial governments as well as the national one were unresponsive, a cooperation with socialists and the communist Farmers Educational League was arranged. Ministers spoke out in condemnation of capitalism.

During her speaking tours Louise stayed with families. She met heavy-accented immigrant farming families and the Empire's dirt farmers of the Soldier Settler schemes. She found internal migrants from Ontario who could not heat their house or provide food for their children. Men and women had to borrow coats and underwear to go out to her meetings. The provincial agricultural minister and other officials betrayed their incomprehension of the extent of poverty when they called the notion of starving farmers "ridiculous." Louise and Henry and their six children lived in the dry belt turned dust bowl. Each year they tried to keep their garden going; each year dust storms blew away soil and seed or parching sun killed the plants. There was not enough water even in deep wells to water the animals. This, the government professed not know. Its officials were of different mentality, different class, different ideology. A small rural newspaper did know. "If the nation is to keep the boys [and girls] on the farms of this country plans will have to be made to make farm life more attractive. To do this the farm home will have to be equipped for modern day life."[31]

When the government finally decided on relief measures, it opted for top-down organization. But people across the small towns objected. Relief was not to be brought in by Big Relief, like the Red Cross, which would buy provisions from Big Business. Relief funds had to be distributed locally so that local storekeepers handled the sales of provisions and remained solvent and able to feed their families. Many of the often decried middlemen like Helgi Einarsson and Gus Romaniuk, were part of the community, if they stayed close to their customers rather than focusing on their private profits only.

Tommy Douglas, after his Winnipeg schooldays, became a printer's apprentice and, studying at Brandon, a Baptist minister in Weyburn, Saskatchewan, not too far off from where the Lucas family lived. He distributed relief in this town where people knew each other, or so they thought. A lawyer from his congregation strongly suggested to him that he sever his connections with Weyburn's association of the unemployed. Tommy Douglas "took him around to some of the homes where there were children who couldn't go to school because they didn't have shoes or clothing, places where they had hardly enough coal, where they hadn't had milk for a week." Taken aback, the lawyer admitted that he had assumed such conditions to be part of the slums of London, "but for it to be happening in the town where I live, I'm ashamed that I don't know this." Just as James Gray and Joseph Wilder in Winnipeg had to take tours to see the section of the town where the rich lived, Weyburn's dignitaries had to be led on guided tours to the areas where the poor lived. Compared to Europe, class distinctions were fewer, and people helped one another, as Iver Andersen and many others realized. But when social spaces separated, "the system" kept some in wealth and relegated others to poverty, and the poor became invisible to the better placed.

In his job as a printer, Tommy Douglas had read much. To earn money he had worked as a paid actor-entertainer. Coming from a trade union family, he was interested in the One Big Union. At the University of Chicago in 1931, he saw fellow students drop out because of poverty and lived among the city's "75,000 homeless transients, mostly decent boys who had come from the same kind of home I had." "This is when I began to read and think and inquire why we were in this mess, ... what's wrong with this economic system." As with Louise and many others, the personal experience and the local poverty led to a systematic critique and to new visions of a better society.

The personal and the public, the individual and the system could not always be easily reconciled. One of Douglas's experiences may help to show why so many of the authors of life-writings seem to have concentrated on the local. A youth gang from the "little shacks on the outskirts of town," children of mentally retarded parents, of unwed mothers, and of broken families came up for sentencing. The sympathetic judge asked the minister for help. Douglas took charge of them, respecting their skills though certainly not condoning them. But one Sunday he had to go off to preach elsewhere. That day the boys interrupted their process of resocialization and broke into a store. Douglas was needed locally, personally, immediately. In this instant, the distant and the local were mutually exclusive. Later, he went into politics and became CCF premier of Saskatchewan. In that position, although he could no longer help delinquent boys in person, he could attempt to alleviate poverty and reform the system.

Louise Lucas repeatedly refused to accept assignments that would have forced her to travel because she had six children at home, but her province-wide activities kept her in the memory of many.[32] Others would have liked to become active, but were hampered by their lack of English or by government repression of foreign radicals. The provincial and national organizations that grew out of the local protest remained part of Canadian political life.[33]

CHAPTER NINETEEN

The Depression Thirties and Discriminatory Forties

For some immigrants the bad years began as early as 1927, but others found secure, if modest, niches throughout the 1930s. The export-driven pole-cutting industry in British Columbia remained expansive. By contrast, farming had to cope with drought in addition to depression. In many families, food was allocated not according to hunger but according to what was available. "[Wartime] rationing, when it came in 1942, was almost meaningless: our coffee, tea, sugar and gasoline had been rationed by circumstances for a dozen years," one family remembered. A few did not have to bother. The daughter of a British official on a cross-Canada trip in October 1929 unconcernedly noted, "There were thousands of stock exchange cables, because of some crisis on Wall Street." Equally oblivious to the crisis caused by the onset of the Depression, Canada's elite continued to advocate deportation of the unemployed and of those non-citizens advocating solutions other than capitalist ones.[1]

Depression Lives

In the 1930s an Alberta farmer "had neighbours who had only one pair of shoes for an entire family of five." A member of the local band did not show up at a wedding: "I found him crying; he was sick and he told me that he does not have a pair of pants to wear ... He told me that he was so depressed that if I did not come to fetch him, he would have done something drastic to himself. He was so broke, neglected and, as an old man over sixty, he was sick of everything, lonely and hungry."[2]

We will first look at some of the immigrants whom we met earlier. In French Quebec, many finally left their farms, Rémi Jodouin and Joseph-Phydime Michaud among them. Departing from his aging parents, Rémi went northward to the mines where he did well but saw others badly exploited. Joseph-Phydime, weighed down by debts, sold his Kamouraska farm in 1934 and moved cityward to become a factory worker. In Montreal the rabbi's daughter, Leah Rosenberg, married by her parents to an incapable husband, had to beg help from her relatives. Realizing with some bitterness that her parents had failed to prepare her for outside life, she mustered her courage, divorced her husband, took in boarders, and took care of her two sons. Moving from job to job, she felt that employers looked her over as they would a race horse before betting on it. In her words, the Depression "ate itself into the very being of people." "To be poor is to be powerless. Poverty is demeaning, demoralizing." In the prairies, the English miner, Bill Johnstone, shared the feeling. "We had produced enough food to feed several families" in a market economy, in which "we didn't earn enough to feed ourselves ... To me these were the years that destroyed men's souls; there was no dignity left in a man." Imploring letters written to Prime Minister R.B. Bennett from across Canada support this view.[3]

James J. Crookes, one of the Home children, felt abandoned. In Toronto he asked "a big, friendly Negro ... about work. He smiled and said 'Join the gang' and shook hands with me." He took Crookes to the Salvation Army. Carola Dziuzynski lived on the margins of poverty but did not go hungry.[4] Child labour received a new lease on life. Russian-born Lydia Litke recalled, "When the farmers ... heard that newcomers with children had arrived, they knew that the children were available for work for little money." During the first winter of 1929-30, she worked for five dollars a month. In 1931 her parents bought a farm for fourteen hundred dollars, indicating that the family was not poor. Both the teenaged daughters had to help clear land and cut trees for logs, and a brother had to hire himself out to earn cash.[5]

Life was not necessarily easier for those who had come earlier. Farming families who could not feed themselves from their own produce had to buy flour of cheapest quality. In shame, they concealed the sacks from the view of their neighbours. "If we raised anything, it sold for nothing. Shoes and clothes were the hardest to obtain." Arthur Stelter, in 1932, had to sell his crop "way below cost," but was able to buy a second-hand binder. Life meant a return to a subsistence economy.[6]

Young people who wanted to marry and set up for themselves faced great hardships, even with family and neighbourly support. Ernest H. Harvey married in 1932: "We learned to do without and to improvise." A bushel of oats sold for three cents, the price of a stamp for a letter. The couple grew their own vegetables, learned to cure and smoke ham and to tan hides for leather. They made and repaired harnesses. "My wife made her own soap and butter and canned Saskatoon berries, chokecherries, and wild high-bush cranberries. Money was almost non-existent. We bartered ... [For] taxes, I undertook to keep about three miles of road in repair. It was a hard, hard life."[7] Walter Chuchla volunteered to work in ethnic organizations and played saxophone at farmer's weddings. He was paid in produce, never in money. He had reason for fear. "At that time, some Poles were being deported from Canada. They were either on relief or were suspected of spreading communist propaganda." Anne Chuchla took in boarders but even so, at times the family was "penniless."[8]

The Depression broke relationships, but could also strengthen supportive ones. Relations could be endangered if communication became impossible; Bill Price could not write to his mother, as the cost of a stamp was beyond his means. In spite of real poverty, people still managed to buy from Eaton's. But "each scrap of string and brown paper" was saved and poor families sent Valentine cards made from scraps. "When the Depression ended and everyone bought Eaton's Catalogue Valentines we felt bereft." The effort that had signalled loving care was now commercialized.[9]

Even in the difficult years, some immigrant families succeeded in establishing themselves as small entrepreneurs. However, those who came in the 1920s with little or no capital had less success than those who had preceded them like Helgi (and Sara) Einarsson, Gus and Emily Romaniuk, or the Destrubé families. Czeslaw H. Chrzanowski, arriving in 1927, saved his earnings from lumbering, harvesting, and a slaughter-house job and, in 1931, invested it in a truck. The Polish community in Edmonton, building a church and a hall, needed him. "I cannot complain, we got something for gas, others worked for as long as a month without pay." Kaspar Halwa in the 1930s bought timber land and two trucks to supply the City of Edmonton with firewood for relief recipients. He and the other driver worked long days. "Much credit goes to my wife, Mary, who took care of the farm-yard and always had meals ready when the trucks stopped on their way to and from the city."

Joseph Lang, from a coal miner's family in Poland, worked underground from the age of fourteen. His wages being part of the family economy, he could not save anything for himself. His mother's brothers and sisters in Canada advanced his fare to join them. He ended up in a "very small coal mine in the Rabbit Hill area, 10 miles south of Edmonton," owned jointly by two uncles, a cousin, and a friend. "My hours were long and I worked very hard. I wanted to repay my debt." He slept in the mine's office and ate with an uncle's family. In the first winter they had to shovel through five kilometres of snow to permit farmers with their teams to "get through for coal." In 1925 his cousin returned to Poland and sold him his share for five hundred dollars – on credit, which he worked off within a year. By 1931, in ever-changing partnerships, the uncles and cousins opened a larger mine, employing thirty men. Joseph made enough money to live comfortably with Lucy Prohonig, whom he married in 1928. A sister helped run the mine's boardinghouse with about fifteen men. Tomasz Opalinski, who worked in a mine which the Lang family purchased from an Italian immigrant, remembered a more negative outcome. In April 1930 the mine "declared bankruptcy and I received absolutely no pay for this work period from October to April."[10]

Discontent was not only directed against provincial governments but also against particular officials. Dorothea Bublitz's husband had long been active in municipal politics and was chosen to distribute relief money. He angered some community members and his house was burnt down. The government of Canada targeted protesters. It jailed, clubbed, and deported rank-and-file immigrant workers as well as union leaders and suspected leftists. Following a pattern established during the Winnipeg General Strike, this was within the law, but as a form of intentional intimidation did not differ from arson. During the 1931 coal miners' strike at Estevan, Saskatchewan, police charged into a parade of strikers' families, killing three, wounding many, arresting more. Farmers and workers joined and organized unions and Farmer-Labour parties.[11]

Dustbowl Experiences

The dustbowl area of southern Saskatchewan was hit doubly hard. People's memories were marked by the years and the geography of misery and desolation. A pastor sent into the area did not give the name of his parish; he just noted it was near the centre of the dust bowl. After a storm, "there were great, ugly, empty patches in the newly sprouted crops." Some men continued to sow, some women to plant their gardens. Year after year they saw their labours destroyed by a storm in a few hours, by the burning sun over months. Farm animals could no longer be fed: "as their body resistance fell low, they were infested with lice ... There was no veterinarian: we couldn't have afforded one anyway." Time abounded, resources were scarce. "My father straightened and reused each bent nail. For a missing bolt he substituted a twist of haywire." Dried manure replaced firewood. "My mother was a virtuoso at 'making do.'" On a foot-powered sewing machine she made "shirts, dresses, dish towels, tablecloths, doilies, pillowcases and opaque windows for chicken coops" from bleached Robin Hood flour sacks.

All aspects of life changed. "Dust seeped under ill-fitting doors and windows." Even in the houses people had to wear handkerchiefs over their mouths. Nancy and James Sadler one spring day did their house cleaning. "That very night the wind got up ... [and] reached gale force." In the morning, "everything in the bedroom was covered with a coat of brown dust." As they got up, the sheets beneath them were white, but their "faces looked as though they had never been washed for years" and on the window-sills dust lay six inches deep.[12]

The Syrian Salloum family in southern Saskatchewan had one good crop in 1928, but thereafter "mother nature refused to send the life-giving rains." Neighbours abandoned their land, formerly self-sufficient farmers became itinerants searching for food. The Salloums were too poor to move. Like Irish, English, and Ukrainian women, Mrs Salloum had brought seeds from their home town of Karoun in the Biqa' Valley, strains adapted to a desert climate. The seeds grew and the family could feed itself. The desert conditions reminded Mrs Salloum of home. Nostalgically "she talked about the orchards and fields of grapes, ... of sunny climates and a land full of people." On the solitary homestead, visitors came but once or twice a year; she was tormented by a longing for her relatives. In the town of Gouvernor they met "a fellow Arab, Albert Hattum, from a neighbouring village in the Biqa' Valley," who farmed north of the town and knew of land for rent in the neighbourhood. The Salloums were able to extract but one crop from the dry soil in 1935, and they had to watch as Gouvernor emptied out and people moved off. In the 1940s the older Salloum sons entered the airforce and the family opened a restaurant in Neville.[13]

Immigrants as Itinerants

Those who rode the trains or wandered across the nation in search of work found life difficult wherever they happened to be, all their efforts and initiative notwithstanding. Phyllis Krommknecht from Germany followed her husband Ali to Canada on borrowed money in 1929. They had been unable to earn a living as workers in Berlin or as farmers on small plots allocated by the government in the eastern territories, thus "the basic decision to go seemed to make itself." The change from Germany to Canada – Ali left in 1928 – was small, a "feeling of strangeness really only came later, [when we] were both on the bum so to speak." Similarly, for Ebe and Hilde Koeppen the true uprooting was not leaving Germany but the loss of their Peace River homestead.

Ali's trip ended in Toronto because his money ran out. With his broken English and the deteriorating urban economy he could not find a steady job: only temporary work on a Manitoba farm, harvest work in Saskatchewan, then freight trains back to Toronto. "As far as we were concerned, the depression was already on in 1928." Ali did manage to rent a small furnished flat before Phyllis arrived.[14] His English improved quickly, and Phyllis learned with the help of "talking movies." Their best friends were a mixed Norwegian-Canadian couple and a Scottish woman. Phyllis worked in a chocolate factory, "a real babel of tongues. Everybody spoke a little broken English, some spoke Italian, others spoke Polish or Ukrainian," one girl Yiddish. When Phyllis found out that their wages of ten dollars a week should have amounted to $12.50, she wrote out a complaint in stilted English. In response, her supervisor shifted her to a different department. Compared to Berlin, Toronto appeared to her "a small and provincial town." In Germany people benefited from an incipient social security system, but in Canada "there was absolutely nothing." It was not much of a consolation that she met "socialists and other decent people" since they were few and "sort of isolated from anything to back them up."

By spring 1930 both were out of work. Ali left to "look around the country" for work and Phyllis searched for a job as a live-in domestic servant. Her Scottish friend Agnes helped with the language. One woman brusquely told her, "I wouldn't dream of hiring a German girl, I don't forget the war that easily." She did find a position and was happy to take care of four children and do the kitchen work. However, she had been pregnant when Ali left and after a few months suffered a dangerous miscarriage. Her supportive employers sent her to a hospital and invited her back afterwards. When she could not pay the hospital bill, the bigoted doctors assumed that they were dealing with an unwed mother and informed the Department of Immigration. When she received notification that deportation proceedings were in the offing, Phyllis left to join Ali in Sault Ste Marie without informing the immigration and deportation bureaucracy of a new address. Ali briefly held a cook's job on a tugboat, Phyllis "helped a very old couple ... But they were so poor that I was embarrassed to take their money." She looked after the children of a family who could pay but refused to, until she took the husband's watch as "security." Soon both were unemployed again, jolted out of even the initial stages of their self-willed acculturation. All they could do was to react at a time when they proactively wanted to chart a future-oriented life-course. Continuity was provided by their personal identities and struggles for at least minimal life chances.

After a few months of odd jobs in Winnipeg, Ali and Phyllis chipped in with two friends, bought an old Model T Ford, and headed for Vancouver. "While the weather was good it was a wonderful trip." The scenery more often than not consisted of abandoned farm houses, although the farmers who still held out "were quite willing to exchange a place to sleep and a meal for a few hours work." Stuck in a tent colony in Calgary's municipal park after an early blizzard, it was decided they would be better off by not clinging together but striking out separately. The two friends moved away, Phyllis used her last money to go on by train, and Ali followed by catching a freight.

"I arrived in Vancouver with twenty-five cents in my pocket and the soles coming off my shoes. They were tacked together with thread." Phyllis had to pawn their wedding rings – she was never able to redeem them. Three days later Ali arrived. Phyllis had taken shelter at the Grey Sisters Refuge, but they now bunked in with unemployed men at a dilapidated house on Wall Street. For food they dug clams, caught crabs, cooked nettles. In retrospect, Phyllis regretted that she did not plant a garden. Next-year country had become a hope for a job next month. They all expected to stay in the house only briefly. The men hiked out into the Fraser valley, got vegetables, took odd jobs, staged wrestling matches, anything that would get them a few dimes or food. Some of them went prospecting, but came back with nothing to show for it and looked "like skeletons." She and Ali got relief until a neighbouring woman told the relief office that Phyllis was "living with a dozen men." "Mrs. McCorky bragged about how she had fixed the bunch of immoral foreigners on her block." Phyllis remembered "pretty puritanical" lives. "For all our progressive talks about free love it was mainly that: talk."

"While none of us ever actually went hungry," there was never any money to spend. "But we enjoyed ourselves as best as we could." Ali told stories of his prospecting trips, others had library cards and read avidly. Most were of some kind of German background. One man, from better circles, kept a diary. Indiscreetly peering into it, another read: "I'm now living with some elements of the lower classes, but I'm not too proud of myself for it, especially when I sit down to eat with them." Immediately the group packed the author's belongings into his suitcase, left it outside the front door with the diary on top, opened at the incriminating passage. "When he came along later in the day the rest of the boys came out on the porch and stood there with their arms folded." Men with folded arms were part of working-class body language and labour movement choreography.

The fear of deportation remained strong. During a second dangerous miscarriage Phyllis did not dare go to a hospital. "We were technically vagrants," neighbours were complaining, petty government officials behaved "high and mighty." Then the unexpected happened: a steady job. Mrs Svensson, a friend of the denunciatory Mrs McCorky, understood that the living conditions in the Wall Street house stemmed from poverty, not immorality. Phyllis gratefully accepted a caretaker's job after three years of hand-to-mouth life. A few months later Ali found a steady slaughterhouse job. But respite was temporary. Within a year Ali, moving constantly between freezers and heating sheds, contracted tuberculosis. The doctor advised "plenty of rest, fresh air and good food." Making do came handy again. Using his knowledge from the prospecting trips the two moved to the Cariboo in 1934. After a few years they opened a small bakeshop in Lillooet but went broke. A son, Jon, was born to them.[15]

Suddenly their family's past and Germany's political present intruded into their already difficult lives. Phyllis's three brothers had been in concentration camps. The sister Erna, after an ear operation in 1937, had been sent to a Nazi doctor, who called her a shirk and ripped off the bandages. She died the next day. In despair, their mother tried to shoot herself. The three brothers implored Phyllis to return to look after her mother. Reluctantly she did return and had to go to Gestapo headquarters for a visa. In February 1938 she and Ali had scraped together enough money for her return fare. In Vancouver in the 1940s, they were slowly able to establish themselves with steady jobs and a home. Their son grew up in a proudly proletarian family. He was to become a local labour historian and collected many first-person accounts from Vancouver workers.[16]

Working-Class Experiences: Camps and Deportations

British, German, and Austrian unions had encouraged working men and women to write about their lives – about the exploitation, they had suffered, and their efforts at self-education. Many of these life-writings were published in order to inspire proletarian readers to follow the example of organization, self-improvement, and conscious pride in class.[17] Neither Canadian nor American unions developed similar traditions. Immigrant life-writings suggest two explanations. First, being part of the working-class for many authors was, at least on the surface, less oppressive than in Europe. To ask for a job did not mean cringing before a boss, though it might imply paying a bribe. On many jobs "no one stood over me"; at others foremen were tough but helpful. Bosses belonged to a different class but mingled with workers and might lend a hand on a difficult job. Secondly, in Europe workers could hardly cross the rigid class barriers and had to organize on a class basis to struggle collectively for improvements. In North America, independent contractor status provided a way to improvement, if a precarious one, as the experiences of Veltri, Einarsson, Hong, and others demonstrate. In the intermediate zone between dependent wage labour and small employer status, social mobility was high, upward as well as downward. Only those who improved their status to contractor or tied into a transposed European working-class culture like Rolf Knight published life-writings.

In factories, the opportunity for upward mobility was usually lacking and working conditions were often degrading, as witnesses had told the Royal Commission on Relations of Labour and Capital in 1889. Bunkhouse men described filthy living conditions, with no recreational facilities, and jobs that had extremely high accident rates. The need to organize was obvious to workers, whether Japanese fishers, loggers in the One Big Union, or factory workers in Hamilton, Oshawa, Trois Rivières. The continental synthesis of the history of the Canadian state and a staple economy has a counterpart in a synthesis of the Canadian labour movement and working-class culture, of the people who built the economy, and created the settlements and workshops across the continent.[18]

Until the Winnipeg General Strike only few life-writings mentioned strikes. Ryuichi Yoshida discussed his union activities, Rémi Jodouin commented on the power of capital. Class-conscious life-writing dates from the 1930s, authored by native-born or English-speaking immigrants or by labour movement activists. Industrial development, the institutional class war from the top down (draconian extension of the War Measures Act and the 1919 changes in the Immigration Act), and depression levels of unemployment led to increased mention of class in memoirs.[19]

Immigrant men and women did not dare apply for relief, as they could be deported if they were not Canadian citizens. For the Polish Brzyski family and other Poles, deportation was part of a long and bitter old-world history. Under tsarist occupation, Polish "rebels" fighting for independence had been deported to Siberia. In 1885 immigrant Poles had been deported by the Prussian government. Polish workers in Prussia became forced labourers during the war years of 1914–18. After 1939 deportation to forced labour in Germany or the Soviet Union dislocated millions.[20]

Antanas Rudinskas in Alberta housed a family which had arrived from Lithuania in 1930. "They were on relief and the government wanted to deport them, but she had run away and was hiding. Anyway, they took the kids and him, and had them all the way back to Winnipeg already, but since they could not find her, they let them go." Fellow Lithuanians had interposed and provided help. "The government deported three or four Lithuanians during that time, and lots more would have been deported but they ran away and hid in the country." For fear of deportation, Irish Nellie O'Donnell had married a brute of a husband. Because of this fear, immigrant workers no longer felt free to ask for help from the government, to organize and demand better wages, to resist harassment. The cost of unemployment, and with it discontent and independent political action, was to be shifted back to the homelands by the country that had been built by immigrants and had collected taxes from them.[21]

The government and the RCMP were confronted with the formation of radical parties and numerous strikes, deportations and persecution notwithstanding. In the Crowsnest Pass, Polish miners who had learnt their English from Welsh co-workers struck. The Canadian working class, like those of most other countries, had internationalized segments in it. The Scottish immigrant, Alex Will, recounted how he and other Vancouver longshoremen fought for "human dignity" and fairness in the hiring halls. They participated in the bitter 1935 strike, and fended off a "dictator sort of guy" who had been hired to break strikes by gang violence. In 1935 large numbers of unemployed organized a march across the nation to demand action from the government in Ottawa. Departing from Vancouver, they had reached Regina when the RCMP, on orders from Ottawa, charged into a fund-raising rally. Local citizens, in sympathy with the men, and the Saskatchewan government intervened. But the march did not continue.

An immigrant farmer also remembered the paranoia. In 1925 the Soviet government "wanted to buy dairy cows and would pay $85 each for good grade dairy cows and up to $120 each for registered stock." But "the next thing we read, ... our country would have no truck with Russia, so we had to go on selling for $10 to $12 each." A Lithuanian insurance club, perhaps of leftist orientation, organized in the 1930s in Edmonton, "lasted nearly until the war but then the communists infiltrated it, and we disbanded. The RCMP were checking all immigrant clubs and arresting people so we just burnt all our papers and quit." The four decades of persecution from the First World War up until the Cold War, prevented autobiographers, Aili Grönlund for example, from mentioning their struggles for a better society.[22]

In 1932 the Conservatives, in power in Ottawa, began to send single men to relief camps administered by the Department of National Defence. Massive protest came from organized labour. In Ontario, the provincial police regularly searched the camps for weapons, fearing direct action by the discontented. An English immigrant man, in a camp near Kenora, was as derisive about the "obvious commies" in camp as about the OPP's fear that "Communism was threatening the country." The men doused the police with water, but it took them longer to find out that the RCMP had an informer in camp. The interned men policed themselves. When two men broke "bush law" by pilfering the trapping cabin of local Natives, they were ordered to pay restitution. The internees retained a pride in craftsmanship, each "making his axe a tool to be proud of." They organized a committee to administer themselves and handle complaints about food or other grievances.

One camp foreman, who was known to have bossed workers at an Oshawa factory, paraded himself "outfitted in mackinaw breaches and coat, with lovely leather calf-high boots." Intending to show his subordinates how to fell trees, he managed to place one on the only telephone wire for tens of kilometres around. The officer in charge, William Lyons from the Defence Department, was "a tyrant." He pointedly told the unemployed, that they were far from home and had better take what they got. He branded an elected three-men committee "trouble makers" and assigned its members to different, separate camps. When the three months' camp stint ended for the men, he refused them the promised train passes, although it was a two-thousand-kilometre walk to the men's home towns and in winter. Like involuntary labour all over the world, the men built their own barracks, had to do bush-clearing jobs with no safety measures, and at twenty cent a day, received "the wages of slave labour."[23]

The situation was just as bad in the West. "In 1934 about one-third of Burnaby's population was on relief," remembered a Home boy. Relief for single men, if paid, was twenty-five cents a day. When sent to camps, men received "free work clothes, tobacco and food and $15 a month ... The top man was usually a major who used unemployed bosses from closed-down construction projects to handle the men. There were no ... uniforms but each man had a number. Men from 15 to 75 years of age cut trails in the forest in the winter and repaired roads in summer." Men too old to work were sent to labour, young men unfamiliar with axes and sledgehammers often injured themselves. Equipment was poor, food worse, housing worst of all. As in the Kenora camp, men without experience were permitted to handle dynamite and accident rates were high. The military officers in charge had not an inkling of what they were doing, according to both the victimized men and outside observers.

Though lacking libraries – a shortcoming no labour or communist hall would have had – the camps were educational experiences. Men organized, developed strike tactics, debated political repression and demanded "the unconditional release of the Communist leaders,"[24] or imagined how a historical vagrant, Jesus Christ, would fare in the camps. Views of a better society, ranging from Social Gospel to Communist theory, were mingled together. The men had more vision for a future Canadian society than all government members taken together.[25]

Ordinary Canadians were bitter. In 1933 a Saskatchewan woman, Clara Leibert, wrote to the prime minister, R.B. Bennett, whom she considered "put in by The Moneyed Men." To her way of thinking, only Agnes McPhail, the first woman MP, was a voice of sanity. She looked back to the First World War and the 1920s. "When I see How these Hard Years Have Affected My Husband, who has always been a Hardworking Man *I am not Red*. But I see Red." War "should never have been allowed and if those who caused The War had been put in The Front Lines the War would have been ended right then. The Moneyed Men are too blame for all the Wars. Returned men did not even know what they had been Fighting." The perceptive Clara Leibert knew that wars were man-made. She could relate the global to the local, the societal to the familial. Her family could not afford a telephone, had forgotten the taste of grapes, raspberries, strawberries, "Tons of Stuff rotting in The Orchards both East & West If We had a Good Government That would not be Allowed." She knew how social views and societal policies evolved: "You in Your Suite of 17 Rooms Furnished in Princly Style Beautiful Rugs etc cannot *Understand* What We women Suffer with Old Slipper and Boots on Cold floors Winter mornings." In the five years from 1930 to 1935, the Bennett administration deported over twenty-eight thousand impoverished immigrants, including British ones; in 1933 one person was deported for every three arriving. Deportation of radicals put the government squarely on the side of capital.[26]

War and Racism: Jewish Exclusion, Japanese Internment

Clara Leibert did not expect that her analysis of war would soon hold true again. On 1 September 1939, the armies of Nazi Germany invaded Poland. Bill Johnstone, the Vancouver Island miner, noted: "With the declaration of war ... money became available for armies, ships, uniforms, coal, steel or whatever was needed to fight the war ... No money for food, but plenty to buy guns; what an indictment against governments!" As war industry picked up speed, the camp "derelicts," as Prime Minister Bennett had called the unemployed, became sought-after workers again. Women workers moved from packing fish to welding ships. Farm produce was in high demand. After a decade of suffering, men and women were happy to have jobs and food for themselves and their children. Few analysed the connections of capitalism, fascism, and war, to persecution for sedition, for exercising the right of free speech, for support of "the enemy," external or internal. While the economic basis of family life, and that of single men and women, improved, the atmosphere of racism and persecution worsened.[27]

The many-cultured country's monocultural or bicultural political elites and national bureaucracy, after intensifying class repression for two decades, now intensified racism. East European immigrants suffered, Jews from Germany in particular and Europeans in general were not admitted, Japanese-Canadians were sent to camps. In Britain, anyone of German origin, whether Jewish or Nazi, was liable to be labelled an enemy alien and would be thrown together in the same compound. Many of these internees were transported to Canadian camps, where the insensitivity towards Jews continued.[28]

A Slovak immigrant, Steve Kuryvial, remembered: "Once a month each of us had to register with the regional RCMP office. We were forced to surrender all our rifles and guns, had to undergo the humiliating procedure of being finger-printed. We were honest, law-abiding citizens, and were known as antifascists." He and other Slovaks suffered because the bureaucracy made no distinction between an enemy state. (Slovakia had become a satellite of Nazi Germany), and people originating from the Slovak culture. Italians, too, as an ethnic group were labelled enemies. Respected contractors and workers had to report to the RCMP. As in 1914, the government action was not totally unjustified. In the Italian community in particular, many supported Mussolini's regime, *prominenti* in particular. In the camps, however, authorities did not single out Nazis, Italian fascists, or Japanese hardliners. It appears that the ethnic groups as a whole were singled out, rather than right-wing activists.

Slovak-Canadians and Czech-Canadians donated their savings for the Czechoslovak army in exile: "everything was more or less subordinated to the antifascist war effort." Communities sent parcels and money to Poland "to help them rebuild their shattered lives" and to the Polish diaspora, whether orphans in Mexico or demobilized soldiers in Scotland. During the war, Anne Chuchla worked in the Red Cross and Walter sold liberty bonds, "even to Germans, and they were buying." The Polish and the German immigrants had become Canadianized; the old country was no longer "home."

Among the sixty million who died in the war, six million were Jews, exterminated by a Nazi machine staffed by executioners from all walks of life. Some planned the railway transports to the camps, others threw gas cans into the packed death chambers, again others pushed the bodies into ovens or mass graves. In the 1930s, when under great difficulties and humiliations, Jewish men and women and their children could still leave Germany, the Canadian immigration bureaucracy, like the Swiss authorities, closed the doors. From 1933 to 1945, Canada accepted a total of five thousand; even Bolivia found room for fourteen thousand and China for twenty-five thousand. As late as the winter of 1945, years after the British secret service had cracked the German codes and eavesdropped on the army reports about death camps and local killing fields, "an anonymous senior Canadian official," asked by journalists how many Jews would be allowed into Canada after the war, callously answered, "None is too many."[29]

Harry Henig from Rypinia, Galicia, reached Canada in 1927 and moved to the Jewish colony in Hirsch, Saskatchewan. During the dust bowl years the fortunes of his uncles and nephews declined. He hitched a ride to Winnipeg, dreaming modestly of a job at three dollars a week. He married Fanny Schiffer in 1932; soon the two owned nothing but a mattress. Fanny's once well-to-do parents, unable to collect rents and thus to keep up with mortgage payments, had lost all. Harry's mother, sister, and family were still in Poland and he began proceedings to bring them over. When the family was finally granted a visa after years of red tape, economic and religious reasons militated against departure. They had come into an inheritance of the equivalent of eight hundred dollars on which they could live "like kings" in Poland. Secondly, the fear of losing their faith lurked in their minds. "How can I sacrifice my religion and forsake all of our rituals and traditions?" Stories circulated that "all of Canada, including Jews is non-kosher ... I have to live out my life here where generations have lived before me." So the family did not come. A last postcard in October 1939 informed Harry of the Russian occupation and "that they were all well." Thereafter, silence. In 1941 the German armies advanced on Russia. After the war, the Red Cross could not locate the family. Finally, Harry's old friend, the local priest's son, informed him that all the Jews of the village had been lined up and gunned down by the Nazi occupation forces. Local peasants had had to dig a mass grave.[30]

In May 1938 the Kohns, a wealthy Jewish family of Bratislava, Czechoslovakia, left for Amsterdam on the day German troops annexed the Sudeten region. From there, three hundred Sudeten-German families fled via Great Britain to Canada. Canadian authorities placed them on marginal land, even though they had been skilled workers and craftsmen. Officials still refused to come to terms with the notion that Canada was more than an agrarian reservoir for world markets. The Kohns had planned their departure carefully. Like the Kurtenbachs moving from the Dakotas to Saskatchewan, they had sent a family member ahead and transferred their assets. Unlike the Henig family in Poland, they did not feel safe in Europe. "With their determination, their wealth, their skills and their family connections, they felt they would have no difficulty" in gaining admission. But, like many other highly qualified Jewish refugees, they were turned down. Candidly the immigration official informed the horrified family that Canada no longer admitted Jews. Another official, not willing to openly fight racism but ready to help turn the system to their advantage, suggested they transfer all investments to Canada, distribute judiciously and discreetly some money, and reapply as Christians. The Kohns had no choice. They took the advice and came to Canada.[31]

About seven months after the Kohns had fled Bratislava, a mere five months before German troops would invade Poland, 907 German Jews left from Hamburg on one of the famous big liners, the *St Louis*. They had lost their possessions, had been humiliated, had to pay for being permitted to leave and had been granted visas for Cuba. However, on arrival, Cuban authorities denied entry, then all Latin American countries refused admission, and finally a hostile United States sent a gunboat to keep the *St Louis* off its shores. Intense efforts to help the refugees by some Canadians and Jewish-Canadians could not prevail. The minister of justice opposed entry, the director of the Immigration Branch of the Department of Mines and Resources, F.C. Blair, emphatically refused admission: "The line must be drawn somewhere." The "voyage of the damned," as the *St Louis*'s odyssey came to be called, ended in Europe. The line that Blair drew led straight to the death camps.[32]

After more than two years of war in Europe, Japanese forces attacked in the Pacific. Along the North American Pacific coast, Japanese-Americans and Japanese-Canadians were suddenly perceived as a military threat. Ryuichi Yoshida worked on a packing boat collecting cod and dogfish for a cod liver oil and fertilizer plant. On 8 December 1941, the captain suddenly called him to the radio: the attack on Pearl Harbor was announced. All twelve hundred Japanese-Canadian owned fishing boats were confiscated, spelling unemployment for the men and their families. Ships with Japanese-Canadian crewmen or workers had to discharge them. Yoshida was questioned, but emphasized that he had come more than thirty years ago and was a naturalized citizen. "What I was afraid of was a riot like in 1907, but worse. Because anti-Japanese feeling was much higher than ever before. I thought that if we did anything to provoke trouble something really horrible would happen. We could all get massacred, women and children, too." Of the community of twenty-three thousand, perhaps thirteen thousand were Nisei, Canadian-born Japanese. Most first-generation Japanese-Canadians kept a low profile, but the Canadian-born second generation questioned why they were being treated in that way. Part of the Japanese elite, those that had opposed the fishermen's Labour Union, turned militaristic and supported the state of Japan.

Yoshida's account of these weeks, although it involved fear of riots, was undramatic, as was his account of much of his life. Interestingly, the RCMP and the army were equally unperturbed. A number of Japanese-Canadians considered subversive had been arrested, so the confiscation of the Japanese-owned fishing boats was considered sufficient as a precautionary measure. However, racists who had demanded the deportation of Japanese earlier saw their chance. The War Measures Act could be used for class purposes, the situation exploited for racist purposes. "The Japanese in British Columbia have from the very beginning been secret agents of Tokyo," a major eastern newspaper editorialized. In Germany, Jews had been said to be agents of international capital (and of Bolshevism for good measure). To fight the "Yellow Peril" often spelled profits for the Euro-Canadian self-styled patriots. While top military officers remained level-headed, British Columbia politicians, pushed for "evacuation." In the First World War, one of the German Wicks brothers had tossed away a spoiled can of milk and had been accused of throwing explosives at a bridge. In the Second World War, Hirozo Fujita and his sons were clearing farmland in the Okanagan. Neighbours claimed that the brush piles could be turned into "flaming beacons" to guide enemy planes.[33]

There were others who did not succumb to racism. Hana Murata had a dressmaking shop on Vancouver's Broadway. Her landlord, who lived above her store, was angry at the "sneak attack" on Pearl Harbor, "but he didn't tell me to get out. He let me know that he'd come and help me if I needed him, so I should just yell for him. That was because a lot of times, people would come and make trouble in the middle of the night, throwing stones and yelling 'Jap, Jap.'" Individually, "though, white people are all pretty nice. The customers kept coming in with their orders as usual." Likewise, Tami Nakamura, from Mission, British Columbia, remembered that there was no discrimination, Canadians and Japanese being in the same strawberry producers' association. While such interaction could not stop the assaults of the racists, public opinion attacked postwar exclusion of Japanese-Canadians from citizenship and their deportation to Japan as a travesty of justice.

But this was not known to those who after January 1942 had to submit to the indignities and property loss of forced leave from the coastal areas. The prime minister decided on evacuation, ostensibly to prevent mob violence against Japanese-Canadians. Within weeks some twenty-two hundred men were sent to road work in the interior of the province, another four thousand to sugar-beet fields in southern Alberta and Manitoba. Families were relocated to abandoned towns along Kootenay Lake, the Slocan valley, or Tashme, east of Hope.

Hana Murata held out as long as possible and was one of the last to leave Vancouver. In camp, she was bored, organized sewing classes, and probably got some rest from her work routine. As early as possible she moved on to Toronto and found a house in the Kensington market Jewish quarter. "The only people who would rent to Japanese were the Jews." She immediately started sewing again. One boss at a fashionable factory refused to hire her: "There's a war on." She insisted: "The war doesn't have anything to do with me. All I want is a job." After checking with authorities, the Jewish boss changed his mind, he "said he'd hire anybody, any nationality, as long as they wanted to work."

Maki Fukushima, the logging contractor's wife, lost her husband. "He wasn't naturalized, so he was classified as an enemy alien." A man who had always been strong and healthy, he could not take the insult; the damage to his identity expressed itself in weakened physical stamina. Under the disgrace of being made an outcast, a slight cold led to asthma, which was aggravated into heart troubles, ending in death. Maki decided to take the family to work on the sugar-beet fields in Alberta. Embittered friends accused her of being a traitor since she cooperated with the Canadian government's relocation program. All she wanted was to keep the family together: her oldest son with a wife and baby, her daughter, and her second son, who had held a good position as bookkeeper of the Fraser Valley Farmer's Association. On the day the family boarded the train, Alberta authorities declared that no more workers were needed. But the Fukushima family had sold their belongings and had nowhere else to go; so they kept moving. Arriving after two days in Lethbridge, "nobody came to meet us, no bosses. They didn't want any Japanese coming. Then it got to be like being sold as slaves. We got taken all across Alberta from west to east, stopping at every station, and family after family got sold off." The "host" village was so small and, probably, so detestable that Maki did not even remember its name even though she spent four years there. Treated like enemies at first, local people came to appreciate the advantage of such semi-unfree labour. When the family decided to leave, the supervisors at first refused to sign the papers. But one after the other, the family was released and moved east.[34]

Takeo Ujo Nakano, in Canada since 1920, worked in a pulp mill at Woodfibre on Howe Sound. During a visit to Japan he had found a wife, Yakie, and in 1933 their first daughter was born. In the mill, Japanese men held the low-paying jobs, whites the better ones. Relations between the groups were "amicable if not close." Takeo Nakano, well educated and a quiet sensitive man, wrote poetry in the *tanka* style. Immigrants had established poetry clubs like those of other ethnicities had formed theatre groups. On 11 March 1942 the Woodfibre Japanese men were ordered to camps. "My wife had some last-minute words for me ... 'When will I see my family again?' ... And my little daughter's bright pink-clad form steadily receded in the distance. This was her first significant parting from her father. The disheartened sloping of her shoulders revealed her loneliness, a child's loneliness." At the Exhibition Ground in Vancouver they were herded into the livestock building, filled by the stench of animal droppings. Takeo Nakano was sent to road work near Yellowhead. For the next years he concentrated on the beauties of nature and the intricacies of *tanka* writing to distract himself from his grief. He was moved to Descoigne road camp, then told that he would be reunited with his family in Greenwood. But just before they could arrive, some men, including Nakano, were ordered to Slocan camp. He was bitter, protested, and argued that a return to the family had been promised. In response, the Security Commission freighted him off to a camp in Angler, Ontario, north of Lake Superior where a group of die-hard Japanese chauvinists tried to set the tone. But men began to apply for work permissions in Ontario which would end internment. In November 1943 Takeo Nakano's application was approved. When he left camp the old men "jeered at us furiously." After a separation of twenty-one months the family greeted each other lovingly. They stayed in Toronto.[35]

In 1949 the last government restrictions on Japanese-Canadians were removed. The dark years of Canadian class and ethnic policies, beginning with the repression of an alleged "Bolshevik menace" in the 1910s, going through the anti-Semitic racism, and culminating in the deportation of the Japanese-Canadians, came to an end. Yet Cold War restrictions lingered on and immigrants from the European Displaced Persons' camps were treated as badly as the female domestics and the harvest labourers of the 1920s.

Shattered Lives: Displaced Persons from Europe

In the late 1940s Canada admitted survivors of the forced labour camps of Nazi Germany who refused to be sent back to communist-ruled East European countries. The group also included a trickle of survivors from Soviet camps, *Volksdeutsche* expelled from Eastern Europe, and those uprooted by wartime ravages. The survivors wanted a chance to live, but were often shunted to Canadian lumbering camps, again as "unfree labour." Until their assignment ended, women and children remained in camps in Germany. For many, life and family projects had to be developed out of a past of desperation and deaths. The German-Jewish Trude Sekely, who grew up in 1920s Munich, looked back on a life history of flight: Paris, 1932, Spain, 1940, and Canada via Portugal in 1944.

When East Central Europe had been occupied by German armies and parts of Poland temporarily by Soviet armies, "there prevailed an aura of sadness among the Polish people [in Canada] ... Their concern about the plight of their families in Poland was justified; one enemy was forcing its way through the front door, the other one through the back ... communication with loved ones in Central Europe had come to a standstill." Hopes, rumours, searches for loved ones, could not overcome the bitter realities. Some were deported "to Germany to work in factories and on farms, while others were marched and hauled away like cattle, in boxcars, to work and die in freezing Siberia." A cousin of Anna Kutera, Leopold, freed from forced labour in Germany after 1945, asked for help to come to Canada. It was only a decade later that he was able to trace his wife of four years, Cecilia, who had been taken to Siberia. After a separation of eighteen years, they were joyfully reunited in Canada in 1958. In 1947 Albert and Anastasia Eskra signed an affidavit to sponsor the remnants of his family, who had been was transported to Russia and separated; a brother had fought in the free Polish army, while other survivors lived in allied camps. From relatives in Poland, Walter Chuchla "found out that except my Parents, everybody was saved." But when Polish Helena and Franek Kojder reached Canada in 1948, they came with a burden of sadness; twenty-two relatives had died in Soviet labour camps.

Women from postwar Europe came singly, admitted only for domestic service regardless of their qualification. These newcomers' process of acculturation and ethnicization differed from that of earlier arrivals. Their memories were of war and persecution rather than of a lived culture and economic constraints. Ties had been broken by larger, man-made forces, – war, persecution, poverty – not by deliberately planned departure.[36] Camp survivors and refugees had to rebuild identities. They would remain emotionally scarred, and passed on their memory of suffering to their children even if they tried to hide it or wanted to forget about it.[37] While the nineteenth century was one of labour migration, the twentieth was one of refugee generation and flight.

PART SEVEN

Perspectives: From Many Cultures to Multiculturalism

By the 1950s the immigrants and their children had achieved modestly comfortable lives. The second, third, and later generations had become part of the mainstream. But the mainstream was not merely the sum total of the input of the diverse British groups and the several French-speaking cultures, as well as that of Native Peoples and Métis. Each and every immigrant had observed, absorbed, or rejected what he or she found. With each person entering those social spaces that in the decades before the First World War became Canada, the dual mainstream and the marginalized Native and Métis societies were reformed, reformulated, challenged, and – with the exception of the First Peoples and Métis – enriched.

Canada's institutional framework had adapted but slightly to the composition of the population. East Europeans had been admitted, but immigrants from Asia were being kept out. In 1947 and 1948 first changes were made in immigration and citizenship legislation, to be completed in the late 1960s with a new immigration law and the first debates on a multicultural society. In these two decades the political leadership and public opinion, or at least segments of it, came to terms with the multiple input to Canada's history. Thus we will summarize the developments that led to the new identity, then review the changes in the legal framework and, finally, the steps towards a policy of non-discrimination and respect for cultural differences.

New migrants began to arrive in a process that involved continuity and change at the same time. The post-1945 refugees from Europe were followed by refugees from communist repression in Hungary in 1956 and Czechoslovakia in 1968. Refugees from communist countries received preferential treatment, but those from the military coup of Auguste Pinochet in Chile were regarded with suspicion. Small numbers of refugees also arrived from the United States in the 1950s. As slaves and Civil War refugees had come till the 1860s, now Quakers opposed to McCarthyism and militarism and opponents of the Vietnam War came. Men and women dislocated in Asia and Africa also came. For example, in 1972 several thousand Ugandan Asian refugees were admitted. In a historical and comparative perspective, they were as highly trained as French Huguenots had been three centuries earlier. In the mid-1970s, the first Southeast Asian refugees came; the Vietnamese of 1975 were usually fairly prosperous, often well educated. As French-speakers, many settled in Quebec. Later the boat people, impoverished and scarred by decades of warfare, arrived. Somalians, Cambodians, West Africans, Sri Lankans, Latin Americans followed.

Labour migration, in seeming continuity, involved the mass migration of Italians in the 1950s and 1960s and later of the Portuguese. But new reservoirs were tapped when women for domestic service were admitted from the Caribbean and, later, from Southeast Asia. More migrants came under manpower and investor-oriented immigration schemes than under programs of refugee admission. However, family-class immigration helped refugees as well as labour migrants to bring in relatives and over time ever more people came from Asia and Africa.

Some Canadians, immigrant or native-born, became uneasy about cultural change. Racist attitudes towards Asian newcomers declined but remained noticeable towards people from the Caribbean and Africa. Economic migrants and refugees from the southern hemisphere, an area that in Western opinion begins south of the United States and the Mediterranean, come in the beginning because of the legacy of colonialism. Later mismanagement and autocratic governments send men and women fleeing, as does population growth combined with lack of jobs and a deteriorating environment. Finally, unequal terms of trade of capitalist world economies, by which the rich industrial, mainly northern third profit from underpaid labour farther south, send men and women in search of better lives.

CHAPTER TWENTY

Years of Change and Redefinition

In the century from the 1850s to the 1940s, identities had emerged in local contexts. Men and women gave "Canada" as their destination, while they then settled in Montreal or on a homestead; or they remained "unsettled" as itinerant labourers and easily dismissible live-in domestics; or they lived in a Chinatown or other ethnic quarter that was a neighbourhood and not a ghetto or tourist attraction. Early immigrants were only concerned to build a new life for themselves in their local and regional economies. They tried to do so without breaks in identities; they looked for continuity as well as change. At the beginning of the twentieth century, when native-born Euro-Canadians became concerned over powerful railway and grain elevator companies or factory owners' autocracy, the immigrants' attention turned to the provincial and national scene, with calls for government regulation. Still, it took decades before the national Cooperative Commonwealth Federation (CCF) was formed in 1932.

Much of this criticism of society came from people of British origin, often third generation or more. At the same time, immigrant groups began to step out of the labelled social slots assigned to them. In the school controversies, Ukrainians stressed their Canadian identity. Many East Central European groups organized politically in response to being termed enemy aliens. While they were achieving recognition in the 1970s, Caribbean-Canadians and Asian-Canadians turned to the government to protest pervasive patterns of racism among Euro-Canadians. Structural change was necessary, and the federal government began to face the need for changes.

Ruptures or Continuities: Canadian Identity in History

In their life-writings only a tiny minority of the ordinary immigrants discussed their citizenship. The contractors and merchants Veltri and Einarsson, the labour migrant Chuchla and the farmer Eskra, Miyazaki, the doctor, and Yoshida, the fisherman, all applied for Canadian citizenship, which at that time meant British citizenship. Canadianization was not an act but a process. At the beginning of the twentieth century, Ukrainians and Icelanders, Japanese and Chinese, in fact the "majority of this cosmopolitan collection" developed a loyalty to Canada. Only among English immigrants, and perhaps Scottish and Welsh ones, was loyalty to Canada supplemented by a loyalty to the Empire. Britishers, many of whom refused to consider themselves immigrant, upon returning "home" realized that they could not longer readjust to the old world on the British isles. Canadians of British origin in the British army in the First World War, wrote back home that they had always been taught they were British, but now realized that they were Canadian. "Many people do not like it at first, but it grows upon one unconsciously." Observers discerned "a very strong feeling of Canadian nationality, which is growing every year."[1]

In contrast, grand white men, a solid wall of Britishers and genteel immigrants on one side and Quebec-Canadian gatekeepers on the other, had constructed a bifurcated identity harking back to the time of the battle of the Plains of Abraham. A backward-looking rhetoric of conquest and assimilation had become a type of ancestor worship. The intellectual gatekeepers who cemented the distinctiveness of the two so-called founding nations, refused to take note of clearly visible alternatives – Irish or Acadian identities, for example.

The elites had later invited the "men in sheepskin coats" with wives and children to populate the new country. But the spokespersons of the self-styled founding peoples agreed, across all their differences, that the newcomers' position as immigrants, ethnics, or allophones was below their own. This ideology, blind to the differences of origin and regional diversity after arrival, is absent from the memories of the life-writings' authors. As regards Euro-Canadians, the threefold division overlooked the heterogeneity of the English, Scottish, Welsh, Cornish, and the Irish. It reduced the French to Quebec, thus negating French contributions from the Maritimes via Manitoba to British Columbia. It assumed that the mass of immigrants after arrival opened their cultural baggage, pulled out old-world identities, and sorted themselves into neatly delineated ethnic groups, each with a few usually self-appointed and always male spokespersons at the helm.

The life-writings present a different national history. In the East, the bicultural Maritimes, and the inward-looking St Lawrence valley, a French cluster existed parallel to an expanse of English, Scottish, United Empire Loyalists or American dots of settlement and an Irish social sphere. Immigrants, including those from the British Isles, entered society from the bottom up and had little or no contact with the elites whose lifestyles and political structures remained distant or even invisible. The settlers pushed the original Amerindian societies into the background. To the north of this settlement belt a second region emerged – a fur-harvesting, logging, and subsequently mining economy with hamlets strung out along railway lines. To the west of the Great Lakes, from the 1870s on, the homesteaders' many-cultured interaction created a third region, hierarchically structured according to ethnicity, gender, and race. The fourth region consisted of a triple economy of the Rockies and the Pacific Coast – mining, agriculture, and fishing – and was as many-cultured as the others. In the northern and the Pacific regions, immigrants and Métis intersected, the Aboriginal cultures forming separate, distinct societies.

All the life-writings emphasize some kind of interaction among people in Montreal factories, northern mines, agricultural subsistence economies, Prairie threshing gangs, railway crews, and Pacific coast fishing. Few of the men and women clung to an imagined past; indeed, several were quite explicit about their critical attitude to the society they had left. Pidgin English or French *patois* became a common language. Among rudimentarily multilingual immigrants from the Balkans and among the mixed peoples from Ukraine, communication was possible without English. English-speaking brokers such as shopkeepers, postmasters or mistresses, foremen, and earlier immigrants or the immigrants' children, mediated contacts with others. The East European experience was not limited to the prairie but included urban wage work and labour organization, domestic service and women's networks. From intercultural contacts, in a process of ethnogenesis, a Canadian people emerged, according to the memories of the immigrants, though they would hardly have phrased it that way.

Canadian society may be viewed as divided into three levels. On the bottom were the immigrants and their children – interactive, accommodative, at times also racist. The top was formed by two mutually exclusive groups. The English or British genteel classes dominated the national institutions and much of the economy. In Quebec an elite of *vieille souche* ancestry and the clergy monopolized institutions whether economic, political or religious. In the middle was a contested as well as cooperative ground in which spokespersons for ethnic groups, business, and labour acted out claims to recognition, demands for access to resources, and influence on cultural institutions, especially the schools. The life-writings, originating mostly from the bottom level, offer clues for a reinterpretation of the threefold British-French-ethnics construct.

English and perhaps Scottish dominance in the institutions was undercut in everyday cultural interaction as well as drawing of boundaries by the fact that English immigrants, who wanted to be accepted as neighbours, had to make quite clear that they had nothing in common with four types of British who refused to acculturate: first, with the remittance men; secondly, with officers and their families of British colonial armies and with administrators who tried to continue lifestyles they could not afford in England; thirdly, with those British visitors or middle-class immigrants who thought they knew everything better than Canadian colonials; and, finally, with British trade union men, who carried their hard-won expectations of wages and hours into a society that demanded flexibility. The pressure was sufficiently strong that English immigrant urban labourers, western settlers, and middle-class people tried to get rid of their accents in order to escape ridicule and labelling. They were not a visible but an audible minority.

British-origin Canadians and English immigrants were caught in multiple layers of contradictory role definitions. First, in imperial ideology, newcomers from the Empire's centre considered themselves better than colony-born English even in the white colonies and Dominions.[2] By migration away from the centre they found their status changed to colonial English who, as green newcomers, ranked below colony or Dominion-born old-timers of many ethnic backgrounds. Secondly, next to imperial position, social status played an important role. Men who came from a genteel background usually lived off parental remittances and developed few capabilities of their own; women could not pretend to status for lack of parental support and adjusted to live on their own. Thirdly, lower-class British immigrants wanted more independence and such aspirations conflicted with role expectations of their middle- and upper-class co-immigrants. Canadians' expectations to make do and work long hours conflicted with their own class as well as imperial ideological discourses. Since many English and Scots arrived with an imperial mentality, some means, and considerable self-confidence, they did not bother to observe their new social environment. Thus they could not learn. Canadians had to tear them harshly out of their preconceived notions.[3]

While the conflation of the multiple British contributions resulted in an expansive view of the British impact, the French impact has been undervalued, as the life-writings show. Francophones were present from Lunenburg, Nova Scotia, to Victoria, British Columbia. The absence of immigrant life-writings in Quebec, the sense of grievance displayed by Quebec autobiographers, and the miscalculation of Quebec elites as regards internal migration – settlement of contiguous but marginal areas rather than to the fertile prairies – reduced the French presence. The role of French-speaking Red River Métis in the development of the West was recognized by early settlers and observers.

While British imperial administration and Quebec culture influenced the emergence of Canada east of the Great Lakes, British-Canadian institutions were but a thin layer farther west. East European, eastern Canadian, American, British, West and North European homesteaders shaped Prairie society. Along the Pacific Coast, Aboriginal cultures with set institutions and English-Métis provincial elites, golddiggers, miners, farmers from many European cultures, prospectors, fishermen, labourers, and farmers of three Asian immigrant groups, formed the social mosaic. Living arrangements reflected cohabitation as well as protective self-segregation in the face of racism and discrimination, but work arrangements and survival in pioneer settings demanded regular coöperation, frequent interaction, or at least occasional contact.

Intra-group life among immigrants and ethnic Canadians was vibrant, too, but as it was considered normal, it was seldom mentioned in the life-writings. Leah Rosenberg moved in Toronto and Montreal Jewish communities, Wilson and Jemima Benson migrated through an Irish social space, Poles and Russian-Germans in the Prairies sought out neighbours with similar language and culture. But their communities incorporated other groups. Only those with different colour of skin were left out, sometimes harshly put down, usually subject to structural discrimination. In the life-writings, Canadians of African origin appeared as individuals, curiosities, only occasionally as neighbours or co-workers. The Aboriginal peoples were mentioned, but in passing.[4] Men and women from Asia experienced institutional discrimination and racism, but on an individual level knocked on doors that were neither open nor inviting but ajar. From their marginal position they had to observe other ethnic groups closely to avoid damage to their own identities. From their segregated lives they came to understand the loneliness of some of the European immigrants and opened doors of emotional support to them.

The building of an ethnic group required the presence of a sufficient number of fellow countrymen or cultural converts to maintain levels of mutual support and spiritual comfort. For Mennonites, Doukhobors, and Jewish farmers, separatism was mandated by particular lifestyles prescribed by religion. Ukrainians and Russian-Germans formed bloc settlements, but in their life-writings describe frequent interaction with other cultural groups. Creating local societies involved establishment of municipal and educational institutions by men and women of different cultures as well as English-speaking children. In urban contexts, individuals and families though living in ethno-specific neighbourhoods and creating ethnic communities, also experienced cultural interference and change by interaction. The "mainstream-in-the-making" was multi-ethnic within the framework of national Anglo-Canadian institutions.

The contested ground in the middle of society is best illustrated by the struggles about schooling of children and attempts to enter English (or French) society. During the 1913 Alberta School controversy, in which the minister of education, J.R. Boyle, and the supervisor of schools objected to certified bilingual teachers and dismissed them, the Ukrainian newspaper *Novyny* angrily noted: "The minister of education lies when he says that Alberta is an English province. Alberta is a Canadian province, where everyone has equal rights, including the Ukrainians." In a poem, "English Culture" written in 1914, a Ukrainian bitterly complained about discrimination: "We help Canada rise/ In Commerce and all things … /We will tell the whole world: /'English culture is peculiar.' "[5]

In the 1930s and early 1940s, Serafina "Penny" Petrone, of Italian background, went to school and to the Collegiate Institute in Port Arthur. Like Fredelle Bruser Maynard and Laura Salverson, she was struck by the English content of the schoolbooks. "Ontario education was British in substance. British and Canadian were synonymous. I memorized the British money system and the British liquid and linear measures. I memorized the achievements of the British around the world," Magna Charta, the steam engine, the defeat of the Boers, Calcutta, the Plains of Abraham, Waterloo, Khartoum. "My heroes were British." Peggy, who became a teacher, quoted from a manual of the Ontario Department of Education of 1934, six and a half decades after an independent Canada had been established. "The teacher should not fail to emphasize the extent, power, and responsibilities of the British Empire, its contributions to the highest form of civilization, the achievements of its statesmen and its generals, and the increasingly important place that Canada holds amongst the Overseas Dominion." Yet while she was thus socialized into a British world, distant from her Italian-Canadian one in Port Arthur, the British section of Port Arthur's society excluded her. At the Collegiate Institute the principal had difficulty spelling her Italian name, Serafina. It was "a closed, predominantly WASP enclave … I lived in the South End – the wrong end of the city." The cliquishness of the students made her life an ordeal. Even when she was invited to a social, she was out of place. More often she would be asked whether, like other "Eyetalians," she stomped grapes with her bare feet. In result, "I tried hard to erase the Italianness that the dominant culture despised." When she graduated in 1941 as the only person of Italian background, there were eleven hundred Italians among Port Arthur's population of twenty-four and a half thousand. The cultural gatekeepers neither permitted others to join their exclusive ranks, nor did they teach Canadian history and culture.[6]

Immigrant groups did produce spokesmen, the ethnic equivalent of the British elites and the Quebec clergy. As political leaders, they needed a solid voting bloc behind them but had to work out compromises with other groups and the dominant Anglo-Saxon institutions. They were brokers. As cultural leaders – teachers, clergy, and journalists – compromise would undercut their own position, including their incomes. Thus they drew boundaries between other cultural groups and the mainstream. They became advocates of cultural purity, of an unwavering adherence to what, according to their memory, had been the lifestyle in the old world. They became gatekeepers trying to prevent young English-speaking or French-speaking group members from leaving the fold and prohibiting access of outsiders to the group. While they helped immigrants to establish themselves, gatekeepers also retarded acculturation. Rarely mentioned in the life-writings, gatekeepers appeared in the ethnic press where boundaries were established, territories staked, conflicts used to strengthen in-group cohesion.

The immigrants' economic contribution to nation-building by establishing family survival economies is evident from the life-writings but only implicitly recognized in the staples history approach. Both men and women were explicit about their part of the work. Even as children they had to contribute as much as their physical and mental capabilities permitted. By class, however, the contribution is not fully reflected; bunkhouse men did not write, and only few women in domestic labour left memoirs. Establishing the material base of life in the new society according to cultural preferences involved constant negotiating between goals in good times, and constant struggle in times of depression. Transcultural context and mainstream society changed with each newcomer, whether Lunenburg merchant, Montreal rabbi's daughter, Toronto female domestic, single homesteader, lonely farming family, Jewish or Chinese shopkeeper in a Prairie town, or Japanese union organizer on the Pacific Coast. The societies all of them built was not "multicultural" in the sense of an avowed policy but it was many-cultured and interactive.

Immigrants as individuals or as cultural groups did not face a bloc of historically-rooted British demanding unconditional conformity or Quebecois prohibiting languages other than French. The thin institutional layer did not have the power to enforce uniformity. But they did face hierarchical power relationships and racial ascription of status. The question answered by the life-writings is: How did the newcomers *participate* across cultural boundaries, how were transcultural practices established? The open question is the connection of the immigrant worlds to the national institutions, what happened to the mainly British top of society?

From Confederation in 1867 to the Citizenship Act of 1947

When autobiographers discussed their naturalization process, they confidently considered themselves Canadian citizens. It is ironic that, had they read the fine print, contemplated constitutional issues, or understood the subordination of the periphery to the core, they would have realized that they had become British subjects. Naturalization legislation in its first comprehensive codification of 1881 was intended to provide "a simple and inexpensive method of naturalization applicable to the whole Dominion and opening wide the door of British citizenship to persons of foreign birth who come to settle in Canada, without at the same time, requiring them to abjure the country of their nativity."[7]

First, the underlying doctrine was populationist: to increase the country's economic potential by encouraging the immigration of producers. This principle, as part of mercantilist policies, had guided Habsburg settlement policies in Balkan territories and recruitment of settlers for the South Russian plains. In 1865 George Brown argued "there is hardly a political or social problem ... that does not find its best solution in a large influx of immigration. The larger our population, the greater will be our productions, the more valuable our exports, and the greater our ability to develop the resources of our country."[8] Thus immigration was administered by the Department of Agriculture and later of Mines and Resources.

The act, secondly, recognized that the settlers' legal and political position must be secure and easy to achieve. Complicated procedures would retard naturalization, insecurity prevent newcomers from investing labour or capital. The law, in keeping with contemporary thought, did not recognize protection of skills and labour power, the only the "property" of artisans and workers. Application of the law was narrow. The intensive debate about political participation of "mechanics" in the United States, of artisans and skilled workers in Europe, conducted in the labour press and in constitutional thought, bypassed Canada, where flexibility and independent contracting set different parameters. Class-conscious British-Canadian elite and power-wielding Quebec clergy combined prevented the emergence of a working-class discourse of democratic participation. After 1878, the Conservatives' National Policy stimulated industrialization, but expected internal migrants from declining rural sectors to form the work force. Industrialists knew better and hired regardless of complexion whomsoever they could get at the lowest wages.[9]

Thirdly, in a forward-looking provision, the act recognized that immigrants would not be ready to dissociate themselves from their culture of origin, or their ties of family still in the old country. This permitted creation of special status slots for specific groups. Mennonites and Doukhobors remained separate in ethno-religious communities, the Icelanders in the "Gimli republic."

Fourthly, in keeping with imperial thought, naturalization blurred the distinction between a subject of a (British) monarchy and a citizen of a (Canadian) state. Did status as a British subject prevent identification with the entity of residence, Canada? Imperial pageantry evoked intense but superficial reactions. In Anglican Lunenburg of the 1850s, royal feast or fast days still had an integrative function, on the prairies of the 1890s it was a holiday with a spectacle of royal colours. In some respects Britishness declined quickly in post-Confereration Canada. The British gentry-style pillars of early Western society, the HBC and Mounties, became outmoded when new people arrived. New institutions, Eaton's "democratic" appeal to mass consumption, and the settler's self-regulation which implied elements of control over other ethnic groups of low status, mirrored the needs and preferences of common people, as well as economic change and a new class structure. In other respects, on the constitutional and educational level, the status of British subject in Canadian society did cause several long-term problems. It remained a hindrance for full participation of Québéquois. Royal pageantry prevented emergence of popular Canadian public rituals. The English or British character of school history, geography, and social studies prevented children of immigrant origin from developing a sense of their own society. The elite's Britishness created difficulties for the emergence of a shared national identity.

The administrative truncation of becoming Canadian was compounded by contemporary views on gender. First, Canadian-born women or, more generally, women born as British subjects "who were married to aliens ... were deemed to hold the citizenship/subjectship of their husbands." Marriage meant subservient status to men and ethnicization for women.[10] Secondly, in the compilation of statistics on ethnic and racial origin, the recognition of ethnic origin through the male line increased the size of all ethnic groups, with a surplus of men who married women of other groups. For example, in 1931, the sex ratio of German-Canadians in the province of Quebec was 145:100. Of 169 children born to German fathers only eighty-one had German mothers (47.9 percent). The other eighty-eight, born by French (forty-one), British (thirty-eight), or mothers of other origin (nine) became Germans in the census figures. Before "multiple origins" became a census category in 1981, among all groups with a surplus of out-marrying males the immigrant segments were augmented by "home-grown" segments.[11] The method of data collection supported concepts of ethnic persistence rather than reflected intergenerational cultural changes.

A bottom-up identity remained opposed to the top-down identity. The absence of a "Canadian ethnic origin" category in the census questionnaires before 1951 meant that men and women who had been Canadianized for generations could not declare themselves ethnically Canadian. Multiple origins were part of the autobiographers' experiences and mentalities: the Polish-origin immigrant with his German-origin Polish-mother-tongue wife; the Galician newcomers who selected Ukrainian, Polish, or German cultural adherence according to their neighbours and the nearest church; the Icelandic immigrant living in common-law union with a Native wife. Subsequent amendments to and changes in the citizenship law of 1881 narrowed access to citizenship rather than embodied the experience of a society "of open doors."

Immigration restrictions were more stringent than the citizenship requirements. The Immigration Act of 1910 excluded numerous categories of "undesirables": criminals, the poor, and non-white people – the latter designated as "those belonging to nationalities unlikely to assimilate and who consequently prevent the building up of a united nation of people of similar customs and ideals." Certain working-class people were excluded, "those who from their mode of life and occupation are likely to crowd into urban centers and bring about a state of congestion which might result in unemployment and a lowering of the standard of our national life." A fourth category, "radicals" and "anarchists," was singled out for special attention after the Winnipeg General Strike.[12]

While the radicals had vision but little power, the government had power and no vision. Twice Conservative prime ministers tampered with citizenship legislation. John A. Macdonald in 1885 excluded from voting Canadians with less than four hundred dollars of annual income, a provision abolished by the Liberals in 1898. His proposal of voting rights for property-holding widows, spinsters, and unmarried women "was quickly disposed of in committee." Amerindians in the East, as "sons of the soil," were deemed "Canadians and British subjects," but Amerindians in the West, as wards of government, were excluded. Also excluded were "Chinese and Mongolians." The "Chinaman," Macdonald opined, "gives us his labour and gets his money, but ... he has no British instincts or British feelings or aspirations." He did not discuss Sikhs, who were British subjects, many of whom had served in imperial armies.

The second manipulation, by the Conservative Borden government, was blatantly partisan. The Military Voters Act of 1917 enfranchised all service personnel regardless of citizenship, age, and ethnicity (including aliens and minors), and all women whose husbands, sons, brothers, or fathers served in the Canadian Expeditionary Force. The Wartime Elections Act, in contrast, disenfranchised citizens naturalized after 31 March 1902 – that is, all immigrants arriving after 31 March 1899, the ethno-religious groups (Mennonites, Hutterites, Doukhobors), and conscientious objectors. Many of these disenfranchised immigrants came from nations engaged in a struggle for self-determination with the enemy empires. Immigrants in the process of Canadianization were thus forced into a secondary minority formation, an ethnic institutionalization to achieve political strength to fight for democratic rights and cultural recognition in Canada.[13]

In 1946, Secretary of State Paul Martin Sr proposed a new Canadian Citizenship bill. At first he was inspired by the classic death-in-war clause granting posthumous membership in a nation. Visiting the Canadian war cemetery at Dieppe, France, in February 1945, he noted: "These brave individuals had come from different ethnic and religious backgrounds. They had come from all over Canada. But one thing united them: they were all Canadians."[14] But he moved beyond the narrow definition. Citizenship, he stated, "means more than the right to vote; more than the right to hold and transfer property, more than the right to move freely under the protection of the state." The concept of citizenship as "the right to full partnership in the fortunes and in the future of the nation." The conservative historian Donald Creighton interpreted this as a radical departure from the past, "a fundamental change in the status of Canadians." But a distinct Canadian identity had existed for a long time and the majority of the members of the House considered the measure overdue. The act brought the written word in line with lived experience, the legal codes with mentalities.

The act's final wording, contrary to Paul Martin's intentions, still left Canadians British subjects. But Canadian identity came first, as it had done for about eight decades for all except a minority from among the British-origin group. Attitudes towards race changed. Restrictions on Chinese-Canadians were removed first, those on Japanese-Canadians in 1948. The cooperation which Chinese and Japanese autobiographers had experienced with co-workers of European origin before the war was not a retrospective idealization of the past but a sign of interaction on the basis of mutual acceptance.[15]

From Racial Restrictions to Non-Discimination, 1967

In the eighteen years before the First World War, more than three and a half million people came to Canada, while the stagnant 1920s and depression 1930s, saw a substantial drop in arrivals. In 1947, when immigration policies were debated in Parliament, Prime Minister Mackenzie King promised a "sustained policy of immigration," taking into account the absorptive capacity of Canada. "Careful selection" in the country's economic interests would prevent "large-scale immigration from the Orient." "Canada is perfectly within her rights [King stated] in selecting the persons whom we regard as desirable future citizens." He concluded that immigration was not a fundamental human right but a privilege.

While affirming this consensus, these same immigrant-receiving countries, in the Cold War context, rebuked communist governments for not permitting free emigration of people. This position implied that emigration was a human right, immigration a matter of domestic policy. This logic permitted migrants to leave but not to arrive.

Discrimination by race and ethnicity in deciding which immigrants to accept had been proscribed in the Charter of the United Nations. As result, receiving countries had to rephrase their laws. The discriminatory continuous journey provision, directed mainly against coloured citizens of the Empire, was abolished. In 1947, Parliament repealed the exclusionist Chinese Immigration Act of 1923, the very title of which reflected racial hypocrisy. But only sponsored family-class immigrants from China were permitted to come. In this debate, the death-in-war clause providing men with access to citizenship had its counterpart in the life-in-the-womb argument used to refuse access to women. Racists argued that sponsored family members would mainly be wives, who then would give birth, thereby flooding the country with even more Chinese. The live-giving powers of women were viewed as a threat to a male-defined British/white/European culture.

In the 1950s, decolonization and increasing self-confidence of the states in the southern hemisphere led to liberation struggles. Economic take-off was offset, however, by continuing dependency between the Third World and the capitalist developed world. Colonial rule and imperial domination changed to exploitation by means of unequal terms of trade, a condition of global apartheid which continues to generate economic migrants by the millions. At the same time, postwar recovery and full employment economies reduced Europe's role as an immigration reservoir for Canada and the United States. The Atlantic migration system, after a short resurgence in the late 1940s and 1950s, declined. The economic development of Southeast Asia, Japan, and India, and the US intervention in Vietnam and Cambodia, increased transpacific connections.

The 1952 Immigration Act reflected none of these changes. Unsponsored immigrants of British, American, and, in a belated departure from previous policies, French origin received priority. As regards sponsored relatives from Asia, "the Immigration Act was really a prohibition act with exemptions," to quote the minister responsible. Parliamentary examination of the haphazard immigration provisions made clear that a comprehensive policy was as overdue as the Citizenship Act had been. In 1967 a points system ended explicit racial discrimination but implicitly assumed that migrants from Latin America, Africa, and Asia would not meet the requirements. The Act of 1978 was intended to "ensure non-discrimination among immigrants on grounds of race, national or ethnic origin, colour, religion and sex."[16]

Policy frameworks clash with the resourcefulness, initiative, and talents of those who want to improve their lives and prospects, within the legal framework of admission if possible, bypassing it if necessary. Those arriving outside of the rules are "illegals," politically speaking. In terms of the gospel of free markets, they are entrepreneurs showing individual initiative. In terms of family economies and prospects for their children, they do the best they can.

Patterns of migration changed under the worldwide shifts of power and economic development. By the mid-1970s, more immigrants arrived from Asia and other non-Western countries than from industrialized Europe. An unforeseen byproduct of the family-class regulation was to increase Asian and Caribbean immigration, as well as that from other Latin American states and Africa. Since sponsored family members often did not enter the labour markets or, owing to the recession, could not enter it, energies were channelled into community-building and development of economic niches that permitted self-employment. The easy access to citizenship offered opportunities to voice discontent within the political system, thus preventing alienation and extra-legal action.

Multiculturalism: Recognition of the Past

The Canadian people are and have been a culturally interactive whole of multiple groups engaged in actively structured courses of development. In 1963 the Royal Commission on Bilingualism and Biculturalism began its work. Its ground-breaking report was released from 1967 to 1970. In October 1971 the Trudeau government announced the policy of multiculturalism.[17] It was cast into legal form in 1988 under a Conservative prime minister. The policy provided for remedial action against cultural hierarchization, discrimination, and racism by governmental institutions, which in themselves had to change from predominantly British- or French-origin composition to a reflection of the origins of Canadian society. An analysis of the quarter-century of multiculturalism demands a distinction between the concept and policy, its implementation, and the daily multicultural interaction.

In the 1960s and 1970s a cross-party consensus accepted diversity as an asset that gave each and every Canadian more options. In its first stage, the goals of the policy on "multiculturalism in a bilingual framework" were: to support those cultural groups "that have demonstrated a desire and effort to continue to develop, a capacity to grow and contribute to Canada"; to "assist members of all cultural groups to overcome cultural barriers to full participation in Canadian society"; to "promote creative encounters and interchange among all Canadian cultural groups in the interests of national unity"; and finally, to "assist immigrants to acquire at least one of Canada's official languages."[18] Ethnic diversity was considered an increment of socio-cultural options.

The second phase began with the concept's implementation. British- and French-dominated bureaucracies and societal structures had to transform themselves to conform to the many-cultured composition of the Canadian people. In the realm of education, new schoolbooks and college texts did justice to the multiple input into Canadian society and helped to generate collective identities that were no longer British- or French-inspired. In programs that began before the multiculturalism policy, new service institutions eased the process of immigrant reception. Just as the working bees of the homesteaders had been, this was help for self-help. Doors were opened, but thresholds had to be crossed on the immigrants' own initiative. When a segment of Canadians reacted with fear and hostility to newcomers with skin colours other than white, the policy also sought to strengthen anti-racism and to ensure equal opportunities for all. The host society tried to take care that newcomers would not be marginalized and become alienated outsiders.[19]

When the policy was first announced, its retentive nature – best described as a desire to celebrate and continue existing diversity – was emphasized over other aspects such as evolution and interaction: "multiculturalism reflects the cultural and racial diversity of Canadian society and acknowledge[s] the freedom of all members of Canadian society to preserve, enhance and share their cultural heritage."[20] The reflection of newcomers on their lives made clear that their diversity of origin was modified by contact and interaction and common experiences in factories or in agriculture.

Changes in attitudes were slow to emerge. When, in keeping with the new citizenship law of 1947, the category "Canadian" was inserted into the census forms in 1951, the bureaucracy remained obstinately British-minded: "Canadian" became a write-in option, which census-takers were to accept only if people insisted. The multiple-origin category, which would have reflected intermarriage and acculturation patterns, was not introduced until 1981. It was claimed by 11 percent of the respondents in 1981 and by 29 percent in 1991. The absence of the categories "Canadian" and "multiple-origin" forced people into ethnic slots. This method, demanded by gatekeepers of the two hegemonic groups as well as those of the ethno-cultural groups, has skewed public discourse on acculturation.[21] A tentative new census questionnaire tested by Statistics Canada in 1988 produced a 35.9 percent mark-in by respondents of a representative sample for "Canadian ethnic origin" and a 53 percent positive response to "Canadian ethnic identity." Canada is less diverse than it appears to some.[22]

CHAPTER TWENTY-ONE

Multicultural Lives in Canada

The policy of multiculturalism provided the framework in which immigrant men and women from a last group of labour migrants from Southern Europe – Italy and Portugal in particular – and new labour migrants and refugees from Asia, the Caribbean, and from other parts of the world, could develop their human and social capital. Their resources upon arrival were often as limited as those of Bill Johnstone, the British miner, who started his first job weakened by hunger, and of Maki Fukushima, who cooked in a lumber camp a day after arrival. For the first time in centuries, Quebec could draw on a French-language immigrant reservoir. Haitians who as slaves had been the first to free themselves and gain independence in 1804, faced a difficult present under a right-wing dictatorship.

The new immigrants shared with the old their resourcefulness, pluck, and mobility. Some of their increasingly TV-induced hopes were as overblown as the CPR's posters of earlier periods. Potential migrants from recently independent colonies first turned to their former imperial countries. France reluctantly accepted Algerians, Vietnamese, West Africans. Britain, the destination of South Asians and sub-Saharan Africans, in the process of losing its colonial empire stripped at first non-white people of citizenship and thus the right to immigrate. Empire-wide mobility of underemployed surplus populations from the former colonies resembled the moves of English "surplus" men and women in the 1920s. That emigration had been encouraged by British population planners, while the new immigration was decried as "invasion." Like France, Britain became multicoloured and multicultured. The West German government concluded labour migration agreements with North African countries but, because of the 1973 rise in oil prices and the resultant economic crisis, they were never implemented. African and Asian refugees did come. Both the United States and Canada, like Sweden and the Netherlands, reacted more openly. Assessing their economic interests in Asia as well as their humanitarian commitments, the two North American societies began a policy of non-discrimination that permitted entry of immigrants other than those from Europe.

Many-Coloured Newcomers

Labour migrants came from across the globe. Italians joined the construction industry with the help of the prewar Italian-Canadian communities. Women from the Caribbean and the Philippines entered the expanding market for domestic labour and caregivers. South Asians entered many walks of life, for example fruit farming in British Columbia. Frank Colantonio, an unskilled labourer from Italy in 1949, became a union organizer in Toronto. Tara Singh Bains, departing in 1953 from India, also began as unskilled worker and invested much time into labour unions in logging work and into religious affairs of his community in Vancouver. Joyce Fraser reached Canada from Guyana in the 1970s hoping to find a job in domestic service. Only Frank still came by boat; the others, like most immigrants after the mid-1950s travelled by plane.[1]

Frank Colantonio came from Molise in southern Italy as one of one hundred and fifty thousand Italians who reached Toronto between the late 1940s and 1965. He spoke the local dialect but during his wartime military service had learned the "good Italian." This was to be of help when he had to talk to Italians from many different localities in Toronto. An uncle had helped him to find a sponsor, a Maltese farmer. Thus Frank settled in the Maltese quarter at Dundas and Annette streets. He worked off his debt to the sponsor and became an unskilled worker in the highly fragmented and mostly non-unionized construction industry. The contractors for whom he worked, squeezed by larger builders, paid but minimal wages. Safety on the work site was of no concern and early in his career Frank saw an Estonian worker die because of an accident. His own helplessness without English induced him to take English lessons within a week after his arrival. His teacher was an acculturated Sicilian war bride who had lived in England. The helplessness of Italian and other construction workers induced him to become a union organizer and concentrate on issues of safety on the job.

While working among Italians and marrying Nella Sabusco from Italy, Frank cooperated with immigrants from Eastern Europe. In the course of his community work, he learned that Jews were not admitted to the Royal York-Kingsway neighbourhood, and dealt with English-Canadian employers and Dutch work crews. When he joined the carpenters' union, the leadership was American or Canadian-born of British origin. Several leaders were tradition-bound and bureaucratically minded; a few, like the Scot Charlie Irvine from the plasterers' union, were activists willing to risk strikes. Most had no knowledge of the multi-faceted Italian community.

Under Irvine's lead, a plasterers meeting in the Croatian hall decided in June 1957 to strike. A contract was negotiated, but for the plasterers only. For the other workers, employment did not differ from prewar railway construction: seasonal labour, long hours, low wages. By law, the men who built the cities had little or no protection. Though by now unionization was permitted, men still feared deportation. A woman, held at a police station for alleged shoplifting, hanged herself, certain that she would be deported. Frank Colantonio had to face ethnic slurs and antagonism to Italians in the labour movement. He left, took odd jobs, then worked with the Italian Immigrant Aid Society. In March 1960 five Italian workers died at an unsafe tunnel construction site. In response to community bitterness as well as to continued exploitation of contract workers, the several construction unions called strikes in 1960 and 1961. Frank returned to the labour movement: "It was a proud moment for me, watching so many Italians who had once been so timid in the face of the boss and deportation threats." He remained committed to his fellow workers but was disgusted at the in-fighting among the union leadership, with its ethnic, anti-Italian undertones.[2]

Tara Singh Bains was sponsored by his sister and brother-in-law and began is life in Canada by working on their farm near Vancouver. He was faced with cultural problems immediately. His nephews suggested to him "that if I shaved, I could make better progress." But he wanted to stay true to his Sikh religion. Tensions in the family mounted. Tara Singh Bains moved to the farm's bunkhouse to do his early morning prayer and singing without disturbing the family. He occasionally went to *gurdwaras*, Sikh temples, but mainly stayed on the farm to work off his debt. In fall he decided to become independent of the family and took a logging job in Nanaimo. He roomed in the old miners' section of the town, where Bill Johnstone had lived, among other Punjabis and Chinese. In the communal living arrangement the day and night shift men divided cooking and *roti*-baking (Indian bread). "We were members of the union, but we had no union strength." For the Punjabi immigrants, too, their lack of power was rooted in the language barrier. They could not express their grievances in union meetings and thus did what the company foreman told them to do.

Tara Singh Bains, like Frank Colantonio, was soon invited to become a union organizer. He, too, had to deal with internal bickering. Some of his opponents tried to connect him to well-known Indian communists and he was questioned by immigration officials. Economically he and his fellow workers were doing well because they lived very modestly. They pooled resources and bought a house. Politically he supported the struggle for a larger immigration quota for people from India: in 1956 it was doubled but remained low; only three hundred were permitted to come annually. Like the Italian migrants, those from India could connect to a small prewar community. Tara Singh's sister had come in the 1920s.

In 1960 Tara Singh Bains went back to India to be reunited with his family after seven years. Like Veltri, he supported improvement projects in his village, but contrary to the most other life-writings, his main concern was with his family obligations and his spiritual life. In 1966 he again set out for Vancouver. At a stopover in England, he travelled to Birmingham to see relatives from his home village who worked in the foundries. The bachelors' community had grown into a family community. In August 1971, Mrs Bains joined her husband, as the oldest son had done earlier. Tara Singh Bains tried to help fellow workers, he became active in the union again, and tried to keep up standards of quality in lumbering work; he wanted companies to be honest and boards graded well. But most of his efforts went into the religious dissentions in the Sikh community, where he remained committed to the traditional ways.[3]

Joyce Fraser, at the age of twenty-six, had an asset in her four children who had to be nurtured and who provided joy. She also had a liability, a husband. For him it was not the children but other women who provided joy. In Guyana, sailors and tourists provided romantic visions of a Canada in which one could obtain wealth; "all you needed was a will to work." The dreams elicited by the stories, for Joyce Fraser, "were the most potent reality I knew." She hated poverty as much as the Russian Jews in the 1880s and the Canadian farmers in the Depression of the 1930s.

She did have female friends in whom she could trust. Her friend Jenny was in Toronto, and trusting friends at home lent her money for her ticket. Her point of arrival was the Toronto International Airport; no days on the ocean gave her time to prepare mentally for the new world. Joyce, who had never travelled out of her own country, watched her more experienced flight companions as carefully as first-time men and women crossing the Atlantic had watched those who knew their way around. It was June 1970. A friendly customs officer wished her "a happy stay in Canada," then Jenny welcomed her.

It was not a sod hut – but an apartment in a basement. She had to sneak in, as Jenny's landlady did not like guests. Joyce and Jenny both worked as domestics, and both were exploited. Food was poor, nothing but hamburgers; old-world food certainly was more varied and tasty. They worked from sun-up to sundown, like American slaves more than a century earlier and like Depression farmers. Fed up, Joyce decided to leave without giving notice. Her employer refused to pay her outstanding wages, as farmers had refused to pay itinerant harvest labourers or

1880s factory owners had refused to pay workers. Jenny, in solidarity, left too. Lugging their suitcases, they were helped by a kindly man, since their dresses showed that they were greenhorns. Times had changed; it was but the colour of their stockings which was out of fashion. "I thought of the warmth and familiarity of my homeland, looked around at my current surroundings and felt very, very lonely, wondering where I really belonged."

Joyce did not belong. At Toronto Airport she had passed customs, not immigration. She was illegal; and she was Black, from Guyana. The four-year-old boy whom she cuddled when she was in service had once said to her: "Mom says white people are better than black people." In an immigrant society she had received help from a white woman and good wishes from a courteous customs officer. The man who had spotted the greenhorn dress was from Trinidad. With the help of a friend from Barbados, he found them a place to stay "in an area where other black people lived." Though Joyce Fraser's experiences in many ways resembled those of European newcomers, including the fear of deportation, she also shared the racist discrimination experienced by Toronto's Black community of the 1900s and the Caribbean community of the interwar years. Canadian society was in the process of opening up, but the process was slow. Some did not bother about colour, but some passed their racism on to their children. Others did not: "I met one woman who had been deported – the child she used to babysit was grief-stricken so the employer wrote to the woman, had her change the name on her passport and sponsored her back." Jenny had no such luck. She returned home with her three Canadian-born children to take care of her sick mother. Neighbours ridiculed her "success": children instead of money. The children did not adjust to her home country. When Jenny attempted to return illegally she was caught and deported.

Joyce Fraser, after a bad time and constant worrying, lived on the margins of criminality. She tried to find roots, calling herself Haile Telatra Edoney. She had to have several identities, a different name for each job, and other names and life-stories for acquaintances. As in the labour movement, stool-pigeons spied among the illegals. When people asked her, "Are you new here?" she would answer, "I lived five years in Montreal." Finally, she found an employer who "treated all his workers with equality and respect and his supervisors did the same ... It was the first company where I had seen so many different races united together." Her persistence, as well as an immigration system that permitted appeals, finally gave her landed status. She got a divorce from her old-country husband and found a new partner from the same culture, brought in her children and, given the new citizenship law, could and did become a citizen.[4]

Contested Culture: Retention or Change?

About fifteen years after Joyce Fraser wrote her story, *Cry of the Illegal Immigrant*, another immigrant yelled, "Don't call me ethnic." Like Joyce Fraser, he wanted to be Canadian. Unlike Joyce, who had a story to tell, East Indian–Trinidadian–Canadian Neil Bissoondath in Quebec used his influence as an author to attack policies that provided the frame for active participation in his chosen society.[5] Joyce had wanted respect, a chance to work and to raise her children. Respect was what the policy was about.

Gatekeepers for a die-hard British segment of society felt their culture, which they still equated with Canadian culture, to be threatened. After high-handed pronouncements, they would probably have dinner in a Chinese restaurant, sit down in a French bistro, or have an espresso in a corner shop. Gatekeepers for a sovereigntist French segment extolled language and school attendance laws as protection for their culture with little regard for other cultures. Gatekeepers of ethnic groups demanded financial allocations and made preservation of culture the task of an ethnic-group bureaucracy. The policy had become contested ground.

A re-examination of the two most important terms of the current debate, "mosaic" and "multicultural," may clarify issues. Most Canadians prefer to live in the Canadian mosaic rather than under Anglo-conformity or a multicultural francophonie. A mosaic, in common understanding, consists of components glued or cemented into a defined space. An ethnic who cannot move out of his or her assigned slot has reason to complain; an English-origin or *pure laine* Québécois child, prevented from participating in other cultural worlds by parents travelling a cultural one-way street, has reason to distance himself or herself from the parental generation's culture. Culture is always in motion. It is as full of colour as a mosaic, as changing as a kaleidoscope, but adds new people constantly.

"Newcomers cling to their cultural ways." This challenge by old-stock Canadians projects onto new Canadians what they themselves practise, retention of an unchanged culture. Does multiculturalism and diversity fragment the country? Is there a canned culture, to be preserved unchanged until its expiration date? Is there a pure culture, passed from generation to generation through either British blood or French language or Canadian lineage? Funding of multicultural activities has not influenced ethnic voting patterns nor has emphasis on heritage reduced intermarriage or naturalization. Again, perceived interest and everyday interaction determine options and life-course projects.

Regionalism has been and is a strong factor in Canadian history and an important component in the formation of identities. The life-writings testify to regional pluralism, as do the debates of the 1990s about identity and unity, about distinctiveness of the provinces. Secondly, social class and status are important in the creation of culture. Toronto or Alberta workers, Quebec, Ontario, or Western farmers, Newfoundland or British Columbia fishermen, college students or entrepreneurs experience different ways of living. Depending on the region and stage of economic development, experiences may overlap; for example, in the past, small farmers spent part of each year as bunkhouse workers; social work students lived in hostels for the unemployed. Interaction in regions where societies were just being established evinced an intensity that crossed social classes and was not found in Quebec City or Victoria. In the present, the emergence of the two-income family has resulted in a demand for cheap domestic labour from abroad. Thirdly, culture is gendered. Middle-class men's norms might restrict their women to homes or mansions, but farm work did not permit this particular type of separation of spheres. Among some ethno-cultural groups families appear in public arenas, among others it is mainly the men. Fourthly, age explains difference. Native-born senior citizens often eye teenagers' lifestyles with critical concern or outspoken hostility; immigrant senior citizens find it difficult to understand the culture of their grandchildren. Culture is not only highly diversified, it is dynamic and has to be negotiated between generations.

None of the many Canadian cultures remained static over time, as is illustrated by the Quiet Revolution in Quebec, which brought new immigrants and new economic options for the native-born; by the dynamic growth of economic connections to Asia experienced in Vancouver and its Hong Kong–Chinese population; by the emergence of Toronto as a banking centre and its South Asian clerks. Whether in the Prairies of the 1900s or the metropolises of the 1990s, culture is an ever-changing interaction of people in specific economies and tradition-framed societies to achieve emotionally, materially, and spiritually comfortable lives, or, in bad times, to survive. Governments and gatekeepers which deny internal diversity can formulate no policies, can provide no remedies for inequality, can create no respect for cultural differences. They become caretakers of monocultural stagnation.

Cultures which immigrants bring with them in their hearts, minds, and everyday practices are as changeable. Old societies, including those of Britain or France, are no models to be re-established. The decision to migrate implies a decision to change. Men and women leave their homelands because they are pushed out, because their options for their future lives are limited, because they want to explore new worlds. Walter Chuchla saw few options in 1920s Poland, Joyce Fraser few in 1970s Guyana. Tara Singh Bains seized economic opportunities but rejected religious change. The old and new worlds were entwined before migration by flows of goods and capital, by power and class structures. Italian and Polish peasants were forced from their tiny plots when the mass production of wheat in the Canadian prairies (and elsewhere) made grain prices in world markets tumble. Guyana and Filipino domestics fled the class structure imposed by European and American colonialism and native elites. Tara Singh Bains had been mobilized into the Indian army with its British traditions and British officers. In contrast to the voluntary migrants, refugees depart because a particular regime becomes life-threatening, not because everyday culture has become intolerable. Ugandan Asians, Cambodian or Vietnamese refugees remained attached to their culture as a way of life but still had to find ways to become part of their new societies.

After migration, immigrant or ethnic lifestyles develop as an exchange between a remembered past, the present in the new society, and the ever-important hope for the future. Newcomers, native-born, and old-stock Canadians face severe psychological strain when confronted with demands to change cultural identities immediately and unconditionally. When Native Canadians were forced to submit to the indignity of cultural surrender by the ancestors of old-stock Canadians, they faced disruption of identities and they never accepted it. When native-born and immigrant Canadians were hurtled into the depths of the Great Depression, they resented the economic assault on "the very being of people," as much as recent newcomers and native-born resent the havoc of the recession after 1973.

Acculturation to a new society's ways of living takes time. So does adaptation by residents to the input of newcomers. Cultures are not switched on or off mechanically. Interaction develops according to needs, as among the homesteaders, or by cultural preference, as when young Canadians choose Caribbean immigrant music, or by economic incentive as when expense-conscious men and women frequent ethnic restaurants rather than Muskoka or Whistler spas. Mono-culturally minded proponents of assimilation who demand of immigrants, "If they chose Canada, they should accept its way," have not understood their own culture's complexities. Furthermore, political exiles and refugees did not chose. They were propelled into Canada by forces beyond their control. Refugees from communist rule in East Central Europe were celebrated as freedom fighters. Do Sri Lankan refugees and Bosnian Muslims in the 1990s have a starting point as helpful as that?[6]

Processes of acculturation are evident all through Canadian history. Early French and Scottish immigrants to Acadia, for example, had to adapt to a new environment and new neighbours. They did not negotiate entry with the resident Micmac people, just as undocumented migrants in the 1990s arrive without asking permission. Did the French and British show respect for the multiple First Nations cultures they entered? In the early 1900s Ukrainians (or Italians or any other ethnic group) were not convinced by British-Canadian models. They founded their own organizations and established a basis in the new society that permitted them at first to survive, and then, to prosper, if economic conditions permitted. All, from First Nations via the founding peoples and pioneer immigrants to newcomers from Africa, Latin America, and Asia have become hyphenated Canadians – in sum total a new mainstream.

Political scientists view diversity of interest or lobby groups as elements of the democratic political processes. Immigrants' self-organization in fully structured ethnic communities is seen as clannishness in the eyes of assimilationists, institutional completeness in sociological terms, and self-help in the terms of economists. From this solid base, newcomers can negotiate with the many-cultured host society and achieve what as individuals they could not have hoped for at home. They finally become Canadians of Ukrainian or Caribbean or other descent, an identity that combines a distant shared past with a common new future. This change involves loss. Gus Romaniuk remembered his neat village when looking at the Manitoba homestead; Maria Campbell introduced her 1973 autobiography, *Halfbreed*: "The house where I grew up is tumbled down and overgrown with brush."[7]

Retention is a slowdown of changes to permit a withering of older identities without psychological damage and to allow the development of new identities without demands for unconditional surrender.[8] Multicultural schools provide ways for children of immigrants to enter the main cultures and routes for children of native-born parents to adapt to many different cultures. Specific heritage courses, whether Polish or British, Caribbean or French, require intergenerational mediators. Children in schools confront their own time, and also are being educated for the future. Respect for the past does not make children mere receptacles for memories of earlier generations. Cultural retention by one generation, often frozen in time or restricted to quaint symbols, shifts the burden of adjustment to the next generation.

Many aspects of so-called heritage culture are remnants of a past that the fathers and mothers of today's Canadians left generations ago: Polish folk dances, Scottish kilts, Oktoberfests. Ukrainian painted eggs,

Bereft of their complex spiritual meaning in their culture of origin, they have become symbols of cultural contributions. With only a superficial resemblance to old-world cultural practices, they now serve a new purpose, – communication with neighbouring people from other cultures. What is being preserved is a Canadian construction of visible aspects of cultures of the past – symbolic ethnicity. Change of formerly lived cultures to symbols indicates integration into a new culture, in which power blocs or excluding boundaries are no longer needed.

Recent immigrant groups, on the other hand, are still close to the cultural practices of their homelands and are still engaged in a process of adaptation. Some cultural practices – Caribbean music, for example – also reach younger Canadians of other cultural backgrounds and young people worldwide. Some economic contributions, of the immigrants from Hong Kong, for example, touch native-born Canadians in many walks of life.

Multicultural Identities

After the 1960s Canada developed a new identity. Quebec changed; its new economic dynamics brought forth calls for *survivance*. In Ontario and elsewhere, schools lost their anglo-exclusionism and the resulting provincialism. Universities moved from a colonial British position in proximity to an overshadowing, powerful neighbouring state to the south to a strong position of their own. Because of the impact on the next generation and thus the future, the changes in education were of particular importance. In 1971 the policy of multiculturalism was announced. By 1996 half of the Canadian population had been born or had immigrated after 1971 and thus has lived its whole life in the new culture.[9]

In the past, allophone immigrants joined the Canadian societies over generations; at present, English-speaking Hong Kong–Chinese and French-speaking Haitians can communicate immediately. The First Nations, whose self-organization has evolved since the 1960s, forced Euro- and other Canadians to recognize that they deserved as much respect as any cultural group, whether early French, 1900s Italian, or recent Jamaican. The immigrant contribution, the policy of multiculturalism, and everyday multicultural interaction provided the "two solitudes" and the "ethnic-group apparatuses" with new options.

Problems of transcultural interaction often involve self-defined white Canadians and their relationship to other races or complexions. The concept of race was a tool of power for empires, British, French, and other, and of hegemonic cultures. The Scottish-Métis British Columbia elite, the dark East Europeans, the olive-skinned Italians, the religiously different Jews, had to portray themselves as white before they could define men and women from other continents summarily as non-white. Visible minorities, Native Canadians, Afro-Canadians, Caribbean-Canadians, and Asian-Canadians have all become part of the society. Free choice of partners by men and women outside socially defined colour boundaries joins multi-ethnic with multicoloured ancestry. To remedy structural and individual Euro-Canadian discrimination against newcomers of different religions, complexions, or alphabet, the designation "visible minorities" was introduced for purposes of equalization policies and affirmative action programs. Two decades later some people assigned to these categories no longer place themselves there. Chinese-origin students do not consider themselves visible, as a study at York University has shown, while students of African or Caribbean background are still being racialized.[10]

Diversity and fragmentation ascribed to immigrants often reflects a generational conflict among Canadians whether native or foreign-born, as a study at the University of Calgary indicates. In political behaviour and choices, older Canadians and older immigrants act alike, as do younger Canadians and younger immigrants. Diversity is generational not ethno-cultural. Young Canadians seem to pay considerably less attention to one, two, or many Canadas than today's older politicians, as other opinion polls show. Ethno-cultural groups have become interest groups, similar to those based on economic status, employer organizations and unions, or, more recently recognized, based on gender.[11] Depending on their length of stay and degree of acculturation, men and women will decide for themselves whether to consider themselves intercultural Canadians, hyphenated ethnics, or recent newcomers.[12]

People of many origins, complexions, and cultures continue to arrive because the larger problems of exploitative terms of trade and global apartheid have not been solved, because the image of the Western world projected in movies and TV programs permits glimpses of wealth, if skewed ones. Immigrants of the 1990s have hopes – like the genteel Britishers who settled in the bush or Montcalm who wanted to defend an empire or Albert Eskra who wanted to establish a farm. Joyce Fraser warns: "The grass isn't greener on the other side, you are more likely to end up with a fistful of dust." Susanna Moodie called that experience "roughing it." Some immigrants would not have moved had they known before what awaited them in hardships and discrimination.

Others never regretted the moves. In 1991, in between the bank towers of downtown Toronto, two German visitors bought hot dogs from a street-corner vendor, who joined their German-language discussion. His parents had come as Baltic Germans after the Second World War, and he considered himself an independent businessman. A day later the same visitors and a Canadian couple of Quebec-Italian and Dutch background, who spoke French among themselves entered a Sri Lankan store. The Sri Lankan shopkeeper joined the French conversation. Surprised, the shoppers tried one-upmanship and added German to the language mix. Undaunted, the shopkeeper's brother conversed in fluent German about his experiences as a worker in southern Germany. If that much choice is available, why restrict oneself to a homogenized culture mandated by a minority with no more than one language, lacking cultural choices, with Wonderbread and McHumburgers for food?

"I was ten years old and didn't speak a word of English. I had to learn it or I would have problems in school." The scene takes place after the dismantling of the British Empire in 1962. Dilip Bhindi, the son of a family of Indian goldsmiths arrived in Uganda where the Indian colony had been established under the Asian contract labour migration system at about 1900. His sister moved to England, the grandmother remained in their home village. Ten years later, President Idi Amin expelled the Ugandan Asians. "The military police were pushing, beating and tormenting people, taking their money, jewelry and anything else of value." People were desperate to get out. As skilled watchmakers, the Bhindi family fit Canadian criteria for refugees and was among the seven thousand Ugandan Indians accepted. On the evacuation flight, the "Canadian government even thought of providing Indian food because many of us don't eat meat." In Montreal, Dilip, now fluent in English and French, translated as go-between for his non-English-speaking father. As Leah Rosenberg had done half a century earlier. Father and son quickly found jobs but had no tools. At the supplier's they realized that they needed $550 but were penniless. The "owner of the store, a lady," verified their story with the prospective employer, then let them have the tools on credit and trust – as in Helgi Einarsson's Winnipeg. Diasporic connections continued. Dilip married a South Asian woman from Kenya to whom he had been introduced by his sister in England. When his father saw a chance to buy a store in Ottawa, a friend in England wired him the money for the initial down payment. In conclusion, Dilip noted: "Multiculturalism really works in Montreal."[13]

Jean Robert Milord's experience in Montreal in 1971 was more negative, involving unfriendly immigration officials and clear racism, his fluent French notwithstanding. Everything was different; he could not enter school, did not find a job, and the food tasted strange. "In Haiti all doors are open. People visit and talk. Here, all doors are closed." Though trained as a medical technician, he had to take odd jobs. In 1971 Black people had a long history in Canada but white people still had a long way to go to end racism.

Racial hierarchies are complex. Meera Shastri, from India, who dreamed of building bridges between two cultures, had her master's degree rejected by a Canadian university and was told to get rid of the red dot on her forehead indicating that she was married. Her first job interview was with a man whose Indian ancestors had migrated to Australia. He spent his time explaining to her that she, the Indian-Indian, and he, the Australian-Indian, had nothing in common. Meera as an immigrant was expected to be submissive, "you are hired not on the basis of your merits, but because of your weakness." This degrading experience she shared with nearly all immigrants from Asia in early twentieth-century British Columbia, but also with European newcomers from non-imperial peoples. Meera stuck out because her English was perfect. Though of Hindu faith, she and her husband decided to have a small Christmas tree for their son.

This combination of heritages was voluntary. But their little son had to realize: "I'm white at home and become brown when I go to day-care." This duality of colours was involuntary, assigned by outsiders. With pressure, the ascribed colour may influence the individual's sense of identity. Three-quarters of a century ago Italians in Montreal were "olive," a quarter-century ago Black Americans fought for Black consciousness: "Black is beautiful." Not blindness, but respect for difference is needed. Cultural interaction is an unending journey.[14]

Notes

PREFACE

1 Dirk Hoerder, "Migrants to Ethnics: Acculturation in a Societal Framework," in Dirk Hoerder and Leslie Page Moch, eds., *European Migrants: Global and Local Perspectives* (Boston: Northeastern University Press, 1996), 211–62, and Hoerder, "Labour Markets – Community – Family: A Gendered Analysis of the Process of Insertion and Acculturation," in Wsevolod Isajiw, ed., *Multiculturalism in North America and Europe: Comparative Perspectives on Interethnic Relations and Social Incorporation* (Toronto: Canadian Scholar's Press, 1997), 155–83.

2 Walter R. Heinz, "Status Passages, Social Risks and the Life Course: A Conceptual Framework," in Walter R. Heinz, ed., *Theoretical Advances in Life Course Research* (Weinheim: Deutscher Studien Verlag, 1991), 9–22; Carol B. Stack and Linda Burton, "Kinscripts," in ibid., 115–29; Martin Kohli, "The World We Forgot: A Historical Review of the Life Course," in Victor W. Marshall, ed., *Later Life: The Social Psychology of Aging* (Beverly Hills: Sage, 1986), 271–303; Helga Krüger, "Statusmanagement und Institutionenregimes. Die Kategorie Geschlecht zwischen Leistung und Zuschreibung" (Research paper, Universität Bremen, September 1995); Nina Glick Schiller, Linda Basch, Cristina Blanc-Szanton, *Towards a Transnational Perspective on Migration: Race, Class, Ethnicity and Nationalism Reconsidered* (New York: New York Academy of Sciences, 1992); Louise A. Tilly and Joan W. Scott, *Women, Work and Family* (New York: Holt, Rinehart and Winston, 1978); Ansgar Weymann and Walter R. Heinz, eds., *Society and Biography. Interrelationships between Social Structure, Institutions and the Life Course* (Weinheim: Deutscher Studien Verlag, 1996).

3 Michael Katz, "The People of a Canadian City: 1851–52," *Canadian Historical Review* 53 (1972), 402–26.

4 Only a few historical studies will be cited to place the immigrants' writings in context. For further literature, see J.W. Berry and J.A. Laponce, eds., *Ethnicity and Culture in Canada: The Research Landscape* (Toronto: University of Toronto Press, 1994); Franca Iacovetta, *The Writing of English*

Canadian History (Ottawa: Canadian Historical Association, 1997); Roberto Perin, "National History and Ethnic History in Canada," *Cahiers de recherche sociologique* 20 (1993); Danielle Juteau, "The Sociology of Ethnic Relations in Quebec: History and Discourse" (mimeographed, Department of Sociology, University of Toronto, 1991).

CHAPTER ONE

1 According to recent archeological evidence, the Basques were pioneers of the fur trade before the French. A theme park is planned at the archeological site in Trois-Pistoles, on the south shore of the St Lawrence. See *Maclean's* magazine, 21 October 1996.

2 William J. Rattray, *The Scot in British North America*, 4 vols. (Toronto: Mclear, 1880–3), 1:24; Ralph Connor, *The Man from Glengarry* (Chicago: F.H. Revell Co., 1901), *Glengarry School Days* (Chicago: F.H. Revell Co., 1902). As early as 1861 Alexander McLachlan had eulogized emigration and forest clearing in his long poem "The Emigrant," in *The Emigrant and Other Poems* (Toronto: Rollo, 1861), 8–89. The oral tradition of Highland Scots has recently been collected and translated: Margaret MacDonell, *The Emigrant Experience: Songs of Highland Emigrants in North America* (Toronto: University of Toronto Press, 1982). See also Robert Sellar, *A Scotsman in Upper Canada: The Narrative of Gordon Sellar* (1915; repr. Toronto: Clark Irwin, 1969).

3 Clifford Sifton in 1897, quoted in John W. Dafoe, *Clifford Sifton in Relation to His Times* (Toronto: Macmillan, 1931), 142; Sifton, "The Immigrants Canada Wants," *Maclean's* magazine, 1 April 1922, cited in Howard Palmer, ed., *Immigration and the Rise of Multiculturalism* (Toronto: Copp Clark, 1975), 35.

4 M.C. Urquhart, K.A.H. Buckley, eds., *Historical Statistics of Canada* (Toronto: Macmillan, 1965), series E 130–42.

5 The settlement of the North American continent, including the contact between European immigrants and Native peoples has most recently been summarized in Helen H. Tanner et al., eds., *The Settling of North America: The Atlas of the Great Migrations into North America from the Ice Age to the Present* (New York: Macmillan, 1995). The best account of Amerindians in Canada is Olive Patricia Dickason, *Canada's First Nations: A History of Founding Peoples from Earliest Times* (Toronto: McClelland and Stewart, 1992). The concept of interacting global migration systems was first developed in Dirk Hoerder, "Migration in the Atlantic Economies: Regional European Origins and Worldwide Expansion," in Dirk Hoerder and Leslie Page Moch, eds., *European Migrants: Global and Local Perspectives* (Boston: Northeastern University Press, 1995), 21–51. A synthesis of immigration is provided by Jean R. Burnet with Howard Palmer, *"Coming Canadians": An Introduction to a History of Canada's Peoples* (Toronto:

McClelland and Stewart, 1988). On United States–Canadian migration, see the dated classic study by Marcus Lee Hansen with John B. Brebner, *The Mingling of the Canadian and American Peoples* (New Haven: Yale University Press, 1940). Canada is placed in a comparative perspective by Walter Nugent, *Crossings: The Great Transatlantic Migrations, 1870–1914* (Bloomington: Indiana University Press, 1992).

CHAPTER TWO

1 J.W. Berry and J.A. Laponce, eds., *Ethnicity and Culture in Canada: The Reseach Landscape* (Toronto: University of Toronto Press, 1994); Jean R. Burnet with Howard Palmer, *"Coming Canadians": An Introduction to a History of Canada's Peoples* (Toronto: McClelland and Stewart, 1988); Dirk Hoerder, "Ethnic Studies in Canada from the 1880s to 1962: A Historiographical Perspective and Critique," *Canadian Ethnic Studies* 26, no. 1 (1994), 1–18.

2 Concise summaries of the development of different types of Canadian life-writings are included in Carl F. Klinck et al., eds., *Literary History of Canada*, 4 vols., 2nd ed. (Toronto: University of Toronto Press, 1976, 1990), and in Norah Story, ed., *Oxford Companion to Canadian History and Literature* (Oxford: Oxford University Press, 1967).

3 Women's autobiographical writing has been juxtaposed to male patriarchal writing. In the texts I have used, borderlines between male and female writing are fluent.

4 Beatrice Didier, *Le journal intime* (Paris: Presses Universitaires Françaises, 1926), 8; Philippe Lejeune, *La pacte autobiographique: Je est un autre, moi aussi* (Paris: Seuil, 1975); Gustav René Hocke, *Das europäische Tagebuch* (Wiesbaden: Limes, 1963). Daniel Shea, *Spiritual Autobiography in Early America* (Princeton: Princeton University Press, 1968); John Burnett et al., eds., *The Autobiography of the [British] Working Class: An Annotated Critical Bibliography*, 3 vols. (New York: New York University Press, 1984–89), xiii-xxxvi; Wolfgang Emmerich, *Proletarische Lebensläufe*, 2 vols. (Reinbek: Rowohlt, 1974). In France, Frédéric LePlay, 1806–82, and his Société d'économie sociale, founded in 1856, developed a working-class biography from a paternalist standpoint. See also Pierre Savard, ed., *Paysans et ouvriers québécois d'autrefois* (Québec: Presses de l'Université Laval, 1968), 9–11.

5 E.P. Thompson, "The Moral Economy of the English Crowd," *Past and Present* 50 (February 1971), 76–135.

6 "Ebe Koeppen's Story," in Rolf Knight, ed., *Stump Ranch Chronicles and Other Narratives* (Vancouver: New Star, 1977), 136.

7 Walter D. Kamphoefner, Wolfgang Helbich, and Ulrike Sommer, eds., *News from the Land of Freedom: German Immigrants Write Home*, transl. by Susan Carter Vogel (German orig., 1988; Ithaca: Cornell, 1991), introduction.

8 Ernesto L. Biagi, *Manuale della Societá italo-americana: Trattato pratico della ritualistica e delle attivité sociali e fraternalistiche* (Philadelphia, 1940); Nuovissimo Segretario Universale, *Manuale teorico pratico per scrivere lettere familiari-commerciali-amorose-suppliche-bilietti d'inviti-ecc. prededuto da regole speciali come scrivere le lettere* (New York, n.d.). Gianfausto Rosoli, "Autobiography and Popular Memory of Italian Immigrants in Canada" (unpublished paper, n.p., n.d.), passim. Herman Ganzevoort, "Dempsey-Tunney and the Emigration Question: Dutch Immigration Correspondents in 1920s Canada," *Canadian Ethnic Studies*. 20, no. 1 (1988), 140–52; and Herman Ganzevoort, ed., "The Last Illusion: Letters from the 'Land of Opportunity,' 1924–1930" (ms., Calgary, 1993).

9 Mary Jo Maynes, "Autobiography and Class Formation in Nineteenth-Century Europe: Methodological Considerations," *Social Science History* 16 (1992), 517–37; David Vincent, *Bread, Knowledge and Freedom. A Study of Working-class Autobiography* (London: Europa, 1980); Carol Poore, *Deutsch-amerikanische sozialistische Literatur, 1865–1900* (Berlin: Akademie, 1987); Susan Jackel, ed., *A Flannel Shirt and Liberty: British Emigrant Gentlewomen in the Canadian West, 1880–1914* (Vancouver: University of British Columbia Press, 1982). The account of a Russian Jew, Michael Usiskin, who had been a worker in London from 1906 to 1911, resembles the working-class self-improvement style, in *Uncle Mike's Edenbridge [Sask.]: Memoirs of a Jewish Pioneer Farmer*, transl. from the Yiddish by Marcia U. Basman (Winnipeg: Peguis, 1983).

10 Daniel Simeoni and Marco Diani, eds., "Biographical Research," special issue of *Current Sociology* 43, no. 2/3 (Autumn-Winter 1995); Pierre Nora, "Between Memory and History: Les Lieux de Mémoire," in Geneviève Fabre and Robert O'Meally, eds., *History and Memory in African-American Culture* (New York: Oxford, 1994), 284–300; Anna R. Burr, *The Autobiography: A Critical and Comparative Study* (Boston: Houghton Mifflin, 1909); Robert Elbaz, *The Changing Nature of the Self: A Critical Study of Autobiographic Discourse* (London: Croom Helm, 1988); James Olney, ed., *Autobiography: Essays Theoretical and Cultural* (Princeton: Princeton University Press, 1980); Roy Pascal, *Design and Truth in Autobiography* (London: Routledge, 1960); Estelle Jelinek, ed., *Women's Autobiography: Essays in Criticism* (Bloomington: Indiana University Press, 1980); Susan Jackel, "Canadian Women's Autobiography. A Problem of Criticism," in Barbara Godard, ed., *Gynocritics: Feminist Approaches to Canadian and Quebec Women's Writing* (Toronto: ECWPress, 1978), 97–110.

11 For the literature by male travellers and sportsmen, see the province entries in Storey, ed., *Oxford Companion to Canadian History and Literature*. Elizabeth Waterston, "Travel Books 1880–1920," in Klinck, *Literary History*, one-vol. ed. (Toronto: University of Toronto Press, 1967), 347–63, provides an analysis of purposes and narrative strategies.

12 M. Elizabeth Aubé, in "Oral History and the Remembered Word: Cultural Determinants from French Canada," *International Journal of Oral History* 10, no. 1 (1989), 31–49, deals with issues of memory and selectivity.

13 W. Burton Hurd, *Origin, Birthplace, Nationality and Language of the Canadian People*, 1921 Census Monograph (Ottawa: Dominion Bureau of Statistics, 1929), and "The Case for a Quota," *Queen's Quarterly* 36 (Winter 1929), 145–9.

14 Timothy D. Adams, *Telling Lies in Modern American Autobiography* (Chapel Hill: University of North Carolina Press, 1990), 2; James C. Holte, ed., *The Ethnic I: A Sourcebook for Ethnic-American Autobiography* (Westport: Greenwood, 1988), 1–8, and "The Representative Voice: Autobiography and the Ethnic Experience," *MELUS* 9 (1982), 25–46; Albert E. Stone, "Autobiography and American Culture," *American Studies: An International Newsletter* 11 (Winter 1972), 27; Philip Abbott, *States of Perfect Freedom: Autobiography and American Political Thought* (Amherst: University of Massachusetts Press, 1987).

15 William I. Thomas and Florian Znaniecki, *The Polish Peasant in Europe and America*, 5 vols. (Chicago, Boston, 1918–1920; repr. in several different editions); [Crashing Thunder/Sam Blowsnake], *The Autobiography of an American [Winnebago] Indian*, ed. Paul Radin (Berkeley: University of California Press, 1920; rev. ed., 1926); *The Polish Memoir Sociology* (Warsaw: Polish Scientific Publications, 1982).

16 William C. Spengemann and L.R. Lundquist, "Autobiography and the American Myth," *American Quarterly* 17 (1965), 501–4; San-ling Cynthia Wong, "Immigrant Autobiography: Some Questions of Definition and Approach," in Paul John Eakin, ed., *American Autobiography: Retrospect and Prospect* (Madison: University of Wisconsin Press, 1991), 161.

17 Michael Woolf, "The Haunted House: Jewish-American Autobiography," in A. Robert Lee, ed., *First Person Singular: Studies in American Autobiography* (London: Vision, 1988), 198–203; G. Thomas Couser, *American Autobiography: The Prophetic Mood* (Amherst: University of Massachusetts Press, 1979), 210–14.

18 Examples of widely circulated immigrant autobiographies include Mary Antin, *The Promised Land: The Autobiography of a Russian Immigrant* (1st ed., 1911; Princeton: Princeton University Press, 1969); Anzia Yezierska, *Bread Givers: A Novel* (1st ed., 1925; New York: Persea, 1975); Jerre Mangione, *Mount Allegro: A Memoir of Italian American Life* (1st ed., 1943; New York: Columbia University Press, 1981); Louis Adamic, *Laughing in the Jungle: The Autobiography of an Immigrant in America* (1st ed., 1932; Salem: Ayer Publishers, 1985).

19 See for example, W. Christopher Atkinson, *The Emigrant's Guide to New Brunswick, British North America* (1842), as well as Alexander Wedderburn (1835), Abraham Gesner (1847), John Stewart (1806), John Lewellin

(1832), S.S. Hill (1839), John S. Springer (1851), Alexander Monro (1855), C. Birch Bagster (1861). See Storey, ed., *Oxford Companion to Canadian History and Literature,* for full citations.

20 Other authors included Anna Jameson and Anne Langton. After his stint as superintendent of the Canada Company, in 1826–9, John Galt, in two novels (London, 1830 and 1831) extolled the characteristics and strengths settlers must possess to overcome the difficulties of frontier life. Thomas McCulloch, "Letters of Mephibosheth Stepsure," *Acadian Recorder,* 1921–2. The letters of a well-to-do Irish immigrant family acquainted with the Traills were published in 1889. See also Frances (Browne) Stewart [1794–1872] *Our Forest Home, Being Extracts from the Correspondence of the Late Frances Stewart,* ed. Eleanor S. Dunlop (Toronto, 1889).

21 Life-writings of early immigrants, whether English, Irish, or Scottish confirm the distinctiveness of the three main English-language cultures as well as of the Cornish and Welsh cultures.

22 Guildo Rousseau, *L'Image des États-Unis dans la littérature québécoise, 1775–1930* (Sherbrooke, Que.: Édition Naaman, 1981).

23 Thomas Chandler Haliburton, *The Clockmaker, Or, The Sayings and Doings of Samuel Slick of Slickville* (Halifax, 1836); Julia Beckwith Hart, *Tonnewonte, Or, The Adopted Son of America* (Watertown, NY, 1825); Frederick Marryat, *The Settlers in Canada,* 2 vols. (London, 1844).

24 George Bourne, *Lorette: The History of Louise, Daughter of a Canadian Nun, Exhibiting the Interior of a Female Convent* (New York, 1834). Anne Sadlier, *Elinor Preston, Or, Scenes from Home and Abroad* (New York, 1851). Bourne had lived in Quebec from 1825 to 1828, Sadlier in Montreal.

25 *Dictionary of Literary Biography* (Detroit: Gale, since 1978), 52: 50–3.

26 Grant Overton, "The Man Called Ralph Connor," in his *American Nights Entertainment* (New York: Apelleton, 1923), 178–88. Connor, *Corporal Cameron of the North West Mounted Police* (1912).

27 See, for example, Nicholas F. Davin, *The Irishman in Canada* (Toronto, 1877).

28 Major publications in ethnic languages predating studies in the official languages include (by year of publication): Abraham Rhinewine, *Der Yid in Kanada,* 2 vols. (Toronto: Farlag Kanada, 1925, 1927); Ödön Paizs, *Magyarok Kanadában. Egy most készülö országról* (Budapest: Athenaeum, 1928); *A Kanadai Magyarság Története* (Toronto: Ruzsa Jeneo, 1940); V.A. Sukhorev, *Istoriya Dukhobotsev* (Grand Forks, B.C., 1944); Benjamin Gutelius Sack, *Geshikhte fun Yidn in Kanade: fun di friste unheybn bis der letster tsayt* (Montreal: Komitet fun fraynt, 1948), as *History of the Jews in Canada,* transl. by R. Novek (Montreal: Harvest, 1965); B.J. Zubrzycki, *Polacy w Kanadzie (1759–1946)* (Toronto: Kongres Polonji Kanadyskiej, 1947); G. Okulevich, *Russkie v Kanade* (Toronto: Federatsii Russkikh Kanadtsev, 1952); Guglielmo Vangelisti, *Gli*

Italiani in Canada (1st ed., 1955; rev. ed., Montreal: Chiesa italiana di N.S. della Difesa, 1958).

29 Rosoli, Autobiography and "Popular Memory," 4.

30 Almost no Native Canadian and Métis life-writings exist. However, see James P. Spradley, *Guests Never Leave Hungry: The Autobiography of James Sewid, a Kwakiutl Indian* (Montreal: McGill-Queen's University Press, 1972); Maria Campbell, *Halfbreed* (1st publ. 1973; Halifax: Goodread, 1983); Irene M. Spry, ed., "The 'Memories' of George William Sanderson, 1846–1936", *Canadian Ethnic Studies* 17, no. 2 (1985), 115–34.

31 My language competency is limited to English, French, and German (exclusive of Mennonite-German). Many immigrants published in English or were translated into English. A Norwegian text was made available to me in summary.

CHAPTER THREE

1 "Témoignages," in Bruno Ramirez, *Les premiers Italiens de Montréal. L'origine de la Petite Italie du Québec* (Montréal: Boréal, 1984), 101–2.

2 Joanna Matejko, ed., *Polish Settlers in Alberta. Reminiscences and Biographies* (Toronto: Polish Alliance, 1979), 38, 49, 121, 146.

3 Ibid., 31; Evan Davies, *Beyond the Old Bone Trail* (London: Cassell, 1960), 4–5.

4 Dirk Hoerder, "The Traffic of Emigration via Bremen/Bremerhaven: Merchants' Interests, Protective Legislation, and Migrants' Experiences," *Journal of American Ethnic History* 13 (1993), 68–101; Hoerder and Horst Rössler, eds., *Distant Magnets: Expectations and Realities in the Immigrant Experience* (New York: Holmes and Meier, 1993); Hoerder with Diethelm Knauf, eds., *Fame, Fortune and Sweet Liberty: The Great European Migration*, transl. Thomas Kozak (Bremen: Temmen, 1992), 9–26.

5 Alexander A. Boddy, *By Ocean, Prairie and Peak: Some Gleanings from an Emigrant Chaplain's Log* (London, 1896), 9, 16; [M.C.S. London], *Adventures in Canada* (London, 1866).

6 Robert Whyte, *The Ocean Plague ...* (Boston, 1848), repr. as *Robert Whyte's 1847 Famine Ship Diary: The Journey of an Irish Coffin Ship*, ed. James J. Mangan (Cork: Mercier, 1994); Robert Scally, "Liverpool Ships and Irish Emigrants in the Age of Sail," *Journal of Social History* 17 (1984), 5–30.

7 Peter O'Leary, *Travels and Experiences in Canada, the Red River Territory, and the United States* (London, 1877), 11–17.

8 James Thomson, *For Friends at Home: A Scottish Emigrant's Letters from Canada, California and the Cariboo, 1844–1964*, ed. Richard A. Preston (Montreal: McGill-Queen's University Press, 1970), 41–8, 60; Cecil J. Houston and William J. Smyth, *Irish Emigration and Canadian Settlement:*

Patterns, Links and Letters (Toronto: University of Toronto Press, 1990), 255–6; Leah Rosenberg, *The Errand Runner: Reflections of a Rabbi's Daughter* (Toronto: Wiley, 1981), 37.

9 Thomson, *For Friends at Home*, 35, 50; Houston and Smyth, *Irish Emigration*, 266–7; O'Leary, *Travels*, 25–30.

10 Houston and Smyth, *Irish Emigration*, 256, 266–7, 269; Aili Grönlund Schneider, *The Finnish Baker's Daughters* (Toronto: Multicultural History Society of Ontario, 1986), 18. The lunch-box issue was also raised when the royal commission of 1904 inquired into the plight of Italians coming to Montreal.

11 O'Leary, *Travels*, 45, 59–60, passim; Boddy, *By Ocean, Prairie, and Peak*, 70, 86; Thomson, *For Friends at Home*, 43, 45. For the trip to Winnipeg and experiences in the immigration sheds of prairie towns, see chapter. 11.

12 Jeanette Vekeman Masson, *Grand-maman raconte la Grosse île* (Ste-Foy: Édition de Liberté, 1981; Engl. transl., 1989); Marianne O'Gallagher, *Grosse Isle: Gateway to Canada, 1832–1937* (Quebec, 1984); *Grosse Île and the Irish Quarantine Tragedy: Report of the Advisory Panel on Grosse-Île* (Quebec, August 1995). Trudy D. Mitic and J.P. LeBlanc, *Pier 21. The Gateway that Changed Canada* (Hantsport, NS: Lancelot Press, 1988).

CHAPTER FOUR

1 New France became Quebec after 1763.

2 Frédéric Mauro, "French Indentured Servants for America, 1500–1800," in Piet C. Emmer, ed., *Colonialism and Migration: Indentured Labour before and after Slavery* (Dordrecht: Nijhoff, 1986), 83–104; Peter Moogk, "Manon's Fellow Exiles: Emigration from France to North America before 1763," in Nicholas Canny, ed., *Europeans on the Move: Studies on European Migration 1500–1800* (Oxford: Oxford University Press, 1994), 244–45.

3 Other sources give somewhat higher figures, 3,000 settlers under Cornwallis, 2,500 foreign Protestants, 35,000 Loyalists. See the diaries of Anna Green Winslow and Rebecca Byles in Margaret Conrad et al., eds., *No Place Like Home: Diaries and Letters of Nova Scotia Women, 1771–1938* (Halifax: Formac, 1988).

4 Jean Daigle, *Les Acadiens des Maritimes* (Moncton: Centre d'études acadiennes, 1980), and Daigle, ed., *The Acadiens of the Maritimes: Thematic Studies* (Moncton: Centre d'études acadiennes, 1982); N.E.S. Griffiths, ed., *The Acadian Deportation: Deliberate Perfidy or Cruel Necessity?* (Toronto: Copp Clark, 1969); C.A. Brasseaux, *The Founding of New Acadia: The Beginnings of Acadian Life in Louisiana, 1765–1803* (Baton Rouge: Louisiana State University Press, 1987). David S. Macmillan, "Scottish Enterprise and Influence in Canada, 1620–1900," in R.A. Cage, ed., *The Scots*

Abroad: Labour, Capital, Enterprise, 1750–1914 (London: Croom Helm, 1985), 46–79. J.B. Brebner, *The Neutral Yankees of Nova Scotia: A Marginal Colony during the Revolutionary Years* (1st pub. 1937; repr. Toronto: McClelland and Stewart, 1969); Stephen Hornsby et al., eds., *The Northeastern Borderlands: Four Centuries of Interaction* (Fredericton: Acadiensis, 1989); Peter Latta, "Eighteenth-Century Immigrants to Nova Scotia: The Yorkshire Settlers," *Material History Bulletin* 28 (Fall 1988), 46–51. Winthrop P. Bell, *The "Foreign Protestants" and the Settlement of Nova Scotia* (1st pub. 1961; repr. Sackville, NB: Centre for Canadian Studies, 1990); Gertrud Waseem, "German Settlement in Nova Scotia," in Peter Liddell, ed., *German Canadian Studies: Critical Approaches* (Victoria: Canadian Association of University Teachers of German, 1983), 56–64; Bernard Bailyn, *Voyagers to the West: A Passage in the Peopling of America on the Eve of the Revolution* (New York: Knopf, 1986).

5 *The Diary of Adolphus Gaetz*, ed. by Charles B. Fergusson (Halifax: Public Archives, 1965).

6 To give another example, Italian-Canadian Olinda Iuticone, born in Montreal in 1904, married a 1920 immigrant.

7 Mather B. DesBrisay, *History of the County of Lunenburg* (2nd ed., Toronto: Briggs, 1895; repr. 1972), on the 1861 "gold rush" on the Avens peninsula, 135–9.

8 William T. Baird, *Seventy Years of New Brunswick Life: Autobiographical Sketches* (Saint John, 1890).

9 This theme was repeated frequently in life-writings. "An entirely English settlement is seldom very progressive. The presence of a few bustling Americans or Canadians creates an atmosphere of push." J. Burgon Bickersteth, *The Land of Open Doors: Being Letters from Western Canada 1911–13* (1st ed., 1914; repr. Toronto: University of Toronto Press, 1976), 244.

10 *Canada Home. Juliana Horatia Ewing's Fredericton Letters 1867–1869*, ed. Margaret Howard Blom and Thomas E. Blom (Vancouver: University of British Columbia Press, 1983).

11 Anon. (attributed to M.C.S. London), *Adventures in Canada. Being two Months on the Tobique, New Brunswick: An Emigrant's Journal* [1851] (London, 1866; repr. 1876?).

12 George M. Grant, *Ocean to Ocean: Sandford Fleming's Expedition through Canada in 1872* (Toronto: Campbell, 1873), 89.

13 The experiences of this period are reflected in many diaries by native-born women. See Margaret Conrad, "Recording Angels: The Private Chronicles of Women from the Maritime Provinces of Canada, 1750–1950" (mimeographed, Ottawa, 1987), surveying diaries in manuscript and reprinted in Alison Prentice and Susan Mann Trofimenkoff, *The Neglected Majority: Essays on Canadian Women's History*, 2 vols. (Toronto: McCelland and Stewart, 1985), 1: 41–60. Conrad et al., *No Place Like Home*, 99–200.

14 When, in 1931, French speakers reached one-third of the province's population, cultural distinctiveness began to recede as more of the population of French origin began to adopt English as their mother tongue.

15 Cyril Harris, *Northern Exposure: A Nova Scotia Boyhood* (New York: Norton, 1963). The Toronto acculturation of emigrants from pockets of poverty in New Brunswick in the 1960s has been described in a semi-autobiographical novel by Sophia Firth, *The Urbanization of Sophia Firth* (Toronto: Peter Martin, 1974).

16 "On Canada's Devil's Island," *Het Vaderland,* March 1929-January 1930. I am grateful to Herman Ganzevoort, of the University of Calgary, for sharing this information with me. Joanna Matejko, ed., *Polish Settlers in Alberta: Reminiscences and Biographies* (Toronto: Polish Alliance, 1979), 177–8.

CHAPTER FIVE

1 Jean-Pierre Poussou, "Les Mouvements migratoires en France et à partir de la France de la fin du XVe siècle au début du XIXe siècle: approches pour une synthèse," *Annales de démographie historique* (1970), 11–78; Peter Moogk, "Manon's Fellow Exiles: Emigration from France to North America before 1763," in Nicholas Canny, ed., *Europeans on the Move: Studies on European Migration 1500–1800* (Oxford: Oxford University Press, 1994), 236–60; François Weil, *Les Franco-Américains, 1860–1980* (Paris: Belin, 1989); Hubert Charbonneau et al., *Naissance d'une population: Les Français établis au Canada au XVIIe siècle* (Paris: Presses Universitaires Françaises, 1987).

2 After having been pardoned, the exiles returned to Canada in 1844–5. Fred Landon, ed., in *An Exile from Canada to Van Diemen's Land* (Toronto: Longmans, 1960), lists eight English-language memoirs. Three others appeared in French: Léandre Ducharme, *Journal d'un exilé politique aux terres australes* (Montréal: Cinq-Mars, 1845); François-Maurice Lepailleur, *Journal d'exil: La vie d'un patriote de 1838 déporté en Australie,* ed. Robert-Lionel Séguin (Montréal: Éditions du Jour, 1972); François-Xavier Prieur, *Notes d'un condamné politique de 1838* (Québec: Brousseau, 1864); English edition: *Notes of a Convict of 1838* (Sydney, Australia: Ford, 1949).

3 Joseph-Guillaume Barthe had advocated French immigration and close intellectual relationships between France and French Canada in his *Le Canada reconquis par la France* (Paris, 1855).

4 Patrice Lacombe, *La Terre paternelle* (1846; repr. Québec, 1877); Antoine Gérin-Lajoie, *Jean Rivard: Le défricheur* (1862; repr. Montréal, 1874): and *Jean Rivard: L'économiste* (1864; repr. as a book, Montréal, 1876).

5 Non-clerical authors did argue along economic lines, as did for, example, Errol Bouchette (*Emparons-nous de l'industrie*, 1901).

6 T.C. Haliburton's history of Nova Scotia (1829) inspired a poem about the expulsion by Longfellow (*Evangeline*, 1847).

7 Benjamin-Antoine Testard de Montigny, *La Colonisation: le nord* (Montréal, 1886); De Bouthillier-Chavigny, *A Travers le Nord-Ouest Canadien: De Montréal aux montagnes rocheuses. Notes de voyage* (Montréal, 1893), 11–12.

8 Guildo Rousseau, *L'Images des États-Unis dans la littérature québécoise, 1775–1930* (Sherbrooke, Que.: Editions Naaman, 1981).

9 The scholarly literature on the French in New England has assumed large proportions. Some of the most important publications, (listed here by year of publication) include: Yolande Lavoie, "Les mouvements migratoires des Canadiens entre leur pays et les États-Unis aux XIXe et au XXe siècle: Étude quantitative," in Hubert Charbonneau, ed., *La Population du Québec: Études rétrospectives* (Montréal: Boréal, 1973), 73–88; Normand Lafleur, *Les "Chinois" de l'Est ou la vie quotidienne des Québécois émigrés de 1840 à nos jours* (Montréal: Lemeac, 1981); Raymond Breton and Pierre Savard, eds., *The Quebec and Acadian Diaspora in North America* (Toronto: Multicultural History Society of Ontario, 1982); Gerard J. Brault, *The French-Canadian Heritage in New England* (Montréal: McGill-Queen's University Press., 1986); Yves Roby, "Quebec in the United States: A Historiographical Survey," *Maine Historical Society Quarterly* 26, no. 3 (Winter 1987), 126–59; Weil, *Les Franco-Américains*; Yves Roby, *Les Franco-Américains de la Nouvelle-Angleterre (1776–1930)* (Sillery: Septention, 1990); Bruno Ramirez, *On the Move: French-Canadian and Italian Migrants in the North Atlantic Economy, 1860–1914* (Toronto: McCelland and Stewart, 1991), French ed.: *Par monts et par vaux. Migrants canadiens-français et italiens dans l'économie nord-atlantique, 1860–1914* (Québec, 1991); Yves Frenette, "La genèse d'une communauté canadienne-française en Nouvelle-Angleterre: Lewiston, Maine, 1800–1880," *Historical Papers* (Québec, 1989), 75–99.

10 Fernand Ouellet, *Histoire économique et sociale du Québec, 1760–1850*, 2 vols. (Montréal: Fidès, 1971); Yves Roby, *Histoire économique du Québec, 1851–1896* (Montréal: Fidès, 1971); Paul-André Linteau, Jean-Claude Robert, et René Durocher, *Histoire du Québec contemporaine* (Montréal: Boréal, 1989); Serge Courville and Norman Séguin, *Rural Life in Nineteenth-Century Quebec* (Ottawa: Canadian Historical Association, 1989).

11 Félix Albert, *Immigrant Odyssey: A French-Canadian Habitant in New England. A bilingual edition of "Histoire d'un enfant pauvre,"* ed. Frances H. Early, transl. Arthur L. Eno, Jr (Orono: University of Maine, 1991).

12 See chapter 8 for the Home children. Yves Landry, *Orphelines en France–Pionnières au Canada: Les Filles du Roi au XVIIe siècle* (Montréal: Lemeac, 1992); Silvio Dumas, *Les Filles du roi en Nouvelle-France. Étude historique avec répertoire biographique* (Québec, 1972).

13 Louise Tilly and Joan Scott, *Women, Work and Family* (New York: Holt, Rinehart and Winston, 1978), is the classic study of family economies.

14 The figures for Quebec (not including the Maritimes) vary from author to author; Lavoie gives 825,000 for 1840–1940, Rouillard, one million. Yolande Lavoie, "Les mouvements migratoires," 78; Gerald Bernier and Robert Boily, *Le Québec en chiffres de 1850 à nos jours* (Québec: Association canadienne-française pour l'avancement des sciences, 1986), 43.

15 Massachusetts Bureau of the Statistics of Labor, *Twelfth Annual Report, 1881*, 469–70; Donna Gabaccia, "The 'Yellow Peril' and the 'Chinese of Europe': Global Perspectives on Race and Labor, 1815–1930," in Jan Lucassen and Leo Lucassen, eds., *Migrations, Migration History, History: Old Paradigms and New Perspectives* (Bern: Lang, 1998), 177–96; Peter S. Li, *The Chinese in Canada* (Toronto: Oxford University Press, 1988), 23–40.

16 *Mémoires de Marie-Rose Girard*, ed. Yvan G. Lepage (Ottawa: Presses de l'Université d'Ottawa, 1918); Rémi Jodouin, *En-D'ssour* (Montréal: Éditions Québécoises, 1973); Lina Madore, *Petit Coin perdu* (Rivière-du-Loup: Castelriand, 1979). Joseph-Phydime Michaud, *Kamouraska, de mémoire ... Souvenirs de la vie d'un village québécois*, recueillis par Fernand Archambault (Paris: Maspero, 1981). The author had to sell his land for debt in 1934 and became a worker and salesman of agricultural machinery. A fifth account, by Marie A. Hamilton [née Bonneau] and Zachary M. Hamilton, *These Are the Prairies* (Regina: School Aids Publishing Co., 1948), is more analytical. The Bonneau family had lived in St Bridget, Co. Iberville. The father began to take railway contracts in 1878, first in Ontario, then near Lake of the Woods, and finally in Regina.

17 Madore, *Petit Coin perdu*, 7. The quote has been contracted from a slightly longer text by the author.

18 The term has been coined by Angelika Sauer, University of Winnipeg, to characterize a segment of the German-Canadians.

19 C. Stewart Doty, ed., *The First Franco-Americans. New England Life Histories from the Federal Writers' Project, 1938–1939* (Orono, Me.: University of Maine Press, 1985); Jacques Rouillard, *Ahoy! Les États: les travailleurs canadiens-français dans l'industrie textile de la Nouvelle Angleterre d'après le témoignage des derniers migrants* (Montréal: Boréal, 1985).

CHAPTER SIX

1 Kerby Miller, *Emigrants and Exiles: Ireland and the Irish. Exodus to North America* (New York: Oxford University Press, 1985).

2 For a critique of historiography, see Donald H. Akenson, *Being Had: Historians, Evidence and the Irish in North America* (Don Mills: PD Meany Publishers, 1985). Donald H. Akenson, *The Irish in Ontario: A Study in Rural History* (Montreal: McGill-Queen's University Press, 1984); Cecil J. Hous-

ton and William J. Smyth, *Irish Emigration and Canadian Settlement: Patterns, Links and Letters* (Toronto: University of Toronto Press, 1990), 190, 206; Bruce S. Elliott, *Irish Migrants in the Canadas: A New Approach* (Montreal: McGill-Queen's University Press, 1988); Scott See, *Riots in New Brunswick: Orange Nativism and Social Violence in the 1840s* (Toronto: University of Toronto Press, 1993). *Censuses of Canada 1665–1871* (Ottawa, 1876), 4: lii, *Canada Census 1971*, 20–1.

3 Robert Whyte, *The Ocean Plague* (Boston, 1848). Edward Laxton's *The Famine Ships: The Irish Exodus to America, 1846–51* (London: Bloomsbury, 1996) is a partially invented story; see review by Donald Akenson in *International History Review (* November 1997), 917–18.

4 "Jane White: Townswoman in Upper Canada," in Houston and Smyth, *Irish Emigration*, 287–301; Bessie Garland, *The Old Man's Darling: A Series of Character Sketches* (Toronto, 1881); *Life's Real Romance: A Picture from Life 1838–83. The Life of Jonathan E. Howard* as recorded by his son Arthur N. Howard (Salt Lake City, 1883[?]).

5 Frances (Browne) Stewart, *Our Forest Home. Being Extracts from the Correspondence of the Late Frances Stewart*, compiled and edited by her daughter Eleanor S. Dunlop (Toronto, 1889).

6 Letters of "Nathaniel and Joseph Carrothers: Upper Canada Pioneers," in Houston and Smyth, *Irish Emigration*, 241–86. In quotations from these letters punctuation has been added and spelling modernized.

7 In the late 1850s, when the Carrothers family occasionally sent photos, it became more difficult to leave women out of the picture altogether. However, sending pictures was also a generational matter; the aging Joseph Carrothers did not go for such innovations.

8 Later, university extension services would provide scientific input.

9 Jonathan E. Howard, born in 1819, travelled across Ireland and England as a master builder. He and his wife emigrated to Quebec in 1860 to her brother in Aston.

10 "Carrothers," 264.

11 Ibid., 278; "Jane White," 294–7.

12 Garland, *Old Man's Darling*, 50–85.

13 Quoted in Houston and Smyth, *Irish Emigration*, 61.

14 Wilson Benson, *Life and Adventures of Wilson Benson* (Toronto, 1876); Houston and Smyth, *Irish Emigration*, 152–5; Michael Katz, *The People of Hamilton, Canada West: Family and Class in a Mid-Nineteenth-Century City* (Cambridge, Mass.: Harvard University Press, 1975), 94–175.

15 According to research by Cecil J. Houston in preparation of a new edition of Benson's *Life and Adventures*, Jemima was only eleven years of age at departure. Benson noted that upon arrival in Canada they posed as brother and sister. It is unclear why the birthdate does not match with Benson's account. For separation of culture by gender and high average age of marriage

among Irish, see Hasia R. Diner, *Erin's Daughters in America: Irish Immigrant Women in the Nineteenth Century* (Baltimore: Johns Hopkins University Press, 1983).

16 Robert F. Harney, ed., *Gathering Place: Peoples and Neighbourhoods of Toronto, 1834–1945* (Toronto: Multicultural History Society of Ontario, 1985), especially J.M.S. Careless, "The Emergence of Cabbagetown in Victorian Toronto," 25–46, and Murray W. Nicolson, "Peasants in an Urban Society: the Irish Catholics in Victorian Toronto," 47–74. James Thomson, *For Friends at Home: A Scottish Emigrant's Letters from Canada, California and the Cariboo, 1844–1964*, ed. Richard A. Preston (Montreal: McGill-Queen's University Press, 1970), 65, 121. I am indebted to Cecil J. Houston and Deborah A. Allen for comments and information on Wilson Benson's life.

17 Peter O'Leary, *Travels and Experiences in Canada, the Red River Territory, and the United States* (London, 1877).

18 "Alexander Robb: Adventurer in British Columbia," [1862–73] in Houston and Smyth, *Irish Emigration*, 302–33.

CHAPTER SEVEN

1 William Weir, *Sixty Years in Canada* (Montreal: Lovell, 1903); James Thomson, *For Friends at Home: A Scottish Emigrant's Letters from Canada, California and the Cariboo, 1844–1964*, ed. Richard A. Preston (Montreal: McGill-Queen's University Press, 1970); Richard Hemsley, *Looking Back* (Montreal, 1930).

2 R.B. Nevitt, *A Winter at Fort Macleod* (Regina: Glenbow Institute, 1974), 7–8.

3 Thomson, *For Friends at Home*, 42–106; Weir, *Sixty Years in Canada*, 26.

4 Hemsley, *Looking Back*, 9–94.

5 Charlotte Erickson, "The Encouragement of Emigration by British Trade Unions, 1850–1900," *Population Studies* 3 (1949–50), 248–73; R.V. Clements, "Trade Unions and Emigration, 1840–80," in ibid. 9 (1955–6), 167–80; Pamela Horn, "Agricultural Trade Unionism and Emigration, 1872–1881," *Historical Journal* 15 (1972), 87–102. See also Lee Shai Weissbach, *Child Labor Reform in 19th-Century France* (Baton Rouge: Louisiana State University Press, 1989).

6 Peter O'Leary, *Travels and Experiences in Canada, the Red River Territory, and the United States* (London, 1877), 56–8.

7 *Census of Canada, 1891*, cited in Susan Mann Trofimenkoff, "One Hundred and Two Muffled Voices. Canada's Industrial Women in the 1880s," *Atlantis: A Women's Studies Journal* 3.1 (Fall 1977), 66–7.

8 *Report of the Royal Commission on Relations of Labour and Capital:* 2 vols. of reports, 5 vols. of evidence (1889), abr. ed., Gregory Kealey, ed.,

Canada Investigates Industrialism (Toronto: University of Toronto Press, 1973), Quebec evidence, 211–313; Trofimenkoff, "Canada's Industrial Women," 66–83; D. Suzanne Cross, "The Neglected Majority. The Changing Role of Women in 19th-Century Montreal," in Susan Mann Trofimenkoff and Alison Prentice, eds., *The Neglected Majority: Essays in Canadian Women's History* (Toronto: McClelland and Stewart, 1977), 66–86; Bettina Bradbury, "The Family Economy and Work in an Industrializing City: Montreal in the 1870s," Canadian Historical Association, *Historical Papers 1979* (Ottawa, 1979), 71–96.

9 *Report of the Royal Commission on Relations of Labour and Capital,* 213, 216–18, 249–57.

10 Ibid., 214–16, 222–3, 240–1; Robert J. Steinfeld, *The Invention of Free Labor: The Employment Relation in English and American Law and Culture, 1350–1870* (Chapel Hill, NC: University of North Carolina Press, 1991).

11 *Report of the Royal Commission on Relations of Labour and Capital,* 230–1, 263–4, 307.

12 During a strike in 1901, the CPR had entered into collusion with Cordasco to bring in strikebreakers.

13 The charity societies which O'Leary had visited could provide accommodation and maintenance for only fifteen to twenty at a time and for no longer than two or three days.

14 *Royal Commission Appointed to Inquire into the Immigration of Italian Labourers to Montreal and the Alleged Fraudulent Practices of Employment Agencies, Report 1904* (Ottawa: Department of Labour, 1905), 44. For an analysis of the report and tensions within the Italian community's elite, see Bruno Ramirez and Michael Del Balso, *The Italians of Montreal: From Sojourning to Settlement, 1900–1921* (Montréal: Editions Courant, 1980).

15 *Report 1904*, xi-xxxvi, 16–18, 28–9.

16 Ibid., 27–8, 45–7, 168. Denise Helly, *Les Chinois à Montréal, 1877–1951* (Montreal: Institut Québécois de recherche sur la culture, 1987).

17 Donald H. Avery, *Reluctant Host: Canada's Response to Immigrant Workers, 1896–1994* (Toronto: McClelland and Stewart, 1995), 25; Bruno Bezza, ed., *Gli Italiani fuori d'Italia, Gli emigrati italiani nei movimenti operai dei paesi d'adozione (1880–1940)* (Milano: Angeli, 1983); Paul C.P. Siu, "The Sojourner," *American Journal of Sociology* 58 (1952–53), 35–44; R. Craig Brown and Ramsay Cook, *Canada 1896–1921: A Nation Transformed* (Toronto: McClelland and Stewart, 1974); D.J. Hall, *Clifford Sifton*, 2 vols. (Vancouver: University of British Columbia Press, 1981, 1985).

18 The oral life-stories were collected in interviews in the late 1970s and early 1980s. Bruno Ramirez, *Les premiers Italiens de Montréal: L'origine de la Petite Italie du Québec* (Montréal: Boréal, 1984), "Témoignages," 87–136, includes eight of about thirty collected by the time of publication.

19 Similar relationships were also maintained between kin in Italy and South America. Samuel L. Baily and Franco Ramella, eds., *One Family, Two Worlds. An Italian Family's Correspondence across the Atlantic. 1901–1922* (New Brunswick, NJ: Rutgers University Press, 1988).

20 "Témoignages," 119, 132–4.

21 Ibid., 92, 100, 104, 107, 110, 135.

22 Ibid., 93, 104, 108, 116, 118; Bettina Bradbury, "Pigs, Cows, and Boarders: Non-Wage Forms of Survival among Montreal Families, 1861–91," *Labour/Le Travail* 14 (1984), 9–46, and *Working Families: Age, Gender, and Daily Survival in Industrializing Montreal* (Toronto, 1993).

23 "Témoignages," 94, 105, 112, 118.

24 Ibid., 111–12, 116, 126, 121–2, 128.

25 Ibid., 93, 95, 100, 115.

26 Leah Rosenberg, *The Errand Runner: Reflections of a Rabbi's Daughter* (Toronto: Wiley, 1981); Gerald Tulchinsky, *Taking Root: The Origins of the Canadian Jewish Community* (Toronto: Lester, 1992). In A.M. Klein's poetry the Montreal of the 1920s to the 1940s is absent. See *Complete Poems*, Zailig Pollock, ed., 2 vols. (Toronto: University of Toronto Press, 1990).

27 Rosenberg, *Errand Runner*, 13. Leah also had four half-siblings from her father's first marriage. In this autobiography, written at about the age of seventy, all names have been changed. Mary Antin, *The Promised Land* (London: Heinemann, 1912), 141–2. By the time of the emigration, America had become "the golden land" (*Errand Runner*, 36). Pierre Anctil and Gary Caldwell, *Juifs et réalités juives au Québec* (Montréal: Institut Québécois de recherche sur la culture, 1984).

28 Rosenberg, *Errand Runner*, 8–36; Elizabeth Waterston, "Travel Books 1880–1920," in Carl F. Klinck, ed., *Literary History of Canada* (Toronto: University of Toronto Press, 1967), 359. Susan A. Glenn, *Daughters of the Shtetl: Life and Labor in the Immigrant Generation* (Ithaca: Cornell, 1990).

29 The Christie Pits riots in 1933 were to show the ugly side of anti-semitism in Toronto, while the non-admission of Jewish refugees from Germany in the 1930s showed the equally ugly anti-semitism of the bureaucratic elite. Leah and her father experienced anti-semitism when a boy threw a stone at the bearded old man. Rosenberg, *Errand Runner*, 50. Stephen A. Speisman, "St. John's Shtetl: the Ward in 1911," in Robert F. Harney, ed., *Gathering Place: Peoples and Neighbourhoods of Toronto, 1834–1945* (Toronto: Multicultural History Society of Ontario, 1985), 107–20, and Speisman, *The Jews of Toronto. A History to 1937* (1st ed. 1979; Toronto: McClelland and Stewart, 1987). Robert J. Brym, William Shaffir, Morton Weinfeld., eds., *The Jews in Canada* (Toronto: Oxford, 1993).

30 Rosenberg, *Errand Runner*, 55–93.

CHAPTER EIGHT

1 Cecil J. Houston and William J. Smyth, *Irish Emigration and Canadian Settlement. Patterns, Links and Letters* (Toronto: University of Toronto Press, 1990), 257–60, 262–4 (spelling of quote modernized by the author).

2 James Thomson, *For Friends at Home: A Scottish Emigrant's Letters from Canada, California and the Cariboo, 1844–1964*, ed. Richard A. Preston (Montreal: McGill-Queen's University Press, 1970), 195–258.

3 George Young, *Leaves from My Life in the Prairie Province, 1868–1884* (Toronto, 1897), 98–9; Johan Schrøder, *Johan Schrøder's Travels in Canada, 1863*, ed. and transl. by Orm Øverland (Norwegian, 1st ed. 1867; Montreal: McGill-Queen's University Press, 1989); Almon J. Cotton, *The Wheat King. The Selected Letters and Papers of A.J. Cotton, 1888–1913*, Wendy Owen, ed. (Winnipeg: Manitoba Record Society, 1985), 3–4; Helge W. Nordvik, "Norwegian Emigrants and Canadian Timber," in Klaus Friedland, ed., *Maritime Aspects of Migration* (Cologne: Böhlau, 1989), 279–92.

4 John C. Geikie, *Adventures in Canada, or, Life in the Woods* (Philadelphia: Porter, 1882); "Emigrant Lady," *Letters from Muskoka* (London: Bentley, 1878); Ann Hathaway, *Muskoka Memories* (Toronto: Briggs, 1904). Geikie gives no date of arrival, but the siblings had been in the country for several years when oil was discovered in Ontario. See also Frederick M. Delafosse (Roger Vardon, pseud.), *English Bloods* (Ottawa: Graphic, 1930), a young Englishman learning pioneer farming in Muskoka District of Ontario, 1878–81.

5 "The Diary of Hanna Aikman (Hammill) Kern", J.H. Holbrook and M.H. Farmer, eds. (mimeographed, Western Ontario Historical Nuggets, no. 26: London: University of Western Ontario, 1958).

6 Anna Leveridge, *"Your Loving Anna": Letters from the Ontario Frontier (1882–1891)*, Louis Tivy, ed. (Toronto: University of Toronto Press, 1972). Gerald E. Boyce, *Historic Hastings* (Belleville, Ont.: Ontario Intelligencer, 1967); G. de P. Glazebrook, *Life in Ontario: A Social History* (Toronto: University of Toronto Press, 1968).

7 Kern, "Diary", 1–12, 24–7.

8 "Emigrant Lady," *Letters*, 26, 30, 71–2; Geikie, *Adventures in Canada,* 37.

9 Anna's letters have been edited by her grandson in his old age, who filled gaps from childhood memory. The editing was sloppy. Dates do not always match. I rely mainly on the letters to reconstruct the family history.

10 Roydon Harrison et al., *The Warwick Guide to British Labour Periodicals, 1790–1970* (Hassocks, GB: Harvester Press, 1977).

11 Joy Parr, "The Skilled Immigrant and Her Kin: Gender, Culture, and Labour Recruitment," *Canadian Historical Review* 68 (1987), 529–51.

12 In Europe Swiss dairymen and dairymaids migrated for centuries across the German-speaking countries, were considered highly skilled, and received good wages. Among British settlers, requests for particular seeds were a recurring theme in letters home. Anna Leveridge's skills were matched by Finnish and Polish immigrant women. See chaps. 9 and 13.

13 The British Home movement was part of a continent-wide new approach to dealing with orphaned, abandoned, or mistreated children in Homes rather than workhouses. The title of one study (Kenneth Bagnell, *The Little Immigrants: The Orphans Who Came to Canada* [Toronto: Macmillan, 1980]), is misleading. Philip Bean and Joy Melville, *Lost Children of the Empire* (London, 1989), point out that child emigration to Australia and Rhodesia continued into the 1950s. The experiences quoted include violence and sexual abuse in Christian Brothers' homes.

14 James Montgomery, *The Chimney-Sweeper's Friend*, ed. Donald H. Reiman (1st ed., London, 1824; New York: Garland, 1978); Robert H. Sherard, *The Child Slaves of Britain* (London: Hurst and Blachett, 1905); A.G. Scholes, *Education for Empire Settlement: A Study of Juvenile Migration* (London: Longmans, 1932); Gail H. Corbett, *The Barnardo Children in Canada* (Peterborough: Woodland, 1981); Gillian Wagner, *Children of the Empire* (London: Weidenfeld, 1982), 85–6.

15 The term "Barnardo children" reflects not only the large number of children from these Homes, but also a male perspective obliterating the input of Miss Rye and other women.

16 In the 1940s children were sent out in a wartime protective measure. Wagner, *Children of the Empire*, 238–58. They were not repatriated. A parliamentary inquiry into their fate began in Britain in 1997. In March 1996 news broke that from 1948 to 1962, at least fifteen hundred Irish children born out of wedlock were taken from their mothers and sent to the United States.

17 The children arrived in Canada between 1871 and 1930. The 106 responses were edited by Harrison in *The Home Children: Their Personal Stories* (Winnipeg: Watson and Dwyer, 1979). Other memoirs include: William R. Price, *Celtic Odyssey*, as told to Eileen S. Hill (Philadelphia: Dorrance, 1970); Claude Theodore, "With Our Own Hands: Margaret Fairley and the 'Real Makers' of Canada," ed. David Kimmel and Gregory S. Kealey, *Labour/Le Travail* 31 (Spring 1993), 258–65, and a letter to R.B. Bennett, in L.M. Grayson and Michael Bliss, eds., *The Wretched of Canada: Letters to R. B. Bennett, 1930–1935* (Toronto: University of Toronto Press, 1971), 70–2.

18 Harrison, *Home Children*, 45, 61, 88. Staff of the Homes also shipped out children without the parents' consent or took children away from mothers and fathers of whose lives they did not approve; see Joy Parr, *Labouring Children. British Immigrant Apprentices to Canada, 1869–1924* (London: Croom Helm, 1980), 67–78.

19 All subsequent quotes are from Harrison, *Home Children*, unless otherwise noted.

20 Price, *Celtic Odyssey*, 3–224.

21 "Name Withheld," Harrison, *Home Children*, 175–81. See also the experiences of Ellen Higgins, 77–9, and Florence Horne, 146–9.

22 Given the stigma attached to Home children, many did not want their own children, their friends in adult life, or their in-laws to know their origin. The past was a burden to be carried alone.

CHAPTER NINE

1 Florence R. Howey, *Pioneering on the C.P.R.* ([Ottawa?], 1938), 12. Early accounts by native-born Canadians include Joshua Fraser, *Shanty, Forest, and River Life in the Backwoods of Canada* (Montreal, 1883); Aeneas McCharles, *Bemocked of Destiny: The Actual Struggles and Experiences of a Canadian Pioneer, and the Recollections of a Lifetime* (Toronto: Briggs, 1908).

2 Howey, *Pioneering*, 18–21, 28–30.

3 F.C. Cooper, *In the Canadian Bush* (London: Heat, 1915), 11–12; Martin Nordegg, *The Possibilities of Canada Are Truly Great: Memoirs 1906–1924*, T.D. Regehr, ed. (Toronto: Macmillan, 1971), 30–2.

4 John C. Geikie, *Adventures in Canada, or, Life in the Woods* (Philadelphia: Porter, 1882), 143–6; Phyllis Harrison, ed., *The Home Children: Their Personal Stories* (Winnipeg: Watson and Dwyer, 1979), 138, 230–1. For the economic and labour background, see Ian Radforth, *Bushworkers and Bosses: Logging in Northern Ontario,1900–1980* (Toronto: University of Toronto Press, 1987).

5 Aili Grönlund Schneider, *The Finnish Baker's Daughters* (Toronto: Multicultural History Society of Ontario, 1986), 44–6, 51–3, 70, 86–91.

6 Gus Romaniuk, *Taking Root in Canada: An Autobiography* (Winnipeg: Columbia, 1954), 59–67.

7 Grönlund Schneider, *The Finnish Baker's Daughters*, 9–11. Varpu Lindstrom-Best, *Defiant Sisters: A Social History of Finnish Immigrant Women in Canada* (Toronto: Multicultural History Society of Ontario, 1988); and Lindstrom-Best, *The Finnish Immigrant Community of Toronto, 1887–1913* (Toronto: Multicultural History Society of Ontario, 1979).

8 Dirk Hoerder, ed., *Josef N. Jodlbauer, Dreizehn Jahre in Amerika, 1910–1923: Die Autobiographie eines österreichischen Sozialisten* (Vienna: Böhlau, 1996).

9 Grönlund Schneider, *The Finnish Baker's Daughters*, 25–40; oral information by Varpu Lindstrom - Best to the author, 21 January 1992. Reino Kero, "The Canadian Finns in Soviet Karelia in the 1930s," in Michael Karni, ed., *The Finnish Diaspora*, 2 vols. (Toronto: Multicultural History Society

of Ontario, 1981); Donald H. Avery, *Reluctant Host: Canada's Response to Immigrant Workers, 1896-1994* (Toronto: McClelland and Stewart, 1995), 60–143; Barbara Roberts, *Whence They Came: Deportation from Canada 1900–1935* (Ottawa: University of Ottawa Press, 1988). See also chapters 18 and 19 below.

10 Harrison, *The Home Children*, 63–4, 261–3.

11 Rémi Jodouin, *En-D'ssour* (Montréal: Éditions Québécoises, 1973), 82–110.

CHAPTER TEN

1 C. Pelham Mulvany, *Toronto Past and Present until 1882: A Handbook of the City* (Toronto: Caiger, 1884; repr. 1970), 9, 33, 39 passim.

2 John C. Geikie, *Adventures in Canada: or Life in the Woods* (Philadelphia: Porter 1882), 20–1; revisiting the city later, it had improved, 376–7. Some Home children were impressed; see Phyllis Harrison, ed., *The Home Children: Their Personal Stories* (Winnipeg: Watson and Dwyer, 1979), 78, 81–5; J. M.S. Careless, *Toronto to 1918* (Toronto: McClelland and Stewart, 1974); Gordon Darroch, "Early Industrialization and Inequality in Toronto, 1861–1899," *Labour/Le Travail* 11 (Spring 1983), 31–61; and Darroch and Lee Soltow, *Property and Inequality in Victorian Ontario* (Toronto: University of Toronto Press, 1994).

3 Ralph Ellison, *Invisible Man* (New York, 1952); Luise Pusch, *Das Deutsche als Männersprache: Aufsätze und Glossen zur feministischen Linguistik* (Frankfurt/M.: Suhrkamp, 1984, repr., 1996), 11.

4 James Rook worked in the garment district in 1929 as a pattern cutter. See Harrison, *The Home Children*, 223.

5 Ann Hathaway, *Muskoka Memories* (Toronto: Briggs, 1904), 9–39.

6 Ibid., 100–3.

7 Harrison, *Home Children*, 144–5.

8 *Reminiscences of a Stonemason*, by a Working Man (London: Murray, 1908), 1–114.

9 Ibid., 115–78.

10 Alice A. Chown, *The Stairway* (1921; repr. Toronto: University of Toronto Press, 1988), 115–22; Gregory S. Kealey, "The Parameters of Class Conflict: Strikes in Canada, 1891–1930," in Deian R. Hopkin and Gregory S. Kealey, eds., *Class, Community, and the Labour Movement: Wales and Canada, 1850–1930* (Wales: Cambrian News, 1989), 213–48; Ruth Frager, "Sewing Solidarity: The Eaton's Strike of 1912," *Canadian Woman Studies* 7 (1986), 96–8; and Frager, "Class, Ethnicity, and Gender in the Eaton Strikes of 1912 and 1934," in Franca Iacovetta and Mariana Valverde, eds., *Gender Conflicts* (Toronto: University of Toronto Press, 1992), 189–228. See also Gregory S. Kealey, *Toronto Workers Respond to Industrial Capi-*

talism, 1867–1892 (Toronto: University of Toronto Press, 1980); John E. Zucchi, *Italians in Toronto: Development of a National Identity, 1875–1935* (Montreal: McGill-Queen's University Press, 1988).

11 R. Eric Smythies, *Around the World in Eighty Years* (Victoria, BC: Morriss, 1968); Adam J. Tolmie, *Roughing It On the Rails* (Bloomfield, Ont.: Silverthorn, 1983).

12 Smythies, *Around the World*, 54–105.

13 Tolmie, *Roughing It*, 1–121.

14 Herbert Reiter, *Politisches Asyl im 19: Jahrhundert. Die deutschen politischen Flüchtlinge des Vormärz und der Revolution von 1848/49 in Europa und den USA* (Berlin: Duncker and Humblot, 1992). Smythies, *Around the World*, 56.

15 Geikie, *Adventures in Canada*, quote 173–5. Sending women away from England did not merely concern Canada out the whole of the empire. See for example, Arthur Grimble, "Women as Empire Builders," *United Empire: The Royal Colonial Institute Journal* 13 (1922), 195–9; Anthony J. Hammerton, *Emigrant Gentlewomen: Genteel Poverty and Female Emigration, 1830–1914* (London: Croom Helm, 1979); Patricia Clarke, *The Governesses: Letters from the Colonies, 1862–1882* (London: Hutchinson, 1985); Joanna Trollope, *Britannia's Daughters: Women of the British Empire* (London: Hutchinson, 1983).

16 Hathaway, *Muskoka Memories*, 36; Tolmie, *Roughing It*, 76. Into the early 1870s, more funds were sent to emigrants in the United States than home by them. *Historical Statistics of the United States* (Washington, DC: Bureau of the Census, 1961), series U 183. Publication in defence of remittance men include Patrick A. Dunae, *Gentlemen Emigrants: From the British Public Schools to the Canadian Frontier* (Vancouver: Douglas, 1981), with the dustjacket blurp: "Most came, however, because they were unable to find suitable vocations on the Old Country. Armed with sporting rifles, walking sticks and cricket bats, resplendent in Norfolk jackets and riding boots, the 'gentlemen emigrants,' as they were known, trooped into the Canadian backwoods and across the western prairies, bringing culture and colour to many pioneer communities." Jessie L. Beattie, *Black Sheep They Were Not: Folklore of Canada* (Hamilton: Fleming, 1981). In late 1920s British Columbia Magnus Pyke had the same experience. Taking a position as a clerk in a bank, he felt pay was calculated on the assumption that his family would support him. He returned to England. Magnus Pyke, *Go West, Young Man, Go West* (Ottawa: Graphic, 1930), 130ff.

17 Hathaway, *Muskoka Memories*, 38; Geikie, *Adventures in Canada*, 4–5; Smythies, *Around the World*, 56–7.

18 Harrison, *Home Children*, 162, 186, 225–6.

19 Benjamin Drew, ed., *The Refugee, or the Narratives of Fugitive Slaves in Canada. Related by Themselves, with an Account of the History and Con-*

dition of the Colored Population of Upper Canada (Boston, 1856; repr. Toronto: Coles, 1972); Tolmie, *Roughing It*, 76.

20 Geikie, *Adventures in Canada*, 351–3, 378–9. Dan Hill, "The Blacks in Toronto," in Robert F. Harney, ed., *Gathering Place: Peoples and Neighbourhoods of Toronto, 1834–1945* (Toronto: Multicultural History Society of Ontario, 1985), 75–105; Robin W. Winks, *The Blacks in Canada: A History* (New Haven: Yale University Press, 1971).

21 Dionne Brand with Lois De Shield, eds., *No Burden to Carry: Narratives of Black Working Women in Ontario 1920s-1950s* (Toronto: Women's Press, 1991), 130, 151.

22 Ibid., 112, 117–18; Harry Gairey, *A [Jamaican] Black Man's Toronto, 1914–1980: The Reminiscences of Harry Gairey*, ed. Donna Hill (Toronto: Multicultural History Society of Ontario, 1981), 7.

23 Brand with De Shield, *No Burden to Carry*, 53–7, 97.

24 Ibid., 40, 45, 48, 93, 131, 161; Dionne Brand, "Black Women and Work: The Impact of Racially Constructed Gender Roles on the Sexual Division of Labour," *Fireweed* 26 (Winter-Spring 1988), 87–92.

25 Dennis W. Mcgill, *Africville: The Life and Death of a Canadian Black Community* (Halifax: Dalhousie University Press, 1974); Brand with De Shield, *No Burden to Carry*, 44.

26 Don Moore: *Don Moore. An Autobiography* (Toronto: Williams-Wallace, 1985), 27–52; Gairey, *Black Man's Toronto*.

27 Marilyn Barber, "The Women Ontario Welcomed: Immigrant Domestics for Ontario Homes, 1870–1930," *Ontario History* 72, no. 3 (1980), 148–72; Murray Nicolson, "Peasants in an Urban Society: The Irish Catholics in Victorian Toronto," in Harney, ed., *Gathering Place*, 47–74.

CHAPTER ELEVEN

1 The Methodist missionary Reverend Alexander Sutherland, in *A Summer in Prairie-Land: Notes of a Tour through the North-West Territory* (2nd ed., Toronto, 1882), noted the covetousness of scheming railway builders with saleable charters and fat contracts, impecunious politicians, and political prophets (iii-iv); John West, *The Substance of a Journal during a Residence at the Red River Colony [1820–23]* (London: S.R. Publishers, 1824; repr. Vancouver: Alcuien Society, 1967), 65–70.

2 De Bouthillier-Chavigny, *A Travers le Nord-Ouest Canadien. De Montréal aux montagnes rocheuses: Notes de voyage* (Montréal, 1893), 20.

3 Alan F.J. Artibise, *Winnipeg: An Illustrated History* (Toronto: National Museum of Civilization, 1977); R.C. Wilson, ed., *Saint-Boniface, Manitoba, Canada, 1818–1968* (St Boniface: Chamber of Commerce, 1967); Jennifer S.H. Brown, *Strangers in Blood: Fur Trade Company Families in Indian Country* (Vancouver: University of British Columbia Press, 1980);

Jennifer S.H. Brown, ed., *The New People: Being and Becoming Métis in North America* (Vancouver: University of British Columbia Press, 1985).

4 Harry Bullock-Webster, *Memories of Sport and Travel Fifty Years Ago* (Ludlow, GB: Meadow Press, 1938), 43–56, 59–62. See also Henry M. Robinson, *The Great Fur Land, or Sketches of Life in the Hudson's Bay Territory* (New York, 1879), a meticulous and laudatory account based on personal travel and compilation from writings of other travellers.

5 Sutherland, *Summer in Prairie-Land*, iii-v, 14–16, 51–2 (emphasis added). A Methodist missionary, the Reverend George Young, was even more biased. See his *Leaves from My Life in the Prairie Province, 1868–1884* (Toronto, 1897).

6 S.A. Archer, ed., *A Heroine of the North: Memoirs of Charlotte Selina Bompas* (London: Society for Promoting Christian Knowledge, 1929), v-xii, 25–36, 60–2, 77.

7 R. Louis Gentilcor ed., *Historical Atlas of Canada*; vol 2: 1880–1891, (Toronto: University of Toronto Press, 1993), plate 18. Other life-writings and travel accounts of the late nineteenth century include William F. Butler, *The Great Lone Land: A Tale of Travel and Adventure in the North-West of America* (1st ed., 1872; London: Law, 1907); W. Henry Barnaby, *Life and Labour in the Far, Far West: Being Notes of a Tour in the Western States, British Columbia, Manitoba, and the North-West Territory* (London, 1883).

8 Irene M. Spry, ed., "The 'Memories' of George William Sanderson, 1846–1936," *Canadian Ethnic Studies* 17, no. 2 (1985), 115–34.

9 Sutherland, *Summer in Prairie-Land*, 5; William Newton, *Twenty Years on the Saskatchewan, N.W. Canada* (London: Stock, 1897), 163–5; Butler, *Great Lone Land*, 69, 76, 98; Harry Piniuta, ed., *Land of Pain, Land of Promise: First Person Accounts by Ukrainian Pioneers, 1891–1914* (Saskatoon, Sask.: Western Producer Prairie Books, 1978), 56, 100; Evan Davies, [as told to] Alec Vaughan, *Beyond the Old Bone Trail* (London: Cassell, 1960), 21; J. Burgon Bickersteth, *The Land of Open Doors: Being Letters from Western Canada, 1911–13* (1st ed., 1914; repr. Toronto: University of Toronto Press, 1976), 7.

10 Laura Goodman Salverson, *Confessions of an Immigrant's Daughter* (1st ed., Toronto: Ryerson, 1939; repr. 1981), 80–1; Joseph E. Wilder, *Read All About It: Reminiscences of an Immigrant Newsboy*, ed. Fred C. Dawkins and Micheline C. Brodeur (Winnipeg: Peguis, 1978), 53–4; Frank G. Roe, *Getting the Know-How: Homesteading and Railroading in Early Alberta*, ed. J.P. Regan (Edmonton: NeWest, 1982), 3; Marcel Durieux, *Ordinary Heroes: The Journal of a French Pioneer in Alberta*, transl. and ed. by Roger Motut and Maurice Legris (Edmonton: University of Alberta Press, 1980), 12–14; Thomas C. Douglas, *The Making of a Socialist. The Recollections of T.C. Douglas*, ed. by Lewis H. Thomas (Edmonton: University

of Alberta Press, 1982), 12; "Gustave Elgert from Volhynia," in Tova Yedlin, ed., *Germans from Russia in Alberta* (Edmonton: Central and East European Studies Society, 1984), 74; Gus Romaniuk, *Taking Root in Canada: An Autobiography* (Winnipeg: Columbia, 1954), 51; Martin Nordegg, *The Possibilities of Canada Are Truly Great, Memoirs 1906–1924*, ed. T.D. Regehr (Toronto: Macmillan, 1971), 54–5.

11 Piniuta, *Land of Pain*, 42, 197–8. See also the account by Vera Lysenko, *Men in Sheepskin Coats: A Study in Assimilation* (Toronto: Ryerson, 1947), 34–6.

12 Salverson, *Confessions*, 39, 42–3.

13 Mary Agnes FitzGibbon, *A Trip to Manitoba; or: Roughing It on the Line* (Toronto, 1880), 15–170.

14 Joanna Matejko and Tova Yedlin, eds., *Alberta's Pioneers from Eastern Europe: Reminiscences* (Edmonton: University of Alberta, 1977), 8; Romaniuk, *Taking Root*, 49–59; Piniuta, *Land of Pain*, 10, 40, 85–8; Michael Luchkovich, *A Ukrainian Canadian in Parliament: Memoirs of Michael Luchkovich* (Toronto: Ukrainian Canadian Research Foundation, 1965), 9; Fredelle Bruser Maynard, *Raisins and Almonds* (1st ed., 1964; repr. Markham, Ont.: PaperJacks, 1973), 82–6.

15 "Tomasz Opalinski: A Businessman and Farmer," Matejko, *Polish Settlers*, 135–40; see 293, and 296 for Poles migrating from the United States to Canada.

16 "Recollections of Pastor Eduard Duesterhoeft," Matejko and Yedlin, *Alberta's Pioneers*, 73–84.

17 Klaas DeJong, *Cauliflower Crown*, ed. Martha Knapp (Saskatoon: Western Producer Prairie Books, 1973), 3–150.

18 Aili Grönlund Schneider, *The Finnish Baker's Daughters* (Toronto: Multicultural History Society of Ontario, 1986), 26; Leah Rosenberg, *The Errand Runner: Reflections of a Rabbi's Daughter* (Toronto: Wiley, 1981), 47–8; Phyllis Harrison, ed., *The Home Children: Their Personal Stories* (Winnipeg: Watson and Dwyer, 1979), 146–9. See also Eliane L. Silverman, *The Last Best West: Women on the Alberta Frontier, 1880–1930* (Montreal: Eden, 1984), 34–5, for experiences in schools.

19 Salverson, *Confessions*, 179–80, 194–6, 203, 219.

20 Douglas, *The Making of a Socialist*, 14.

21 Maynard, *Raisins and Almonds*, 70–8; James H. Gray, *The Boy from Winnipeg* (Toronto: Macmillan, 1971), 34–41.

22 Bernd Baldus and Meenaz Kassam, "'Make Me Truthful, Good, and Mild': Values in Nineteenth-Century Ontario Schoolbooks," *Canadian Journal Sociology* 21 (1996), 327–58; Jill Ker Conway, *The Road from Coorain* (New York: Vintage, 1989).

23 Laura, too, was placed with an uncle once. She remembered this period as more happy than the home. Offers for adoption had also been made to the Leveridge family and that of Félix Albert.

24 Salverson, *Confessions,* 81–2, 91, 179, 261.
25 Matejko, *Polish Settlers*, 31, 114–20, 151–61.
26 Laura Salverson no longer mentioned her husband George when describing her work on her first novel, *The Viking Heart* (1923). In this regard, her memory is similar to that of men writing about their work and hardly mentioning wives or children.
27 Salverson, *Confessions,* 83–93.
28 Ibid., 139, 146–7, 217–19. Mennonite girls noted that each additional baby meant more work for the older girls. See Lawrence Klippenstein and Julius G. Toews, eds., *Mennonite Memories: Settling in Western Canada* (Winnipeg: Centennial, 1977), 224.
29 Salverson, *Confessions,* 313–79. The tone of her autobiography had many Icelandic qualities to it, similar to that of Helgi Einarsson, a fisherman-entrepreneur on the northern shores of Lake Manitoba.
30 Hugh G.G. Herklots, *The First Winter: A Canadian Chronicle* (London: Dent, 1935), 14, 24–50, 67–8, 73–4, 162–3; Bickersteth, *The Land of Open Doors*, 94: Veronica Strong-Boag, "Introduction" to Nellie L. McClung, *In Times Like These* (1915; repr. Toronto: University of Toronto Press, 1972); Gray, *Boy from Winnipeg*, 26.
31 "To us there was no distinction between Canada and the United States – it was all America, the land across the sea, full of hope, freedom, and the opportunity for a better life." Wilder, *Read All About It*, 7.
32 Ibid., 56–7, 90–1.
33 Gray, *Boy from Winnipeg*, 112, 119–20.
34 Dorothy Livesay, *Beginnings: A Winnipeg Childhood* (Winnipeg: Peguis, 1973; repr. Toronto: New Press, 1975), 6, 45, 72, 91–3. In the 1930s Dorothy Livesay became involved in leftist politics, was a peace activist, and published poetry and short stories. Wilder, *Read All About It*, 80.
35 Douglas, *The Making of a Socialist*, 6–19, 29.
36 Gray, *Boy from Winnipeg*, 89, 94–6, 117–19; Livesay, *Winnipeg Childhood*, 25–31.
37 Gray, *Boy from Winnipeg*, 126–38; D.C. Masters, *The Winnipeg General Strike* (Toronto: University of Toronto Press, 1950).
38 This memory may reflect family conversation more than Dorothy Livesay's experiences. Born in 1909, she was five years old at the beginning of the war. Livesay, *Winnipeg Childhood*, 69, 85–6, 95–9.

CHAPTER TWELVE

1 J. Burgon Bickersteth, *The Land of Open Doors: Being Letters from Western Canada, 1911–13* (1st ed., 1914; repr. Toronto: University of Toronto Press, 1976), 113; Christian F.J. Galloway, *The Call of the West: Letters from British Columbia* (London: Adelphi, 1916), 20.

2 The CPR later used priests as recruiting agents. A Father Van Aken from Montana was sent to the Netherlands in 1908, claimed his commission but fled after the settlers he brought to Strathmore lost their stake. See Willem DeGelder, *A Dutch Homesteader on the Prairies: The Letters of Willem DeGelder, 1920–13*, transl. and ed. Herman Ganzevoort (Toronto: University of Toronto Press, 1973), viii, 28.

3 George M. Grant, *Ocean to Ocean: Sandford Fleming's Expedition through Canada in 1872* (Toronto: Campbell, 1873), 90–9.

4 Marie A. Hamilton [née Bonneau] and Zachary M. Hamilton, *These Are the Prairies* (Regina: School Aids, 1948), 7, 261; Maryanne Caswell, *Pioneer Girl* (Toronto: McGraw Hill, 1964) [no pagination, letters without dates, letters numbered by author], letters no. 6 and 7; *Letters of Lovisa McDougall, 1878–1887*, ed. by Elizabeth M. McCrum (Edmonton: Provincial Archives, 1978), 15. It merits critical attention that Marie was four years old when she arrived and Maryanne a girl of fourteen. Their memory was remarkably developed for the age. [Barbara H. Anderson], *Two White Oxen: A Perspective of Early Saskatoon, 1874–1905*, ed. George W. Anderson and Robert N. Anderson (Lethbridge: privately printed, 1952). P. Turner Bone, *When the Steel Went Through: Reminiscences of a Railroad Pioneer [1882–92]* (Toronto: Macmillan, 1947), 62–3; *The Wheat King: The Selected Letters and Papers of A.J. Cotton, 1888–1913*, ed. Wendy Owen (Winnipeg: Manitoba Record Society, 1985); see also John P. Pennefather, *Thirteen Years on the Prairies: From Winnipeg to Cold Lake Fifteen Hundred Miles* (London: Kegan Paul, 1892).

5 Bickersteth, *The Land of Open Doors*, ix-xix, 99–110.

6 Dirk Hoerder, "From Dreams to Possibilities: The Secularization of Hope and the Quest for Independence," in same and Horst Rössler, eds., *Distant Magnets: Expectations and Realities in the Immigrant Experience* (New York: Holmes and Meier, 1993), 1–32. Frank Carrel, *Canada's West and Farther West* (Quebec: Telegraph, 1911), 28; Bickersteth, *The Land of Open Doors*, 25. For the continuing hopes in the 1930s, see Jean Burnet, *Next-Year Country: A Study of Rural Social Organization in Alberta* (Toronto: University of Toronto Press, 1951), 5.

7 Billie L. Allen, *Dew upon the Grass* (Saskatoon: Modern Press, 1963).

8 *Letters of Lovisa McDougall*, 49, 59, 67, 70. Ruth M. Buck, in *The Doctor Rode Side-Saddle* (Toronto: McClelland and Stewart, 1974), 89, 116, reported that her father John "Grace" Matheson, Anglican missionary on the Sekaskooch Indian Reserve near Fort Pitt, also had to be a trader, builder, and rancher to keep the mission and hospital financed. He did not draw a salary.

9 James G. MacGregor, *North-West of 16* (1st ed., 1958; repr. Edmonton: Hurtig, 1968), 13–15.

10 Hamilton, *These Are the Prairies*, 53–7; *Letters of Lovisa McDougall*, 73–6.

11 Anderson, *Two White Oxen*, 22, 52, 120–29. Edward Ffolkes, *Letters from a Young Emigrant in Manitoba*, ed. Ronald A. Wells (1st ed., 1883; Winnipeg: University of Manitoba Press, 1981), (1st edition anonymous, letters in second edition attributed to E. Ffolkes who arrived in Manitoba in 1881). H.E. Church, *An Emigrant in the Canadian Northwest* (London: Methuen, 1929). In 1886, Church and his brother came to Ontario to learn farming but were used as labourers and taught nothing.

12 Hamilton, *These Are the Prairies*, 128, 180–1, 195–7, 216–17, 219, 228, 233.

13 Joanna Matejko and Tova Yedlin, eds., *Alberta's Pioneers from Eastern Europe: Reminiscences* (Edmonton: University of Alberta, 1977), 16, 28.

14 Harry Piniuta, ed., *Land of Pain, Land of Promise: First Person Accounts by Ukrainian Pioneers 1891–1914* (Saskatoon: Western Producer Prairie Books, 1978), 121–35. Peter Svarich published memoirs about his life in 1901 on three different occasions: in the 1950s, in 1953, and in 1974. The accounts vary somewhat. In one he departs for British Columbia in fall 1901, in the others this is not mentioned. The evening-class activities are only mentioned once. William A. Czumer, *Recollections about the Life of the First Ukrainian Settlers in Canada*, transl. by Louis T. Laychuck (Ukrainian original, 1942; Edmonton: Canadian Institute of Ukrainian Studies, 1981).

15 Anna M. Martellone, "Italian Mass Emigration to the United States, 1876–1930: A Historical Survey," *Perspectives in American History* n.s. 1 (1984), 379–423; Gianfausto Rosoli, "Italian Migration to European Countries from Political Unification to World War I," in Dirk Hoerder, ed., *Labor Migration in the Atlantic Economies: The European and North American Working Classes During the Period of Industrialization* (Westport, Ct.: Greenwood, 1985), 95–116; Bruno Bezza, ed., *Gli Italiani fuori d'Italia: Gli emigrati italiani nei movimenti operai dei paesi d'adozione (1880–1940)* (Milano: Angeli, 1983).

16 Robert F. Harney, "Preface," *The Memoirs of Giovanni Veltri*, ed. by John Potestio (Toronto: Multicultural History Society of Ontario, 1987), 1st published as *Ricordanze Autobiografiche* (Cosenza: Grimaldi, 1955), 7.

17 Veltri, *Memoirs*, 7–76. Veltri did not once mention that Italy was fascist at this time.

18 Joanna Matejko, ed., *Polish Settlers in Alberta: Reminiscences and Biographies* (Toronto: Polish Alliance, 1979), 36–8, 145.

19 Edwin A. Alm, *I Never Wondered* (Vancouver: Evergreen, 1971), 15–103.

20 "Arnt Arntzen's Story," in Rolf Knight, ed., *Stump Ranch Chronicles and Other Narratives* (Vancouver: New Star, 1977), 25; Bill Johnstone, *Coal Dust in My Blood: The Autobiography of a Coal Miner* (Victoria: Royal British Columbia Museum, 1993), 77; Bickersteth, *Land of Open Doors*, 199.

21 Alm, *I Never Wondered*, 48–9, 63, 93, 112–13, 118, 154, 244–5.
22 Gus Romaniuk, *Taking Root in Canada: An Autobiography* (Winnipeg: Columbia, 1954), 9–94.
23 Bickersteth, *Land of Open Doors*, xiv-xv; Romaniuk, *Taking Root*, 56.
24 Bickersteth, *Land of Open Doors*, 120–52, 133–4, 212. Bone, in *When the Steel Went Through*, 105–6, mentioned a strike in 1884 because men had not been paid.
25 Bickersteth, *Land of Open Doors*, 154–5, 195; Basil Stewart, *The Land of the Maple Leaf. Or, Canada As I Saw It* (Toronto: Musson, 1908), 140–2; Slovak and Polish workers quoted in David Montgomery, "Nationalism, American Patriotism, and Class Consciousness among Immigrant Workers in the United States in the Epoch of World War I," in Dirk Hoerder, ed., *"Struggle a Hard Battle" – Essays on Working-Class Immigrants* (DeKalb, Ill., 1986), 346. See also quotes in Ewa Morawska, *For Bread with Butter: The Life-Worlds of East Central Europeans in Johnstown, Pennsylvania, 1890–1940* (Cambridge, Mass.: Harvard University Press, 1986).
26 Bickersteth, *The Land of Open Doors*, 215–16.
27 Robert E. Johnson, *Peasant and Proletarian: The Working Class of Moscow in the Late Nineteenth Century* (New Brunswick, NJ: Rutgers, 1979), and Johnson, "Family Relations and the Rural-Urban Nexus: Patterns in the Hinterland of Moscow, 1880–1900," in David L. Ransel, ed., *The Family in Imperial Russia. New Lines of Historical Research* (Urbana: University of Illinois Press, 1978), 263–79.

CHAPTER THIRTEEN

1 Publications before the First World War include: John J. Rowan, *The Emigrant and Sportsman in Canada: Some Experiences of an Old Country Settler* (London, 1876); Thomas Moore, *A Tour Through Canada, in 1879, with Remarks on the Advantages It Offers for Settlement to the British Farmer* (Dublin, 1880); *The Visit of the Tenant-Farmer Delegates to Canada in 1890* ([Ottawa?], 1891); Basil Stewart, *The Land of the Maple Leaf: Or, Canada as I Saw It* (London: Routledge, 1908); F.W. Grey, *Seeking a Fortune in America* (London: Smith, 1912).
2 The life-writings will by cited in chronological order of the arrival of the settlers; those of merchants, contractors, labourers will not be cited again. Eliane L. Silverman, in *The Last Best West: Women on the Alberta Frontier, 1880–1930* (Montreal: Eden, 1984), presents oral history regardless of ethnicity.
3 1874 and later: Lawrence Klippenstein and Julius G. Toews, eds., *Mennonite Memories: Settling in Western Canada* (Winnipeg: Centennial, 1977). See Royden Loewen, *Family, Church and Market: A Mennonite Community in the Old and New Worlds, 1850–1930* (Toronto: University of Toronto Press, 1993).

4 Tova Yedlin, ed., *Germans from Russia in Alberta: Reminiscences* (Edmonton: Central and East European Studies Society, 1984).

5 Harry Piniuta, ed., *Land of Pain, Land of Promise: First Person Accounts by Ukrainian Pioneers, 1891–1914* (Saskatoon: Western Producer Prairie Books, 1978); Joanna Matejko and Tova Yedlin, eds., *Alberta's Pioneers from Eastern Europe: Reminiscences* (Edmonton: University of Alberta, 1977); 1896: Peter Humeniuk, *Hardship & Progress of Ukrainian Pioneers: Memoirs from Stuartburn Colony and Other Points* (Steinbach: Derksen, 1976); 1907: Michael Luchkovich, *A Ukrainian Canadian in Parliament. Memoirs of Michael Luchkovich* (Toronto: Ukrainian Canadian Research Foundation, 1965); 1912: Gus Romaniuk, *Taking Root in Canada: An Autobiography* (Winnipeg: Columbia, 1954). See also Andrew Suknaski, *Wood Mountain Poems*, edited by Al Purdy (Toronto: Macmillan, 1976), especially "Homestead 1914," 19–26; Lubomyr Luciuk and Stella Hryniuk, *Canada's Ukrainians: Negotiating an Identity* (Toronto: University of Toronto Press, 1991).

6 Joanna Matejko, ed., *Polish Settlers in Alberta: Reminiscences and Biographies* (Toronto: Polish Alliance, 1979).

7 1905: Israel Hoffer, "Reminiscences," *Saskatchewan History* 5, no. 1 (Winter 1952), 28–32; 1910: Abe L. Plotkin, *Struggle for Justice: The Autobiography of Abe L. PLotkin* (New York: Exposition, 1960); 1911: Michael Usiskin, *Uncle Mike's Edenbridge [Sask.]: Memoirs of a Jewish Pioneer Farmer*, transl. from the Yiddish by Marcia U. Basman (Winnipeg: Peguis, 1983); 1927: Harry Henig, *Orphan of the Storm*, ed. Lawrence F. Jones (Toronto: Pitt, 1974). Eli Mandel, *Out of Place* (Don Mills: Musson, 1977), on the colonies in southern Saskatchewan.

8 1902: Emil Julius Meilicke, *Leaves from the Life of a Pioneer: Being the Autobiography of Sometime Senator Emil Julius Meilicke* (Vancouver, 1948; repr. Regina: Canadian Plains Research Centre, 1997); 1902: Joseph Prechtl, "My Homesteader Experience," in Richard J.A. Prechtl, *Take the Soil in Your Hands* (Saskatoon: Herrem, 1984), 5–26; 1907: Karl A. and Franziska Peter, eds., "The Kurtenbach Letters: An Autobiographical Description of Pioneer Life in Saskatchewan Around the Turn of the Century," *Canadian Ethnic Studies* 11, no. 2 (1979), 89–96.

9 1893: Klaas DeJong, *Cauliflower Crown*, arranged by Martha Knapp (Saskatoon: Western Producer Prairie Books, 1973); 1920: Willem DeGelder, *A Dutch Homesteader on the Prairies. The Letters of Willem DeGelder 1920–13*, transl. and ed. Herman Ganzevoort (Toronto: University of Toronto Press, 1973).

10 Danish 1910: Julie Feilberg, "Letters Home from a Danish Family in the Prairies," ed. Jorgen Dahlie, *Canadian Ethnic Studies* 8, no. 2 (1976), 93–5, from *Hjemliv paa Praerien – De Derovre: En Raekke Breve Fra Canada*, ed. Henning F. Feilberg (1st ed., 2 vols., 1912 and 1917; 1-vol. ed., Copenhagen: Nordisk Forlag, 1927). Norwegian, 1908: Ole Hjelt, *Nybyggerliv*

paa praerien [Pioneer Life on the Prairie] (Instow, Sask.: Forfatterens Forlag, 1920).

11 1906: Marcel Durieux, *Ordinary Heroes: The Journal of a French Pioneer in Alberta*, transl. and ed. Roger Motut and Maurice Legris (Edmonton: University of Alberta Press, 1980), French edition: *Un héros malgré lui* (St Boniface, Man.: Éditions des Plaines, 1986); 1906: *Pioneering in Alberta: Maurice Destrubé's Story*, ed. James E. Hendrickson (Calgary: Historical Society of Alberta, 1981); 1910: Gaston Giscard, *On the Canadian Prairie* (French orig: *Dans la Prairie Canadienne*), bilingual ed., transl. Lloyd Person, ed. George E. Durocher (Regina: Canadian Plains Studies Centre, 1982).

12 Welsh, 1904: Evan Davies, [as told to] Alec Vaughan, *Beyond the Old Bone Trail* (London: Cassell, 1960). Scottish, English, 1906: James G. MacGregor, *North-West of 16* (1st ed., 1958; repr. Edmonton: Hurtig, 1968). English, 1889: W.M. Elkington, *Five Years in Canada* (London: Whittaker, 1895); 1894: Frank G. Roe, *Getting the Know-How: Homesteading and Railroading in Early Alberta*, ed. J.P. Regan (Edmonton: NeWest, 1982); 1894: Claude Gardiner, *Letters from an English Rancher*, ed. Hugh A. Dempsey (Calgary: Glenbow Alberta Institute, 1988); 1899: Edna T. Parson, *Land I Can Own: A Biography of Anthony Tyson and the Pioneers Who Homesteaded with Him at Neidpath, Saskatchewan* (Ottawa: privately printed, 1981); 1906: Leslie H. Neatby, *Chronicle of a Pioneer Prairie Family* (Saskatoon: Western Producer Prairie Books, 1979); 1909: Monica Hopkins, *Letters from a Lady Rancher* (Halifax: Goodread, 1983); 1909: James M. Minifie, *Homesteader: A Prairie Boyhood Recalled* (Toronto: Macmillan, 1972); *c.* 1910: Harold Baldwin, *A Farm for Two Pounds: Being the Odyssey of an Emigrant* (London: Murray, 1935); 1911: Edward A. Wharton, *A Manitoba Chore Boy: The Experiences of a Young Emigrant Told from His Letters* (London: Religious Tract Society, 1912); 1910s: Elinor M. Eliot, *My Canada* (London: Hodder and Stoughton, 1915).

13 Stewart, *Canada as I Saw It*, vii, 135, 151. J. Burgon Bickersteth, *The Land of Open Doors: Being Letters from Western Canada, 1911–13* (1st ed., 1914; repr. Toronto: University of Toronto Press, 1976), 64.

14 Giscard, *On the Canadian Prairie*, 36, 40–1; Silverman, *Last Best West*, 86–91.

15 Sarah E. Roberts, *Alberta Homestead: Chronicle of a Pioneer Family*, ed. Lathrop E. Roberts (Austin: University of Texas Press, 1968), 164–7.

16 Destrubé, *Pioneering in Alberta*, 125; James H. Sadler, *The Hard Way to Goshen* (n.p., n.d.), 39–40, 48.

17 Matejko and Yedlin, *Alberta's Pioneers*, 8; Roe, *Getting the Know-How*, xiv; Robert Collins, *Butter Down the Well: Reflections of a Canadian Childhood* (Saskatoon: Western Producer Prairie Books, 1980), 55–6; Agatha Karpinski: "I had no-where to go and no-one to talk to," Matejko,

Polish Settlers, 154; Peter Chapman, ed., *Where the Lardeau River Flows* (Victoria: Provincial Archives, 1981), 18.

18 Davies, *Old Bone Trail*, 38, 78; Bickersteth, *The Land of Open Doors*, 179–80.

19 Roe, *Getting the Know-How*, 25–7.

20 Edward Ffolkes, *Letters from a Young Emigrant in Manitoba*, ed. Ronald A. Wells (London, 1883; new ed., Winnipeg: University of Manitoba Press, 1981), 21; DeGelder, *Dutch Homesteader*, xii-xiv; Monkman: *Canada Year Book of 1871*, 132.

21 Peter, "The Kurtenbach Letters," 89–96.

22 Durieux, *Ordinary Heroes*, 18, 27, 45–54.

23 Matejko, *Polish Settlers in Alberta*, 23–9; Matejko and Yedlin, *Alberta's Pioneers from Eastern Europe*, 73.

24 Klippenstein and Toews, *Mennonite Memories*, 99. If need be, Mennonites hired Ukrainian or other harvest help (p. 213).

25 Yedlin, *Germans from Russia*, 2–7, 10, 127.

26 Ibid., 13, 28, 31, 64–65, 71, 77; Matejko and Yedlin, *Alberta's Pioneers*, 1–5 passim.

27 Paul Mingus, ed., *Sounds Canadian: Languages and Cultures in Multi-Ethnic Society* (Toronto: Martin, 1975), 32. Matejko, *Polish Settlers*, 47. The Canadian-Ukrainian *Novyny*, 22 August 1913, like the whole press, sharply attacked authorities. Quoted in William A. Czumer, *Recollections about the Life of the First Ukrainian Settlers in Canada*, transl. by Louis T. Laychuck (Ukrainian original, Edmonton, 1942; Edmonton: Canadian Institute of Ukrainian Studies, 1981), 106–10.

28 Matejko, *Polish Settlers*, 30–5.

29 Ibid., e.g. 29, 44, 152; Yedlin, *Germans from Russia*, e.g., 41, 59, 103; Matejko and Yedlin, eds., *Alberta's Pioneers*, 44.

30 Piniuta, *Land of Pain*, 37–52; Czumer, *Recollections*, 52–3.

31 Thomas C. Douglas, *The Making of a Socialist: The Recollections of T.C. Douglas*, ed. Lewis H. Thomas (Edmonton: University of Alberta Press, 1982), 46, 50; Yedlin, *Germans from Russia*, 99, 103. The best study of social groups as actors in the process of developing a national consciousness is Miroslav Hroch, *Social Preconditions of National Revival in Europe* (Cambridge: Cambridge University Press, 1985).

32 Theodor H. von Laue, "Russian Peasants in the Factory, 1892–1904," *Journal of Economic History* 21 (1961), 61–80; Robert E. Johnson, "Peasant Migration and the Russian Working Class: Moscow at the End of the Nineteenth Century," *Slavic Review* 35 (1976), 652–64; Franco Ramella, "Between Village and Job Abroad: Italian Migrants in France and Switzerland," in Dirk Hoerder et al., eds., *Roots of the Transplanted*, 2 vols. (Boulder: East European Monographs, 1994), 2: 271–88.

33 Matejko, *Polish Settlers*: Biedrawa 32–3, Kolber 102–5; see also Opalinski, 1928, ibid. 137–8; Arnold Dyck, "Aus meinem Leben", in *Collected Works – Werke*, ed. Victor G. Doerksen et al. (Steinbach: Manitoba Mennonite Historical Society, 1985), 1: 497–9; Yedlin, *Germans from Russia*, 27–8.

34 Sadler, *The Hard Way to Goshen*, 10–11; Matejko and Yedlin, eds., *Alberta's Pioneers*, 95; Matejko, *Polish Settlers*, 35, 105.

35 Edwin A. Alm, *I Never Wondered* (Vancouver: Evergreen, 1971), 87; Matejko and Yedlin, eds., *Alberta's Pioneers*, 44; Gardiner, *Letters from an English Rancher*, 58; Bickersteth, *The Land of Open Doors*, 91–5.

36 Bickersteth, *The Land of Open Doors*, 244; Durieux, *Ordinary Heroes*, 70. Georgina Binnie-Clark, in *Wheat and Woman* (1st ed., 1914; Toronto: University of Toronto Press, 1979), again and again commented upon makeshift work. Edward F. Fripp, *The Outcasts of Canada: Why Settlements Fail, a True Record of 'Bull' and Bale-Wire* (Edinburgh: Blackwood, 1932); Cecilia Danysk, "Showing These Slaves Their Class Position: Barriers to Organizing Prairie Farm Workers," in David Jones and Ian MacPherson, eds., *Building Beyond the Homestead* (Calgary: University of Calgary Press, 1985), 163–79; David P. McGinnis, "Farm Labour in Transition: Occupational Structure and Economic Dependency in Alberta," in Howard Palmer, ed., *The Settlement of the West* (Calgary: University of Calgary Press, 1977), 174–86.

37 Lucy Lindell, comp., *Memory Opens the Door to Yesterday. History as Told by Pioneers of the Central, West-Interlake Area [Manitoba]* (Eriksdale, Man.: n.p., 1970), 64; Romaniuk, *Taking Root*, 40; an embroidered flour sack as tablecloth is exhibited in the Ukrainian Museum and Archives in Cleveland, Ohio. Matejko, *Polish Settlers*, 147, 150, 164.

38 Matejko, *Polish Settlers*, 146; Gardiner, *Letters from an English Rancher*, 59; John Grossmann, "Streiflichter vom Rande der Zivilisation. Die Erlebnisse eines deutschen Heimstätters im Peace-River-Gebiet," *German-Canadian Yearbook* 1 (1973), 191–244, and 2 (1975), 193–246. Binnie-Clark, *Wheat and Woman*, e.g., 30, 35, 307; Magnus Pyke, *Go West, Young Man, Go West* (Ottawa: Graphic, 1930), 108–13.

39 Jane Thompson," 'I never intended to Marry': Tales of Single British Women in Western Canada, 1880–1950" (Ph.D. research in progress, University of Toronto, 1997); Robert Jefferson, *Fifty Years on the Saskatchewan* (Battleford, Sask.: Canadian Northwest History Society, 1929), 15–16; William Newton, *Twenty Years on the Saskatchewan, N.W. Canada* (London: Stock, 1897), chapter on "Emigrants and Emigration"; Grey, *Seeking a Fortune*, 46; Roe, *Getting the Know-How*, 62–9; Eliot, *My Canada*, 22, 187–91; Alexander A. Boddy, *By Ocean, Prairie and Peak: Some Gleanings from an Emigrant Chaplain's Log* (London, 1896), 87; Destrubé, *Pioneering in Alberta*, 73.

40 Piniuta, *Land of Pain*, 27–48, 87, 97, 131; Luchkovich, *A Ukrainian Canadian in Parliament*, 24–5.

41 Donald B. Smith, "A History of French-Speaking Albertans," in Howard Palmer and Tamara Palmer, eds., *Peoples of Alberta: Portraits of Cultural Diversity* (Saskatoon: Western Producer Prairie Books, 1985), 84–108; Giscard, *On the Canadian Prairie*, xi-xv; Durieux, *Ordinary Heroes*, 43 79, 93–4. Richard Lapointe and Lucille Tessier, *Histoire des Franco-Canadiens de la Saskatchewan* (Regina, 1986), is an uncritical survey.

42 Piniuta, *Land of Pain*, 72; Yedlin, *Germans from Russia*, 64, 74; Matejko, *Polish Settlers*, 156; Beth Hatefutsoth, *A Century of Jewish Settlement in Western Canada* [exhibition catalogue] (Tel Aviv: Goldman Museum, 1980); Max Rubin, "Alberta's Jews: The Long Journey," in Palmer and Palmer, *Peoples of Alberta*, 328–47.

43 Matejko, *Polish Settlers*, 136; Yedlin, *Germans from Russia*, 102; Bickersteth, *The Land of Open Doors*, 30; *The Memoirs of Giovanni Veltri*, ed. John Potestio (Toronto: Multicultural History Society of Ontario, 1987), 40. William W. Calderwood, "Pulpit, Press, and Political Reactions to the Ku Klux Klan in Saskatchewan," in Susan Mann Trofimenkoff, ed., *The Twenties in Western Canada* (Ottawa: National Museum of Canada, 1972), 191–229.

44 Marie A. Hamilton and Zachary M. Hamilton, *These Are the Prairies* (Regina: School Aids, 1948), 186; H.E. Church, *An Emigrant in the Canadian Northwest* (London: Methuen, 1929), 33–7; Roe, *Getting the Know-How*, 38–9; Grant MacEwan, *John Ware's Cow Country* (Edmonton: Institute of Applied Art, 1960). R. Bruce Shepard, *Deemed Unsuitable: Blacks from Oklahoma* (Toronto: Umbrella, 1997); Colin A. Thomson, *Blacks in Deep Snow: Black Pioneers in Canada* (Don Mills, Ont.: Dent, 1979); Howard Palmer and Tamara Palmer, "The Black Experience in Alberta," in Palmer and Palmer, *Peoples of Alberta*, 365–93.

45 Eliot, *My Canada*, 149; Yedlin, *Germans from Russia*, 15; Sadler, *The Hard Way to Goshen*, 14; Fredelle Bruser Maynard, *Raisins and Almonds* (1st ed. 1964; repr. Markham, Ont.: PaperJacks, 1973), 57–60; Collins, *Butter Down the Well*, 86–9 (quote slighty rearranged by author); J. Brian Dawson, "The Chinese Experience in Frontier Calgary, 1885–1910," in A.W. Rasporich and H.C. Klassen, eds., *Frontier Calgary: Town, City and Region, 1875–1914* (Calgary: McClelland and Stewart West, 1975), 124–41.

46 Destrubé, *Pioneering in Alberta*, 98–9; Frampton and Henderson, *The Long Long Trail*, 61–2.

47 Phyllis Harrison, ed., *The Home Children: Their Personal Stories* (Winnipeg: Watson and Dwyer, 1979), 41–5.

48 *The Wheat King: The Selected Letters and Papers of A.J. Cotton, 1888–1913*, ed. Wendy Owen (Winnipeg: Manitoba Record Society, 1989), 10–13.

49 Frampton and Henderson, *The Long Long Trail*, 55.

50 Matejko and Yedlin eds., *Alberta's Pioneers*, 44; Bickersteth, *Land of Open Doors*, 229; Piniuta, *Land of Pain*, 49–50; Baldwin, *A Farm for Two Pounds*, 42, 135, 244–8. Howard Palmer, *Patterns of Prejudice: A History of Nativism in Alberta* (Toronto: McClelland and Stewart, 1982); Palmer and Palmer, *Peoples of Alberta*.

51 Anne K. Chuchla, "The Martin J. Pieronek Family," in Matejko, *Polish Settlers*, 140–4.

52 "Childhood Memories of Anna Kutera," in ibid., 114–20.

53 Yedlin, *Germans from Russia*, 16; Matejko and Yedlin eds., *Alberta's Pioneers*, 9. Jacqueline Dowd Hall et al., *Like a Family: The Making of a Southern Cotton Mill World* (Chapel Hill: University of North Carolina Press, 1987).

54 Matejko, *Polish Settlers*, 30–1, 152–3.

55 Roe, *Getting the Know-How*, 16; Giscard, *On the Canadian Prairie*, 21; Matejko, *Polish Settlers*, 88, 293.

56 Eliot, *My Canada*, 57; Yedlin, *Germans from Russia*, 55.

57 Davies, *Old Bone Trail*, 148–51; Eliot, *My Canada*, 59–63.

58 Ffolkes, *Letters from a Young Emigrant*, 19.

59 Davies, *Old Bone Trail*, 164. The original submissions to the competition may be found at the University of Saskatchewan, Library, Special Collections, Morton Manuscript Collection. The period covered ranges from *c.* 1880s to the 1920s.

60 Veronica Strong-Boag, "Introduction," to Nellie L. McClung, *In Times Like These* (1915; repr. Toronto: University of Toronto Press, 1972). The province of Quebec passed woman's suffrage only in 1940. Linda Kealey and Joan Sangster, eds., *Beyond the Vote: Canadian Women and Politics* (Toronto: University of Toronto Press, 1989).

61 Ruth M. Buck, *The Doctor Rode Side-Saddle* (Toronto: McClelland and Stewart, 1974), vi, 24–5, 86–7, 104–14; Romaniuk, *Taking Root in Canada*, 231–9, on a doctor and his wife in Riverton, Manitoba.

62 Laura Goodman Salverson, *Confessions of an Immigrant's Daughter* (1st ed., 1939; repr. Toronto: University of Toronto Press, 1981), 123–4.

63 Bickersteth, *Land of Open Doors*, 91; Davies, *Old Bone Trail*, 81; Roe, *Getting the Know-How*, 121–3.

64 Church, in *An Emigrant in the Canadian Northwest*, noted that even in ranching country, in Calgary "it was the regular custom to leave your 'gun' at the livery stable with your horse and saddle outfit"(p. 34).

65 Matejko, *Polish Settlers*, 88, 293; Davies, *Old Bone Trail*, 120–3.

66 Bickersteth, *Land of Open Doors*, xvi, 24, 62, 80–3.

67 Matejko, *Polish Settlers*, 37, 46, 57, 157.

68 Dorothea E. Bublitz, *Life on the Dotted Line* (New York: Vantage,

1960), 30–1; Benedykt Heydenkorn, ed., *Memoirs of Polish Immigrants in Canada* (Toronto: Futura, 1979), 240; Silverman, *Last Best West*, 23, 29–30.

69 Matejko, *Polish Settlers*, 151–7.

CHAPTER FOURTEEN

1 Lucy Lindell, comp., *Memory Opens the Door to Yesterday: History as Told by Pioneers of the Central, West-Interlake Area [Manitoba]* (Eriksdale, Man., 1970), 64.

2 Laura Goodman Salverson, *Confessions of an Immigrant's Daughter* (1st ed., Toronto: Ryerson, 1939; repr. 1981), 44–7; Jessie L. Beattie, *Along the Road* (Toronto: Ryerson, 1954), 28–39; E.W. Nuffield, *With the West in Her Eyes: Nellie Hislop's Story* (Winnipeg: Hyperion, 1987), 27.

3 James H. Gray, *The Boy from Winnipeg* (Toronto: Macmillan, 1971), 65.

4 Marie Ets Hall, ed., *Rosa: The Life of an Italian Immigrant* (Minneapolis: University of Minnesota Press, 1970), 17–18, 26, 113, 118, 124, 141; Louis Adamic, *Laughing in the Jungle* (New York, 1932), 5. See also Matjaz Klemencic, "The Image of America among Yugoslav, esp. Slovene Migrants: Promised Land or Bad Jobs," in Dirk Hoerder and Horst Rössler, eds., *Distant Magnets: Expectations and Realities in the Immigrant Experience* (New York: Holmes & Meier, 1993), 199–221; Dirk Hoerder, "German Immigrant Workers' Views of 'America' in the 1880s," in Marianne Debouzy, *ed., In the Shadow of the Statue of Liberty: Immigrants, Workers and Citizens in the American Republic, 1880–1920* (Vincennes: University de Paris VIII, 1988), 17–33.

5 Joanna Matejko and Tova Yedlin, eds., *Alberta's Pioneers from Eastern Europe: Reminiscences* (Edmonton: University of Alberta, 2nd ed., 1978), 57.

6 D.E. Macintyre, *Prairie Storekeeper* (Toronto: Martin, 1970), 1–19.

7 Ibid., 21–34.

8 Ibid., 28–48, 99–100. In, *Pioneering in Alberta: Maurice Destrubé's Story*, ed. by James E. Hendrickson (Calgary: Historical Society of Alberta, 1981), 56, Destrubé also had to deal with butter delivered in payment by poor housekeepers, in his case an Englishwoman.

9 Fredelle Bruser Maynard, *Raisins and Almonds* (1st ed. 1964; repr. Markham, Ont.: PaperJacks, 1973), 28–30 passim.

10 Habeeb Salloum, "Reminiscences of an Arab Family Homesteading in Southern Saskatchewan," *Canadian Ethnic Studies* 15, no. 2 (1983), 130–8. Baha Abu-Laban, *An Olive Branch on the Family Tree: The Arabs in Canada* (Toronto: McCelland and Stewart, 1980).

11 Helgi Einarsson, *A Manitoba Fisherman*, transl. by George Houser (Icelandic orig., Reykjavik, 1945; Winnipeg: Queenston, 1982), 1–143. Ice-

fishing was described in Gaston Giscard, *On the Canadian Prairie* (French orig: *Dans la Prairie Canadienne*; bilingual ed., transl. Lloyd Person, ed. George E. Durocher; Regina, Sask.: Canadian Plains Studies Centre, 1982), 22–9.

12 Einarsson, *A Manitoba Fisherman*, 142–3.

13 Gus Romaniuk, *Taking Root in Canada: An Autobiography* (Winnipeg: Columbia, 1954), 149–217, 276–7.

14 Einarsson, *Manitoba Fisherman*, 91–103, 106–8; Destrubé, *Pioneering in Alberta*, 55–63, 98–9; Giscard, *On the Canadian Prairie*, 69–70.

CHAPTER FIFTEEN

1 Marie A. Hamilton and Zachary M. Hamilton, *These Are the Prairies* (Regina: School Aids, 1948), 22; *Letters of Lovisa McDougall, 1878–1887*, ed. by Elizabeth M. McCrum (Edmonton: Provincial Archives, 1978), 21; Claude Gardiner, *Letters from an English Rancher*, ed. by Hugh A. Dempsey (Calgary: Glenbow Alberta Institute, 1988); Tom Telfer in Milly Charon, *Between Two Worlds: The Canadian Immigrant Experience* (1st ed., 1983; rev. ed., Montreal: Nu-Age Editions, 1988); 79. Recent studies include E.E. Rich, *The Fur Trade and the Northwest to 1857* (Toronto: McClelland and Stewart, 1967); Douglas Mackay, *The Honourable Company* (New York, 1970); Peter C. Newman, *The Company of Adventurers* (Markham, Ont.: Viking, 1985).

2 Nora Kelly and William Kelly, *The RCMP: A Century of History, 1873–1973* (Edmonton: Hurtig, 1973); R.C. Macleod, *The North-West Mounted Police and Law Enforcement, 1873–1905* (Toronto: University of Toronto Press, 1976); William R. Morrison, *Showing the Flag: The Mounted Police and Canadian Sovereignty in the North, 1894–1925* (Vancouver: University of British Columbia Press, 1985); Keith Walden, *Visions of Order: The Canadian Mounties in Symbol and Myth* (Toronto: Butterworths, 1982).

3 Adam J. Tolmie, *Roughing It on the Rails* (Bloomfield, Ont.: Silverthorn, 1983), 17; Lina Madore, *Petit Coin Perdu* (Rivière-du-Loup: Castelriand, 1979), 90; Joanna Matejko, ed., *Polish Settlers in Alberta: Reminiscences and Biographies* (Toronto: Polish Alliance, 1979), 65.

4 Luta Munday, *A Mounty's Wife: Being the Life Story of One Attached to the Force but Not of It* (London: Sheldon, 1930), vii-28; Maryanne Caswell, *Pioneer Girl* (Toronto: McGraw-Hill, 1964); letter 12; Alexander A. Boddy, *By Ocean, Prairie and Peak* (London, 1896), 95; Hamilton, *These Are the Prairies*, 32, 125–6, 224. [Capt.] Ernest J. Chambers, *The Royal North-West Mounted Police: A Corps History* (Montreal: Mortimer, 1906), includes illustrations of the elaborate pageantry of the uniforms.

Frank G. Roe, *Getting the Know-How: Homesteading and Railroading in Early Alberta*, ed. J.P. Regan (Edmonton: NeWest, 1982), 35. Harry Piniuta, ed. and transl., *Land of Pain, Land of Promise: First Person Accounts by Ukrainian Pioneers, 1891–1914* (Saskatoon: Western Producer Prairie Books, 1978), 32–3; Abe L. Plotkin, *Struggle for Justice: The Autobiography of Abe L. Plotkin* (New York: Exposition, 1960), 83–5.

5 Other observers commented on the profits made by supplying the force, "large and lucrative contracts." R.B. Nevitt, *A Winter at Fort Macleod* (Calgary: Glenbow Institute, 1974); Alexander Sutherland, *A Summer in Prairie-Land* (2nd ed., Toronto, 1882), 33; Sydney Hutcheson, *Depression Stories* (Vancouver: New Star, 1976), 14; *R.C.M.P. Security Bulletins: The Early Years, 1919–1929*, ed. Gregory S. Kealey and Reg Whitaker (St John's: Canadian Committee on Labour History, 1994), 11–24, passim.

6 Hamilton, *These Are the Prairies*, 121; *Letters of Lovisa McDougall*, 26–7, 54.

7 Matejko, *Polish Settlers*, 44, 49–50; Joanna Matejko and Tova Yedlin, eds., *Alberta's Pioneers from Eastern Europe: Reminiscences* (Edmonton: University of Alberta, 1977), 40; Thomas C. Douglas, *The Making of a Socialist: The Recollections of T.C. Douglas*, ed. by Lewis H. Thomas (Edmonton: University of Alberta Press, 1982).

8 Caswell, *Pioneer Girl*, letter 12; J. Burgon Bickersteth, *The Land of Open Doors. Being Letters from Western Canada, 1911–13* (London, 1914; repr. Toronto: University of Toronto Press, 1976), 89; Hamilton, *These Are the Prairies*, 128.

9 *The Memoirs of Giovanni Veltri*, ed. by John Potestio (Toronto: Multicultural History Society of Ontario, 1987), 26, 47, 58, 62, 76; Matejko, *Polish Settlers*, 37.

10 A.M. Klein, *Complete Poems*, 2 vols. (Toronto: University of Toronto Press, 1990), 2: 650.

11 Roe, *Getting the Know-How*, 58; *Historical Atlas of Canada*, 3 vols. (Toronto: University of Toronto Press, 1987–93), 2: 42. One diarist noted that grain-threshing machines were sold to Russia and Germany in 1912. Evan Davies, *Beyond the Old Bone Trail* (London: Cassell, 1960), 154.

12 James H. Sadler, *The Hard Way to Goshen* (n.p., n.d.), 6; Raymond M. Patterson, *The Buffalo Head* (Toronto: Macmillan, 1961), 7; Hamilton, *These Are the Prairies*, 128, 195.

13 John J. Rowan, *Emigrant and Sportsman in Canada* (London, 1876), preface, 1–9.

14 Bickersteth, *The Land of Open Doors*, 86; Gus Romaniuk, *Taking Root in Canada: An Autobiography* (Winnipeg: Columbia, 1954), 36.

15 At the end of their stories, many noted: "Canada gave me a chance." But during their earlier years they never reflected on "Canada."

16 Romaniuk, *Taking Roots*, 36; Davies, *Beyond the Old Bone Trail*, 137.

17 Tova Yedlin, ed., *Germans from Russia in Alberta: Reminiscences* (Edmonton: Central and East European Studies Society, 1984), 55, 61.

18 Bickersteth, *The Land of Open Doors*, 33–4, 96; Yedlin, *Germans from Russia*, 60; Matejko, *Polish Settlers*, 29, 42, 58, 97, 150, 287; Matejko and Yedlin, eds., *Alberta's Pioneers*, 14, 40, 42, 57, 67.

19 Matejko, *Polish Settlers*, 46–7, 54, 59, 326.

20 Karl A. Peter and Franziska Peter, eds., "The Kurtenbach Letters: An Autobiographical Description of Pioneer Life in Saskatchewan Around the Turn of the Century," *Canadian Ethnic Studies* 11, no. 2 (1979), 89–96.

21 Helgi Einarsson, *A Manitoba Fisherman* (Winnipeg: Queenston, 1982), 143–5.

22 See in general: Joy L. Santink, *Timothy Eaton and the Rise of His Department Store* (Toronto: University of Toronto Press, 1990); George G. Nasmith, *Timothy Eaton* (Toronto: McClelland & Stewart, 1923); John M. Bassett, *Timothy Eaton* (Don Mills, Ontario: Fitzhenry and Whiteside, 1976). Willem DeGelder, *A Dutch Homesteader on the Prairies: The Letters of Willem de Gelder, 1920–13*, transl. and edited by Herman Ganzevoort (Toronto: University of Toronto Press, 1973), 22; Robert Collins, *Butter Down the Well: Reflections of a Canadian Childhood* (Saskatoon: Western Producer Prairie Books, 1980), 15–16; Fredelle Bruser Maynard, *Raisins and Almonds* (1st ed., 1964; repr. Markham, Ont.: PaperJacks, 1973), 42.

23 By 1907 the T. Eaton Company employed a total of nine thousand men and women in all its locations.

24 Joseph E. Wilder, *Read All About It: Reminiscences of an Immigrant Newsboy*, ed. Fred C. Dawkins and Micheline C. Brodeur (Winnipeg: Peguis, 1978), 77–8; James H. Gray, *The Boy from Winnipeg* (Toronto: Macmillan, 1971), 4, 65–6, 112.

25 Gray, *The Boy from Winnipeg*, 53–4, 114; Elinor M. Eliot, *My Canada* (London: Hodder & Stoughton, 1915), 20; Marcel Durieux, *Ordinary Heroes: The Journal of a French Pioneer in Alberta*, transl. and ed. by Roger Motut and Maurice Legris (Edmonton: University of Alberta Press, 1980), 14; Harry Gairey, *A Black Man's Toronto, 1914–1980: The Reminiscences of Harry Gairey*, ed. Donna Hill (Toronto: Multicultural History Society of Ontario, 1981), 16.

26 Vera Lysenko, *Westerly Wild* (Toronto: Ryerson, 1956), 86, 115, 189; Bickersteth, *Land of Open Doors*, 16; Aili Grönlund Schneider, *The Finnish Baker's Daughters* (Toronto: Multicultural History Society of Ontario, 1986), 103; Collins, *Butter Down the Well*, 132; Harry Henig, *Orphan of the Storm*, ed. Lawrence F. Jones (Toronto: Pitt, 1974), 96; Matejko, *Polish Settlers*, 116.

27 Schneider, *The Finnish Baker's Daughters*, 48; Collins, *Butter Down the Well*, 129, 133.

28 Douglas, *The Making of a Socialist*, 31–2; Gairey, *A Black Man's Toronto*, 9.

29 Tamara J. Palmer, "Ethnic Response to the Canadian Prairies, 1900–1950," *Prairie Forum* 12 (Spring 1987), 49–74.

30 Veronica Strong-Boag, Introduction, in Nellie L. McClung, *In Times Like These* (1915; repr. Toronto: University of Toronto Press, 1972), vii-xx.

31 Isabel Bassett, Introduction, in Emily Murphy, *Janey Canuck in the West* (1st ed., 1910; repr. Toronto: McClelland and Stewart, 1975), ix-xxiii.

32 Frederick Niven, *Canada West* (London and Toronto: Dent, 1930), 34–46. Niven's personages might be compared with William Kurelek's of the 1950s and 1960s: *Someone with Me: The Autobiography of William Kurelek* (Ithaca: Cornell, 1973; rev. ed. Toronto: McClelland and Stewart, 1980); Kurelek and Joan Murray, *Kurelek's Vision of Canada* (Edmonton: Hurtig, 1983). See his *A Prairie Boy's Summer* (1975), *Lumberjack* (1974), and others. Later literary representations include Robert W. Service, *Ploughman of the Moon: An Adventure into Memory* (New York: Dodd, 1945), and Wallace E. Stegner, *Wolf Willow: A History, a Story and a Memoir of the Last Plains Frontier* (1st ed. 1955; repr., Toronto: Macmillan, 1977).

33 Quoted in Donald Avery, "The Radical Alien and the Winnipeg General Strike of 1919," in J.M. Bumsted, ed., *Interpreting Canada's Past*, 2 vols (Toronto: Oxford University Press, 1986), 2: 224.

CHAPTER SIXTEEN

1 "Alexander Robb: Adventurer in British Columbia," in Cecil J. Houston and William J. Smyth, *Irish Emigration and Canadian Settlement: Patterns, Links and Letters* (Toronto: University of Toronto Press, 1990), 302–33.

2 Jakob Stricker, *Erlebnisse eines Schweizers in Kanada* (Zurich: Orell Fuessli, 1935), 62; Conrad Kain, *Where the Clouds Can Go*, ed. Monroe Thorington (New York: American Alpine Club, 1935). Kain's multi-ethnic experiences had begun in Austria, where he had worked with Italian, Slovak, and German construction workers. Like British Columbian packers, he had guided high-ranking people and was dismissed from his job in a quarry because his employer felt that he was moving beyond his class and place. Harry Piniuta, ed. and transl., *Land of Pain, Land of Promise: First Person Accounts by Ukrainian Pioneers, 1891–1914* (Saskatoon: Western Producer Prairie Books, 1978), 135–6.

3 Martin Nordegg, *The Possibilities of Canada Are Truly Great, Memoirs 1906–1924*, ed. T.D. Regehr (Toronto: University of Toronto Press, 1971), 5–60.

4 De Bouthillier-Chavigny, *A Travers le Nord-Ouest Canadien: De Montréal aux montagnes rocheuses. Notes de voyage* (Montréal, 1893), 13–14; Alexander Sutherland, *A Summer in Prairie-Land: Notes of a Tour Through the North-West Territory* (2nd ed., Toronto, 1882), 15–17; Raymond M. Patterson, *The Buffalo Head* (Toronto: Macmillan, 1961), 5–6; Marcel Durieux, *Ordinary Heroes: The Journal of a French Pioneer in Alberta*, transl. and ed. by Roger Motut and Maurice Legris (Edmonton: University of Alberta Press, 1980), French ed.: *Un héros malgré lui* (St Boniface, Man.: Éditions des Plaines, 1986), 28–9; Christian F.J. Galloway, *The Call of the West: Letters from British Columbia* (London: Adelphi 1916), 22; oral testimony by two German immigrants in post-Second World War Toronto, in the Multicultural History Society of Ontario oral history collection. I am grateful to Christiane Harzig for this reference.

5 Kain, *Where the Clouds Can Go*, 60–1, 227–8.

6 *The Memoirs of Giovanni Veltri*, ed. by John Potestio (Toronto: Multicultural History Society of Ontario, 1987), 38–9.

7 Nordegg, *The Possibilities of Canada*, 78–235; Martin Nordegg, *To the Town that Bears Your Name: A Young Woman's Journey to Nordegg in 1912*, transl. by Maria Koch, introd. by W. John Koch (Edmonton: Brightest Pebble, 1995), 101–9; W. John Koch, *Martin Nordegg: The Uncommon Immigrant* (Edmonton: Brightest Pebble, 1997). For the First World War, see Gerhard P. Bassler, *The German Canadian Mosaic Today and Yesterday: Identities, Roots, and Heritage* (Ottawa: German-Canadian Congress, 1991), 61–7.

8 Gaston Giscard, *On the Canadian Prairie* (French orig: *Dans la Prairie Canadienne*), transl. Lloyd Person, ed. George E. Durocher (Regina: University of Regina, 1982), 4, 49, 69–70.

9 Max Otto, *In kanadischer Wildnis: Trapper- und Farmerleben* (Berlin, 1923; 5th ed., 1924) and *In Kanadas Urwäldern und Prärien: Erlebnisse eines Trappers und Farmers* (Berlin, 1925; 4th ed., 1926).

10 Joanna Matejko, ed., *Polish Settlers in Alberta: Reminiscences and Biographies* (Toronto: Polish Alliance, 1979), 328.

11 Gus Romaniuk, *Taking Root in Canada: An Autobiography* (Winnipeg: Columbia, 1954), 91.

12 Walter F. Chuchla, "Personal Experiences from 1904 till 1978," in Matejko, *Polish Settlers*, 49–79, 265–9, especially 98, 171; Allen Seager, "Class, Ethnicity, and Politics in the Alberta Coalfields, 1905–1945," in Dirk Hoerder, ed., *"Struggle a Hard Battle": Essays on Working-Class Immigrants* (DeKalb, Ill.: Northern Illinois University Press, 1985), 304–26.

13 "The Martin J. Pieronek Family," in Matejko, *Polish Settlers*, 140–4.

14 Bill Johnstone, *Coal Dust in My Blood: The Autobiography of a Coal Miner* (Victoria: Royal British Columbia Museum, 1993), 7–165; Reg Whitaker, *Canadian Immigration Policy since Confederation* (Ottawa: Canadian Historical Association, 1991), 10.

CHAPTER SEVENTEEN

1 Sylvia Van Kirk, *"Many Tender Ties": Women in Fur Trade Society in Western Canada, 1670–1870* (Winnipeg: Watson, 1980); Van Kirk, *Towards a Feminist Perspective in Native History* (Toronto: Ontario Institute for Studies in Education, 1987); Adele Perry, "Mixed-Race Relationships and Colonial Discourse in British Columbia, 1858–1871" (doctoral research in progress, York University, 1996). George Bowering, *Bowering's British Columbia: A Swashbuckling History* (Toronto: Viking, 1996); Hugh J.M. Johnston, ed., *Pacific Province: A History of British Columbia* (Vancouver: Dougal, 1996).

2 Walter Moberly and Noel Robinson, *Blazing the Trail Through the Rockies: The Story of Walter Moberly and His Share in the Making of Vancouver* (n.p.: News-Advertiser [1915]), 48.

3 William Newton, *Twenty Years on the Saskatchewan, N.W. Canada* (London: Stock, 1897), vi, 180–4.

4 Jean Bruce, *The Last Best West* (Toronto: Fitzhenry and White side, 1976), 12–13; Howard Hiroshi Sugimoto, *Japanese Immigration, the Vancouver Riots and Canadian Diplomacy* (New York: Arno, 1978), 26; Hugh Johnston, *The Voyage of the 'Komagata Maru': The Sikh Challenge to Canada's Colour Bar* (Vancouver: University of British Columbia Press, 1989).

5 *The Reminiscences of Doctor John Sebastian Helmcken*, ed. Dorothy Blakey Smith (Vancouver: University of British Columbia Press, 1975), xi-xxxvi. See also William J. MacDonald, *A Pioneer 1851* (Victoria: privately printed, 1915).

6 Eric Duncan, *From Shetland to Vancouver Island* (Edinburgh: Oliver, 1937), 158–61, 187; and *Growing Up in the Valley: Pioneer Childhood in the Lower Fraser Valley* (Victoria: Provincial Archives, 1983), 15–16, 27–31 passim; Peter Chapman, ed., *Where the Lardeau River Flows* (Victoria: Provincial Archives, 1981), 39; Victor Casorso, *The Casorso Story: A Century of Social History in the Okanagan Valley* (Okanagan Falls: Rima, 1983).

7 H.E. Church, in *An Emigrant in the Canadian Northwest* (London: Methuen, 1929), helped set up a school district in Comox, Vancouver Island, in 1898, and was "shocked" that a female teacher "had a large and very apparent proportion of negro blood," 89.

8 Duncan, *From Shetland to Vancouver Island*, 103, 126, 134.

9 John Johnson, *Childhood, Travel and British Columbia* (privately printed, *c.* 1907), 11–15, 30, 142–7, 174–5.

10 Georgina Binnie-Clark, *Wheat and Woman*, with an introduction by Susan Jackel (1st ed., Toronto, 1914; repr. Toronto: University of Toronto Press, 1979); Susan Jackel, ed., *A Flannel Shirt and Liberty: British Emigrant Gentlewomen in the Canadian West, 1880–1914* (Vancouver: University of British Columbia Press, 1982); Monica Hopkins, *Letters from a Lady Rancher* (Halifax: Goodread, 1983).

11 *A Pioneer Gentlewoman in British Columbia: The Recollections of Susan Allison*, ed. by Margaret A. Ormsby (Vancouver: University of British Columbia Press 1976), ix-xvii, 1–17.

12 Quoted in ibid., xviii-xix.

13 These so-called outlaws, the three McLean boys, were the sons of an HBC trader and his wife, the daughter of a Native chief. Their sister, raised in a convent, beautiful and "most accomplished," and a white man of high standing fell in love. When she became pregnant he left her for another woman. It is said that after that the young men took to drinking and terrorizing the neighbourhood. The young woman, with her child, returned to her mother's people.

14 Ibid., 30–72.

15 Kay Anderson, *Vancouver's Chinatown: Racial Discourse in Canada, 1875–1980* (Montreal: McGill-Queen's University Press, 1991); Patricia Roy, *A White Man's Province: British Columbia Politicians and Chinese and Japanese Immigrants, 1858–1914* (Montreal: McGill-Queen's University Press, 1991); Peter Ward, *White Canada Forever: Popular Attitudes and Public Policy Towards Orientals in British Columbia* (Montreal: McGill-Queen's University Press, 1978).

16 Moberly and Robinson, *Blazing the Trail*, 42–3.

17 Hugh Tinker, "Indians in Southeast Asia: Imperial Auxiliaries," in Colin Clarke, Ceri Peach, and Steven Vertovec, eds., *South Asians Overseas: Migration and Ethnicity* (Cambridge: Cambridge University Press, 1990), 39–56.

18 Christian F.J. Galloway, *The Call of the West: Letters from British Columbia* (London: Adelphi, 1916), 256–8, 276; Martin A. Grainger, *Woodsmen of the West* (1st edition, 1908; repr. introduced by Rupert Schieder, Toronto: McClelland and Stewart, 1964), 32, 79; Basil Stewart, *The Land of the Maple Leaf: Or, Canada As I Saw It* (London: Routledge, and Toronto: Musson, 1908), 128–35; Rolf Knight and Maya Koizumi, *A Man of Our Times: The Life History of a Japanese-Canadian Fisherman [Ryuichi Yoshida]* (Vancouver: New Star, 1976), 57.

19 Knight and Koizumi, *A Man of Our Times*; Tomoko Makabe, *Picture Brides: Japanese Women in Canada*, transl. by Kathleen C. Merken (Japanese orig., Tokyo, 1983; Toronto: Multicultural History Society of Ontario, 1995), includes the reminiscences of Maki Fukushima, Hana Murata, Yasu Ishikawa, Tami Nakamura, Miyo Hayashi; Daphne Marlatt and Maya Koizumi, *Stevenson Recollected: A Japanese-Canadian History* (Victoria: Provincial Archives, 1975); Masajiro Miyazaki, "My Sixty Years in Canada" (mimeographed, n.p., 1973).

20 W.M. Hong, *And So ... That's How It Happened: Recollections of Stanley-Barkerville, 1900–1975*, ed. by Gary Seale and Eileen Seale, originally edited by J. R. Hambly (Wells, BC: privately printed, 1978); May Lee, "Chinese Canadian Women: Our Common Struggle," *Canadian Ethnic Studies*

19, no. 3 (1987), 174–84. A fictional account is Ruthanne L. McCunn, *Thousand Pieces of Gold* (1981, Boston: Beacon, 1988).

21 Tara Singh Bains and Hugh Johnston, *The Four Quarters of the Night: The Life-Journey of an Emigrant Sikh* (Montreal: McGill-Queen's University Press, 1995); Norman Buchignani and Doreen Indra, *Continuous Journey: A Social History of South Asians in Canada* (Toronto: McClelland and Stewart, 1985).

22 Hong, *That's How It Happened*, 1–27.

23 Miyazaki, "My Sixty Years in Canada," 1–31.

24 Marlatt and Koizumi, *Stevenson Recollected*, 1–34.

25 Makabe, *Picture Brides*, 37–65; Knight and Koizumi, *A Man of Our Times*, 36; Galloway, *The Call of the West*, 278.

26 C.L. Cowan, *The Trail of the Sky Pilot* (Toronto: Poole, 1929), 8–9; Chapman, *Where the Lardeau River Flows*, 27, 30; J. Burgon Bickersteth, *The Land of Open Doors: Being Letters from Western Canada, 1911–13* (1st ed. 1914; repr. Toronto: University of Toronto Press, 1976), 3; Edward F. Fripp, *The Outcasts of Canada* (Edinburgh: Blackwood, 1932), 4; [Margaret A.D. Phillips and John N. Phillips], *Letters From Windermere, 1912–1914*, ed. by R. Cole Harris and Elizabeth Phillips (Vancouver: University of British Columbia Press, 1984), xii-xiii; John T. Bealby's *Fruit Ranching in British Columbia* (London, 1909; 2nd ed. London: Black, 1911) is a booster book for land sales. See also Charles W. Holliday, *The Valley of Youth* (Caldwell, Idaho: Caxton, 1948).

27 "Arnt Arntzen's Story," in Rolf Knight, ed., *Stump Ranch Chronicles and Other Narratives* (Vancouver: New Star, 1977), 11–28.

28 Chapman, *Where the Lardeau River Flows*, 17, 23, 28, 30–1, 39–41. Near Pemberton, the Swiss immigrant Jakob Stricker logged poles. *Erlebnisse eines Schweizers in Kanada* (Zurich: Orell Fuessli, 1935), 92–132. See also *Alex Lord's British Columbia, Recollections of a Rural School Inspector, 1915–36*, ed. John Calam (Vancouver: University of British Columbia Press, 1991).

29 *Gioconda Maglio. A Biography by Her Family* (Nelson, BC: privately printed, 1983[?]), 1–19. I am grateful to Gabriele Scardellato for the reference and a copy of the booklet.

30 Fripp, *Outcasts of Canada*, 1–19, 30–69, 74.

31 Walter Wicks, *Memoirs of the Skeena* (Saanichton: Hancock, 1976).

32 Oral testimony by Liz Brown, Heilsuk Nation, 1992, exhibited in "Cannery Days," Pam Winter, curator, University of British Columbia, Anthropology Museum, 1993. See also Homer Stevens and Rolf Knight, *Homer Stevens: A Life in Fishing* (Madeira Park, BC: Harbour, 1992). Stevens, born in 1923 of European and Coastal Indian ancestry, started fishing in 1936 and became treasurer of the fishermen's union at the age of twenty-five.

33 Knight and Koizumi, *A Man of Our Times*, 15–72.

34 Denise Chong, *The Concubine's Children: Portrait of a Family Divided* (Toronto: Penguin, 1994).

CHAPTER EIGHTEEN

1 Reg Whitaker, *Canadian Immigration Policy since Confederation* (Ottawa: Canadian Historical Association, 1991), 7–9, and Whitaker, *Double Standard: The Secret History of Canadian Immigration* (Toronto: Lester, 1987).

2 In Canada, too, same administrators and military leaders developed authoritarian policies. According to a top-secret Canadian scorched-earth policy plan of 1942 to limit potential German invasion troops to wastelands, seven cities, St John's, NFL, Halifax, Sydney, and Shelburne, NS, Saint John, NB, and Gaspé and Quebec City, Que., were to be ruthlessly destroyed, its inhabitants evacuated. See Toronto *Globe and Mail,* 1 June 1998; *Archivist,* July 1998.

3 Joanna Matejko, ed., *Polish Settlers in Alberta. Reminiscences and Biographies* (Toronto: Polish Alliance, 1979), 82–4.

4 "Diseased persons" were declared inadmissible in 1902. J. Burgon Bickersteth, *The Land of Open Doors: Being Letters from Western Canada, 1911–13* (London, 1914; repr. Toronto: University of Toronto Press, 1976), 4–5.

5 John Grossmann, "Streiflichter vom Rande der Zivilisation. Die Erlebnisse eines deutschen Heimstätters im Peace-River-Gebiet," *German-Canadian Yearbook* 1 (1973), 191–244, and 2 (1975), 193–246.

6 Tova Yedlin, ed., *Germans from Russia in Alberta: Reminiscences* (Edmonton: Central and East European Studies Society, 1984), 147, 159, 101, 194, 110; Matejko, *Polish Settlers,* 50, 121–2; Anna Baerg, *Diary of Anna Baerg 1916–1924,* transl. and ed. by Gerald Peters (Winnipeg: CMBC Publications, 1985), 143–51.

7 Matejko, *Polish Settlers*, 39, 84–86, 102; Benedykt Heydenkorn, ed., *Memoirs of Polish Immigrants in Canada* (Toronto: Futura, 1979), 62; Stjepan Bradica, "A Croatian Immigrant on the Frontier," ed. Anthony W. Rasporich, *Canadian Ethnic Studies* 8, no. 2 (1976), 99.

8 Matejko, *Polish Settlers*, 32–3, 102, 124, 137.

9 Canada, Special Joint Committee on Immigration, *Minutes of Proceedings and Evidence* (Ottawa, 1966–8), 14.

10 Godfrey E. Mappin, "Migration as a Paying Proposition," *United Empire: The Royal Colonial Institute Journal* 13 (1922), 323–26; Stephen Constantine, ed., *Emigrants and Empire: British Settlement in the Dominions between the Wars* (Manchester: Manchester University Press, 1990); Anthony J. Hammerton, *Emigrant Gentlewomen: Genteel Poverty and Female Emigration, 1830–1914* (London: Croom Helm, 1979); Joanna Trollope, *Britannia's Daughters: Women of the British Empire* (London: Hutchinson, 1983).

11 Marion Cran, *A Woman in Canada* (Toronto: Musson, 1912), e.g., 10–28, 53; Ella C. Sykes, *A Home Help in Canada* (London: Smith, 1912), e.g., vii-xv, 41. See also Elizabeth K. Morris, *An Englishwoman in the Canadian West* (Bristol: Arrowsmith, 1913), who travelled *c.* 1910 and gave advice on servant migration. These women, as regards race and class, remained in the framework of their male predecessors. James E. Ritchie had noted in 1884 in Montreal: "It is curious the airs the raw servant-girls from Ireland give themselves out here." *To Canada with Emigrants: A Record of Actual Experiences* (London: Unwin, 1885), 61. Basil Stewart, *The Land of the Maple Leaf: Or, Canada As I Saw It* (London: Routledge, and Toronto: Musson, 1908), 189.

12 Nellie O'Donnell (name changed),"This Is What It Was All About," in Sheelagh Conway, ed., *The Faraway Hills Are Green: Voices of Irish Women in Canada* (Toronto: Women's Press, 1992), 133–46. Sykes, *Home Help in Canada*, 10. From the wide range of scholarly literature see, e.g., Marilyn Barber, "The Women Ontario Welcomed: Immigrant Domestics for Ontario Homes, 1870–1930," *Ontario History* 72, no. 3 (1980), 148–72; Varpu Lindstrom-Best, "Tailor-Maid: the Finnish Immigrant Community of Toronto before the First World War," in Robert F. Harney, ed., *Gathering Place: Peoples and Neighbourhoods of Toronto, 1834–1945* (Toronto: Multicultural History Society of Ontario, 1985), 205–39; Genevieve Leslie, "Domestic Service in Canada, 1880–1920," in Janice Acton et al., eds., *Women at Work: Ontario 1850–1930* (Toronto: Canadian Women's Educational Press, 1974), 71–125.

13 Peggy Holmes, *It Could Have Been Worse*, ed. Joy Roberts (Don Mills, Ont.: Collins, 1980); Kathleen R. Strange, *With the West in Her Eyes: The Story of a Modern Pioneer* (New York: Dodge, 1937); Robert Collins, *Butter Down the Well: Reflections of a Canadian Childhood* (Saskatoon: Western Producer Prairie Books, 1980).

14 Collins, *Butter Down the Well*, 10–44, 94–125.

15 Holmes, *It Could Have Been Worse*, 16–61; James H. Walker, *A Scotsman in Canada* (Toronto: Cape, 1935), 73.

16 Strange, *With the West in Her Eyes*, 3–10 passim.

17 Grossmann, "Streiflichter," 1: 191–244, 2: 193–246;

18 Alfred Fitzpatrick, *The University in Overalls: A Plea for Part-Time Study* (Toronto: Hunter-Rose, 1920), 14.

19 Other immigrants and temporary migrants into the Peace River District included Mary Percy Jackson; see P. J. Andrews, ed., *On the Last Frontier. Pioneering in the Peace River Block: Letters of Mary Percy Jackson* (Toronto: General Board of Religous Education, 1933), and Jackson, *Suitable for the Wilds: Letters from Northern Alberta, 1929–1931*, ed. Janice D. McGinnis (Toronto: University of Toronto Press, 1995); Monica Storrs, *God's Galloping Girl: The Peace River Diaries of Monica Storrs, 1929–1931*, ed.

W.L. Morton and Vera K. Fast (Vancouver: University of British Columbia Press, 1979). See also Ida Scharf Hopkins, *To the Peace River Country and On* [n.p., n.d.], who migrated as child from Ontario to Winnipeg and in 1929 to Peace River.

20 Isaiah Bowman, *The Pioneer Fringe* (New York: American Geographical Society, 1931); C.A. Dawson and R.W. Murchie, *The Settlement of the Peace River Country: A Study of a Pioneer Area* (Toronto: Macmillan, 1934).

21 Cran, *A Woman in Canada*, 73–5.

22 Walker, *A Scotsman in Canada.*

23 See also the autobiography of a Swiss itinerant labourer and contractor; Jakob Stricker, *Erlebnisse eines Schweizers in Kanada* (Zuerich: Orell Fuessli, 1935).

24 Penny Petrone, *Breaking the Mould: A Memoir* (Toronto: Guernica, 1995).

25 Bradica, "A Croatian Immigrant," 95–102.

26 S. Manoe Hansen, "[Iver Lassen Andersen] An Emigrant Destiny," transl. Birgit Langhammer, *Canadian Ethnic Studies* 19, no. 1 (1987), 96–117; G.H. Westbury, *Misadventures of A Working Hobo in Canada* (London: Routledge, Toronto: Musson, 1930), 93–9.

27 Albert Eskra, "A Difficult Life," in Heydenkorn, ed., *Polish Immigrants in Canada*, 51–136.

28 Edwin A. Alm, *I Never Wondered* (Vancouver: Evergreen, 1971), 52, 86, 122; Gus Romaniuk, *Taking Root in Canada: An Autobiography* (Winnipeg: Columbia, 1954), 133–7; Helgi Einarsson, *A Manitoba Fisherman*, transl. from the Icelandic by George Houser (Winnipeg: Queenston, 1982), 138.

29 Willem DeGelder, *A Dutch Homesteader on the Prairies: The Letters of Willem DeGelder, 1910–13*, transl. and ed. by Herman Ganzevoort (Toronto: University of Toronto Press, 1973), 48–9; Bickersteth, *The Land of Open Doors*, 61–2; Evan Davies, [as told to] Alec Vaughan, *Beyond the Old Bone Trail* (London: Cassell, 1960), 146–7, 154; William A. Czumer, in *Recollections about the Life of the First Ukrainian Settlers in Canada*, transl. by Louis T. Laychuck (Ukrainian orig., Edmonton, 1942; Edmonton: Canadian Institute of Ukrainian Studies, 1981), 59–61, 71–3, noted that when "enlightened young people" came and did not go to church, they "were labelled 'socialist' by the clergy."

30 Ole Hjelt, *Nybyggerliv paa praerien* [Pioneer Life on the Prairie] (Instow, Saskatchewan: Forfatterens Forlag, 1920). I am grateful to William Jenkins for a summary of the book. See also Aksel Sandemose, *Ross Dane* (Kobenhavn, 1928; transl. by Christopher Hale, Winnipeg: Gunnars, 1989).

31 *Hanna Herald*, 18 February 1943, quoted in Jean R. Burnet, *Next-Year Country: A Study of Rural Social Organization in Alberta* (Toronto: University of Toronto Press, 1951), 17.

32 Thomas C. Douglas, *The Making of a Socialist. The Recollections of T.C. Douglas*, ed. by Lewis H. Thomas (Edmonton: University of Alberta Press, 1982), e.g., 55–8, 65.

33 Donald Avery, *"Dangerous Foreigners": European Immigrant Workers and Labour Radicalism in Canada, 1896–1932* (Toronto: McCelland and Stewart, 1983); "Ethnic Radicals," special issue of *Canadian Ethnic Studies* 10, no. 2 (1978).

CHAPTER NINETEEN

1 Robert Collins, *Butter Down the Well: Reflections of a Canadian Childhood* (Saskatoon: Western Producer Prairie Books, 1980), 138; Katherine Götsch-Trevelyan, *Unharboured Heaths* (Toronto: McClelland and Stewart, 1933), 53.

2 Joanna Matejko, ed., *Polish Settlers in Alberta: Reminiscences and Biographies* (Toronto: Polish Alliance, 1979), 60, 81.

3 Leah Rosenberg, *The Errand Runner: Reflections of a Rabbi's Daughter* (Toronto: Wiley, 1981), 106–27; Bill Johnstone, *Coal Dust in My Blood: The Autobiography of a Coal Miner* (Victoria: Royal British Columbia Museum, 1993), 66; L.M. Grayson and Michael Bliss, eds., *The Wretched of Canada: Letters to R.B. Bennett, 1930–1935* (Toronto: University of Toronto Press, 1971). Jean R. Burnet, *Next-Year Country: A Study of Rural Social Organization in Alberta* (Toronto: University of Toronto Press, 1951).

4 Phyllis Harrison, ed., *The Home Children: Their Personal Stories* (Winnipeg: Watson & Dwyer, 1979), 143, 250; Matejko, *Polish Settlers*, 82–8.

5 Tova Yedlin, ed., *Germans from Russia in Alberta: Reminiscences* (Edmonton: Central and East European Studies Society, 1984), 131–3.

6 Gus Romaniuk, *Taking Root in Canada: An Autobiography* (Winnipeg: Columbia, 1954), 40; Yedlin, *Germans from Russia,* 21–3; Joanna Matejko and Tova Yedlin, eds., *Alberta's Pioneers from Eastern Europe: Reminiscences* (Edmonton: University of Alberta, 2nd ed., 1978), 58 (Daniel Svanda).

7 Harrison, *The Home Children,* 169 (Walter Henry Miles), 215–17.

8 Matejko and Yedlin, eds., *Alberta's Pioneers,* 65, 69–70. Edith Pringle from Ireland and her husband attempted to farm under a Canadian unemployed-to-homestead scheme. Edith Pringle, "They Were the Dirty Thirties," in Sheelagh Conway, ed., *The Faraway Hills Are Green: Voices of Irish Women in Canada* (Toronto: Women's Press 1992), 161–6.

9 William R. Price, *Celtic Odyssey,* as told to Eileen Sheila Hill (Philadelphia: Dorrance, 1970), 223–4; Matejko, *Polish Settlers*, 81; Collins, *Butter Down the Well,* 72, 115. Several of the letter-writers to R.B. Bennett stressed that they used their last cents to buy the stamp for the letter.

10 Matejko, *Polish Settlers*, 44–7, 89–91, 120–3, 138–9; see also Charles Mamczasz, road contractor, 129–31.

11 Dorothea E. Bublitz, *Life on the Dotted Line* (New York: Vantage, 1960), 50. Thomas C. Douglas, *The Making of a Socialist: The Recollections of T.C. Douglas*, ed. by Lewis H. Thomas (Edmonton: University of Alberta Press, 1982), 32–33, 64–76 passim.

12 Matejko and Yedlin, eds., *Alberta's Pioneers,* 78; Collins, *Butter Down the Well,* 56–7, 72–3; James H. Sadler, *The Hard Way to Goshen* (n.p., n.d., pagination added), 62–5. See also Yedlin, *Germans from Russia,* 103; Burnet, *Next-Year Country,* 6–7.

13 Habeeb Salloum, "Reminiscences of an Arab Family Homesteading in Southern Saskatchewan," *Canadian Ethnic Studies* 15, no. 2 (1983), 130–8.

14 Phyllis Knight, *A Very Ordinary Life: As Told to Rolf Knight* (Vancouver: New Star, 1974), Toronto episode, 99–116; the Krommknechts, whose name might be translated as "villein" or "menial servant," changed their name to Knight in the 1930s, 165.

15 Ibid., 116–42.

16 Ibid., 174–87.

17 From among the numerous publications, the following provide a starting point: Richard Klucsarits and Friedrich G. Kürbisch, eds., *Arbeiterinnen kämpfen um ihr Recht. Autobiographische Texte rechtloser und entrechteter "Frauenspersonen" in Deutschland, Österreich und der Schweiz des 19. und 20. Jahrhunderts* (Wuppertal: Hammer, n.d.); Walter Köpping, ed., *Lebensberichte deutscher Bergarbeiter* (Frankfurt: Gutenberg, 1984); Wolfgang Emmerich, *Proletarische Lebensläufe*, 2 vols. (Reinbek: Rowohlt, 1974); Mary Jo Maynes, *Taking the Hard Road: Life Courses in French and German Workers' Autobiographies in the Era of Industrialization* (Chapel Hill: University of North Carolina Press, 1995).

18 From the wealth of studies only a few with a broad coverage will be cited. Jacques Ferland, Gregory S. Kealey, and Bryan D. Palmer, "Labour Studies," in Alan F.J. Artibise, ed., *Interdisciplinary Approaches to Canadian Society: A Guide to the Literature (*Montreal: McGill-Queen's University Press, 1990), 9–38, provide the best overview. See also Craig Heron, *The Canadian Labour Movement: A Short History* (Toronto: Lorimer, 1989); Bryan D. Palmer, *Working-Class Experience: The Rise and Reconstitution of Canadian Labour, 1800–1980* (Toronto: Butterworth, 1983); Donald H. Avery, *Reluctant Host: Canada's Response to Immigrant Workers, 1896–1994* (Toronto: McClelland and Stewart, 1995); Avery and Bruno Ramirez, "European Immigrant Workers in Canada: Ethnicity, Militancy and State Repression," in Dirk Hoerder et al., eds., *Roots of the Transplanted* (Boulder: East European Monographs, 1994), 2: 411–40; Desmond Morton with Terry Copp, *Working People: An Illustrated History of Canadian Labour* (Ottawa: Deneau and Greenberg, 1980); Laurel S. MacDowell and Ian Radforth, eds., *Canadian Working Class History: Selected Readings* (Toronto: Canadian Scholars' Press, 1992).

19 On Native-born workers see: Alfred Edwards, "The Mill: A Worker's Memoir of the 1930s and 1940s," introduction by John Manley, *Labour/Le Travail* 36 (1995), 253–98; Margaret Fairley, "With Our Own Hands: Margaret Fairley and the 'Real Makers' of Canada," eds. David Kimmel and Gregory S. Kealey, *Labour/Le Travail* 31 (Spring 1993), 253–85; Homer Stevens and Rolf Knight, *Homer Stevens: A Life in Fishing* (Madeira Park, BC: Harbour Publications, 1992); Frank Colantonio, *From the Ground Up: An Italian Immigrant's Story*, afterword by Craig Heron (Toronto: Between the Lines, 1997). On Native-born radicals, including the CCF, see: Leo Heaps, *The Rebel in the House: The Life and Times of A[braham] A[lbert] Heaps, M.P. [1889–1954]* (London: Niccolo, 1970; rev. ed. by Frank English, Markham, Ont.: Fitzhenry and White side, 1984); Peter Hunter, *Which Side Are You On Boys ... Canadian Life on the Left* (Toronto: Lugus, 1988); Davis Lewis, *The Good Fight: Political Memoirs, 1909–1958* (Toronto: Macmillan, 1981); Len Scher, *The Un-Canadians: True Stories of the Blacklist Era* (Toronto: Lester, 1992); Bryan D. Palmer, ed., *A Communist Life: Jack Scott and the Canadian Workers Movement, 1927–1985* (St John's: Committee on Canadian Labour History, 1988); Lloyd Stinson, *Political Warriors: Recollections of a Social Democrat* (Winnipeg: Queenston, 1975). On Immigrant radicals and unionists, see: *Yours in the Struggle. Reminiscences of Tim Buck*, ed. William Beeching and Phyllis Clarke (Toronto: New Canada, 1977); Bill Johnstone, *Coal Dust in My Blood*; J. Donald Wilson and Jorgen Dahlie, eds., "Ethnic Radicals," special issue of *Canadian Ethnic Studies* 10, no. 2 (1978), with "Ethnic Radicals – Eyewitness Accounts," 95–106 (Tomo Cacic, Ole Hjelt, Pavlo Krat, Matti Kurikka, A.B. Makela, Arthur Puttee, Sam Scarlett, John Witta).

20 See, for example, the biography of the Kojder family in Apolonja Maria Kojder and Barbara Glogowska, *Marynia, Don't Cry: Memoirs of Two Polish-Canadian Families* (Toronto: Multicultural History Society of Ontario, 1995), 1–138.

21 Matejko and Yedlin, eds., *Alberta's Pioneers*, 96; Matejko, *Polish Settlers*, 40, 85, 119–20; Knight, *A Very Ordinary Life*, 115; Nellie O'Donnell, "This Is What It Was All About," in Conway, *The Faraway Hills Are Green*, 133–46; Rolf Knight and Maya Koizumi, *A Man of Our Times: The Life History of a Japanese-Canadian Fisherman* (Vancouver: New Star, 1976), 55.

22 Rolf Knight, ed., *Along the No. 20 Line: Reminiscences of the Vancouver Waterfront* (Vancouver: New Star, 1980), 128–37; Douglas, *The Making of a Socialist*, 32–3; Fairley, "With Our Own Hands," 264. Fredelle Bruser Maynard in Winnipeg joined a radical students' circle; see *Raisins and Almonds* (1st ed., 1964; repr. Markham, Ont.: PaperJacks, 1973), 135–56. Barbara Roberts, *Whence They Came: Deportation from Canada, 1900–*

1935 (Ottawa: University of Ottawa Press, 1988); Jonas Pasukonis, in Matejko and Yedlin, *Alberta's Pioneers*, 93.

23 Adam J. Tolmie, *Roughing It On the Rails* (Bloomfield, Ont.: Silverthorn, 1983), 77–99; Grayson and Bliss, eds., *The Wretched of Canada*, xv-xvi. The Kapuskasing unemployment camp was described as a First World War internment camp by Philip Yasnowskyj in Harry Piniuta, ed. and transl., *Land of Pain, Land of Promise: First Person Accounts by Ukrainian Pioneers, 1891–1914* (Saskatoon, Saskatchewan: Western Producer Prairie Books, 1978), 170–95. Carmela Patrias, *Relief Strike: Immigrant Workers and the Great Depression in Crowland, Ontario, 1930–1935* (Toronto: New Hogtown Press, 1990).

24 The leaders of the Communist party had been imprisoned. According to several reports, guards in the Kingston Penitentiary had attempted to murder Tim Buck.

25 Harrison, *The Home Children*, 143; Edmund D. Francis, ed., *Why? The Diary of a Camp Striker* ([1935] n.p.).

26 Grayson and Bliss, eds. *The Wretched of Canada*, 60–2; Roberts, *Whence They Came*, 128–9, 192.

27 Bill Johnstone, *Coal Dust in My Blood*, 139.

28 Robert H. Keyserlingk, "Breaking the Nazi Plot: Canadian Government Attitudes Towards German Canadians, 1939–1945," in Norman Hillmer, Bohdan Kordan, Lubomyr Luciuk, eds., *On Guard for Thee: War, Ethnicity, and the Canadian State, 1939–1945* (Ottawa: Canadian Committee for the History of the Second World War, 1988), 53–70; David J. Carter, *Behind Canadian Barbed Wire: Alien and German Prisoners of War Camps in Canada, 1914–1946* (Calgary: Tumbleweed Press, 1980); Paula Jean Draper, "The Accidental Immigrants: Canada and the Interned Refugees," *Canadian Jewish Historical Society Journal* 10, nos. 1–2 (1978), 1–38, 80–112; Bohdan Kordan and Peter Melnycky, *In the Shadow of the Rockies: Diary of the Castle Mountain Internment Camp, 1915–1917* (Edmonton: Canadian Institute of Ukrainian Studies, 1991); Donald Avery, "Canada's Response to European Refugees, 1939–1945: The Security Dimension," in Hillmer et al., *On Guard for Thee*, 179–216.

29 Irving Abella and Harold Troper, *None Is Too Many: Canada and the Jews of Europe, 1933–1948* (Toronto: Lester, 1983), ix. Thomas E. Wood, Stanislaw Jankowski, *Karski: How One Man Tried to Stop the Holocaust* (New York: Wiley, 1994); Richard Breitman, "The Allied War Effort and the Jews, 1942–43," *Journal of Contemporary History* 20 (1985), 135–56, and research in progress on recently released documents of the British National Security Agency; Alan Davies and Marilyn F. Nefsky, *How Silent were the Churches? Canadian Protestantism and the Jewish Plight during the Nazi Era* (Waterloo: Wilfrid Laurier Press, 1997). Memoirs of survivors who reached Canada include Sandra Oancia, *Remember: Helen's Story*

(Calgary: Detselig, 1997) and Eva Brewster, *Vanished in Darkness: An Auschwitz Memoir* (Edmonton: NeWest, 1984).

30 Harry Henig, *Orphan of the Storm*, ed. Lawrence F. Jones (Toronto: Pitt, 1974),109–23. Harry and Fanny lived by storekeeping and peddling in those areas where the Brusers had also tried their luck, then moved to Toronto.

31 Andrew Amstatter, *Tomslake: History of the Sudeten Germans in Canada* (Saanichton, BC: Hancock Howe, 1978); Jonathan F. Wagner, "Flight and Beyond: Canada's Anti-Nazi Sudeten German Refugees and Their Descendants" (manuscript [Minot: Minot State University, 1995]); Abella and Troper, *None Is Too Many*, x-xi, 1–2. The story of the Kohn family is based on interviews.

32 G. Thomas and M.M. Witts, *The Voyage of the Damned* (New York: Stein, 1974); Abella and Troper, *None Is Too Many*, 63–4.

33 Ken Adachi, *The Enemy That Never Was: A History of the Japanese Canadians* (Toronto: McClelland and Stewart, 1976), 199–346, quote 208; Ann G. Sunahara, *The Politics of Racism: The Uprooting of Japanese Canadians during the Second World War* (Toronto: Lorimer, 1981); Peter Ward, *White Canada Forever: Popular Attitudes and Public Policy Towards Orientals in British Columbia* (Montreal: McGill-Queen's University Press, 1978); Knight and Koizumi, *A Man of Our Times*, 73–86. Life-writings and literary reflections on the experiences include Takeo Ujo Nakano with Leatrice Nakano, *Within the Barbed Wire Fence. A Japanese Man's Account of His Internment in Canada* (Toronto: University of Toronto Press, 1980); Muriel Kitagawa, *This Is My Own: Letters to Wes & Other Writings on Japanese Canadians, 1941–1948* ed. Roy Miki (Vancouver: Talonbooks, 1985); Joy Nozomi Kogawa, *Obasan* (1st ed., 1981; Markham, Ontario: Penguin, 1983); Keibo Oiwa, ed., *Stone Voices. Wartime Writings of Japanese-Canadian Issei* (Montreal: Vehicule, 1991); Barry Broadfoot, *Years of Sorrow. Years of Shame. The Story of the Japanese Canadians in World War II* (1st ed. 1977; Markham, Ont.: PaperJacks, 1979).

34 Tomoko Makabe, *Picture Brides. Japanese Women in Canada*, transl. by Kathleen C. Merken (Toronto: Multicultural History Society of Ontario, 1995), Maki Fukushima, 58–62, Hana Murata, 82–8.

35 Nakano, *Within the Barbed Wire Fence.*

36 Mark Wyman, *DP: Europe's Displaced Persons, 1945–1951* (Philadelphia: Balch, 1988): "Childhood Memories of Anna Kutera," Matejko, *Polish Settlers*, 119–20, Chuchla, 64–71; Matejko and Yedlin eds., *Alberta's Pioneers*, 41–4; Eskra: Heydenkorn, *Memories of Polish Immigrants*, 122; Milly Charon, *Between Two Worlds: The Canadian Immigrant Experience* (1st ed., 1983; rev. ed., Montreal: Nu-Age, 1988), 257–72, 274–81. Peter Chapman, ed., *Where the Lardeau River Flows* (Victoria: Provincial Archives, 1981), 73; Wsevolod W. Isajiw, *The Refugee Experience. Ukrainian*

Displaced Persons after World War II (Edmonton: Canadian Institute of Ukrainian Studies, 1992); Milda Danys, *DP: Lithuanian Immigration to Canada after the Second World War* (Toronto: Multicultural History Society of Ontario, 1986).

37 See the novel by Kerri Sakamoto, *The Electrical Field* (Toronto: Knopf Canada, 1997).

CHAPTER TWENTY

1 J. Burgon Bickersteth, *The Land of Open Doors: Being Letters from Western Canada, 1911–13* (London, 1914; repr. Toronto: University of Toronto Press, 1976), 86; Christian F.J. Galloway, *The Call of the West: Letters from British Columbia* (London: Adelphi, 1916), 278; research in progress on soldiers' letters by Robert Craig Brown, University of Toronto, 1996.

2 The former British colonials to the south had conceptualized this issue in the War of Independence that led to the formation of the United States of America.

3 Britishness assumed a further dimension when the ethnically East Indian British army officers reached British Columbia. See also Terence L. Craig, *Racial Attitudes in English-Canadian Fiction* (Waterloo, 1987).

4 Few politicians or scholars have bothered to learn any of the Aboriginal languages to understand their contribution.

5 William A. Czumer, *Recollections about the Life of the First Ukrainian Settlers in Canada*, transl. by Louis T. Laychuck (Ukrainian orig., 1942; Edmonton: Canadian Institute of Ukrainian Studies, 1981), 104–12, 118–19.

6 Penny Petrone, *Breaking the Mold: A Memoir* (Toronto: Guernica, 1995), 165–91.

7 Alfred Howell, *Naturalization and Nationality in Canada* (Toronto: Carswell, 1884), 3, quoted in Robert Craig Brown, "Full Partnership in the Fortunes and in the Future of the Nation," *Nationalism and Ethnic Politics* (Fall 1995), 10. I have relied on this succinct summary. See also William Kaplan, ed., *Belonging: The Meaning and Future of Canadian Citizenship* (Montreal: McGill-Queen's University Press, 1993), and Kaplan, *The Evolution of Citizenship Legislation in Canada* (Ottawa: Multiculturalism and Citizenship Canada, 1991).

8 Reg Whitaker, *Canadian Immigration Policy since Confederation* (Ottawa: Canadian Historical Association 1991), quote on p. 3.

9 Vic Satzewich, *Racism and the Incorporation of Foreign Labour: Farm-Labour Migration to Canada since 1945* (London: Routledge, 1991).

10 Brown, "Full Partnership," 10.

11 Albert Moellmann, *Das Deutschtum in Montreal* (MA thesis, McGill University, 1934; Jena: Fischer, 1937), 115–16. Cf. *Census 1931*, Table III.

12 Whitaker, *Canadian Immigration Policy*, 11–14.

13 Brown, "Full Partnership," 10–11, 18–20; Galloway, *The Call of the West*, 256–8, 276.

14 Brochure on the celebration of "50 Years of Canadian Citizenship," Citizenship and Immigration Canada, "It Means the World to Us" [Ottawa, 1997].

15 Privileged status of British subjects was abolished in 1976, the residence requirement reduced from five to three years. Brown, "Full Partnership," 11–12; unpublished paper by Patricia Roy, University of Victoria, February 1997.

16 Whitaker, *Canadian Immigration Policy*, 17–21; Brown, "Full Partnership," 16–18; Freda Hawkins, *Canada and Immigration: Public Policy and Public Concern* (Montreal: McGill-Queen's University Press, 1988), 71–173.

17 Some critics charged that the then Liberal prime minister, Pierre Elliott Trudeau, imposed the policy upon a less than receptive majority of the electorate. However, the B & B Commission met during Lester B. Pearson's term of office.

18 "Announcement of Implementation of Policy of Multiculturalism within Bilingual Framework," Canada, House of Commons *Debates*, 8 October 1971, 8545–8, 8580–5.

19 Other issues still demand attention: refugee admission, definition of functional families, review of deportations, and deportation of Canadian-socialized criminal offenders to their parents' cultures of origin.

20 An Act for the Preservation and Enhancement of Multiculturalism in Canada, 21 July 1988, section 3.1.

21 The clause "if a person insists" was dropped from the instruction manuals in 1981. See *Canadian Census Ethno-Cultural Questions, 1871–1991* (Ottawa: Statistics Canada, 1991). Warren E. Kalbach, *The Impact of Immigration on Canada's Population*, 1961 Census Monograph (Ottawa, 1970), App. E: "Instructions to Census Enumerators for Obtaining Ethnic Origin and Birthplace Data in Censuses of Canada, 1931–61," 442–53.

22 *Ethnic Origins* 1991 Census (Ottawa: Statistics Canada, 1993). Because of the influence of ethnic gatekeepers and the political establishment, these options were not included in the 1991 census. Monica Boyd, *Measuring Ethnicity: The Roles of People, Policies and Politics and Social Science Research* (Lectures and Papers in Ethnicity No. 11, University of Toronto, Department of Sociology, February 1994); Gordon E. Priest, *Ethnicity in the Canadian Census* (Toronto: University of Toronto, Department of Sociology, 1990).

CHAPTER TWENTY-ONE

1 Frank Colantonio, *From the Ground Up: An Italian Immigrant's Story*, afterword by Craig Heron (Toronto: Between the Lines, 1997); Tara Singh

Bains and Hugh Johnston, *The Four Quarters of the Night: The Life-Journey of an Emigrant Sikh* (Montreal: McGill-Queen's University Press, 1995); Joyce C. Fraser, *Cry of the Illegal Immigrant* (Toronto: Williams-Wallace, 1980).

2 Colantonio, *From the Ground Up*, 22–148; John E. Zucchi, *Italians in Toronto: Development of a National Identity, 1875–1935* (Montreal: McGill-Queen's University Press, 1988); Franca Iacovetta, *Such Hardworking People: Italian Immigrants in Postwar Toronto* (Montreal: McGill-Queen's University Press, 1992).

3 Bains and Johnston, *Life-Journey of an Emigrant Sikh*, 45–150; Norman Buchignani and Doreen Indra, *Continuous Journey: A Social History of South Asians in Canada* (Toronto: McClelland and Stewart, 1985).

4 Fraser, *Cry of the Illegal Immigrant.*

5 Neil Bissoondath, *Selling Illusions: The Cult of Multiculturalism in Canada* (Markham, Ont.: Penguin, 1994).

6 Ibolya (Szalai) Grossman, *An Ordinary Woman in Extraordinary Times* (Toronto: Multicultural History Society of Ontario, 1990).

7 Maria Campbell, *Halfbreed* (1st publ., 1973; Halifax: Goodread, 1983), 1.

8 Wsevolod W. Isajiw, *Ethnic Identity Retention*, Ethnic Pluralism Paper, No. 125, Department of Sociology, University of Toronto, July 1981, republished in revised form as chapter 2 in Raymond Breton, Wsevolod W. Isajiw, Warren E. Kalbach, Jeffrey G. Reitz, *Ethnic Identity and Equality: Varieties of Experience in a Canadian City* (Toronto: University of Toronto Press, 1990).

9 For a perceptive discussion, see Danielle Juteau, *Changing Forms of Nationness in the Canadian Context: The Quebec Case* (Saskatoon: University of Saskatchewan, January 1994).

10 York University, Institute for Social Research: J. Paul Grayson with Deanna Williams, *Racialization and Black Student Identity at York University* (1994); Grayson with Tammy Chi and Darla Rhyne, *The Social Construction of 'Visible Minority' for Students of Chinese Origin* (1994); Grayson, *Race on Campus: Outcomes of the First Year Experience at York University* (1994).

11 James S. Frideres, "Edging into the Mainstream? Immigrant Adults and Their Children" (unpublished paper, University of Calgary Nov. 1994).

12 The Angus Reid Group for Multiculturalism and Citizenship Canada, *1991 Attitude Survey Multiculturalism and Citizenship*, June-July 1991; Jeffrey G. Reitz and Raymond Breton, *The Illusion of Difference: Realities of Ethnicity in Canada and the United States* (Toronto: Howe Institute 1994); Wsevolod W. Isajiw, "Multiculturalism and the Integration of the Canadian Community," *Canadian Ethnic Studies* 15, no. 2 (1983), 107–17; John Goldlust and Anthony Richmond, "*Factors Associated with Commitment to and Identification with Canada,*" 132–53, in Wsevolod

W. Isajiw, ed., *Identities: The Impact of Ethnicity on Canadian Society* (Toronto: Martin, 1977).

13 Milly Charon, *Between Two Worlds: The Canadian Immigrant Experience* (1st ed., 1983; rev. ed., Montreal: Nu-Age, 1988), 303–13. See also the personal account, in Thomas P. Melady and Margaret B. Melady, *Uganda: The Asian Exiles* (Maryknoll, NY: Orbis, 1976).

14 Ibid., 212–18, 283–92.

Index

Note: names of the migrants creating societies have been indexed separately.

Acadia. *See* Nova Scotia
Acadians. *See* French-Canadians
acculturation xiii, 130, 132, 147, 177, 181, 185, 193, 214, 226, 264, 277, 283, 287, 294, 303–3; of English 111–14, 283–4
adoption. *See* family economy
Afro Canadians 7, 41, 44, 71, 87, 94, 114–17, 122, 124; associations of 116–17; heterogeneity of 115, 117, 208, 220, 260; refugees ("fugitive slaves") 65, 114; in the West 144, 163, 165–6, 201–2
Alberta. *See* Prairies
American Canadians 151, 181, 188; as criminals 167, 188, 191, 222; criticism of 141
Angler 276
Arntfield 103
Ashmont district 245
Asian Canadians 163, 205, 222–6, 231–4; exclusion 219, 234, 240; as Orientals xii, 158, 216, 222, 227–31, 291
Aston 62
Atlantic world 5, 77, 78, 157
Austrian Canadians 207

Banff 207
Barnardo, Thomas J. 91–4
Barrie 115
Basques in Newfoundland 7, 39
Belgian Canadians 74–5, 151, 164, 211
Belleville 93
Bennett, R.B. 269–70
Bissoondath, Neil 300
Blaine Lake 251
Blairmore 214
bloc settlement. *See* Prairies
boardinghouses 79, 103–4, 106, 111, 171, 176, 213, 260; *see also* camps, bunkhouses
British Columbia 5, 166, 205, 218–36; fruit-ranching in 228
British Empire 223; citizens from Asia 219; citizenship 288–91; dismantling of 306; imperial economy 230; imperial ritual 141, 193–4, 200, 207, 221,245, 289
British stock 221, 223, 239, 242
Britishness 151, 283–4, 289; Anglo-Saxon self-image 203
Brockville 65, 91
Bruderheim 197
bunkhouse 138, 145–9
Burnaby 269
Byelorussian Canadians 198

Calgary 140, 165–6, 175, 215
camps (construction, lumbering, railway) 96–104, 126–7, 160, 226, 228
Canadian Geological Survey 207–8
Canadianization xiii,15, 23, 65–6, 71, 82, 95, 114, 144, 159, 160, 184, 194–5, 198, 201, 209, 237, 246, 250, 271, 281, 289, 291; ethnogenesis 283; mainstream-in-the-making 285
capitalism 185–9, 230, 255–6
Cardinal (Edwardsburg) 73, 85–6
Caribbean Canadians. *See* Afro Canadians
charity 77, 110, 173–4, 192
Charteris 92–3
Chinese Canadians 7, 124, 133, 135, 139, 140, 147, 165–7, 180, 216, 221–36, 245–6, 251, 301
citizenship 211, 214, 223, 234, 240, 273–4, 281, 287–91, 293; and death-in-war clause 291–2; and life-in-the-womb clause 292; law of 1947 291; naturalization 224–5, 287–91, 300
class: class consciousness 11–12, 58, 61, 63–4, 66–7, 72, 78, 89, 91, 102, 112, 113, 127, 132,

134, 136, 146, 160, 162, 178, 192, 195, 197, 199, 200, 202–3, 215, 217, 221, 225, 230, 243, 246, 250, 252, 256, 265–6, 273, 287–9, 301; and deference 106; among the English 162, 283–4; and ethnicity 10
Cobalt 103
Coleman 168, 213–15
Connor, Ralph 24–5, 51, 203, 227
Cooperative Commonwealth Federation, farmer-labour parties 225, 234, 257, 262, 281
Craigellachie 220
Croatian Canadians 248, 297; Yugoslav 104
Crowsnest Pass 143, 207, 212–15, 268
cultural practices xiii, 301; barriers 200, 287, borderlands; 157, 161; conflict 230, 236, 248; and the life cycle 301; retention 157, 300–4; symbols 303
Cumberland 216
Czech Canadians 162, 252, 271

Danish Canadians 151, 248–50
Dawson, George M. 207–8
democracy of consumption 199
deportation: of Acadians 40, 52; of 1837–8 rebels 57; of Japanese 273–6; of labourers and radicals in the 1920s–40s 114, 233, 238, 244, 249–50, 261, 267, in the 1950s 297, 299
Depression 167, 229, 233, 235, 244, 252, 259–70, 302, militancy 214–15; work camps 111, 226–70
Deutsches Kanada Syndikat 207–11
Dinant 216
discrimination and prejudices 129, 143, 163, 233, 250–1, 273, 275, 292, 297; and UN charter 292
discrimination by Anglo-Saxon/Celtic peoples 122, 135; against Afro-Canadians 115; against English 122; against First Peoples 106, 122, 128, 137; against French 122; against Hunkies 129, 227–31, 247; against Irish 59, 65, 71; against Jews 82–3, 129, 133, 165, 181, 231, 296: *see also* racial stereotyping
Displaced Persons from Europe 104, 276–7
Doukhobor Canadians 125, 157, 167
Drydor 252
Dundas 87
Dunmore 157
dustbowl years 256, 262–3, 272
Dutch Canadians 47–8, 127–8, 151, 154, 230, 296

East European Canadians 203, 271, 276–7
East Indian Canadians. *See* South Asian Canadians
Eaton's 13, 109–10, 152, 179, 189, 190–1, 199–202, 216, 261, 289
economics of survival 196–9
Edmonton 126, 138–9, 141–2, 156, 159, 188, 198, 211, 215–16, 241, 249–50, 261, 268
education 13–14, 83, 92–3, 100–1, 116, 128, 132, 140, 141, 169, 225, 228–9, 235, 254–5, 294, 303; among Afro-Canadians 116; in camps 269; among Finns 100; and librairies 213, 265, 269
educational problems: Alberta school controversy 158, 286; British bias in school texts 130, 286; in Finland 128; in Iceland 182; in the Netherlands 127
emigration agents 31–2
emigration, assisted 127
emigration ports, 29–32; Bremen 31, Hamburg 227; Liverpool 29, 67, 108, 165, 240
enemy aliens xii, 111, 135, 192–3, 211–12, 271, 281
English Canadians 8–9, 41, 45–6, 73–4, 97, 105–11, 132, 142, 151, 215–16, 221, 227–31, 242–3, 248, 283; criticism of 111–14, 163–4, 249–50; intergenerational strategies 112–13, 163–4; loyalty to empire 281; remittance men 45–6, 97, 111–13, 122; social composition 283–4; social roles 284; unemployed sent 114; workers 144
English-speaking peoples, heterogeneity of xii, 8, 24, 85, 89, 113, 282
Estevan 157, 262
Estonian Canadians 102, 296
ethnic ascription 231; conflict 80, 214; diversity 51 294, 300; divisiveness xiii; elites 78, 271, 273, 304; hierarchies 162; *see also* interaction, cultural
ethnic groups 271, 282, 285, coherence of 82; construction of 158–9; deconstruction of 9; formation of xii
ethnic identities xii, 10–14; multiple origins 289–90, 294, 306
ethno-political group 9, 41;

Gimli republic 288; *see also* United Empire Loyalists
ethno-religious groups 285, 288, 290; *see also* Doukhobor Canadians, Mennonite Canadians
Euro-Canadians 123, 167, 225–6, 305; *see also* ethnic groups
everyday life: communication in stores 80, 83, 176–81; dresses from flour bags 101, 162, 201, 214, 244; food 72, 77, 80, 84, 90, 100, 107, 109, 127, 134, 135, 154, 161, 265, 297

Fairford 182
fairs, agricultural 61–2, 86, 90
families in sheepskin coats 12, 204, 282
family economies 28, 53, 61, 65, 67, 76, 79, 88–9, 91, 107, 122, 132, 151, 154, 156, 168–70, 226, 234, 252, 293; and children, adoption 52–3, 130, 185; daughters sent into other families 125, 140; intergenerational change 102, 234, live-in help of children 88–9; reversed gender roles 83, 99, 131; surrogate mother 79
Faraday 89
farmers' cooperatives 254, 255, 256
fascism 238, 251, 271–3
Fenn 245–6
Fernie 192
Filipino Canadians 302
Finnish Canadians 97–104, 146, 151, 154, 232
First peoples 5–7, 9, 39, 46, 71, 73, 119, 123, 125, 134, 139, 163, 167, 173, 181–5, 191, 205, 218–23, 231–4, 268, 283, 302, 304; Cree 122; first-coming immigrants 7–10, 114; heterogeneity of 222, 303; Micmac 303; Nez Percé 222; Saulteaux 167; Sioux 192; Six Nations 6–7; Stony 208; two solitudes 304; *see also* English-speaking peoples, French-speaking peoples
Fleming, Sandford 137
Fort Saskatchewan 158
Fort Simpson 122
Fort William 99, 148, 248
foreign Protestants 41
Fraser river 227, 265, 275
Fredericton 41, 44, 46
French-Canadians 8, 71–2, 103–4, 151, 193; in British Columbia 219, 220, 229; in the Maritimes 39–41, 47–49; in the prairies 56, 124, 144, 154–5, 164–5, 179, 208, 211, 252; in the St Lawrence valley 49–57, 96; and war and conscription 56, 110–1, 164–5
French-English relations 49, 71, 104,
French-speaking peoples; Haitians 295; heterogeneity of xii, 8, 24, 165, 282; Vietnamese 280

Gaelic-speakers 8, 58, 72, 113, 119
Galicians 127, 141, 142, 158, 201, 222, 272; *see also* Ukrainian Canadians, Jewish Canadians
gatekeepers 240, 286, 294, 300; as brokers 286–7; British and French 282–3, 300; ethnic 198, 282
gender 10, 289:
– female xiii, 289; feminism 202–3, 245; as pioneer type 23; political activities 255–6; political rights 171–2; suffrage 171–2, 202–3; women as authors 23–5; women's labour 74–5, 89–90, 162;
– gender cultures 301; problems 208; relations 45; roles 66; spheres 17; women in men's minds 98, 150, 201–2;
– male independence 122; masculinity 122, 162–3, 173, 192, 247–8, 250; marginal men 208–10, 232; orphan hero 46;
Genier 55
German Canadians 8–9, 41–4, 122, 135, 140, 151, 158, 193, 207–12, 263–5, 289, 305; heterogeneity of 157, 276; Russian Germans 126–7, 151, 154, 156–7, 166, 240, and World War I 209, 211–12, 232, 274, and World War II 217
Gimli 130, 196, 288
Glengarry 8, 203
Goderich 63
gold rush 43, 67, 73, 85, 88, 205, 218–20
government:
– local 14, 190, 196, 198, 285; mail service 13, 196; road work 13, 196, 260, school districts 197; taxes 45, 60, 64, 196, 253;
– national 13, 199, 255, 265; monocultural bureaucracy 270, 294, 301; and private capital 199, 253, 269–70; and relief camps 268–9; and repression 237, 267–8, 270
– provincial 188–90, 193, 207, 209, 268; and politics of protest 196, 253–8
Gouvernor 182, 263
Grandview 181
Greek Canadians 176, 220
Groulx, Lionel 51

Haitian Canadians 306
Halifax 115, 117, 126
Hamilton 249, 267
Hatzic 220
Hazenmore 182
Hinton 149, 216
Hirsch 157, 272
historiography xi, 9, 14–16, 20–1, 22, 25, 84, 267; conservative 291; and census data 20–1, 289–90, 294; deconstruction 9
Hoffer 157
Home children 90–5, 98, 103–4, 108, 111, 114, 131, 161, 169
Hope 221
Hungarian Canadians 161
Hudson's Bay Company 5–6, 121–2, 119–23, 139, 183, 190–1, 215–16, 218–19, 221, 228

Icelandic Canadians, 124–5, 128–9, 130–3, 182–99
identities 15, 21, 79, 82, 129, 158, 181, 246, 260, 264, 275, 281, 285, 299, 301, 302–3, 304–7
immigrants xii, 9, 239, 241:
– assisted passage 78, 164, 27, 243–4; recruitment by posters and fraud 76, 119, 148, 153–4, 227;
– travel experiences 27–35, 123–6, 148, 212, 215, 240–5, 296; colonist cars 124, fraudulent land sales in west 137, 164, 228; immigration stations in Winnipeg and prairie towns 124–5, 140–1
immigration: bureaucracy 271–3; laws 292, 299; policy 242, 264, 290, 299; undocumented 293, 299, 303
immigration ports: Grosse Isle 30, 35; Halifax 32, 212, 219; Montreal 32–3; Quebec City 32, 219, 241; Vancouver 205, 219
independent lives 60, 63, 64, 80, 89–90, 134, 164, 187, 197, 199, 243, 246, 251
interaction, cultural 29–30, 57, 62, 94, 115, 77, 96–7, 117, 144, 146, 149, 154, 157–9, 163, 165, 169,182, 197, 203, 205, 216, 220, 222, 229–34, 245, 250, 283, 294, 299, 302; among the several British peoples 7–8, 24, 113
intercultural mediation: by immigrant children 79, 83, 197; by librarians 132, 135, 197; by teachers 83, 129, 158, 172, 183–4, 186, 197, 232
intercultural relations 108, 122–3, 132–3, 161, 163–8; brokers and middlemen 160, 176; transcultural 29, 144
intermarriage 6–7, 158, 168, 185, 193, 218–21, 252, 294, 300
Irish Canadians 8–9, 24, 73–4, 122, 125, 144, 165, 200, 243–4; famine migrants 30, 58–9, 73, 93; Protestants and Catholics 58–9; *see also* discrimination and prejudice
Italian Canadians 71, 74–81, 96, 105, 126, 142–4, 151, 176, 211, 229, 249, 286, 296–7

Japanese Canadians 181, 224–6, 232–4; internment 273–6
Jewish Canadians 9, 71, 82–4, 105, 111, 151, 175, 180–1, 201, 203, 274–6; Belgian Jews 230; exclusion of 271–3; German Jews 207–11, 220; in the prairies 144, 157, 159, 163, 165; *see also* discrimination and prejudice

Kamouraska 259
Kapuskasing 244
Kenora 268
King, William Lyon Mackenzie 291
Kingston 65
Kiriak, Ilya 16
Kootenay Lake region 227, 274

labour: agents 76–9; and bosses 104, 106, 113, 215, 266; of children 74–5, 90–5, 134, 169–70; and foremen 75, 81, 99, 104, 109, 116, 161, 266, 297; fraud about wages 149
labour markets 29 193, 195; internationalized 126–7, 227, 249; theory 74
labour militancy 81, 113, 146, 149, 230, 232, 248, 250, 254, 268–9; march on Ottawa 251, 268; repression 75, 78, 110, 136, 202, 204, 237, 251; strikes 80, 109, 149, 141, 142, 192, 215, 225–6; unions 66–7, 74 n.5, 77, 105, 109, 113, 116, 131, 134, 146, 201–2, 214, 217, 225, 228, 232–4, 257, 267–8, 296–8; Winnipeg general strike 135–6; *see also* radicals
labour, unemployment 103, 108, 154, 161, 164, 183, 247, 249, 250, 256, 264, 270
labour, wages 61, 72, 75–6, 106–8, 114, 127, 225, 247, 254, 269, 296; as straight money 150, 182–3, 233
labour, working conditions: bound labour 75, 274–6;

hours 74–5, 107, 109, 225; unhealthy and unsafe 103, 131, 146, 269, 296–7
Lachute 71
Lake Winnipeg 148, 199
language skills 43, 54, 72, 79–80, 83, 94, 100, 102, 104, 122, 130, 132, 141, 151, 155–6, 158–9, 164–5, 174, 197, 213, 231, 249, 255, 258, 264, 268, 283, 297, 306; as barrier 79, 200; Manitoba language crisis 165; multilingualism 158, 169
Leduc 158, 217
Ledwyn 196
Lethbridge 276
life-writings 71; as sources 16–26; literary traditions 23–5, 54; and memory 153, 167, 282, 303; of migrants 53–7, 85–6, 99, 172, 284 and national 196, 282–3; participant observer accounts 19–20, proletarian 287, 266–7
Lillooet 266
Lithuanian Canadians 161, 267–8
Leofeld 154
London, Ont. 85
Lunenburg 41–4

Madoc 88
Maltese Canadians 296
Manitoba: Selkirk colony 9, 119; Red River colony 119, 123; *see also* Prairies
Mankota 167–8
Mannville 241
Markdale 66
Marlboro 148
marriage: long-distance 102, 170, 225–6; markets 29; migration 170–1; war brides 244, 296
Martin, Paul Sr. 291
McPhail, Agnes 270
Medicine Hat 166
Mennonite Canadians 125, 151, 157, 161, 240
mental maps 78, 144
Métis 6, 119, 123, 125, 131, 133, 154, 163, 191, 205, 218–19, 222, 283–5, 303; rebellion 6, 50, 119
migration:
– in Asia 295; Asian contract labour system 205, 306;
– in the British Empire 89–90, 110–13, 134, 151, 194, 215, 220–2, 242–6, 295, 302, Empire Settlement 224, 242–8; and disabled soldiers 239, 242–6, 256; and surplus women 195;
– Canadian internal 9, 43, 66, 78, 96, 127, 140, 211, 220; rural 145, 160, 263; rural-urban 150, 160, 216, 245; urban 77, 80; transcontinental 205, 220;
– in Europe and Russia 5–6, 28, 79, 87, 145, 157–8, 160, 178, 205, 219, 295, 298; in the British isles 64–5;
– internal: of Maritimers 47–8, 216, 220; of French-Canadians 6, 50–2, 55, 62; of Métis 119; to the West 77, 86, 131, 140, 171–2, 183;
– via Latin America 73, 97, 110, 115–17, 296–9;
– labour itinerancy 64–6, 86–7, 90, 127, 141, 145–50, 156, 160–1, 168, 203–4, 216, 247–51, 263–6;
– return migration: to Britain 73, 109, 110; to Europe 164–5, 212; to Ireland 60, 65; to Japan 226; to Russia/Soviet Union 101, 246;
– from US 41, 62, 78, 87, 99, 123, 141, 164, 167, 210, 221–2, 255, 279; refugees from civil war 71, 114;
– to US 53–5, 109, 126, 130, 143, 145, 184, 211, 225; of Afro-Canadians 115; of French-Canadians to New England 10, 50–5; of Irish 58–9; of Maritimers 47;
– worldwide 28, 73, 77, 110, 143, 178, 220, 246, 295, 306; of African Canadians 115; impact of trade or recession 5, 13; in labour diasporas 77–8, 251, 271
Millbridge 88
model town 210–11
Montreal 63, 69–84, 91, 105, 122, 123, 126, 142, 178, 194, 230–1, 247, 306
Moose Jaw 140, 166, 179–80, 194, 245, 254, 256
Moose Lake 139
moral economy 14, 176, 185–9, 199, 247
Mundare 156
multicultural(ism) 287, 293–4, 300, 304–7
Muskoka district 86–7
mutual aid 116, 160, 188, 198–9, 213, 255, 285, 297

Nanaimo 220, 235, 297
nation-building 153, 156, 175, 193–5, 202, 287
national economy 188, 202
national identity 10–11, 281–7
nationalism 138, 172, 203, 284; Canada First movement 11–14; National Policy 288
Nelson 229
Neville 263
New Brunswick 92

New Westminster 219, 221, 226–7
Newfoundland 40
next-year country 100, 164, 180, 200, 246, 255, 265
Niagara 91
Nisku 158
Niven, Frederick 203
Noranda–Rouyn 56
Nordegg 210–11
North West Company 5, 119, 218
North-West Mounted Police 45, 112, 190–2, 207; as a myth 191, 289; RCMP 214–15, 233, 238, 268, 271, 271
Norwegian Canadians 29, 86, 163, 167, 181, 220–1
Nova Scotia 40–3, 92, 117, 130

occupations: boarding-house keeper 79; businessman/woman, entrepreneurs, traders 41–3, 54–5, 71, 74, 78, 107, 146, 176–81; cannery workers 224–5, 231–4; construction 67, 76–7, 94, 108; contractor 143, 176, 210, 220, 266, 296; domestic, 67, 72, 116–17, 125, 224, 242–3, 264, 277, 296, 301; garment and millinery 106–7, 117; governess 106–7, 113, 221; lumbermen 56, 97–8, 201–2, 298; midwife 130, 201, 225, 234, 245; miners 103–4, 169, 205, 209–17; newsboy 133–4; pedlars, 54–5, 65, 74, 174, 176–7, 182, 199, 215, 220; prostitution 140, 145–6, 228, 235; raftsmen, 33, 65, 97; skilled crafts 60, 71, 75, 115, 127, 131, 179–80, 306; teachers 56, 71, 140
Okanagan valley 222–3, 228, 230, 274
Ontario 69, 85–95, 96–104, 130
open-door concept 290, 294, 306
Orangeville 66
Oshawa 249, 267, 269
Ottawa 123, 268, 306; valley 50–1, 60

Peace River district 159, 246, 263
Peterborough 59–60, 62, 91, 108
Polish Canadians 48, 128, 151, 157, 159, 181, 193, 198, 212–15, 248, 251–3
Port Alberni 226
Portage-la-Prairie 247
poverty 63, 74, 79, 81, 86, 127, 130, 136, 160, 162, 186, 202, 227, 230, 256, 259–70, 298
Prairies and prairie life 137–204; bloc settlements 151, 157–8, 208, 285; failure 245–6; harvest crews 160–1; socials 166, 172–3, 179, 183, 193
Prince Albert 123, 251
Prince Edward Island 40
Prince George 227–8
Prince Rupert 232
Princeton 222

Qu'Appelle Valley 179
Quebec 49–57, 71, 91, 121, 164, 171; Quebec City 67, 105, 126, 247
Quiet Revolution 301

Rabbit Hill 169, 261
race and colour, 115–16, 219, 230, 249
racial stereotyping xii, 25; of Indians 44, 46; of Negroes xii, 43, 44, 46; of non-white Europeans xii, 149
racism 151, 167–8, 195, 216, 224, 234, 240, 270, 306; conflict 225–6; decline of 291–3; racist mob action 221, 273
radicals 134, 192, 198, 204, 214–15, 230, 237, 247–52, 254–6, 258, 264, 268, 269, 290, 297; *see also* labour militancy
railways: construction 11–12, 44, 46, 56–7, 77, 85–6, 96–99, 123–4, 126, 143–50, 155, 160, 209; CPR 76–7, 96, 117, 119, 137, 142, 179, 194, 196, 227, 239, 244, 247; and local economy 62–3, 66, 151, 254; trunk lines 11–12, 33–4, 45–7, 127, 137, 142, 205
refugees 16, 277, 279–80, 302, 306
Regina 138, 140–1, 192, 268
relief 167, 256, 265, 267–8
religion 81, 92, 122, 159, 165, 254; Catholic 49, 80, 155, 165, 272–3; Catholic-Protestant tension 40–1, 24, 51–2, 58; Hindu 307; Huguenot 40; Jewish 82–4, 272–3; missionaries 122, 135, 138–9, 140, 148, 224; Presbyterian 72, 227; Protestant 43; Orthodox 159, 164; Sikh 297–8
Rivière-du-Loup 52–4
Riverton 148, 186, 199
Roblin, Dufferin 202
Roy, Gabrielle 16
royal commissions: on bilingualism and biculturalism 293; on Chinese and Japanese immigration 240; on Italians in Montreal 76–81; on labour and capital 74–6, 237, 267; on the Winnipeg general strike 136
Russian Canadians 147, 169, 248
Rye, Maria S. 91

Saguenay region 76
St Boniface 119–22, 164, 181
Saint John 46
Saskatchewan. *See* Prairies
Saskatoon 138, 147, 241
Scandinavian Canadians 71, 154, 166
Scottish Canadians 8, 24–5, 40–1, 44–5, 65, 72–3, 85–6, 91, 103, 121, 153, 159, 141, 220, 247–8, 268, 296
Selkirk 130, 199
Shamrock 166
Short, Arthur W. 75
Sifton, Clifford 12, 204; Sifton family 182–3, 237
Similkaneen region 221–2
Skeena river 224, 231, 234–6
Slocan valley 274
Slovak Canadians 162, 271
Smart, James A. 78
Smith, Adam 253
Smith Falls 103
social gospel 269
social hierarchies 134, 135, 161, 208, 210–1, 223, 251, 257; awareness/observation of 114–16, 284–5; invisibility of women 106, 115; visible/audible minorities 284, 304, 305
social space xi, 10, 23, 37–48, 60, 121–3, 126, 190, 218–22, 226, 257, 285, 290, 301
South Asian Canadians 124, 219, 224, 296, 301, 306
Sri Lankan Canadians 306
Stettler 155, 165
Strathcona 141
Steveston 225–6, 233
Sudbury 207, 249, 250
Swan River 172, 182
Swedish Canadians 145–6, 151, 228–9
Swiss Canadians 119, 151, 207, 228–9
Syrian Canadians 182, 240, 263

Testard de Montigny, B.-A. 75–6
Thunder Bay 96, 143–4
Timmins 98–103, 225, 244
Tobique river 46
Toronto 65, 69, 82, 91, 105–17, 200–2, 243, 250, 263–4, 274–5, 276, 296–9, 301
Trois Rivières 267
Trudeau, Pierre-Elliott 293

Ugandan Asian Canadians 306
Ukrainian Canadians 16, 105, 124–5, 141–2, 147, 151, 154, 158–9, 163–4, 211, 213, 215, 253; *see also* Galicians
United Empire Loyalists 7, 9, 41, 85, 114
Vancouver 219, 231, 234–6, 264–5, 275–6, 296–8, 301
Victoria 219, 226

Wabanum 212, 216
Welsh Canadians 93, 123, 170, 173, 233
Westminster 60
Weyburn 256
whiteness 166, 168, 181, 192, 195, 218, 230, 234, 304
Winnipeg 25, 67, 69, 76, 91, 111, 119–36, 143, 144, 147–8, 163, 165, 176–7, 181–9, 191–2, 194, 199, 200–1, 208, 227, 241, 246–8, 256, 258, 264, 267, 272
Wolseley 179
Woodfibre 275
Woodsworth, James S. 25, 135, 192

Yankees 44, 46, 62
Yellowhead 276

Index of Migrants

Albert family 52–5, 85–6
Allison, John Fall and Susan 221–2, 228
Alm, Edwin 138, 145–6, 162, 183, 208, 224, 250
Andersen, Iver L. 248–51
Andreychuck family 156, 216
Armstrong, merchant 183–8
Arntzen, Arnt 227
Aylestock, Addie and Viola 116

Baczynski, Anna 28, 162
Baerg, Anna 240
Bains, Tara Singh 296–8, 302
Baird, William T. 44, 53
Beattie, Jessie 177
Beguin, Ruth 227
Benson, Wilson and Jemima 64–6, 85, 114, 195, 285
Bhindi, Dilip 306
Bickersteth, J.B. 138, 148–50, 254
Biedrawa, George 131–2, 159, 241
Bielesh, George 144, 194
Binnie-Clarke, Georgina 196
Blackman, Violet 116
Bompas, Charlotte Selina 122–3
Bonneau family 138, 140, 166, 192, 194
Bradica, Stjepan 248–9
Bratsberg, Carrie 162
Bruser family, Fredelle Bruser Maynard 22, 25, 125, 129, 165–6, 178, 180, 188
Brzyski, Stanley 28, 241, 267
Bublitz, Dorothea 174, 262
Bullock Webster, Harry 121–2

Campbell, Maria 262
Carrothers family 27, 60–2, 85, 95
Carson, Winnie 227–8
Caswell, Maryanne 138, 140
Chan Sam family 234–6
Charron, Theophile 75
Chown, Alice 109–10
Chrzanowski, Czeslaw H. 157, 261
Chuchla, Walter and Anne 28, 195, 212–15, 260–1, 271, 277, 302
Clark, Billy 153
Cohn, Martin. *See* Nordegg, Martin
Coleman, William 113
Collins, Robert 166, 244
Colontonio, Frank 296–7
Cooper, F.C. 97
Cordasco, Antonio 76–7
Cotton, A.J. 167
Cowan, C.L. 221
Cran, Maria, observer 242–3
Crookes, James J. 250

Dalton, Patrick J. 75
D'Amico, Constanzo 78
Davies, Evan 170, 254
DeGelder, William 154, 254
DeJong, Klaas 127–8, 130
Derrigan, Ms 106–7
Destrubé family 152, 165, 188
Dmytriw, Nestor 159, 164
Douglas, Tommy C. 129, 134, 196, 225, 255–7
Duesterhoeft, Eduard 126
Duncan, Eric 220
Durieux family 27, 155, 165, 253
"Dutchie" 208–10
Dziuzynski, Carolina 240–1, 260

Einarsson, Helgi 182–8, 196, 198–9, 256
Emigrant Lady (pseud.) 86
Eskra, Albert and Anastasia 248, 251–4, 277
Ewing, Juliana 18, 44–5

FitzGibbon, Agnes, 125
Fortier, factory owner, 75
Fraser, Joyce 298–300, 302, 305
Fridel, Waclaw 212
Fripp/Shadwell family 229–31, 244
Fujita, Hirozo 274
Funicelli, Antonio 78
Fukushima, Maki 226–7, 249, 275, 295

Gaetz family 41–4, 53, 61
Gairey, Elma and Harry 115, 201–2

Gardiner, Claude 191
Garland, Bessie 63
Geike family 86, 88, 114
Genyk, Kyrylo 124
Girard, Marie-Rose 55
Giscard, Gaston 211
Grant, George M. 137
Gray, James 133–4, 177, 225, 258
Grönlund family 34, 99–105, 128, 181, 268
Grossmann, John 163, 240, 246
Gudmundson family 125, 130–2, 186–7, 196; *see also* Salverson

Halwa, Kaspar 141, 159, 261
Hathaway family 86, 105–8
Hattum, Albert 263
Helmcken, Sebastian 219
Hemsley, Richard 71, 73–4
Henig, Harry 165, 272
Henry, Finnish immigrant 98
Herklots, Hugh 132
Hislop, Nelli 177
Hjelt, Ole 254
Home children: Thomas Loach, George McDonald, Jack W., Ellen Higgins, Harry Jeffery, George Mackie, James Wilde, W.B. Cartledge, Len Weston, William R. Price, Margaret Cleaves, Agnes McFadden, Emily Boys, J.L. Churcher 90–5; Patrick Markham, Allan Slade 98; William Gwilliam 103; John Cameron 103; Lily E. Clapham 108; Fred Sanders 115; Florence Horne, 128; Henry Thomas 167; Bill Price 261
Hoffer, Israel 165
Holmes, Peggy 244–5
Hong, Bill 224
Howey, Florence R. 96–7

Irvine, Charlie 296–7
Iuticone, Olinda 78

Jankovskis, Janis 141
Jenny, Guyana immigrant 298–9
Jodouin, Rémi 56–7, 103–4, 128, 214, 256, 267
Johnson, John 220–1
Johnstone, Bill and Dorothy 215–16, 270, 295

Karpinski, Agatha 131, 169–70, 174–5
Kern, Hannah 86–7
Knight family 263–5
Knull, Bertha 170
Koeppen, Ebe 18, 263
Kohl, Ms 167
Kohn family 272–3
Kojder family 277
Kolber, Albert 161, 241–2
Krommknecht. *See* Knight
Kupsch, Lydia 197
Kurtenbach family 154–5, 198
Kuryvial, Steve 271
Kutera, Anna 131, 201, 277

Lalieu, Leopold 76
Lamb, T.H.P 139
Landry, Noel 179–80
Lang, Joseph 28,261
Leibert, Clara 269–70
Leveridge family 27, 86, 88–90, 95, 139, 253
Linkiewich, Frank 241
Lisowyks family 148
Litke, Lyia 260
Livesay, Dorothy 134, 136
Loiselle, Georgina 75
London, M.C.S. 45–6, 111
Lacas, Louise 255–8
Luchkovich, Michael 125, 164

MacGregor, James G. 140
Macintyre, D.E. 178–80
Madore, Lina 55–6
Maglio family 229
Maki, Helga 102
Manzo, Nicola 78
Marcogliese, Michele 78
Massey, Eli 75
Matti, Finnish immigrant 102
Mauro, Vincenzo 27
McAleer, Bertha 116
McClung, Nellie L. 171, 202
McDougall family 138–9
Michalski, merchant 213
Michaud, Joseph-Phydime 259
Milord, Jean R. 306
Mikko, Finnish immigrant 98
Mills, Ms 171
Miron, Edouard 75
Miyazaki, Masajiro 224–5, 232, 239
Moberly, Walter 219, 221, 223
Monaco, Vincenzo 78–9, 100
Monkman, Joseph 154
Moore, Don 117
Murata, Hana 274–5
Murphy, Emily 171, 203
Muzury, George 167–8

Nakano family 275–6
Nehring, Ludwig 158
Nevitt, R.B. 192
Nordegg, Martin 207–11

O'Donnell, Nellie 243–4, 247, 267
O'Leary, Peter 30, 32, 66–8, 74, 121, 124
Olsekiv, Osyp 151
Opalinski, Tomasz 126, 165, 241, 262
Oswald, Julius 158

Patterson, Raymond 195
Pépin, Albert 103–4
Pepolenski, Katie 128
Petrone, Serafina 249, 286
Pieronek family 168–9, 213–14
Plachner, Jan 145
Plotkin, Abe 165

Pozza, Anna 78
Prohonig, Lucy 262

Reino, Finnish immigrant 98
Robb, Alexander 205
Roe, Frank 124, 153, 166
Romaniuk, Gus 98–9, 104, 138, 147, 161, 186, 195, 212, 256, 303
Roseman, Erdman 158
Rosenberg, Leah 82–4, 128, 259–60, 285
Rudinskas, Antanas 161, 267

Sadler family 152, 166, 195, 262
Salloum family 263
Salverson, Laura 19, 22, 25, 125, 128, 177; *see also* Gudmundson family
Sanderson, George W. 123
Sawczuk, Steve 228
Schiffer, Fanny 272
Sekely, Trude 276
Shastri, Meera 307
Smythies, Eric and Ruth 110
Stelter, Arthur 157, 169, 260
Stewart, Frances (Browne) 59–60, 63–4
Stonemason (pseud.) 108–9
Strange family 244–6
Sutherland, Alexander 122, 125
Svanda, Daniel 178
Svarich, Peter 141–2
Suzuki, Etsu and Moto 225, 233
Sykes, Ella C. 242–3

Tamura, Toshiko 233
Tarasco, Raffaele 78
Thomson, James 71, 85, 89, 100, 109, 205
Thorvaldsson, Sveinn 199
Tolmie, Adam 110–11

Usiskin, Michael 165

Veltri, Giovanni, 138, 143–4, 155, 183, 194–5, 224

Wachowicz family 125, 169
Walker, James 230, 245, 247–9
Ware, John 165
Weir, William 71
White, Jane 62–3
Wicks family 231–4
Wilder family 124, 133, 200, 258
Will, Alex 268
Worchuk, Steve 181
Wróblewski family 48

Yoshida, Ryuichi 232–4, 267, 273
Yuen, W.K. 166–7, 188

Zinkowsky, Dmytro 196